PHP MySQL Website Programming

Problem – Design – Solution

Chris Lea
Mike Buzzard
Jessey White-Cinis
Dilip Thomas

Apress™

PHP MySQL Website Programming

Problem – Design – Solution

© 2002 Apress

ISBN (pbk): 1-59059-150-X

Printed and bound in the United States of America 345678910
Trademarked names may appear in this book. Rather than use a trademark symbol with every occurrence of a trademarked name, we use the names only in an editorial fashion and to the benefit of the trademark owner, with no intention of infringement of the trademark.

Distributed to the book trade in the United States by Springer-Verlag New York, Inc., 175 Fifth Avenue, New York, NY, 10010 and outside the United States by Springer-Verlag GmbH & Co. KG, Tiergartenstr. 17, 69112 Heidelberg, Germany.
In the United States: phone 1-800-SPRINGER, email orders@springer-ny.com, or visit http://www.springer-ny.com. Outside the United States: fax +49 6221 345229, email orders@springer.de, or visit http://www.springer.de.

For information on translations, please contact Apress directly at 2560 Ninth Street, Suite 219, Berkeley, CA 94710. Phone 510-549-5930, fax 510-549-5939, email info@apress.com, or visit http://www.apress.com.

Credits

About the Authors

Chris Lea

Chris Lea is, on his better days, a developer. He started out on the East Coast, going to school at UNC-CH and getting a BS in Physics with Highest Honors and Distinction. Fortunately, he managed to escape graduate school and made it to sunny Los Angeles, which is where he currently spends most of his time. If you track him down, it's likely that he will be playing around with Linux, Apache, PHP, and other related bits of software. For fun he sees his friends, plays his guitar, and harasses Mike Buzzard over instant messenger. If you're so interested that you want (almost) daily updates, you can visit his personal web site at http://www.chrislea.com.

Mike Buzzard

Mike Buzzard is a self-taught applications developer currently residing in San Francisco, CA. He is a partner member of Cuban Council, a freelance collective of programmers and designers based in the US and Denmark. Mike spends most of his time building web-based software solutions utilizing a wide array of languages, platforms and databases for the entertainment industry as well as the online design community world-wide. Mike's work history ranges from software development companies to the architecture and engineering services where his efforts have always been focused toward online applications development. In his spare time, Mike occasionally guest lectures at Stanford University where he instructs students in PHP and MySQL for solving course projects involving art, product design and communications.

Mike can be reached via email: nonsense@blather.org

Mike would like to thank his family for always supporting his non-conventional methods, the contributors and editors of this book for the highly educational experience, Jessey White-Cinis, the finest friend and coding companion anyone could ever ask for. And lastly, Mike would like to thank everyone who has always believed in him by continuously encouraging his pursuits far beyond his own exaggerated confidence.

Jessey White-Cinis

Jessey White-Cinis is a freelance contractor currently living in Los Angeles, CA. His expertise lies primarily in core level web programming and development, however, he also has an extensive background in *NIX system administration. Jessey began his career in Kansas as a developer for OneMain.com (now Earthlink) at the age of seventeen. At the age of nineteen, Jessey moved back to his hometown of Los Angeles to work as a webmaster, developer and system administrator for Epitaph Records. Now twenty-one, Jessey enjoys working on a wide variety of web development projects while maintaining close professional relationships with his former employers. In his 'free time', Jessey enjoys traveling, mountain biking and writing and producing his own music.

Jessey would like to thank the editors, reviewers and contributors of this book for providing guidance, support and patience throughout the writing process. He would also like to thank Mike Buzzard for continually being the best friend, supporter and work companion anyone could ever hope for, Heather Fremling for sticking by him through insane work hours and helping him to 'stringulate his porpoises', Chris Lea for his contribution and confidence, Nathan Morton for starting him on this path by saying "Hey, have you seen this crazy PHP thing?" and all of his friends and family for being there through thick and thin and vinyl clothing.

Dilip Thomas

Dilip Thomas hails from the sleepy little town of Cochin, set in God 's own country. He is employed full time with Wrox Press, as a Content Architect on their Open Source Editorial and Research group – Saltmarch, and has been instrumental in shaping the PHP line of books for Wrox. He is committed to the PHP community, and much of his thrill comes from peering into that community from a philosophical perspective. He first got hooked onto Open Source in his sophomore days in college, and has been playing the role of a technology evangeliser ever since. His interests also lie in the Apache Jakarta projects and Open Standards technology in general. Before work with Wrox Press came calling, he was spotted organizing bungee jumping shows to flustered audiences in his favorite city of Bangalore.

Dilip can be reached via email: dilipt@graffiti.net

Dilip would like to thank his brother, for being the guiding light and inspiration in his life - "Deepak, you are the best". He cannot thank his beautiful wife, enough, for all her love, and the wonderful moments that she has bought into his life – "Indu, you are a darling". A lot of thanks are also due to his mentor and friend, John Franklin for introducing him to Wrox and placing confidence and trust in him – "John, you are a star". He would also like to thank Paul Cooper for being a wonderful manager, Vijay Tase for the wonderful setup at work, and the little Saltmarch team for shaping his ideas into what we call 'books'. And how can he forget the wonderful 'PITS KIDS', for showing him the other side of life – "See you guys in CBH".

Table of Contents

Table of Contents

Table of Contents

Table of Contents

Table of Contents

Introduction

Welcome to PHP MySQL web site design. This book shows the development process for a web site using a specific set of technologies: the PHP scripting language, the MySQL database system, and the Apache web server.

PHP is a powerful scripting language specifically designed to create web applications. MySQL is a fast and popular open source relational database that integrates well with PHP and is suited for building dynamic and e-commerce sites. Apache is an Open Source project that runs on both Linux and Windows and is one of the leading web servers.

Unlike other books, what we're working towards is a complete 'application-driven' site. Therefore, the chapters in this book are not standalone descriptions of how to create different things. They are instead related, and you are encouraged to read the book sequentially to get the most out of it.

Before we go any further, we should have a clear idea of what we mean when we talk about an 'application-driven' site. When we say this, what we mean is that pages will typically be functional rather than static. They will have the capacity to allow users to manipulate or display data of various sorts in real time in the database. Sometimes, this will mean adding, modifying, or deleting actual data. Other times, it will mean displaying that data on a page for consumption.

The web site we are creating in this book is called DVD Life, and is available for you to see at http://apress.mediatemple.net. Although the primary focus of the web site is on content, we have also included a shopping cart module that is complete with 'check out' features.

What Does This Book Cover?

The chapters in this book follow a problem-design-solution pattern. First, we identify what we need to achieve, then we sketch out how we will achieve it, and finally we build the software using PHP and MySQL.

Most chapters involve building a 3-tier system, with data, business, and presentation layers. We will also see how to build separate modules so that they integrate well into the whole site.

Chapter 1 looks at the web site as a whole. We identify the problem that it is trying to solve, and discuss how we will go about solving it. We then come up with a solution – which involves building and integrating the modules detailed in the later chapters.

Chapter 2 covers some of the critical design issues that affect the course of development. It covers information that our base architecture will provide to the modules, how errors will be handled, the need for different kinds of users on the site, the layout of the directory structure, and the coding conventions and naming schemes for our application.

Chapter 3 provides a complete definition for what our User Interface (UI) should look like, and how it will be constructed with some help from the utility functions.

Chapter 4 will detail the base architecture we covered in Chapter 2, that will provide user and session classes for the application modules to make use of.

Chapter 5 looks at developing a solution for managing our site visitors by providing visitor accounts. This will get us started to look at the applications that are dependent on this architecture for managing secure content. Furthermore, understanding the involvement of users and session management will enable us to implement secure applications for content management into our system.

Chapter 6 looks at using the visitor's accounts to enable them to share comments to news publications in the web site. Here we build a newsfeed application and look at plugging it into both our CMS and web site frameworks.

Chapter 7 looks at some ways to extend the existing content for syndication by using RSS to provide a standard distribution of our newsfeed via XML.

Chapter 8 will dive back in and create a system for displaying banner advertisements and look at the different options that are available for implementing reliable, practical, and effective advertising systems into a web site.

Chapter 9 defines the problems associated with implementing a visitor poll into our web site and then looks at designing a solution into a functional application that seamlessly plugs into our CMS architecture for easy management.

Chapter 10 looks at how to create discussion forums to provide a nice community building aspect to the site, which allow users to interact and communicate with one another on our web site, and encourages visitors to register with the site so that they can interact with the forum beyond the read-only access offered to anonymous users.

Chapter 11 shows how to provide a great way to get across information in a simple and controlled fashion, by adding a newsletter module to our web site.

Chapter 12 shows how to design, build, and implement a product management system and cookie-based shopping cart.

Chapter 13 will be an extension of the shopping cart chapter and will detail the check out process and many of the problems involved with online purchases, data security, and credit card transactions.

Chapter 14 features a review of the finished site and takes a peek into the future. We will also look at the concept of 'refactoring' and leave it up to you, the programmer, to decide if any of the refactoring ideas would be beneficial in your own applications.

Who Is This Book For?

This book is for developers who have a reasonable knowledge of PHP, and want to apply that knowledge to building web sites. Furthermore, although we assume a reasonable knowledge of MySQL, anyone who has a conceptual familiarity with databases can make full use of this book.

You will also get the most from this book if you have read a decent amount of Apress's *Beginning PHP4 (ISBN 1-861003-73-0)*, or *Professional PHP4 (ISBN 1-861006-91-8)*.

What You Need To Use This Book

To run the code samples in this book you need to have the following:

❑   Linux or Windows 2000, Windows XP.

❑   PHP 4.2 or later. We have tested all the code using PHP 4.3, although most of the code is backward compatible, and should work with earlier releases of PHP 4.

❑   MySQL 3.23 version or later.

❑   Apache 1.3.x version.

Conventions

To help you get the most from the text and keep track of what's happening, we've used a number of conventions throughout the book.

For instance:

> **Important, not-to-be-forgotten information, which is directly relevant to the surrounding text, come in boxes like this.**

While advice, hints, and background information come in this type of font.

As for styles in the text:

❑   When we introduce them, we **highlight** important words

❑   We show keyboard strokes like this: *Ctrl-K*

❑   We show filenames and code within the text like so: `<element>`

❑   Text on user interfaces and URLs is shown as: Menu

We present code in two different ways:

```
In our code examples, the code foreground style shows new, important,
    pertinent code
while code background shows code that is less important in the present
    context or has been seen before.
```

Customer Support

We always value hearing from our readers, and we want to know what you think about this book: what you liked, what you didn't like, and what you think we can do better next time. You can send us your comments by e-mail to feedback@apress.com. Please be sure to mention the book title in your message.

How to Download the Sample Code

When you visit the Apress site at http://www.apress.com, simply visit the Downloads section. The files that are available for download from our site have been archived using WinZip. When you have saved the attachments to a folder on your hard drive, you need to extract the files using a de-compression program such as WinZip or PKUnzip. When you extract the files, the code is usually extracted into chapter folders. When you start the extraction process, ensure that your software (WinZip, and PKUnzip, for example) is set to use folder names.

Errata

We've made every effort to ensure that there are no errors in the text or in the code. However, no one is perfect and mistakes do occur. If you find an error in one of our books, like a spelling mistake or faulty piece of code, we would be very grateful for your feedback. By sending in errata you may save other reader hours of frustration, and of course, you will be helping us provide even higher quality information. Simply submit the problem at the book's page on www.apress.com, and your information will be checked and posted on the errata page for the title, or used in subsequent editions of the book.

Building a PHP MySQL Web Site

In this book we are going to build an application-driven PHP MySQL web site. The web site will consist of a number of modules, which will all fit together to produce the finished product – DVD Life.

> *In an 'application-driven' site the pages will typically be functional rather than static. They will have the capacity to allow users to manipulate or display data of various sorts in real time in the database. Sometimes, this will mean adding, modifying, or deleting actual data. Other times, it will mean displaying that data on a page for consumption.*

We'll build each module in a standard fashion, and hence we'll structure each chapter as follows:

- ❑ Identify the **Problem** – What tasks do we need to accomplish? Are there any restrictions that we need to take into account?

- ❑ Produce a **Design** – Decide on what features we need to solve the problem and get an idea of how the solution will work

- ❑ Build the **Solution** – Build the code based on the design discussion

With any such project, there is often more than one way to solve a particular problem. Throughout the book, we'll try to present the most optimal solution to the problem. This means that we'll try to create a maintainable codebase that will use object-oriented (OO) techniques when handling aspects of the problem that are easily represented as objects, and procedural techniques to handle procedural tasks. Additionally, we will focus on creating a site that can be deployed in a typical Internet Service Provider (ISP) setup, where we do not necessarily have control over every aspect of our web server.

> **Our DVD Life application is online at http://apress.mediatemple.net.**

In keeping true to our goal of developing this application in a standard environment, the server we're using to host the site is an off-the-shelf appliance server that was donated to this project by Media Temple (http://www.mediatemple.net), a Los Angeles-based ISP. The authors and the publisher would like to thank the Media Temple staff and Demian Sellfors, in particular, for this gracious contribution.

An appliance server is a specialized server that is designed for ease of installation and maintenance. Appliance servers have their hardware and software bundled in the product, so all applications are pre-installed. The appliance is plugged into an existing network, and can begin working almost immediately with little configuration. Furthermore, the web server is generally configured with standard and useful software such as Apache, MySQL, Perl, and PHP.

What We're Trying to Do

An amazing number of projects start out poorly and consequently end poorly because there was not a clear idea from the outset regarding the project goals. Obviously, we would like to avoid falling into this trap, so let's think about the things that we're trying to accomplish with this book.

Development of a Typical Application

The primary goal of this book is to go through the development of a typical PHP web application. By typical, we mean that it'll involve the creation of functionality that is used on many different kinds of sites.

Use of a Typical Hosting Environment

In addition to looking at some of the common kinds of programming tasks, we're going to develop this application using the sort of hosting platform that we're likely to encounter in the real world – specifically, the kind of shared hosting environment that any client might have set up at an ISP. The most typical thing that we'll encounter is the Apache web server, the MySQL database, and the PHP scripting language configured according to the policies of the ISP.

Therefore, the examples in this book won't make a whole lot of assumptions about how much configuration is possible on our machine. Everything is designed to work with a typical ISP setup. We'll talk more about the specific assumptions in Chapter 2, but a few of the obvious ones are:

- ❑ Lack of GD graphics library support
- ❑ Use of PHP's safe mode
- ❑ Lack of access to the `httpd.conf` or `php.ini` configuration files

Use of Good Programming Practices

We'll also demonstrate good coding practices throughout the book. This applies to both the overall design of the application as well as the specific syntaxes and standards that we'll be using. At all times, we'll strive to write code that is 'readable' as opposed to being overly 'clever'.

Also, for all our classes we will use the phpDocumentor style of commenting to allow for the automatic creation of API documentation. So we'll need to write clear, well-commented code that adheres to the conventions available at http://phpdocu.sourceforge.net/.

Finally, we will have a consistent variable naming scheme that will help us keep different kinds of variables distinct in our heads. We'll include more specific detailing and examples in Chapter 2, where we plan the site.

What We're Not Trying to Do

Now that we know what we're trying to get out of this book, we should take a moment and clarify the things that this book is not attempting to be. This is an important and very often overlooked piece of thinking. No program has ever performed every task for every person, but many programs have died trying.

A PHP Tutorial

This book isn't intended to teach the PHP language. We're assuming that readers are already comfortable with the PHP syntax, structures, operators, variables, and so on.

It would be a good idea to look at the books available, such as *Beginning PHP4* (*ISBN 1-861003-73-0*) and *Professional PHP4 (ISBN 1-861006-91-8)* from *Apress*.

An HTML, CSS, or JavaScript Tutorial

This book is focused on showing the reader how to develop an application using PHP and MySQL. Since the application is a web site, however, a certain amount of HTML and related coding needs to be done, and we're assuming that the reader is familiar with the technologies used.

For reference on JavaScript, refer to *Professional JavaScript 2nd Edition* from *Apress* (*ISBN 1-861005-53-9*). For reference on HTML, refer to *HTML 4.01 Programmer's Reference* from *Apress* (*ISBN 1-861005-33-4*).

A UNIX or Linux Administration Guide

This application is being developed on a Linux machine in a shared hosting environment. The administration of such a computer is an enormous task, and certainly exceeds the scope of this book. Therefore, we'll only be talking about configuration issues that are specific to the application we're developing. As said earlier, we're using a typical server, so it's unlikely that we'll need to worry about any issues that we don't talk about here.

For more information on Linux, refer to *Linux Network Administrator's Guide, Second Edition* from *O'Reilly* (*ISBN 1-56592-400-2*).

The Problem

Our site will cater to DVD enthusiasts. So it should endeavor to provide content for DVD lovers – this will come in the form of news stories that talk about current events in the DVD market, new releases, advances in technology, and the like.

There will be a **newsletter** that users can choose to get via e-mail. To get news across to the widest possible audience, we'll **syndicate the news** into a standard RSS feed XML format. This will enable others to syndicate the news items, and attract visitors to the DVD site by having it referenced elsewhere on the Internet. To develop a sense of community, we'll create a **discussion board** where users can create and respond to various topics. We'll also provide a **poll** where users can vote on DVD-related subjects and see the results. Additionally, we'll serve **advertisements** to potentially generate revenue for the site. Finally, we'll provide a **shopping area**. Here, users who are logged in can add DVDs, DVD players, and accessories to a cart and buy them.

We should pause at this point to note that this isn't going to be an enterprise scale application. The codebase that we'll develop would not be sufficient to handle a web site the size of Amazon. However, we'll write code that is designed to scale up reasonably. Moreover, some of the features that we'll be implementing, like e-commerce, could easily have an entire book devoted to them.

We're going to define a methodology for creating a web site. Specifically, we'll identify problems, surmise a solution to each of the problems, and then implement those solutions with code using modern development practices.

The Design

Now that we've outlined what our site needs, let's look at how we can provide it. The issues in the problem section can be summarized as follows:

- ❑ Examine a common structure for the site's User Interface (UI)
- ❑ Develop a useful and extensible base architecture for sessions, users, and user management
- ❑ Create a system to publish content to the site
- ❑ Provide syndication of the content to others
- ❑ Establish and foster a user community through discussions forums
- ❑ Create a poll where users can vote on topics
- ❑ Create a newsletter system that users can subscribe to
- ❑ Create a banner advertisement system
- ❑ Provide a shopping area for the users

Let's talk about each of these in detail.

The User Interface (UI)

Each page of the site will have a consistent feel defined by common interface elements. The use of technologies such as Cascading Style Sheets (CSS) will also help us to maintain the 'look-and-feel' for the site. The pages will be built using a common set of templating functions that will simplify the construction.

The Base Architecture

We're going to need more advanced and abstracted tools than just a bunch of native PHP functions. We need a base architecture that allows us to build advanced functionality on top of it. In this way, new application modules can be created that are distinct, but that also share a common way of doing certain things. In practice, this means that we're going to use a common set of classes, functions, and UI elements that are used pervasively throughout the site. The other applications will also make sure of this functionality to avoid having to re-write code already in use.

Content Publication

We need to devise a system that lets certain users put news stories on the site via a web-based publication system. This sort of dynamic content is almost mandatory if we want to keep the site interesting for our users. We should also allow users to react to the stories that are published so that they feel more involved with the site's operation.

Syndication

We want to get our news to as many people as possible, and not just those who happen to be looking at our site. To accomplish this, we'll need to syndicate our news in an easily-accessible format so that other web sites may utilize it in their content, and hence direct visitors to our site. The idea of syndicating news content basically means making it accessible in a presentation-agnostic way to other devices. We will accomplish this by generating an RSS feed, which is an XML format specifically designed for this kind of operation.

Advertising

Selling banner advertisements to generate revenue is a common scheme for many sites. We should be able to display banner advertisements that highlight products that are of interest to DVD enthusiasts. Naturally, our system should keep track of how many displays and clicks a certain banner advertisement gets.

Online Polls

Polls where users can vote on different topics are ubiquitous today. Numerous sites have polls on various topics. They are in such widespread use because they tend to be popular items. We could provide this functionality to our users. Beyond the fact that they are popular, we could use the polls to gauge users' opinions about DVD-related topics, reaction to industry events, and even improvements to the site. Further, certain users should be allowed to put up a topic for discussion on the poll.

Discussion Forums

Site visitors like to feel that they are part of a larger community. A good way to foster this attitude is to provide a discussion forum where the users can talk with each other about DVD-related topics. Therefore, we could provide this kind of application on our site.

Site Newsletters

To keep interested users informed about the latest happenings at DVD Life, we could send them periodic e-mail updates. Users should be able to choose whether they want to receive such e-mails. In our newsletter, we can tell the users about new products, features, or particularly exciting stories.

Online Shopping

We want to be able to sell products to our users. The users should be able to choose from a selection of products, put the desired ones into a cart, submit payment information, and have their orders logged in our system for shipping. The system should, of course, be able to handle secure transactions so that our users' payment information is safe from prying eyes. We'll use the Payflow Pro functionality in PHP to facilitate the use of credit cards.

The Solution

We've identified what we want to accomplish with DVD Life, and have sketched out some rough ideas of how to provide it. Now we'll look at how to build our solution. This really encompasses the whole of the book. In this section, we'll look at how each chapter relates to the initial problem and design.

Site Elements

In Chapter 2, we'll lay out detailed specifications of how we're going to build the various application modules and diagram the major portions of the site architecture. Doing this effectively will involve a discussion of how and why we intend to separate the database, code, and UI elements.

Additionally, we'll talk about the standards we intend to employ. In particular, we'll describe the syntax to be used and the ways in which we'll develop the PHP objects to help us develop the application.

The User Interface (UI)

In Chapter 3, we'll code the shell of the UI for DVD Life. This will involve more than just HTML and CSS; hence, we're also going to use PHP to help us manage the common parts by breaking up our pages into distinct areas, and using PHP to automatically generate the parts that are mostly redundant. Once the shell is in place, we can go back and develop the PHP classes that will provide the logic needed to generate the application-specific interface parts.

User and Session Management

In Chapters 4 and 5, we'll start with the serious PHP coding needed to develop the base architecture. Since it's a user-centric site, the base will be designed accordingly to help us manage our users. This means creating functionality that lets us identify specific users via an authentication mechanism, and track them using a suitable method of sessioning. This information will be made available to the other modules so that the users can interact with them in a cohesive way.

In addition, this will allow for different types of users, like:

❑ Web masters – They have administrative access to the administrative features of the site. In fact, there will be a permissions system that will give specific web masters access to specific administrative pages that will be defined in Chapter 5.

❑ Users – They have created an account and can subsequently log in to post comments about news articles, put up topics for discussion, and so on. As mentioned earlier, the users class will let us very easily access things such as the user's name and ID via the session information. The users class (created in Chapter 4) will provide us with an easy way to check if a person on a given page has the permissions necessary to be there or not, and then we can take appropriate action.

❑   Visitors – They visit the site but aren't logged in. Consequently, certain site features, such as commenting on news stories, are not available to them.

Dynamic News Content

With the base architecture in place, we'll develop a module that will allow for the creation of new news stories on the web site, in Chapter 6. Web masters will be allowed to post new stories to the site, and users will be able to make comments about the story.

To help the web masters, a special administrative area (CMS) will be created that will allow them to add, modify, and delete stories easily via the Web.

Syndication

With our news module in place, we'll now be able to construct a module for syndication in Chapter 7. It will take the latest stories and put them into the widely used RSS format.

> Short for **RDF Site Summary** or **Rich Site Summary**, RSS is an XML format for syndicating web content. A web site, that wants to allow other sites to publish some of its content, creates an RSS document and registers the document with an RSS publisher.

A user that can read RSS-distributed content can use the content on a different site. Syndicated content includes data such as news feeds, event listings, news stories, headlines, project updates, excerpts from discussion forums, and even corporate information.

Advertising

This module, created in Chapter 8, will allow the placement of banner advertisements on the site. Banners will be displayed pulling specific images randomly from a pool. Our module will also keep track of display and click statistics for individual advertisements. There will be an administration area (CMS) that allows web masters to add or remove banners from the pool.

Online Polls

In Chapter 9, we'll develop a polling application module. It will allow visitors to vote on different subjects and view the results. The accompanying administration area will allow web masters to create new polls and make them active on the site. The classes that handle the polls will be designed specifically to disallow poll spoofing, or falsifying of results.

Discussion Forums

The forums, created in Chapter 10, will allow users to create new topics and respond to existing topics. Visitors will have read-only abilities. The admin for this module will allow web masters to remove any unwanted threads.

Site Newsletters

We will develop a newsletter mailing system in Chapter 11. Web masters will be able to create, modify, store, and send e-mail newsletters to users. The recipients can choose whether they would like to get the e-mail. The newsletters will have some personalization, like the ability to choose between plain text and HTML, for each user. It'll also allow users to easily unsubscribe if they wish.

Online Shopping

This part of the site will allow users to pick items from our inventory, put them in a shopping cart, and buy them. The corresponding admin will allow for the addition of new items to the inventory, including pictures, SKU numbers, and a description of each product.

Summary

This chapter has provided a high-level outline of what we'll be building for our site in this book. We should definitely note that there is a great deal of code already available that does some of the things we are going to be doing in the book. For example, the phpBB discussion forum is excellent and available for free, and could probably be adapted here for use if desired. We are choosing not to do this because we want to examine and understand the process of developing such applications ourselves. In the rest of the chapters we will investigate and demonstrate the development process rather than modify existing code for our purposes.

It's worth downloading the completed code and database from the Apress web site, because the book does not describe every detail of the web site. Therefore, it's best to obtain the code download before we begin, so that you can refer to it as we go through the book.

> **The code for the book is available from http://www.apress.com.**

Now we're ready to start laying out the structure for this site. The next chapter will cover the base architecture of the web site, directory structure, and the programming standards used for the web site.

2

Planning the Web Site

In Chapter 1 we looked at the DVD Life web site as a whole. We identified the problem that we would try to solve, and discussed how to go about solving it. We also came up with a solution – building and integrating the modules discussed in the later chapters.

Now it's time to start thinking about how we are going to put this site together. Along with this process, we need to have an understanding of how the different parts of the site are going to interact, if indeed there is any need for them to. Determining these things is going to require planning.

There is a widespread opinion regarding the amount of planning that must go into such a project. Some developers feel that the best thing to do is to start writing code, knowing that it'll need changing as the programming goes along based on new developments. Others feel that every aspect of the site should be fully considered, discussed, diagrammed, and so on before any kind of actual programming should begin. And of course there are lots of people who fall somewhere in between these two extremes. Naturally, the real world constraints of projects don't allow for total planning, yet we should try to plan as much as possible before starting.

What are some of the considerations we need to keep in mind while planning? For starters, how many people will work on the project? Small teams who are in close contact can often get away with less planning because they can adapt quickly if anything changes. Likewise, larger teams often need more planning in place to help keep everybody together. How big is the site? Clearly, a tiny project probably does not need a full treatment of UML diagrams to be successful.

> The Unified Modeling Language™ (UML) is the industry-standard language for specifying, visualizing, constructing, and documenting the artifacts of software systems. It simplifies the complex process of software design, making a "blueprint" for construction.

In any case, the ideas written down during the planning phase of a project often constitutes a significant portion of the overall available documentation. Therefore, it's certainly in our best interests to get the results of the planning down in writing.

In this chapter we'll walk through the planning process to build a fairly comprehensive idea of what the site will look like when it's done, from a development standpoint.

The Problem

We must get our heads around some of the high-level specifications for our DVD Life web site. This kind of foundational planning can be many things to different people, and it's not always the most 'fun' part of the job. Nevertheless, it's an important part of the process for any non-trivial application and as good developers we need to pay attention to it.

What We Need to Know

We need to have an understanding of the following issues:

- ❑   What must the base architecture provide us?
- ❑   How will we keep track of the users?
- ❑   What will the directory structure look like?
- ❑   How will the database, application code, and User Interface (UI) interact?
- ❑   What programming standards will be used, and why?

Let's discuss each of these issues in detail.

Base Architecture

There is certain information that all of our application modules will need easy access to. So we need to understand what that information is and decide upon a common way of providing it – this will form the 'base architecture'.

Keeping Track of Users

HTTP is called a stateless protocol because each command is executed independently, without any knowledge of the commands that came before it. This is the main reason why it's difficult to implement web sites that react intelligently to user input. This shortcoming of HTTP is being addressed in a number of technologies, including ActiveX, Java, JavaScript, and cookies, among others. This situation is undesirable for our purposes, since we need to be aware of things like whether or not our users are logged into the site from page to page.

The way around this problem in our application is to implement user sessions. A session is a sequence of service requests by a single user using a single client to access a server. The information maintained in the session across requests is called **session state**. Session state may include both information visible to the user (shopping cart contents, for example) and invisible application control information (user preferences, for example).

We can use several mechanisms to store session state in the client tier of a web application – some of these are to store the state in a cookie, rewrite URLs to include the encoded state, keep the state in hidden form variables, or implement native PHP sessions.

Rewriting URLs and keeping hidden form variables all the time can get complicated quickly, so often the decision is between using cookies or native PHP sessions. In our application, we are going to store the state in a cookie. This approach, like any other, has both advantages and disadvantages:

❑ Advantages

   ❑ Potentially lower server resource usage

   ❑ Client sessions can survive a server crash

   ❑ Improved scalability and easy failover in clusters

❑ Disadvantages

   ❑ Persistent cookies may be readable by unauthorized users

   ❑ Client-side data can be modified

   ❑ Greatly increased communication overhead

   ❑ Complex implementation

   ❑ Limited data size

For more information about sessions and cookies, refer to Chapter 8 of Professional PHP4 from Apress (ISBN 1-86100-91-8).

In this case, it was the server resource usage factor that that made the developers decide to use cookies to maintain state. As noted, we are trying to develop a site that could easily be deployed at a typical ISP setup. If the site becomes popular and is getting a large amount of traffic, it's very feasible that we could exceed resources such as disk space that are allotted to us in a shared hosting environment.

Directory Structure

For organizational purposes, it's convenient to put the files meant for different functionality of the site into distinct directories. Developing a consistent, sensible directory structure will help us stay on top of our development process. Also, keeping the code in distinct files and directories, separated according to their intended function, makes the codebase more modular so that it's easier to edit in the future.

Application Layers

In addition to physically separating files into different directories, modern applications typically have a clean separation of the application layers. This means that the data, the application code, and the UI are kept as distinct as possible. We need to understand how this will work within the context of our site.

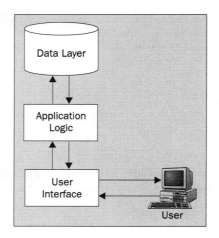

Coding Standards

We'll also need to discuss the issue of coding standards – the naming conventions, how the code should be commented, and so on. These issues must be resolved before development commences, or else we run the risk of too many styles that can make maintenance a nightmare.

This may seem like a small point, but in reality it's absolutely not. For example, the following snippet highlights some of the worst things that a development team can do:

```
function fooFunction($s) {
    if( $s == '' ) {
        return 0;
    }
    else {
        return stripslashes($s);
    }
}

function bar_function($sVariable) {
    if( !strcmp($sVariable,'') ) {
        return FALSE;
    }
    else {
        return stripslashes($sVariable);
    }
}
```

What's the problem, you ask? Well, for starters, the functions do not follow a common naming scheme. One uses capitalization and the other uses underscores. The arguments also aren't using a common naming convention. Six months down the road when you need to change something in your code, these sorts of discrepancies create huge headaches. To avoid that problem, we will define and follow coding conventions to use throughout.

The Design

Now that we've considered the high-level code-centric issues that need to be addressed, let's begin the design process. There should be a common methodology that developers can adhere to when deciding how to go about the development of different parts of the application. For example, some tasks can be accomplished with both object-oriented (OO) and procedural techniques. When trying to decide which way to go, programmers should have guidelines to help them choose. This will help to ensure that similar problems are solved in similar ways which makes the codebase, as a whole, easier to understand.

This is generally not an issue if there is only one developer for a particular project, who would decide on a certain set of conventions and go about development in a consistent manner. But as soon as there are multiple people involved, it's best to have a common set of design goals. In fact, many software companies have these goals put up on posters where everybody can see them easily. It's important to remember that it's typically harder to go back and work on old code than it is to write new code. However, since we can certainly anticipate having to go back and work on or extend things once in a while, we want to have the most maintainable codebase possible.

Let's take a look at some of the concepts that form the core of a well-planned site:

❑ **Scalability**
We want our application to be able to support more than a handful of users. Therefore, we should avoid operations that put a great deal of strain on the system whenever possible. Examples of such operations might include poorly formed SQL that puts unneeded strain on the database system.

❑ **Flexibility**
There is a set of modules that we intend to build for this site, but it's certainly possible that we'll want to add more in the future. Our foundation should be general enough to allow this. This means that our modules should not interoperate needlessly, which would create interdependencies that could be broken. Also, our base architecture should provide general information that would likely be used by any future applications.

❑ **Code Reusability**
We want to encourage code reuse whenever possible. This will speed up the development time and will keep us from 'reinventing the wheel'. Accordingly, we'll modularize the code as much as possible. Functions that are used in many places on the site will be located in a central place. Also, classes will be defined to implement reusable data objects that are capable of providing our applications with requested information easily.

❑ **Separation**
Our modules are distinct applications in their own right. Therefore, they should only interact with each other if and when they need to. Changes to the code of a particular module should not affect the others.

❑ **Usability**
Strangely, this is often left out of the design guidelines. Our site should be user-friendly – there should not be extraneous buttons to click on, or confusing menus.

❑ **Configuration**
It should be simple to configure this site to run in a new environment. There should be a small number of files that need to be tweaked if the site is moved.

❏ **Error Handling**
We would like to avoid having an almost blank screen with a complicated error message showing up if anything goes wrong. We should try to create a comfortable user experience whenever possible.

If we are conscious of these design goals at all times, the result will be a site that runs efficiently, is extensible, is easy to maintain, and that users will have a good time browsing around.

The Solution

In the earlier sections we talked about the problems we need to address, as well as some of the considerations we need to make while building this web site. Now it's time to start talking about how we are going to put all of these pieces together.

The Base Architecture

Having a solid base architecture helps to build good application modules. This scenario is as relevant in architectural constructions as it is in building web applications. For instance, if the building has a solid foundation, then constructing the rest of it would be easy, whereas if the foundation is faulty, then a lot of the building time and resources would be spent in making up for these shortcomings. Another reason for determining this architecture is so that we aren't continually re-implementing the same code in different areas of the application.

There are specific pieces of information that all the sections of our web site will need. These include.

❏ The ability to be logged in or out of the site

❏ Information about the user on a specific page stored in sessions

❏ An easy way of dealing with any errors that come up

❏ Functions to handle common tasks such as form input validation

❏ A simple way to configure global parameters such as the database DSN, administrative e-mail address, and other values that are constant throughout the site

Let's look at how we can implement these requirements.

Logging Into the Site

Each user will have a login and password specific to him or her. When entered correctly into a login form, a cookie will be set for that user. If this cookie exists, the user will be considered 'logged in'. This cookie will also be used for sessioning, which we'll talk about in the *User Sessions* section. The methods that will be used to facilitate checking the logins, adding new users, and so on will be part of a **users** class.

User Sessions

In addition to the users class, we'll have a **sessions** class. In good OO style, the sessions class will actually be an extension of users, to retain that functionality. It'll have methods to store different data in the session cookie, like the specific user's username and permissions.

This cookie will have a predefined and reasonable timeout, so if the users leave their computer sitting around for a day they will find themselves logged out when they return. However, we'll provide a mechanism that automatically refreshes this cookie when they visit any page on the site. So as long as they keep browsing around at any normal rate they will remain logged in. This 'normal rate' will be easily configurable, but we'll set the timeout at half an hour for our web site.

Of course, this automatic refresh will have ways of validating the user's credentials to prevent session spoofing. Spoofing or hijacking occurs when an unauthorized person gets hold of the information needed to pretend to be someone they aren't. For our purposes, this would mean changing the value of the cookie stored on their system to try and become somebody else as far as the web site was concerned. Our validation methods will make this very hard to do, so our site users should be safe. This will be covered in detail in Chapter 5.

Error Handling

The base architecture will introduce a $ERROR **global array variable** into the namespace. All of the methods in the users class will attempt to trap any errors and store the messages in the array. The architecture will also have a method that allows for the easy display of these errors to the user, without bringing page execution to a halt.

The advantage of this is that the users will never be stuck looking at a screen devoid of anything but a cryptic (to them) error message. They will, however, be able to see the errors so that they can ideally report them back to the web master.

Common Function Library

There are some functions that do not really belong in a class of some sort, but which are nonetheless useful in many places. A perfect example of this is a function that checks to see if a string is a valid e-mail address or not.

We'll develop a small library with these kinds of functions so that we may reuse them later on in the site as needed.

Configuration of Global Parameters

There is nothing more aggravating than having to hunt through a bunch of different files looking for some constant parameter that needs to be changed. However, in any medium-sized application, there are always at least a dozen or so such variables. These tend to be things such as a system DSN, the web master's e-mail address, or global instance variables.

In our system, we'll put all such variables into a single configuration file. This way, if we need to change anything, we should have an easy time doing it. Also, if we need to redeploy the site on a new machine, we should just have to update the values in this one file. There is one additional file that we'll use to set path information – the .htaccess file, which we'll discuss in the *Configuration* section later in the chapter.

The Two Faces of DVD Life

Chapter 1 mentions that for most of the different application modules we'll be writing, there will be a corresponding 'administrative' section. This section will allow administrative users to make changes to the site with different tools.

There are two faces to DVD Life:

❑ The public section where any user can come and look around

❑ The private section where the administrators can keep the site content updated

Different User Types

As far as the site is concerned, there are three different user types:

❑ Visitors – They are users who are not logged in

❑ Users – They are users who are logged in, but do not have any administrator privileges

❑ Web masters – They are users who are logged in with administrator privileges

Visitors can browse around, but can't contribute anything to the site – that is, they can't post opinions on the message boards, respond to any of the news articles, shop, or sign up for the newsletters. A person should obviously be logged in for instances like shopping. It would, however, be possible to give a visitor the ability to do things like post on the message boards anonymously if we wanted to. The reason that we're not letting the users do so is because for our example web site, we want to provide an incentive to register with DVD Life.

Users are those who are logged in, but do not have any web master privileges. They gain the abilities listed above that the visitors lack. However, they cannot do things like post news stories or control the banner advertisements.

Finally, there are the web masters. They have the ability to use the administration tools for some or all of the application modules on the site. We'll see later in Chapter 4 how to develop a system that allows a fine-grained control over which administrators are allowed to use the different tools. For example, an administrator John might be able to post news stories but cannot control the banner advertisements, whereas an admin Doe might be in the opposite situation.

Implementation

To integrate the three different classes of users into the site, we'll break them down into two groups:

❑ Users and Visitors
   If a person is registered with the site, there will be a cookie-based session mechanism that defines a cookie on the browser when they log in. So to distinguish between visitors and users, all we need to do is check for the existence of that cookie, like this:

```
if( isset($_COOKIE["cUSER"]) ) {
    // user is logged in code
} else {
    // visitor is not logged in code
}
```

❑ Web masters
This group is slightly complicated – the cookie-based sessions are still there, but we need a more intricate system of permissions that will keep track of which web masters are allowed to use which administrative tools. This is known as 'User-Based Policy Roles'. Basically, for a specific web master, there will be a lookup table that indicates what administrative functionality is available to them. We'll discuss this in detail in Chapter 4. The application will check these records when the administrative user attempts to use particular tools and will act accordingly.

Directory Structure

A well-thought-out directory structure helps us with our design goal of separation. We want to keep our modules distinct from each other. Therefore, it makes sense to keep the files that define those modules as separate as possible.

Directory Tree Depth

There are several schools of thought on how deeply-nested good directory structures should be. Some developers believe that you should in general only go one directory down from the server root. Others think that you should nest as deeply as you need to in order to keep files and applications completely separate.

The advantage to 'shallow' structures is that everything is right there for us to see, if necessary. On the other hand, 'deep' structures can make it more easy and obvious to compartmentalize the code. One has to consider issues such as the size of the codebase, the number of developers, and the complexity of the application(s) at hand when choosing how to arrange the directories and files. Additionally, there is the issue of relocation. For example, can the site easily be moved into a subdirectory of the web server's root directory, or are we assuming that the site will start at the server root? Note that we're assuming the latter, meaning that our code is being designed so that it's deployed in the web server's root directory.

Regardless of the particular implementation used, the reason for defining a directory structure is so that the developer can easily understand how a page being visited relates to the files needed to generate that page. This in turn means that the developer should understand where different functional pieces of the code, like classes or templates, are housed.

What We'll Use

At the highest level, we can break the site down into three categories in terms of the directories. The approach that we're going to take will consistently go two directories down from the server root in each of these three levels.

The top three levels are:

❑ User pages
❑ Admin pages
❑ Shared code

Our application modules, being the entities with which regular users interact, will all fall under one directory, called **site**. The admin tools used to control the site will all fall under a different directory, called **core**. Finally, there will be a place to put other files, such as shared function libraries and custom classes, called **_lib**.

Here is a diagrammatic representation of the directory structure:

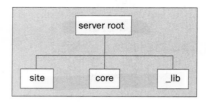

Now, we are going to further subdivide these directories to keep the code organized. Under the `site` directory, we'll have subdirectories for each of the modules we are going to have to build:

Subdirectory	Description
accounts	Will allow users to create a user account, or log in if they already have one. Also, it'll have functionality to set preferences.
login	Will house the files that define the web master login bit for the site.
forums	Will house the files that define the discussion forums for the site.
news	Will house the files that define the news content for the site. Users will be able to post comments.
polls	This is where the online polls will be made available.
products	Here, the products available for sale on the site can be seen.
shopping_cart	Here, users can see the items that they have in their cart, modify the cart's contents, and check out.

The same sort of hierarchy will exist under the `core` directory with a few additions:

Subdirectory	Description
news	This is where web masters will be able to post new news stories to the site
ads	Here, web masters can create new banner advertisements, and see reports about the current banners
forums	This will allow web masters to police the content on the forums in case they need to delete any unwanted threads
products	Web masters will go here to add, edit, or delete products that appear on the site
polls	This is where new polls can be created
newsletters	This is where web masters will be able to add, edit, or view the newsletters
users	Here, web masters can be added or deleted, and their administrative permissions can be modified
settings	This is where web masters can modify personal settings such as their password

The extra folders here exist because there are certain things like advertisements that the web masters need to control, but that the users just see without any real interaction.

We'll subdivide _lib, like this:

Subdirectory	Description
_base	Includes the common function libraries that will exist, along with the global configuration file
_classes	Includes the custom classes that we'll be writing throughout the book
doc	Includes any documentation notes we want to keep for ourselves
_sql	Includes any MySQL creation files that we might need to reference
_bin	Includes the e-mail send daemon

Additionally, there will be a _img directory, where we'll keep the graphics and the banner advertisement images for the site.

The full spread of directories looks like this:

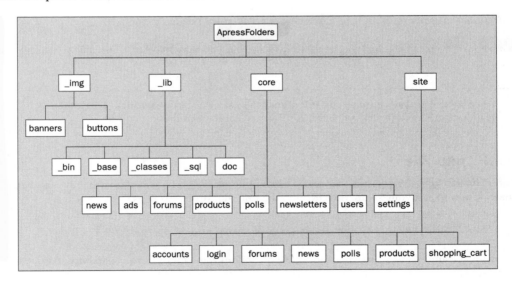

Configuration

We would like the configuration of this site to be as simple as possible. Here we'll use two files that will need to be adjusted when deploying this web site. The first is the .htaccess file located in the web server's root directory, and the second is the config.php global configuration file located in the /_lib/_base directory.

The .htaccess File

The Apache web server can be configured to allow user-specific changes to the default configuration options. This is typically done by placing a file, named .htaccess, in the directory where we want the changes to take effect. Any configuration changes we make will cascade to lower directories unless they are overridden by other .htaccess files.

We'll use the .htaccess file to do two things:

❑ To set the value of PHP's include_path, which is the listing of directories that PHP will go through when it's looking for a file that we have included in a piece of code.

❑ To ensure that the register_globals directive is set to Off. We'll talk more about why this is needed in the *HTTP Request Variables* section later in the chapter.

Our .htaccess file contains the following.

```
php_value include_path
".:/usr/lib/php/:/var/www/html/_lib/_base:/var/www/html/_lib/_classes:/var/www/htm
l/site:/var/www/html/core:/var/www/html/pear"

php_value register_globals "Off"
```

Note that the value for include_path should all be on one line in the file.

Our web server's root directory is /var/www/html, but you may need to adjust this to comply with your setup.

> Here we are assuming that your ISP allows the use of .htaccess files. This practice is ubiquitous enough that we feel it is a safe assumption to make.

The config.php File

This file defines global values that are used throughout our site. You will probably have to change some of these values to suit your setup. Specifically, the line that reads:

```
define("DSN", "mysql://root:@localhost/apress");
```

will almost certainly have to be changed to use the values that work for your database. Also, you might want to set the value that defines the default e-mail address to an address of your choosing.

The Database, Application Code, and UI

Modern applications tend to be divided (as much as possible) into three distinct classes of functionality:

❑ Data layer

❑ Application codebase, often referred to as Application or Business Logic

❑ User Interface (UI), often referred to as Presentation

This is done for web applications because it's a design model that tends to foster the development of maintainable and scalable sites. Also, on larger development teams, it allows people to specialize. For example, the programmers can focus mostly on programming, and the interface designers can focus on the UI. Each of these has a well-defined purpose in and of itself.

The Data Layer

The data layer is generally the data in the database, along with any data-centric logic like stored procedures. This can involve data stored in more than one database, or even more than one machine. The central issue for us here will be the database schema or table layout.

Because we are developing a site that could be deployed in a standard ISP hosting situation, we'll just have a single database to worry about, since that is often what we are presented with in a shared hosting environment.

> *The database for our application is called 'apress'.*

Also, we have chosen to use MySQL, which does not support stored procedures. So for us, the data layer is really just that – the data that we'll be putting into our database tables. However, we should note that the lack of stored procedures does not mean that we're going to have SQL code splattered all over our pages. Instead, our SQL will be encapsulated in classes whose methods will therefore effectively emulate stored procedures for us.

The Application Code Layer

The application code layer (**application logic layer**) also has a discreet function. Half of its job is to provide clear and useful ways of getting data out of the data layer, formatting it if necessary, and passing it on to the UI where it'll be seen by the user.

The other half deals with getting input from the browser and placing what it finds into the data layer for later use. This is not as simple as it sounds, however. There are always considerations for things like data validation, by ensuring that the user's input is actually something that should be stored. The application code layer also may play some role in maintaining data consistency, by ensuring that the relationships between different tables in the database are maintained properly.

> *For an excellent reference on these issues, refer to Beginning PHP4 Databases from Apress (ISBN 1-861007-82-5).*

Our application code will consist of function libraries and classes that will be stored under the _lib directory we talked about in the *Directory Structure* section. The bulk of this will be classes to represent different things such as users, forums, polls, and shopping carts. Each of these is an example of something that is easily thought of as an object, so it makes sense to create classes to represent them. Wherever possible we'll make use of the PEAR classes included with PHP to keep from duplicating the functionality that is already well-developed and available to us.

Much of the rest of this book will be devoted to creating these files in ways that achieve the goals stated above.

The User Interface (UI)

The UI is the part of the web site that defines what the user will actually see. This usually consists of a collection of HTML or XHTML files, CSS definitions, and JavaScript functions. Note that in this book, we'll not be using any browser-specific JavaScript functions, since we want the site to function properly on all popular browsers. We'll work on the UI in Chapter 3.

> *HyperText Markup Language (HTML) is an SGML (Standard Generalized Markup Language) application conforming to International Standard ISO 8879, and is widely regarded as the standard publishing language of the World Wide Web. Extensible HyperText Markup Language (XHTML) is a family of current and future document types and modules that reproduce, subset, and extend HTML 4. CSS is a technology specification published by the W3C that is implemented in modern browsers. JavaScript is a scripting language that is supported by all major browsers like Netscape and Internet Explorer.*

Programming Standards

Agreeing on and consistently using a set of programming standards is essential to creating clear and maintainable code. All the developers for a particular project need to implement a set of standards that is clearly defined at the start of the work, especially because it's easy to become lax about following a common set of standards when you are in the middle of a project. Many times, when we are working away, it's bothersome to have to stop and properly document a function. However, when we come back to that function three months later we'll be pleased that we did.

Another point we should remember is that there are a great number of coding standards that one might employ. For example, some people think that functions should always use mixed case naming. Others think that underscores are a better way of separating the words that make up a function name. There isn't a 'universally-best' scheme; the critical thing, however, is that we pick one and use it consistently through the codebase.

In the next few sections we'll lay out the scheme for the code in the upcoming chapters.

Program Variables

All variables should easily be identifiable by their name, and make use of a mixed case naming convention. Furthermore, variables should be prefixed with a data type character that identifies their assumed type. This ensures that developers will understand the expected type for the variable and will further explain the purpose of its usage.

Additionally, variables in a class that are intended to be private will have a leading underscore – a 'private variable' is one that is only supposed to be accessed directly by the class that it's defined in. Likewise, a 'private method' is a method that is only supposed to be called internally by the class it is defined in.

Finally, the defined constants will be all uppercase.

Here is a listing:

Program Variable	Naming Convention
String variable	$sVarName
Integer variable	$aVarName
Array variable	$aVarName
Object instance	$oVarNmae
Private member variable	$_sVarName
Defined constant	CONSTANT

HTTP Request Variables

PHP version 4.2.0 and higher has the register_globals configuration turned to Off, by default, for security reasons. With register_globals set to On, a user could potentially override the correct setting for a particular variable by doing things such as defining a new GET variable via the URL. This is not possible with register_globals set to Off, which is why we used the .htaccess file to force this issue earlier.

> **For more information on this topic, refer to the PHP 4.1.0 release notes at http://www.php.net/release_4_1_0.php.**

By turning off the ability for any user-submitted variable to be injected into the PHP code, the amount of variable poisoning a potential cracker may inflict is reduced. They will have to take the additional time to forge submissions, and our internal variables are effectively isolated from the user-submitted data.

With the reister_globals turned off, however, the variables that are part of HTTP requests are not immediately available anymore with this configuration. They can, however, be accessed using the superglobal arrays that were introduced in PHP 4.1.0. Here is a listing of PHP's superglobals that we'll use in our application:

Superglobal Array	Description
$_GET	Form variables sent through GET
$_POST	Form variables sent through POST variables
$_COOKIE	HTTP cookie variables
$_SESSION	HTTP variables registered by the session module
$_FILES	Uploaded file variables
$_SERVER	Server variables, like REMOTE_ADDR
$_ENV	Environment variables

Refer to http://www.php.net/manual/en/printwn/language.variables.predefined.php for more information.

Functions

All functions should be named such that their usage is easily identifiable to a developer. The following sections will detail the primary development implementations and their standards.

Naming

All functions will be named with a mixed case naming convention. Functions should be named so that they provide a clear and obvious context of their usage, like this:

```
function getActiveUserId($iUserId) {
    // code
    return TRUE;
}
```

Private member functions will be named with an underscore notation similar to variables, like this:

```
function _checkUserName($sUserName) {
    // code
    return FALSE;
}
```

Commenting

To take advantage of the benefits of self-documenting code implemented with phpDocumentor, we need to provide clear, well-commented code that adheres to the conventions available at http://phpdocu.sourceforge.net/.

> phpDocumentor is a JavaDoc-like automatic documentation generator for PHP written in PHP. It's the most versatile tool for documenting PHP.

This means that there are comments attached to each function with a short description, a summary of the arguments for the function, and information about the return type, like this:

```
/**
 * Sets the name
 *
 * @param string the name to set
 * @return boolean
 * @access public
 */

function setName($sName) {
    // code to set name
    return TRUE;
}
```

Classes

Classes will be built to provide the maximum level of functionality and reuse by organizing a logical object hierarchy. Objects will be treated as such and will be comprised of functions that specifically relate to the object and its intended use. Objects should extend other objects whenever there is a shared function that can be taken advantage of.

In particular, we'll be making use of certain PEAR objects that are native to newer PHP installs. In the event that a shared object is extended, the resource reference will be implemented into the child class. We can use the `require_once` statement to ensure that only a single instance of our resource class will be introduced on a linear object reference.

Naming

Classes will be defined in files named with the **class.classname.php** convention. So if we define a `users` class, we would put the code for that class into a `class.users.php` file. Furthermore, there will only be one class defined per file. This will help keep things clean and separate, especially for reference purposes.

Summary

We've covered quite a lot in this chapter. We started by considering some of the critical design issues that will affect the course of development. These included what information our base architecture will provide to the modules, how errors will be handled, the need for different kinds of users on the site, the layout of the directory structure, and the coding conventions and naming schemes for our PHP application.

Having done that, we delved into the implementation details. We identified that the base architecture will provide a type of cookie-based session implementation. Errors will be handled in a uniform way designed not to be disruptive to the person visiting the site. There will be three different types of people that come to the site – defined as visitors, users, and web masters. Furthermore, the web masters will have a more finely grained level of access control that defines what administrative functionality they will have available. Finally, we dissected the directory structure that we'll use, and defined coding standards that we'll make use of.

Of course, this means that it's finally time to start some actual coding. In the next chapter, we'll start by defining what our UI should look like and how it will be constructed with some help from the utility functions.

3

Designing the User Interface

In Chapters 1 and 2, we discussed the elements required to build a useful web application. Our site is going to be viewed by end users, and they are going to need something to look at. This will require the construction of a User Interface (UI) with which they can interact to make use of our programs.

This chapter will look at some of the basic strategies that are employed when going through the process of interface design. These include:

❑   The purpose, benefits, and implementation of Cascading Style Sheets (CSS)

❑   Developing reusable page elements that can be deployed on many pages easily

❑   Establishing a way of error handling that shows us the problems without detracting too much from the user experience

In this chapter we'll first identify the initial problem relating to our front-end (UI). Then we'll move on to designing a solution to this problem. Finally we'll cover the actual code and implementation of this solution.

The Problem

At some point, we'll need to create the presentation layer of our application. We could use a text editor and start writing; however, we would need to edit many pages to make a single global change if all the pages were constructed in an independent manner – a problem that crops up if the application logic is not properly separated from the presentation. To avoid this maintenance nightmare, we'll build a solid UI that is simple to modify and maintain. We can achieve this only with careful planning and the use of good design techniques.

We'll also need to pay careful attention to the user experience. This involves following sound usability guidelines and principles, and is a critical factor in the success of the site. Put simply, if users don't like the way something is presented, they won't be inclined to stay at, or come back to, our site. There are several factors that could turn a user off, such as:

❑ Unclear navigation

❑ Outdated content

❑ Aesthetically unappealing site

❑ Long load time due to excessive graphics

❑ Improper rendering, in a specific browser, due to flawed code

There are many web sites out there that provide similar content. So we need to understand our target audience and provide things that they are interested in. Furthermore, we need to do it in a way that looks good.

The problem that must be solved in this chapter is the creation of a solid foundation for the UI that we can employ throughout the design of this application. This UI should strive to meet the following set of goals at all times:

❑ The site should be easily modifiable and maintainable

❑ The site should present information clearly to the user

❑ The site should be aesthetically appealing to the user

❑ Care should be taken to separate logic and UI as cleanly as possible

In the next section, we'll explore the design principles that will help us solve our problem while meeting the stated goals.

The Design

Now that we've identified that our problem is the lack of a solid UI, let's go about laying down a solid foundation that we can extend to create the site's UI.

Now, as anyone who has ever gone through a full development cycle will tell us, no amount of planning will ever account for the small changes that are essential, as we get further into the process. The best we can do is to create a **flexible design** that'll allow us some room to make changes. Here are a few things we can do in the coding and basic designing that will help us achieve flexibility:

❑ Use CSS to classify different elements and styles on the pages such as headers, footers, background colors, and font styles. CSS is also used to define themes for the overall presentation that can easily be reused across the desired pages.

❑ Create reusable elements that appear on many or all of the pages and include them where needed at runtime. Some perfect examples of this would be common navigational elements, behind the scenes code for checking cookies, and logging referrers.

❑ Design the interface to be uncluttered, meaning that there should not be extraneous links or design elements that distract the user from the site's content.

In *The Problem* section, we mentioned the need to create a UI that is attractive as well as functional. The reality is that the general browsing public is not interested in how well the backend of a web site is coded as long as it works. If the UI is hard to understand, then the users wouldn't find it easy to locate what they want, not to mention the fact that they don't even like looking at the site.

> **Excellent articles about UI design are available on the Web. Insightful comments can often be found at http://www.zeldman.com/, http://www.alistapart.com, and http://www.webstandards.org.**

The first step in creating the UI is usually the generation of graphical **comps**, which are graphics that demonstrate what a typical page might look like. Once a nice looking design has been created, we can code a non-functional shell. We'll first make a static HTML page that can be rendered in a browser to see what things will look like – this is the procedure that we'll follow when building this site.

Programmers generally prefer to write everything by hand using Homesite or XEmacs. The code in the chapters in this book will reflect this fact. There are many other less code-centric programs to help you with your UI design – Macromedia's Dreamweaver and Microsoft FrontPage, for example. Text editors were chosen because the graphical options available tend to produce bloated and non standards-compliant HTML that may not render correctly in some browsers. Conversely, text editors can support context-based tag selection based on the DTD you're using, thus ensuring well-formed markup (like Emacs with PSGML mode, for instance).

The following is a screenshot of a sample mock-up for the newsfeed comp. It doesn't do anything at this point, but we can gather some useful information about the UI elements needed from it:

We'll develop this particular page, including the PHP code needed to utilize the reusable parts, in *The Solution* section. All other pages on both the user and administration site are put together in a similar manner, so if you understand how we get this page together, then the functionality of the rest will be clear.

Browser Issues

In the early days of the Internet, developers normally used Netscape Navigator since this browser offered support for the available standards. This meant that developers could read the freely available specifications for HTML and design pages based on these specifications, and the pages would render in the browser as expected.

Later, both Netscape and Microsoft started building browser functionality that was not compatible with the published standards, or with the other company's browser. With version 4 (Netscape and Microsoft), the browsers degraded when they were hit with code they didn't understand, since they supported existing standards incorrectly. For example, the way that tables were rendered was not the same in terms of how cellpadding was implemented even when presented with identical HTML.

> *cellpadding is a feature of a table in HTML that controls the area around the contents of the table's cells by allowing for more whitespace. Alternatively, cellspacing provides more space between the cells. The two can be used together, which gives the author flexibility in designing the table.*

However, the newest browser releases from Microsoft, Netscape, the Mozilla project (which produces the rendering engine used by Netscape), and Opera are all compliant with the current standards. The issue of cross-browser support these days lies largely in the decision to support, or not support, the Netscape 4.x browser line.

> When generically referring to standards, we are actually talking about the published specifications available from the World Wide Web Consortium (W3C). For more information, refer to http://www.w3c.org.

Choosing Supported Browsers

Some of the issues that we should consider when choosing a browser are:

❑ The demography of the target audience – Are they likely to be tech-savvy, which might indicate a willingness to upgrade to the newest browser versions? Or are they more likely to just stick forever with whatever came with their computer?

❑ Use of site elements that are supported by the browsers that we want to target – For example, Microsoft Internet Explorer 6 (IE 6), which is the newest release at the time of writing, still does not have complete support for the PNG (Portable Network Graphics) image format.

❑ Diversity of the platforms in the userbase – For example, if we were developing a site about Macintosh hardware, we would certainly not want to use any features specific to the Windows version of IE, as we would be damaging the user experience for a substantial part of our user base.

❑ Time required for developing and maintaining the UI – Supporting older browsers requires much more time. This is partially due to the fact that we'll be forced to use older development models, and partially due to the time required to make sure they work.

❑   Any accessibility issues needed to be addressed – This may be much harder to do in older browsers.

Note that choosing the browser is something we need to decide on before we begin planning the UI. If halfway through the design we are forced to go back and support another browser, it may send us right back to the drawing board.

In this book, we aren't going to support older browsers such as the Netscape 4.x series. We'll talk mostly about the PHP parts of site development, and the extra effort needed to support old and inferior browsers is not worth the effort. Our site should render correctly and identically in the new versions of Microsoft IE, Mozilla, Netscape, Phoenix, and Chimera.

Cascading Style Sheets (CSS)

CSS provides developers a way to separate content from presentation on web pages. It's important to state the importance of the proper use of CSS when designing a UI.

CSS is a technology specification published by the W3C that is implemented in modern browsers, especially those browsers based on the Mozilla rendering engine, such as Chimera, Phoenix, Galeon, and the Netscape 6 and 7 series. For more information about Mozilla, refer to the web site http://www.mozilla.org.

For example, if we want all the text in the navigation elements to be 10 point, bold Verdana in bright green, we could accomplish this using the old (non-CSS) and new ways.

With the old method of coding, the code might look like this:

```
<div>
    <font size="10" color="#00ff00" face="Verdana">
        <b>
            Navigation Text
        </b>
    </font>
</div>
```

For every navigation element on the site, we would have to code the <font> and <b> tags by hand, which is a tedious task. More importantly, clients may come back and ask us to change the background for all the navigation elements to gray. So we'd have to change the opening of every element like this:

```
<div style="background: #66666;">
    ...
</div>
```

Thus a lot of time would be spent in making changes every time they were needed. Compare doing that to using an External Style Sheet (ESS) to define a class for navigation elements. The equivalent HTML code would look like this:

```
<div class="nav_element">
    Navigation Text
</div>
```

It's easy to agree that this is a nicer way of doing things. Furthermore, if we need to make a global change to the appearance of these elements, we can just edit the single file that defines the class. The change will propagate instantly and globally across the site with little effort. From a programmer's perspective, this is somewhat like having a global configuration file that defines parameters used in many places in the code. If we want to make any changes to such a parameter, we can just edit the global configuration file and the changes will take place everywhere.

We'll use this as a paradigm for working with the display. It's clear that we should try to generate a set of common display types, or classes, that'll be used regularly in various parts of the site. All these will be defined in a single external file that can be included into our HTML markup. One of the advantages of this approach is that it's easy to add new classes later on.

Looking at our basic comp, we can start to pick out the classes that we'll want to define. It's common to have a large number of comps. In fact, on larger sites, it's common to see over a hundred distinct classes.

For example purposes, here's the public newsfeed comp for our web site:

We'll need to implement the following CSS style classes:

- ❑ Basic Body – This style will provide the basic background color, text color, and font information for everything within the `<body>` of the site.

- ❑ Header – A class to define what the page header or title looks like. In our comp, this corresponds to the DVD Life Newsfeed text.

- ❑ Copy – Just a standard set of display information about generic bits of text. For example, the text just below the header.

- ❑ Error Display – This is one that we can't see from our comp. However, we'll use it to show any errors (that we trap) to the user.

❑ Banner Advertisement – Here, we'll put in any information about how the banner advertisements should be shown.

❑ News Headline – In the earlier screenshot, it's shown that each news story has an associated headline. Naturally, we'll want a style to describe what those headlines look like.

❑ Separator – The dotted lines that separate different stories can and should be handled via CSS, since they're part of the presentation.

❑ Logo – This is the text, in the upper left of the web site, that gives the name of the site. We want control over its presentation as it'll be useful if we ever need to change the logo.

This will provide us with a good starting point for our stylesheet definitions. There is a possibility that we'll need new classes as we get further along with the development. Fortunately, as we'll see, adding additional classes is trivial – we'd only need to add a few lines into the text file.

Reusable Page Elements

We can conceptually divide the UI into four areas:

❑ Header

❑ Navigation

❑ Main Content

❑ Footer

Visually, these fall into place (roughly) as shown here:

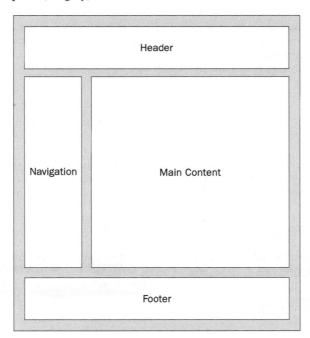

Let's look at each of these, and see what qualifies as reusable.

The Header

The header is that part of the page where the banner advertisement sits. All visitors will see these banners, which will be dynamically generated in the advertisements module detailed in Chapter 8. Therefore, this part of the page is a reusable element.

The Navigation

The main navigation consists of the links on the left-hand side of the page. The user can go to different parts of the site by clicking on these links. This is the same for everybody (it only differs between the registered and non-registered users of the site), so it's reusable.

It's particularly important that we reuse this navigation component for several reasons:

❑   It's well suited for it, since each user sees the same navigation on all parts of the site

❑   If there is a problem, such as a link changing, we don't want to have to fix that link on every page where the navigation is used

❑   In the future, if we were to add or remove one of the application modules, we wouldn't want to have to change the navigation on each page where it's used

By using a common component, we greatly improve our ability to have an extensible and maintainable implementation. Since that is one of the principal design goals, we should certainly implement things this way.

The Main Content

Right now, we have some sample news stories. In Chapter 6 where we develop the newsfeed, we'll look at how to dynamically generate content. This content will be specific to a particular part of the site, and will have substantially different functionality, which we'll see when we get to topics such as the discussion forums in Chapter 10. So clearly, it's not something that we can reuse.

The Footer

There is some bit of HTML code that closes out the page. In this case, that's all it does, but it's still reusable and should be treated as such.

This is also true from the standpoint of extensibility. In the future, we may decide to put up another banner at the top of the site, or decide that we want another banner to appear at the bottom of the site – with a reusable component, we could easily add this in on all pages at the same time.

Building the Page

Now we know which parts should be reused, and which the application module generates. The idea is that when a given page is called, it'll pull the header, navigation, and footer from some common place, and the specific application will fill in the main content. The functionality for the reusable parts will be provided in the /site/tpl_unsecure.php file, which we'll code in *The Solution* section of the chapter.

As mentioned in Chapter 2, all our application modules fall into the `site` directory.

The 'tpl' part of the filename is meant to indicate that this file provides template functionality, meaning that it gives us a way to deploy the reusable components we have mentioned. The 'unsecure' part is not meant to indicate that this file in some way leaves anything open to attack. Instead it indicates that the site can make use of this file for users and visitors who do not have any administration (web master) privileges. There is a corresponding file for the administrative part of the site called /site/tpl_secure.php that'll only allow those with web master privileges to use it.

Error Handling

We need a consistent way to trap any errors that occur when the pages execute. Furthermore, this should happen in a user-friendly way, a point that is often overlooked by developers.

Nothing is more disconcerting to the standard user than seeing a DB Error:syntax error output, and the following page generates such an error message:

```php
<?php

// import file that contains the configuration values for the application
require_once("config.php");

// import the PEAR::DB class
require_once("DB.php");

$db = DB::connect(DSN);

$sql = "SELECT *
        FRM
            apress_forums
        WHERE
            1";

$oTmp = $db->query($sql);

if( DB::isError($oTmp) ) {
    die($rsTmp->getMessage());
}
?>
```

Note that we've referred to the apress_forums table, which hasn't been defined yet (it's created in Chapter 10 that deals with discussion forums). It's not important at the moment. The thing to pay attention to is the obvious syntax error caused by misspelling the SQL word **FROM** as **FRM**. The PEAR_ERROR object will notify us that the problem was caused by a syntax error, but the important issue is how we deal with that error.

We can use die() to trap errors, but it leaves the user thinking that the whole site is down. Moreover, the users can do nothing outside of clicking their back button or typing in a new URL to get out.

Instead, we will create functions that trap these errors, which will give us an easy way of displaying them on the page. This way, the user knows something is wrong, but is left with the ability to at least click on other links to go to other parts of the site.

The Solution

In this chapter, we first identified the need for a UI that'll serve as a foundation for the presentation layer of our application. After that, we discussed some of the design considerations that will help us get to our goal. With all of this in mind, let's start with some code to create the UI elements that we need.

We'll work on three things in this section:

- ❑ The CSS file that will define the presentation of the UI

- ❑ The tpl_unsecure.php file that will provide functionality needed to implement reusable parts of our pages

- ❑ The error handling functions that will trap errors and present them for review without having the site break down

Styles

We'll use CSS wherever possible to help separate content from presentation in the application. We do this by defining CSS classes that can be applied to the appropriate UI elements. By consistently applying the same classes to similar elements throughout the site, we'll ensure a unified look and feel.

The benefit of using CSS is evident when we need to make a global change to a display element in the site. All we need to do is correct the CSS file, and the corresponding change will immediately take effect everywhere that style is used. This relieves us of the burden of tracking down each instance and changing it by hand.

— PORTAL . CSS

We'll put all our styles into the _lib/apress.mt.css file, under our web server's root directory. The HTML will simply include this file to make use of the classes that we'll define.

As detailed in Chapter 2, the _lib directory contains files like the shared function libraries and custom classes.

The first thing we'll do is to create a style definition for the <body> element:

```
body {
    margin: 0;
    font: 10px verdana, geneva, arial, sans-serif;
    color: #000000;
    background-color: #FFFFFF;
}
```

Now, we'll set the page margins to zero pixels, define a default font size, face, and color, and set the default background color of the page to white. Then we'll provide a default style for the <td>, <th>, and <font> tags, as well as for a generic .bod class just in case we need it later:

```
td, th, .bod, font {
    font: 10px verdana, geneva, arial, sans-serif;
    color: #000000;
}
```

We'll force the <b> and <strong> tags to look the same:

```
b, strong {
    font-weight: bold;
}
```

We'll override the default behavior of the <a> tag, meaning that links will not show up displayed using the browser defaults that the user has set. We define our own font information, as well as removing the underline that typically appears. This will help us to get a consistent look and feel within the UI:

```
a {
    font: 10px verdana, geneva, arial, sans-serif;
    color: #485C98;
    text-decoration: none;
}
```

We'll also want to control what the link looks like when the user's mouse is hovering over it:

```
a:hover {
    color: #687FC0;
}
```

So far, most of what we've been doing is setting our site specific values for existing tag elements. However, looking at our earlier discussion of the elements of the UI, it's clear that we'll need to create some custom styles.

We'll start with the logo, which is the part where we identify our site to the viewers:

```
.logo {
    font: 15px Georgia, Times;
    color: #FFFFFF;
    font-weight: bold;
    text-align: center;
    width: 122px;
    height: 19px;
    background-color: #22397A;
    position: absolute;
    top: 15px;
    left: 0px;
    z-index: 10;
}
```

Next we create the header style, which will be applied to the title of the application module we're looking at on any given page:

```
.header {
    font: 12px verdana, geneva, arial, sans-serif;
    color: #485E9C;
    font-weight: bold;
    padding-top: 5px;
    padding-bottom: 5px;
}
```

This will be followed by the section style, which can be seen in our comp defining what'll be the news headlines:

```
.section {
    font: 11px verdana, geneva, arial, sans-serif;
    color: #000000;
    font-weight: bold;
    padding-top: 5px;
    padding-bottom: 5px;
}
```

We'll also need a style to tell us what the copy for the news stories look like:

```
.copy {
    font: 10px verdana, geneva, arial, sans-serif;
    color: #000000;
    padding-bottom: 5px;
}
```

There are a few more things that we need to take care of. The first is a style for the banner advertisements to make sure that they're padded properly from the rest of the page elements:

```
.banner {
    padding-top: 15px;
    padding-bottom: 10px;
}
```

We'll also want to use CSS to generate the dotted lines that separate the different stories. Here we are using a simple graphic to create the separator. Clearly, this could be implemented by just creating a graphic and putting it into the HTML where needed.

There are two reasons why it's better to use a style. First, it's a presentation element, so by creating it with a style we get all of the control available in CSS. Second, it's good to use CSS to control presentation whenever possible – by using CSS, we can create a much smaller graphic and implement is as a background image that the browser will repeat for us. The style we want to use looks like this:

```
.dotrule {
    background-image: url(../_img/bg_15dot_rule.gif);
}
```

Next, we'll create an error style. This will be used when any errors occur and we need to make the user aware of them. We'll make the text for this class bright red:

```
.error {
    padding-top: 15px;
    color: #990000;
}
```

Finally, we need one more class for the paging graphics on the lower right side of the site. Later we'll see how these will be used to let the visitor scroll through the news stories:

```
.paging {
    padding-top: 5px;
    padding-bottom: 5px;
}
```

This use of CSS is straightforward. We've now defined a set of page defaults and classes that can be applied to generate a consistent look and feel for the site.

> **Full documentation for CSS is available at the W3C site. CSS1 is detailed at http://www.w3c.org/TR/REC-CSS1, and CSS2 is detailed at http://www.w3.org/TR/REC-CSS2/.**

As we progress into the development of the applications, we'll need to define some new classes for new elements as they appear. These new classes will go into the same file and won't have any effect on the ones we just created.

Reusable Page Elements

We'll now think about how we'll involve reusable page elements in our site where possible. In *The Design* section, we identified three areas that are the same for every page:

- ❑ Header
- ❑ Navigation
- ❑ Footer

With this in mind, let's look at what the code for this kind of page might look like. Our comp was for the newsfeed section, so we'll continue using that as our test case. This is the /site/news/index.php file:

```php
<?php

//File Location: /site/news/index.php

// include the tpl_unsecure.php file that has the needed
// functions for the rest of this page
require_once("tpl_unsecure.php");

// generate the header information
setHeader();

// start a new page with a banner advertisement
openPage(TRUE);
?>
```

Now we put the desired text in the main content section of the site:

```html
<!-- main content -->
<table border="0" cellpadding="0" cellspacing="0">

    <tr>
        <td><div class="header"><?php echo ENTITY; ?> Newsfeed</div></td>
    </tr>
```

```
    <tr>
        <td><div class="copy">To view news articles,
        select a news type from the list below.</div></td>
    </tr>

    <tr>
        <td><div class="error"><?php writeErrors(); ?></div></td>
    </tr>
</table>

<table width="608" border="0" cellpadding="0" cellspacing="0">
    <tr>
        <td><div class="section">Something about DVD's</div></td>
    </tr>
    <tr>
        <td><div class="copy">This is some test news....</div></td>
    </tr>

    <tr>
        <td class="dotrule"><img src="../../_img/spc.gif"
        width="1" height="15" alt="" border="0" /></td>
    </tr>
    .....

    <tr>
        <td align="right"><div class="section">
        <!--| paging |-->

        <table width="35" border="0" cellpadding="0" cellspacing="0">
            <tr>
                <td width="15"><img src="../../_img/buttons/btn_prev.gif"
                width="15" height="15" alt="" border="0" /></td>
                <td width="5"><img src="../../_img/spc.gif"
                width="5" height="1" alt="" border="0" /></td>
                <td width="15"><img src="../../_img/buttons/btn_next.gif"
                width="15" height="15" alt="" border="0" /></td>
            </tr>
        </table>

        <!--| paging |-->
        </div></td>
    </tr>
</table>

<?php

// print out footer information
closePage();
?>
```

The part designated as main content is static at this point, with the minor exception of some PHP to print out the version number. All of the work for the header, navigation, and footer is handled by these three functions:

❑   setHeader()

❑   openPage()

❑   closePage()

These will be defined in the `tpl_unsecure.php` file that's included at the beginning of the script.

The Template Framework File

Let's now define the three functions – `setHeader()`, `openPage()`, `closePage()` – that will live in the `tpl_unsecure.php` file, in the `/site` directory under the server root. Let's start the script:

```php
<?php

// File Location: /site/tpl_unsecure.php
```

The `elements.php` file, which is included next, is located in the `/_lib/_base/`, but we don't need to write out the full path because of the `.htaccess` file (detailed in Chapter 2). We'll talk more about this file in the *Error Handling* section. For now, we'll use some of its error handling functions here. To create the page header, we need a simple function that prints out the start of our page – it's effectively just a big print statement. However, it does dynamically include certain things such as the version and page title. More importantly, it also dynamically generates some JavaScript that'll alert the user to any exceptions that have been caught.

> As mentioned in Chapter 2, the `.htaccess` file is used to set the value of PHP's `include_path`, which is the listing of directories that PHP will go through when it's looking for a file that has been included in a piece of code. Our web server's root directory is `/var/www/html`, but you may need to adjust this to comply with your setup.

Let's continue with the script:

```php
// contains reusable generic elements such as error display functions
require_once("elements.php");
```

In the above section of `tpl_unsecure.php` script, all of the constants that are printed to the screen are defined in the `/_lib/_base/config.php` file. This file is required by the `/_lib/_base/funcs.php` file which in turn is required by the `/_lib/_base/elements.php` file. The following diagram will help to make things clearer:

config.php ⟶ funcs.php ⟶ elements.php ⟶ tpl_unsecure.php

By including `/_lib/_base/elements.php` , we get access to all the predefined constants too. Furthermore, `elements.php` provides a `writeExceptions()` function that generates some JavaScript code to alert the user of any values stored in the global `$EXCEPTS` array, which will trap and hold any exceptions that are thrown.

You may be wondering why we have so many different files that are getting included. It might seem easier just to put all of the code needed by `tpl_unsecure.php` in one place (or in `tpl_unsecure.php` itself) to decrease the complexity of the include hierarchy. The reason not to do this is that we never want to include more code than needed for a given task. Doing so requires increased server resources which is never desirable. The `tpl_unsecure.php` file may well make use of the page elements defined in `elements.php`. However, it's unlikely that we would need those in one of the data objects we'll be defining in future chapters. So for those objects, we might just want to include the `funcs.php` file.

Here is the code for the `setHeader()` function:

```php
// render page header
function setHeader() {

    // the writeExceptions() function is defined in the elements.php file
    $sExceptions = writeExceptions();
    print '

    <?xml version="1.0" encoding="ISO-8859-1">
     <!DOCTYPE html PUBLIC "-//W3C//DTD XHTML 1.0 Transitional//EN"
     "http://www.w3.org/TR/xhtml1/DTD/xhtml1-transitional.dtd">
    <html xmlns="http://www.w3.org/1999/xhtml" xml:lang="en" lang="en">

    <!--| version ' . VERSION . ' |-->

    <head>
        <meta http-equiv="Content-Type" content="text/html;
        charset=iso-8859-1" />
        <title>' . TITLE . '</title>
        <link href="' . SITE_DIR . '_lib/apress.mt.css"
        rel="stylesheet" media="screen" />
        <script language="javascript"
        src="' . SITE_DIR  . '_lib/apress.mt.js"
        type="text/javascript"></script>
        <script language="javascript" type="text/javascript"><!--
        ' . $sExceptions . '
        // --></script>
    </head>
    ';
} // end setHeader()
```

[handwritten annotations: Portal.CSS, Portal.JS]

Note that with the DOCTYPE we are defining, we're telling the browsers to interpret our pages as XHTML instead of HTML.

The `openPage()` function generates the HTML that displays the navigation, and optionally the banner advertisement. We say 'optionally' because we're going to build in the ability to turn off banner advertisements for any particular page. There is a Boolean variable (`$bBanner`) passed to `openPage()` – if it's set to TRUE, then the banner is displayed.

Here is the `openPage()` function that puts HTML onto the page:

```php
// render page opening
function openPage($bBanner = FALSE) {

    // $sBanner holds the HTML for the banner advertisement, if we want one.

    if( $bBanner ) {

        $sBanner = '
         <tr>
             <td align="center"><div class="banner">
             <img src="../../_img/banners/lg_blank.gif"
               width="467" height="60" alt="" border="0" /></div></td>
         </tr>';
```

```
    } else {
        $sBanner = '';
    }
```

Note that at the moment, there is just a static GIF (Graphics Interchange Format) file that is displayed if we open the page with a banner. On the completed site, we'll want banners to display dynamically from an available pool. We'll add this functionality to tpl_unsecure.php in Chapter 8, which deals with banner advertisements. For now though, putting in this static value will suffice to understand how we are approaching things.

The next section of the script prints out the header and menu:

```
    // now print out the header and menu
    print '

    <body>

        <!--| framework |-->
        <table width="740" border="0" cellpadding="0" cellspacing="0">
        <tr>

            <td width="119" bgcolor="#E2E2E2" valign="top">
            <!--| menu |-->
            <table width="119" border="0" cellpadding="0" cellspacing="0">
            <tr>
                <td colspan="2"><img src="../../_img/spc.gif"
                width="1" height="54" alt="" border="0" /></td>
            </tr>

            ......

            </table>
            <!--| menu |-->
            </td>

            <td width="3" bgcolor="#D4D3D3" rowspan="2">
             <img src="../../_img/spc.gif"
              width="3" height="1" alt="" border="0" /></td>

            <td width="15" rowspan="2"><img src="../../_img/spc.gif"
             width="15" height="1" alt="" border="0" /></td>

            <td width="603" valign="top" rowspan="2">

                <!--| content |-->
                <table width="603" border="0"
                 cellpadding="0" cellspacing="0">' . $sBanner . '
                <tr>
                    <td>
                    <!--| section |-->

    <br />';

    } // end openPage()
```

The `openPage()` function generates the same, consistent navigation for any page where it's used. Moreover, looking at the HTML it generates, we can see that the CSS styles defined in the previous section are being used where appropriate. If in the future, we wanted to change, add, or delete some part of the navigation, we could just do it here in this one function, and it would affect all of the pages that use it.

The `closepage()` function really is just a `print()` statement at this point. Remember that we're handling the footer this way because we want the flexibility to make global changes to the bottom of the page in the future:

```
// render page closing
function closePage() {
    print '
                        <!--| section |-->
                        </td>
                </tr>
                </table>
                <!--| content |-->
            </td>
        </tr>

        <tr>
            <td width="122" height="2" bgcolor="#CBCACA">
            <img src="../../_img/spc.gif"
              width="1" height="2" alt="" border="0" /></td>
        </tr>
        </table>
        <!--| framework |-->

        <div class="logo">' . ENTITY . '</div>

    </body>
    </html>
    ';
} // end closePage()
```

Here we generate the functionality to display the header, navigation, and footer for our pages in a convenient and reusable way. The sample news that we used will be replaced later dynamically by the newsfeed module.

We still need to look at the `writeErrors()` and `writeExceptions()` functions that we used in the `tpl_unsecure.php` file. We'll take care of that in the next section.

Error Handling

In the earlier section, we used a few undefined functions to help keep track of errors or exceptions that occur in the execution of our application. It's time now to put these down in code and see what they do.

> *PEAR_ERROR or an extended version is really the best method to store and retrieve error messages. In our application, we do use PEAR_ERROR everywhere we can, and, once we get the error messages, trap them in our own way so that we can display them in reasonably friendly ways.*

The first of these is the `writeErrors()` function, which is defined in the `elements.php` file – it contains functions that write HTML where needed into our reusable elements.

The first lines of this file are:

```
<?php

//File Location: /_lib/_base/elements.php

// utility functions
require_once ( "funcs.php"; )
```

The `funcs.php` file is located in the same directory as `elements.php`, and serves two purposes. First, it provides some useful utility functions that may be needed when generating display elements in `elements.php`. Second, `funcs.php` includes the global configuration file (`/_lib/_base/config.php`) that introduces useful global variables into the namespace.

The `writeErrors()` function looks at the `$ERRORS` global array and generates HTML to display any information it finds:

```
// write user errors (usage: must be called inside the HTML body)
function writeErrors() {

    global $ERRORS;

    if( count($ERRORS) ) {

        print "<strong>Error_</strong><br />";

        while( list($key, $value) = each($ERRORS) ) {
            print($value)."<br />";
        }
    }
}
```

On examining the mock output (which will later be replaced by the newsfeed) we can see that whatever is generated by `writeError()` goes within the error CSS class that we created earlier. So if there are any such errors, they'll be bright red and easily visible to the user.

Next is the `writeExceptions()` function that is used to generate a JavaScript popup that will be displayed if there are exceptions that the user needs to be aware of. For example, if they verify improper data, the functions that validate this data would throw exceptions, and the user would be greeted by a popup on the next page telling them what they did wrong:

```
// write exception errors
// (usage: must be called in JavaScript tags inside the HTML head)
function writeExceptions() {

    global $EXCEPTS;

    $sReturn .= "// exception reporting
    function trace() {
        var msg = \"\";";

        if( count($EXCEPTS) ) {
            $sMsg = "";
            while( list($key, $value) = each($EXCEPTS) ) {
```

```
            $sMsg .= "msg = msg + \"".str_replace("\n", "",
                    addslashes($value))."\\n\";\n";
        }
        $sReturn .= $sMsg;
    }

$sReturn .= "\t
    if( msg != \"\" ) {
        alert(msg);
    }
}
document.onload = trace();\n";

    return $sReturn;
}
```

The function may seem slightly messy, since we're using PHP to write JavaScript, and there are many things (curly braces, for instance) that we need to keep track of. However, it's not a complicated function. It does a similar thing with the global $EXCEPTS array that writeErrors() did with the $ERRORS array. It's just that in this case, the resulting problems are reported into a JavaScript function that's defined and executed when the page loads.

Summary

This wraps up our examination of the UI construction for the site. The sections of the site used by other modules, and the administrative side of the site, are built in exactly the same way. In this chapter we created a file that uniformly creates the header, navigation, and footer HTML for any given page. This makes sense because those pieces of the page are the same for all of the applications on this site. For example, a user in the shopping area will see the same navigation as a user who is voting on a poll. Thus all the applications will make use of the same reusable components where possible. Then, the application in question will populate the main content area with data specific to the module being used on the given page.

Having read this chapter, you should now be familiar with the following concepts:

❑   Using CSS styles to define presentation

❑   Creating a system of reusable display components

❑   Handling errors in a user-friendly fashion

In the next chapter, we'll develop our base architecture that'll provide user and session classes for the application modules to make use of.

4

Managing Users and Sessions

When building a web site containing a great deal of content, we should provide a simplified, secure, and intuitive method for managing that content. By developing and employing a management interface (Content Management System or CMS) for our web site, we can delegate certain roles to assigned users (web masters) who can then contribute to specific sections of the web site. Providing a CMS environment enables us to reduce the time allotted for minding content, and increases the potential for consistency throughout the site.

To begin defining the administrative CMS application, we need to understand how we want our web masters to interact with the system, at what level we want to restrict access, and how we must manage the web masters within the secure realm. We know right away that we must provide a security architecture that requires an authentication process, and regular validation throughout the entire CMS framework. We also know that we want to provide a framework that is easy to extend and manage through the potential growth of our site and its offerings.

In this chapter, we will:

- ❑ Identify some of the potential problems and issues involved with providing a CMS and its userbase
- ❑ Illustrate the problems
- ❑ Produce an initial design concept for how to solve them
- ❑ Write the necessary software to solve these problems

The Problem

Our web site has been defined as a DVD enthusiast's web site. That being known, we need to determine the types of content that we're going to serve. Primarily, we'll focus on dynamic content that ensures up to date, syndicated information to evolve a community based on capturing the 'what's new?' audience. Since this content will be provided by different contributors throughout various applications within the site, we'll need a security layer that enables multiple access permissions for each application. Once we have such a pluggable security architecture in place, we'll be able to easily integrate new applications into our environment, and utilize the different security features that are available within.

We may not want all the site content to be visible to all the web masters, so it would be essential to make provisions for restricted content visibility as well. By defining a set of permissions for each application, we can easily regulate the web master's level of interaction there within. Applying this notion properly will also reduce the potential for overwriting web master content changes and submissions. In this case, where some web masters will merely be contributors and others will act as editors/publishers, we need to make certain that our application content can be stored in multiple states. We'll also have to allow items to be published upon creation and then un-published (staged) by the publishers. This practice could be reversed if we need more control over the content management workflow; however, for our site we'll assume that our publishers are trusted individuals.

Now that we understand some of the basic rules that our CMS must adhere to, let's consider the usability factors that will greatly affect how web masters enter data into the system. If we build a slap-dash application that provides little or no content entry guidelines then we can assume that web masters will potentially feel confused within the administrative tools. In such a case, it's likely to assume that without continual updates and content management, our site visitors won't be overly enthusiastic about returning to the site. Therefore, we need to take care of the interaction aspects of our forms and actions as well as their functionality in order to maintain an even balance of form and function throughout the CMS. We should also be concerned with the importance of clear, contextual, and concise error handling and application feedback for our users – if we do not maintain an intuitive level of user error reporting then we could sacrifice the usability and intended usage of the CMS.

Finally, we must utilize a templating system that will allow for rapid deployment of new applications into our system. By reducing our pages to simple function calls that generate abstracted code, we can simplify and streamline our development and management process. This system will also allow us to produce a dynamic menuing system that renders according to a users' access permissions.

The management interface should strive to meet the following set of goals. It should:

❏   Develop a security architecture that allows multiple access permissions for each application

❏   Define application permissions to restrict content visibility

❏   Maintain clear, contextual, and concise error handling and application feedback

❏   Utilize a templating system to produce a dynamic menuing system that renders according to a web master's access permissions

The Design

When defining the CMS, we need to be aware that there are different ways to design the security architecture correctly. We should simplify the design while maintaining focus on two key aspects – page-level security and access-level security. We could easily over-engineer this process with an investment of time and resources; however, it will be beyond the scope of our needs. We'll be building a three-tiered web site consisting of a data layer (the database), a business layer (the data objects), and a presentation layer (the UI). Each of these tiers will be discussed in our design and illustrated in our solution as the chapter evolves.

Now that we've established our high-level design problem considerations, let's define these rules and/or requirements. Typically, once we begin coding it's assumed that we have a clear, general understanding about all the application requirements and how they may or may not affect one another in the code.

Often times, in larger software companies or projects, the requirements definition phase is a long, tedious process that involves several departments to ensure well-defined feature/functionality lists, application requirements, platform and design requirements, as well as potential support requirements. To ensure that we stay focused on our delivery goals we shall simplify these definitions to the basic application design and briefly discuss the feature/functionality aspects from which we can easily derive our other requirements.

Feature and Functionality Aspects

The following is a list of the key functionality and features that need to be built into the CMS design:

❑   User login and password reminder functionality

❑   Thorough login authentication with intuitive error handling

❑   Page-level dynamic menuing and authentication verification

❑   User settings accessibility for managing web master account information

❑   Page-level controls for web master activity such as adding, editing, deleting, and publishing content based on their application permissions

❑   Logout option to absolutely disable an active web master session

As we are working within a web application, we cannot maintain state like we would in a normal desktop application. Therefore we would need to develop a way to manage a web master session that we can reliably depend on for consistent validation of a web master's activity. We'll use cookies to store some general web master information, as well as, some pseudo-encrypted information about the web master account, which will enable us to effectively cascade our applications around the web master's access permissions in a lightweight manner.

Rather than using the built-in security features and options available through most web server environments, we'll create our own security realm. This is the best option for web sites that need to provide a custom set of rules that apply more in part to their functionality, rather than just accessibility. Therefore, although there are security options available within our web server environment, we shall build a portable application that could easily be re-deployed (if necessary) without being too dependent on our platform's user and group configuration.

Here's a diagrammatic representation of how we want our web master access to function:

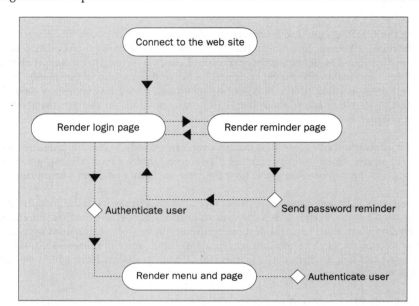

Note that the login page has to be reached by an absolute URL
(http://apress.mediatemple.net/site/login/index.php, in our case) to gain access to the CMS
login. This is very common with CMS systems since they are meant for a restricted set of users.

Our pages throughout the site will rely on HTML forms for user input. Each page will have the necessary code to handle the request method and appropriately execute the necessary functions based on the request type. The $op operation variable, which is captured and assigned in the /_lib/_base/elements.php file can be referenced throughout the underlying hierarchy. This variable enables us to conditionally switch between different activities in our page.

The following diagram shows how a typical request is handled in our application pages:

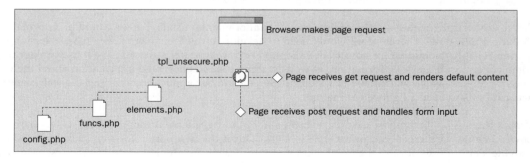

Designing the Data Layer

As mentioned earlier, we are developing a three-tiered application, which consists of a data layer, a business layer, and a presentation layer. For our design, we'll begin with the foundation of our application – the data layer.

The data layer will consist of three tables that will manage web masters, permissions, and applications within the database:

❑ `apress_admin_users` to store the web master's information

❑ `apress_admin_apps` to reference the applications within the CMS system

❑ `apress_admin_perms` to store relationships between web masters and their assigned applications

In an active account, a web master is associated with applications that are then associated with permissions in a one-to-many relationship. These simple relationships would ultimately define the web master's access privileges. We can set the following permissions:

❑ 0 – No access

❑ 1 – View Only access

❑ 2 – Create and View access

❑ 3 – Manage, Create, and View access

Thus, by having a single permission identifier we can set conditions based on the identifier, to enable/disable user access and activity throughout the applications.

In our application, we'll use a simple set of tables that interrelate based on the web master's unique identifier and any correlating application, and permissions referenced therein:

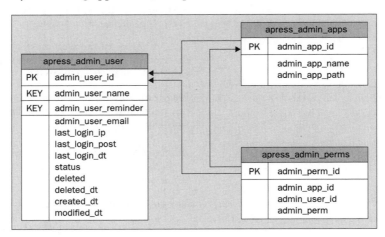

This simple table structure not only provides for better performance but also enables greater flexibility. Next we'll detail the design definitions for each of our tables and how they are interrelated in the security model.

The Admin Users Table

The `apress_admin_users` table is the core of the CMS administration security model as it houses all of the users and the basic attributes needed within the system:

Field	Type	Description
admin_user_id	INT(10)	The unique identifier for each web master in the system.
admin_user_name	VARCHAR(50)	The unique login name given to each web master for authentication. This field has an index to improve the performance of queries as it is often referenced during authentication.
admin_user_pass	VARCHAR(50)	The web master's encrypted user password string. This field is also indexed for the increased performance of queries during repetitive authentication that occurs throughout the CMS.
admin_user_remind	VARCHAR(100)	A non-encrypted or plain text copy of the web master's password that can be e-mailed to him/her once the password reminder form has been accurately completed.
admin_user_email	VARCHAR(100)	The web master's unique e-mail address.
last_login_ip	VARCAHR(15)	The last IP address from which the web master logged in.
last_login_host	VARCHAR(100)	The last host name from which the web master logged in, if available.
last_login_dt	DATETIME	The date and time of the last successful login for each web master.
status	INT(1)	Flag indicator of the web master's status within the system. This can have a value of 0/1 as it's a simple Boolean comparative.
deleted	INT(1)	Flag indicator to determine whether a record has been 'soft deleted' or not. This too is a Boolean comparative. *A soft delete does not actually remove the record from the database; instead it flags it as deleted so that it's not displayed on the public web site.*
deleted_dt	DATETIME	The soft delete date and time, if deleted.
created_dt	DATETIME	The date that the web maser record was created.
modified_dt	DATETIME	The date time value of the last edit made to a web master record.

Each web master is referenced by the `admin_user_id` column, which is indexed along with the `admin_user_name` and `admin_user_pass` columns.

The Admin Applications Table

The `apress_admin_apps` table is the application store that contains its display name and site-relative path references to all of the applications within the CMS:

Field	Type	Description
admin_app_id	INT(2)	A unique identifier for each application record. This field is referenced by the `apress_admin_permissions` table to map relationships to each user.
admin_app_name	VARCHAR(50)	The plain text name of the application to be used in the menu.
admin_app_path	VARCHAR(100)	The site root relative application path where the files are stored. This is used during the authentication process to ensure that a web master has appropriate access to a set of files and actions.

The Admin Permissions Table

The `apress_admin_permissions` table is a mapping of user permissions to admin applications – all the user access privileges are stored within, to easily query a user's full permission set or a single reference to an isolated application request:

Field	Type	Description
admin_perm_id	INT(10)	A unique identifier for each application entry. This field is referenced by the permissions table mapped to each web master.
admin_app_id	INT(10)	The unique identifier of the applications table will be placed in this field to create a relationship to a web master.
admin_user_id	INT(10)	The unique identifier for a user will be placed in this field to create a relationship to an application.
admin_perm	INT(1)	The integer value that represents the level of access or permission that a user has to the related application.

Designing the Data Objects

Now that we have considered our database design, we can move on to our data object class designs. The data objects for our security architecture are PHP classes that are placed within our hierarchy and contain all of the data access functionality needed to be used within the site applications.

Implementing the data objects allow us to abstract the data layer from the presentation layer, so to use the data objects we would just need to instantiate a class and call its members. Our essential task is to provide a wrapper interface to our database content through the use of class objects that can be written to handle the data precisely. These data objects will constitute the business tier in our application hierarchy – they'll interface the database directly, and also handle some formatting and manipulation of the data within each data object.

We should design data objects to allow for as much code reuse as possible. Often, we may write a function that performs a series of tasks and later realize that some of those tasks would be better stored in an independent function that can be called by other members in the class. A class member would be any function or variable defined within that class, or any inherited classes, which can be referenced within the same namespace.

In order to adhere to good programming practices when engineering the class objects, try to think of them as real world objects with real world behaviors. Applying this notion will aid and guide you through your development decisions and ensure a more positive result.

The Users Class

As mentioned in Chapter 2, each user for the CMS system will be assigned a user name and password for accessing the applications within. When the web master logs into the application, a session will begin that will be used to continually validate and associate the web master session with administrative activities.

The users class handles all of the functionality that we could perform on/with a web master. This includes creation, management, and removal of web masters within the context of our security realm. It is important to note that since our session class will extend to our users class, we can define certain members within our users class that will be inherited by the session class, thus providing as much reuse and organization as possible in our code.

Here is a listing of the members of the class:

users Class Member	Description
_iUserId	Property containing the web master's unique identifier.
_oMail	Property containing the PEAR::Mail object reference.
_oConn	Property containing the PEAR::DB object reference.
users(userid[optional])	Constructor method which instantiates any parent objects.
_resetPassword()	Resets a web master's password.
_userExists(username)	Returns a Boolean check to see if the string web master name exists in the database.
_emailExists(email)	Returns a Boolean check to see if the string web master's e-mail already exists in the database.
_notifyUser(emailbody)	Sends an e-mail to the set web master. Accepts a string as the e-mail address body text.

users Class Member	Description
_setPerms(permissions)	Accepts an array of the web master's permissions.
setUserId(userid)	Accepts a numeric user ID and sets the class member variable to that ID.
getUser()	Returns an array of user information.
getUsersCount()	Returns a numeric value representing the number of active web masters in the database (used for pagination).
getUsers(sort, rows[optional])	Accepts a string for the sort column and an optional numeric value for the row number to begin with, and returns an array of active web masters.
getApps()	Returns an array of the available applications in the system. This information can be used to create/modify the web master permissions for each application.
addUser(userdata)	Accepts an array of web master information and adds a web master to the system
editUser(userdata)	Accepts an array of web master information and updates a web master in the system
updateSettings(userdata)	Accepts an array of web master data and updates the web master settings in the database
deleteUser()	Updates the web master in the database by setting the web master status to 'deleted'
activateUser()	Updates the web master in the database by setting the web master status to 'active'
deactivateUser()	Updates the web master in the database by setting the web master status to 'inactive'

The Session Class

The session class is used to perform session related tasks, which are directly related to a web master, for instance. This class simplifies the security model by abstracting the menuing system and the authentication process, which are all interdependent.

The following diagram shows a simplified view of our security realm. As you can see, there are several file dependencies in an organized hierarchy:

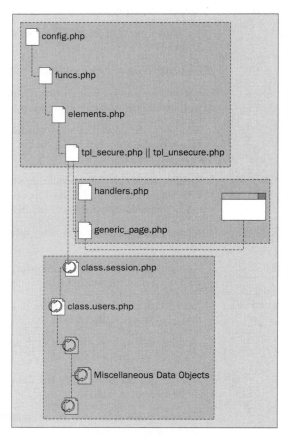

Now let's take a look at the different methods contained within the session class. Remember, that this session class will extend to the users class, so we will have access to all the members of that class by means of inheritance:

session Class Member	Description
_oUser	Property containing the web master's object reference
_sFilePath	Property containing the truncated file path, which was passed in the HTTP request
session()	Constructor method with instantiates any parent objects
_setSession()	Accepts an array of arguments, which are imploded into a string and then set in the session variable
_authenticate()	Validates web master access to the system

session Class Member	Description
_updateLogin()	Updates the web master login history on completion of a successful login
login(userdata)	Accepts an array of web master credentials to the process
getPerms()	Accepts an array of web master credentials to retrieve real-time application access information
getMenu()	Returns an array of accessible menu information for the specified web master

The Solution

Now that we have looked at the problems that need to be addressed, and the considerations that we need to be aware of while building our web site's CMS, let's start putting all these pieces together to build a secure, usable session and user management environment.

These are the primary aspects of our solution:

❏   Multi-user application environment
❏   Multi-level page and activity permissions
❏   Session-based authentication and access validation
❏   Pluggable/scaleable application architecture

This table describes the location and functional purpose of each file:

> As detailed in Chapter 2, the _lib directory contains files like the shared function libraries and custom classes. It includes a _base subdirectory that includes the common function libraries and the global configuration file, a _sql subdirectory that includes the MySQL creation files, and a classes subdirectory that includes the custom classes that are written through the book. All our application modules fall into the site directory, and its login subdirectory houses the files that define the CMS login bit for the site. The core directory includes the admin tools used to control the site. It includes a users subdirectory where web masters can be added/deleted and their administrative permissions can be modified, and a settings subdirectory where web masters can modify personal settings, like their password.

File Name	File Path	Description
config.php	/_lib/_base/	Configuration values for the application.
funcs.php	/_lib/_base/	Utility functions for the application.
elements.php	/_lib/_base/	Reusable generic elements such as error display functions. This file also assigns the common GET variables of $op and $id.

Table continued on following page

File Name	File Path	Description
tpl_unsecure.php	/site/	Template framework file for pages outside the CMS application. It implements banner advertisements into the page framework.
tpl_secure.php	/core/	Template framework file for pages inside the CMS application.
handlers.php	/_lib/_base/	Data input validation functions.
index.php	/site/login/	Page that provides login form for web masters.
logout.php	/site/login/	Page that provides logout functionality disabling a web master session.
reminder.php	/site/login/	Page that provides the account reminder form for web masters.
index.php	/core/users/	List page for web masters in the CMS system.
form.php	/core/users/	Form for adding and editing web masters in the CMS system.
settings.php	/core/settings/	Form for changing web master account settings during an active session.
class.users.php	/_lib/_classes/	Data object for the web master's logic.
class.session.php	/_lib/_classes/	Data object for session logic.
apress_admin_users.sql	/_lib/_sql	SQL create script for the apress_admin_users table.
apress_admin_apps.sql	/_lib/_sql/	SQL create script for the apress_admin_apps table.
apress_admin_perms.sql	/_lib/_sql/	SQL create script for the apress_admin_perms table.

All the above listed scripts are available as part of the book's code download from http://www.apress.com.

Now that we have clearly defined both the database and the data object design, and reviewed the files that are going to be used throughout, we can begin constructing and implementing our web master management and security solution.

Implementing the Data Layer

We shall hand-code the SQL scripts to create the tables. Any text editor will work just fine to successfully complete this step, although using an editor with some sort of color coding will help to ensure that the scripts are syntactically proper as well as formatted correctly. For our application we'll be using MyISAM table types to take advantage of the locking mechanisms within. You may choose to apply different table types to your application based on the different features that each provide. For more information regarding the different table type options and their features refer the documentation on the MySQL web site at http://www.mysql.com/doc/en/Table_types.html.

apress_admin_users

This table houses all of the web masters and the basic attributes needed within the system:

```
CREATE TABLE apress_admin_users (
    admin_user_id     INT(10)       NOT NULL auto_increment,
    admin_user_name   VARCHAR(50)   NOT NULL default '',
    admin_user_pass   VARCHAR(50)   NOT NULL default '',
    admin_user_remind VARCHAR(100)  NOT NULL default '',
    admin_user_email  VARCHAR(100)  NOT NULL default '',
    last_login_ip     VARCHAR(15)   default NULL,
    last_login_host   VARCHAR(100)  default NULL,
    last_login_dt     DATETIME      default NULL,
    status            INT(1)        NOT NULL default '1',
    deleted           INT(1)        default '0',
    deleted_dt        DATETIME      default NULL,
    created_dt        DATETIME      NOT NULL default '0000-00-00 00:00:00',
    modified_dt       DATETIME      NOT NULL default '0000-00-00 00:00:00',
                      PRIMARY KEY (admin_user_id),
                      KEY admin_user_name_ref (admin_user_name),
                      KEY admin_user_pass_ref (admin_user_pass)
) TYPE=MyISAM;
```

Note that we have specified NOT NULL for most fields, since they require entry by the user.

apress_admin_apps

This table contains the display name and site-relative path references to all of the applications within the CMS:

```
CREATE TABLE apress_admin_apps (
    admin_app_id   INT(2)        NOT NULL auto_increment,
    admin_app_name VARCHAR(50)   NOT NULL default '',
    admin_app_path VARCHAR(100)  NOT NULL default '',
                   PRIMARY KEY (admin_app_id)
) TYPE=MyISAM;
```

apress_admin_perms

This table is a mapping of web master permissions to administer applications:

```
CREATE TABLE apress_admin_perms (
   admin_perm_id INT(10) NOT NULL auto_increment,
   admin_app_id  INT(10) NOT NULL default '0',
   admin_user_id INT(10) NOT NULL default '0',
   admin_perm    INT(1)  NOT NULL default '1',
                 PRIMARY KEY (admin_perm_id)
) TYPE=MyISAM;
```

Implementing the Data Objects

Now that we have the data layer in place, we can proceed with creating the data objects. We now know how we want our data objects to behave, we can also assume what properties we'll want them to have, so let us begin constructing them.

Based on the coding standards discussed in Chapter 2, we have a clear set of rules regarding how we should code, so now it's just a matter of writing conforming code.

class.users.php

In this PHP script we'll look at the functions for the users class and how we simplified our design to reuse as much code and functionality as possible:

We shall open our class with includes for all of the files that our class is dependent on. Then, we'll write a constructor method to instantiate any default member properties as well as any inherited objects:

```php
<?php

// File Location: /_lib/_classes/class.users.php

// the Mail.php, and DB.php scripts are in the PEAR library, and
// they'll include and extend the PEAR.php class object automatically.
require_once("Mail.php");
require_once("DB.php");

/**
 * handles web master functions
 */
class users { // open the class definition

    /**
     * class member variables
     *
     * @var integer
     * @access private
     * @see setUserId()
     */
    var $_iUserId;
```

```
/**
 * PEAR mail object
 *
 * @var object
 * @access private
 */
var $_oMail;

/**
 * PEAR::DB object
 *
 * @var object
 * @access private
 */
var $_oConn;
```

The constructor instantiates and assigns any base PEAR objects that we'll need, and optionally assigns a value for the _iUserId member. The constant variable DSN is defined in the configuration file in the _base directory:

```
// CONSTRUCTOR
/**
 * class constructor
 *
 * @param integer user ID [optional]
 * @access public
 */
function users($iUserId = '') {

    // implement PEAR::Mail object
    $this->_oMail =& Mail::factory("mail");

    if( Mail::isError($this->_oMail) ) {

        // catchExc() is defined in the funcs.php file
        catchExc($this->_oMail->getMessage());
    }

    // implement db object
    $this->_oConn =& DB::connect(DSN);

    if( DB::isError($this->_oConn) ) {

        catchExc($this->_oConn->getMessage());
    }

    // set unique identifier
    if( is_int($iUserId) ) {

        $this->setUserId($iUserId);
    }
}
```

Our private methods are obvious through their naming convention. Class members in PHP do not really have a scope as far as being private or public, but it helps to denote them that way so we can clearly understand their usage. We have opted to prefix all of our private members, be it variables or methods, with an **underscore character**. This practice makes it easy to quickly identify if a method can be called from outside of the class hierarchy, or if it's intended to be used only by other class members.

The _resetPassword() function generates a new password for a web master, updates the database reference, and e-mails the new login information to the affected web master:

```
/**
 * reset user password
 *
 * @return boolean
 * @access private
 */
function _resetPassword() {

    // generate random unique password
    $sPasswordRemind = substr(md5(uniqid(rand(1, 100000))), 3, 8);

    // encrypt password
    $sPassword = substr(md5($sPasswordRemind), 3, 8);
```

Note that the password is automatically generated and then encrypted using the MD5 algorithm along with the uniqid() function which is seeded or prefixed by a random number between 1 and 10000. We are shortening out password length to 8 characters from the number 3 position so that our string is not too long. We don't want to confuse the user by sending a 32 character password string.

Let's continue with the script:

```
    // update user account record
    $sql = "UPDATE ".PREFIX."_admin_users
        SET
            admin_user_pass='".$sPassword."',
            admin_user_remind='".$sPasswordRemind."',
            modified_dt=(NOW())
        WHERE
            admin_user_id=".$this->_iUserId;

    if( DB::isError($rsTmp = $this->_oConn->query($sql)) ) {

        catchExc($rsTmp->getMessage());
        return FALSE;
    }

    // send user e-mail
    $sBody = "Your ".ENTITY." password has been reset.\r\n\r\n";
    $sBody .= "Your new password is ".$sPasswordRemind;

    return $this->_notifyUser($sBody);
}
```

The _userExists() function is a verification function which ensures that a unique record is being passed for a web master name. This function is replicated for the web master's e-mail address as well:

```php
/**
 * verify unique web master name
 *
 * @param string $sUser web master name
 * @return boolean
 * @access private
 */
function _userExists($sUser) {

    $sql = "SELECT
                admin_user_id
            FROM
                ".PREFIX."_admin_users
            WHERE
                admin_user_name='".$sUser."' AND
                deleted=0";

    if( DB::isError($rsTmp = $this->_oConn->query($sql)) ) {

        catchExc($rsTmp->getMessage());
        return FALSE;
    }

    // return number of matches
    $return = $rsTmp->numRows();
    return $return;
}

/**
 * verify unique e-mail address
 *
 * @param string $sEmail e-mail address
 * @return boolean
 * @access private
 */
function _emailExists($sEmail) {

    $sql = "SELECT
                admin_user_id
            FROM
                ".PREFIX."_admin_users
            WHERE
                admin_user_email='".$sEmail."' AND
                deleted=0";

    if( DB::isError($rsTmp = $this->_oConn->query($sql)) ) {

        catchExc($rsTmp->getMessage());
        return FALSE;
    }

    // return number of matches
    $return = $rsTmp->numRows();
    return $return;
}
```

The `_notifyUser()` function is an abstraction of potentially redundant code. Instead of scattering the mail object calls throughout our class we have created a new function for it:

```php
/**
 * send e-mail notification
 *
 * @param string $sBody e-mail body
 * @return boolean
 * @access private
 */
function _notifyUser($sBody) {

    // assign mail properties
    $aUser = $this->getUser();
    $aHeaders["To"] = $sRecipients = $aUser["Email"];
    $aHeaders["From"] = ENTITY." Admin <".EMAIL.">";
    $aHeaders["Subject"] = ENTITY." System Account Notification";
    $aHeaders["Priority"] = "3";

    // try to send mail
    if( Mail::isError($mailTmp = $this->_oMail->send($sRecipients,
                                                      $aHeaders,
                                                      $sBody)) ) {

        catchExc($mailTmp->getMessage());
        return FALSE;
    }
    return TRUE;
}
```

The `_setPerms()` function assigns the web master permissions. Instead of running a series of updates in the table, we delete the old permissions and reassign the new ones. This practice ensures that if new applications have been added to the system, they will not be overlooked when updating a web master as well as alleviating us from having to do a constant check against all the permissions for each web master. We can be certain that there will always be a relatively small number of records since this is a CMS environment with a controlled userbase:

```php
/**
 * set user permissions
 *
 * @param array permissions
 * @return boolean
 * @access private
 */
function _setPerms($aPerms) {

    // check perms array
    if( count($aPerms) ) {

        $sql = "DELETE
                FROM
                    ".PREFIX."_admin_perms
                WHERE
```

```
                            admin_user_id=".$this->_iUserId;

            if( DB::isError($rsTmp = $this->_oConn->query($sql)) ) {

                catchExc($rsTmp->getMessage());
                return FALSE;
            }

            // loop through permissions array
            while( list($key, $val) = each($aPerms) ) {

                // add new permission record
                $sql = "INSERT INTO ".PREFIX."_admin_perms (
                                admin_user_id,
                                admin_app_id,
                                admin_perm
                    ) VALUES (
                                ".$this->_iUserId.",
                                ".$key.",
                                ".$val."
                    )";

                if( DB::isError($rsTmp = $this->_oConn->query($sql)) ) {

                    catchExc($rsTmp->getMessage());
                    return FALSE;
                }
            }

            return TRUE;
        }
    }
```

Since we're working with a web master in this class, we have created a setter for the web master's unique identifier. This function allows us to define the targeted user for any function that we may call within the class:

```
/**
 * set the _iUserId variable for the class
 *
 * @param integer $iUserId unique identifier
 * @access public
 */
function setUserId($iUserId) {

    if( is_int($iUserId) ) {

        $this->_iUserId = $iUserId;
    }
}
```

In the event that a web master forgets his/her password, they should be provided a reminder via e-mail, if he/she is able to furnish the valid web master name–e-mail address match. This method takes care of the password reminder functionality:

```
/**
 * send password reminder
 *
 * @param array $aArgs web master values
 * @return boolean
 * @access public
 */
function sendReminder($aArgs) {

    $sql = "SELECT
                admin_user_id,
                admin_user_email
            FROM
                ".PREFIX."_admin_users
            WHERE
                admin_user_name='".$aArgs["User Name"]."' AND
                status=1 AND
                deleted=0";

    if( DB::isError($rsTmp = $this->_oConn->query($sql)) ) {

        catchExc($rsTmp->getMessage());
        return FALSE;
    }

    if( $rsTmp->numRows() > 0 ) {

        $aRow = $rsTmp->fetchRow(DB_FETCHMODE_ASSOC);

        if( strcmp($aRow["admin_user_email"], $aArgs["Email"]) ) {

            // catchErr() is defined in the funcs.php file
            catchErr("User email does not match account information");
            return FALSE;
        }

        // set class member unique identifier and get user data
        settype($aRow["admin_user_id"], "integer");
        $this->setUserId($aRow["admin_user_id"]);
        $aUser = $this->getUser();

        // build e-mail body
        $sBody = "Your ".ENTITY." account login information
                is:\r\n\r\n";
        $sBody .= "User Name: ".$aUser["User Name"]."\r\n";
        $sBody .= "Password: ".$aUser["Password Reminder"];

        return $this->_notifyUser($sBody);

    } else {

        catchErr("Cannot find user account information");
        return FALSE;
    }
}
```

The `getUser()` function retrieves a single user from the database. It's better to accept and return the data as an array, that way we have more flexibility with the results than we would with a result set:

```php
/**
 * get a user single user by ID
 *
 * @return array user data
 * @access public
 */
function getUser() {

    $sql = "SELECT
                admin_user_id,
                admin_user_name,
                admin_user_pass,
                admin_user_remind,
                admin_user_email,
                last_login_dt,
                last_login_ip,
                last_login_host,
                status,
                created_dt,
                modified_dt
            FROM
                ".PREFIX."_admin_users
            WHERE
                admin_user_id=".$this->_iUserId;

    if( DB::isError($rsTmp = $this->_oConn->query($sql)) ) {

        catchExc($rsTmp->getMessage());
        return FALSE;
    }

    // assign result to array
    $aRow = $rsTmp->fetchRow(DB_FETCHMODE_ASSOC);

    // build user array to return
    $return["User Id"] = $aRow["admin_user_id"];
    $return["User Name"] = $aRow["admin_user_name"];
    $return["Password"] = $aRow["admin_user_pass"];
    $return["Password Reminder"] = $aRow["admin_user_remind"];
    $return["Email"] = $aRow["admin_user_email"];
    $return["Login Date"] = strtotime($aRow["last_login_dt"]);
    $return["Login Address"] = $aRow["last_login_ip"];
    $return["Login Host"] = $aRow["last_login_host"];
    $return["Status"] = $aRow["status"];
    $return["Created Date"] = strtotime($aRow["created_dt"]);
    $return["Modified Date"] = strtotime($aRow["modified_dt"]);

    // get permissions for the web master
    $sql = "SELECT
                app.admin_app_id,
```

```
                        perm.admin_perm
                FROM
                        ".PREFIX."_admin_apps app,
                        ".PREFIX."_admin_perms perm
                WHERE
                        perm.admin_app_id=app.admin_app_id AND
                        perm.admin_user_id=".$this->_iUserId."
                ORDER BY
                        app.admin_app_id";

    if( DB::isError($rsTmp = $this->_oConn->query($sql)) ) {

        catchExc($rsTmp->getMessage());
        return FALSE;
    }

    // build permissions array to return
    while( $aRow = $rsTmp->fetchRow(DB_FETCHMODE_ASSOC) ) {

        $return["Perms"][$aRow["admin_app_id"]] = $aRow["admin_perm"];
    }

    return $return;
}
```

To display a paginated list of the returned items (instead of one long list) in the CMS administration page, we'll need to know the total number of records. This function takes care of that functionality:

```
/**
 * get users count for paging
 *
 * @return integer record count
 * @access public
 */
function getUsersCount() {

    $sql = "SELECT COUNT(admin_user_id) AS user_cnt
            FROM
                    ".PREFIX."_admin_users
            WHERE
                    deleted=0 AND
                    admin_user_name != 'admin'";

    if( DB::isError($iCnt = $this->_oConn->getOne($sql)) ) {

        catchExc($iCnt->getMessage());
        return FALSE;
    }

    return $iCnt;
}
```

The getUsers() function gathers all of our active users into an indexed associative array. Again, to utilize the pagination functionality, we need to query the active users based on the current page cursor position and a sort column:

```php
/**
 * get users list
 *
 * @param string $sSort sort key
 * @param integer $iPage [optional] cursor
 * @return array user data
 * @access public
 */
function getUsers($sSort, $iPage=0) {

    // get a list of all users
    $sql = "SELECT
                admin_user_id,
                admin_user_name,
                admin_user_pass,
                admin_user_remind,
                admin_user_email,
                status,
                created_dt,
                modified_dt
            FROM
                ".PREFIX."_admin_users
            WHERE
                deleted=0 AND
                admin_user_name != 'admin'
            ORDER BY
                ".$sSort."
            LIMIT ".$iPage.", ".ROWCOUNT;

    if( DB::isError($rsTmp = $this->_oConn->query($sql)) ) {

        catchExc($rsTmp->getMessage());
        return FALSE;
    }

    // loop through result and build return array
    $i = 0;
    while( $aRow = $rsTmp->fetchRow(DB_FETCHMODE_ASSOC) ) {

        $return[$i]["User Id"] = $aRow["admin_user_id"];
        $return[$i]["User Name"] = $aRow["admin_user_name"];
        $return[$i]["User Password"] = $aRow["admin_user_pass"];
        $return[$i]["User Password Reminder"] =
                                    $aRow["admin_user_remind"];
        $return[$i]["User Email"] = $aRow["admin_user_email"];
        $return[$i]["Status"] = $aRow["status"];
        $return[$i]["Created Date"] = strtotime($aRow["created_dt"]);
        $return[$i]["Modified Date"] = strtotime($aRow["modified_dt"]);
        ++$i;
    }
    return $return;
}
```

In the web master management section of the CMS, we need to know what applications are available in the architecture so that we can create and modify web master permissions. To do so, we'll need to return an array list of applications within the system:

```
/**
 * get applications list
 *
 * @return array applications data
 * @access public
 */
function getApps() {

    $sql = "SELECT
                    admin_app_id,
                    admin_app_name
                FROM
                    ".PREFIX."_admin_apps
                ORDER BY
                    admin_app_id";

    if( DB::isError($rsTmp = $this->_oConn->query($sql)) ) {

        catchExc($rsTmp->getMessage());
        return FALSE;
    }

    $i = 0;
    while( $aRow = $rsTmp->fetchRow(DB_FETCHMODE_ASSOC) ) {

        $return[$i]["App Id"] = $aRow["admin_app_id"];
        $return[$i]["App Name"] = $aRow["admin_app_name"];
        $return[$i]["Perm"] = 0;
        ++$i;
    }
    return $return;
}
```

There are several steps to adding a web master – first, we'll need to insert the web master's account information into the database (apress, as mentioned in Chapter 2), and then grab the unique identifier of that web master. Once we have the unique identifier, we must assign the web master permissions and notify the web master of the new account as well:

```
/**
 * add a new user record
 *
 * @param array $aArgs user data
 * @return boolean
 * @access public
 */
function addUser($aArgs) {

    // generate random unique password
```

```
$sPasswordRemind = substr(md5(uniqid(rand(1, 100000))), 3, 8);

// encrypt new password
$sPassword = substr(md5($sPasswordRemind), 3 , 8);

// check for existing user name
if( $this->_userExists($aArgs["User Name"]) ) {

    catchErr("This user name already exists");
    return FALSE;

// check for existing e-mail
} else if( $this->_emailExists($aArgs["Email"]) ) {

    catchErr("This email address already exists");
    return FALSE;
```

We'll lock the apress_admin_users table prior to inserting the new record and then unlock this table after we have successfully added the account record. This locking query ensures that when we capture our unique identifier after the insert, we can be sure that no other records have been added that would provide an inaccurate identifier return:

```
} else {

    // lock tables to capture unique identifier
    $sql = "LOCK TABLES ".PREFIX."_admin_users WRITE";

    if( DB::isError($rsTmp = $this->_oConn->query($sql)) ) {

        catchExc($rsTmp->getMessage());
        return FALSE;
    }

    // add new user record
    $sql = "INSERT INTO ".PREFIX."_admin_users (
                    admin_user_name,
                    admin_user_pass,
                    admin_user_remind,
                    admin_user_email,
                    status,
                    created_dt,
                    modified_dt
            ) VALUES (
                    '".$aArgs["User Name"]."',
                    '".$sPassword."',
                    '".$sPasswordRemind."',
                    '".$aArgs["Email"]."',
                    1,
                    (NOW()),
                    (NOW())
            )";
```

```
            if( DB::isError($rsTmp = $this->_oConn->query($sql)) ) {

                catchExc($rsTmp->getMessage());
                return FALSE;
            }

            // get unique identifier for a new record
            $sql = "SELECT MAX(admin_user_id)
                    FROM ".PREFIX."_admin_users";

            if( DB::isError($iUserId = $this->_oConn->getOne($sql)) ) {

                catchExc($iUserId->getMessage());
                return FALSE;
            }

            $sql = "UNLOCK TABLES";

            if( DB::isError($rsTmp = $this->_oConn->query($sql)) ) {

                catchExc($rsTmp->getMessage());
                return FALSE;
            }

            // set member variable for the unique identifier
            settype($iUserId, "integer");
            $this->setUserId($iUserId);

            // set permissions values
            $this->_setPerms($aArgs["Perms"]);

            // build user e-mail
            $sBody = "Your ".ENTITY." account has been created.\r\n";
            $sBody .= "Your login information is:\r\n\r\n";
            $sBody .= "User Name: ".$aArgs["User Name"]."\r\n";
            $sBody .= "Password: ".$sPasswordRemind;

            return $this->_notifyUser($sBody);
        }
    }
```

Editing a web master account is much simpler than adding one. Since we already know the web master's unique identifier, we can reduce much of the code needed to perform this task. Again, since we have abstracted much of the reusable code into class functions, we can make simple calls to those functions knowing what our passed data is going to be:

```
/**
 * edit an existing user record
 *
 * @param array user data
 * @return boolean
 * @access public
```

```
    */
    function editUser($aArgs) {

        // update user record
        $sql = "UPDATE ".PREFIX."_admin_users
                SET
                    admin_user_email='".$aArgs["Email"]."',
                    modified_dt=(NOW())
                WHERE
                    admin_user_id=".$this->_iUserId;

        if( DB::isError($rsTmp = $this->_oConn->query($sql)) ) {

            catchExc($rsTmp->getMessage());
            return FALSE;
        }

        // check to reset user password
        if( $aArgs["Reset"] ) {

            // reset user password
            $this->_resetPassword();
        }

        // update user permission records
        $this->_setPerms($aArgs["Perms"]);
        return TRUE;
    }
```

The updateSettings() function is similar to the editUser() function, however, it's to be called when a web master updates his own account, so we don't have to worry about reassigning permissions or resetting passwords:

```
/**
 * update user settings
 *
 * @param array user data
 * @return boolean
 * @access public
 */
function updateSettings($aArgs) {

    // initialize SQL filter
    $sFilter = "";

    if( !empty($aArgs["Password"]) ) {

        // generate new password and add SQL filter
        $sPasswordRemind = $aArgs["Password"];
        $sPassword = substr(md5($sPasswordRemind), 3 , 8);
        $sFilter = " admin_user_pass='".$sPassword."',
        admin_user_remind='".$sPasswordRemind."',";
```

```
        }

        // update user record
        $sql = "UPDATE ".PREFIX."_admin_users
                SET
                    admin_user_email='".$aArgs["Email"]."',".$sFilter."
                    modified_dt=(NOW())
                WHERE
                    admin_user_id=".$this->_iUserId;

        if( DB::isError($rsTmp = $this->_oConn->query($sql)) ) {

            catchExc($rsTmp->getMessage());
            return FALSE;
        }

        return TRUE;
    }
```

The remaining functions provide simple updates to the user account for changing the user's state within the system:

```
    /**
     * delete a user record
     *
     * @return boolean
     * @access public
     */
    function deleteUser() {

        $sql = "UPDATE ".PREFIX."_admin_users
                SET
                    deleted=1,
                    deleted_dt=(NOW())
                WHERE
                    admin_user_id=".$this->_iUserId;

        if( DB::isError($rsTmp = $this->_oConn->query($sql)) ) {

            catchExc($rsTmp->getMessage());
            return FALSE;
        }

        $this->deactivateUser();
        return TRUE;
    }

    /**
     * activate a user record
     *
     * @return boolean
     * @access public
     */
```

```php
    function activateUser() {

        $sql = "UPDATE ".PREFIX."_admin_users
             SET
                 status=1
              WHERE
                 admin_user_id=".$this->_iUserId;

        if( DB::isError($rsTmp = $this->_oConn->query($sql)) ) {

            catchExc($rsTmp->getMessage());
            return FALSE;
        }

        // build user e-mail
        $aUser = $this->getUser();
        $sBody = "Your ".ENTITY." account has been activated.\r\n";
        $sBody .= "Your login information is:\r\n\r\n";
        $sBody .= "User Name: ".$aUser["User Name"]."\r\n";
        $sBody .= "Password: ".$aUser["Password Reminder"];

        return $this->_notifyUser($sBody);
    }

    /**
     * deactivate a user record
     *
     * @return boolean
     * @access public
     */
    function deactivateUser() {

        $sql = "UPDATE ".PREFIX."_admin_users
             SET
                 status=0
              WHERE
                 admin_user_id=".$this->_iUserId;

        if( DB::isError($rsTmp = $this->_oConn->query($sql)) ) {

            catchExc($rsTmp->getMessage());
            return FALSE;
        }

        // build web master e-mail
        $sBody = "Your ".ENTITY." account has been deactivated.";

        return $this->_notifyUser($sBody);
    }
} // close the class definition
?>
```

class.session.php

Now let's take a look at the `session` class, which extends the `users` class. As mentioned earlier, this class depends on certain members (`_iUserId`, and `setUserId`) from the `users` class to operate properly.

We shall open our class with includes for all of the files that our class is dependent on:

```php
<?php

// File Location: /_lib/_classes/class.session.php

require_once("class.users.php");

/**
 * user access security
 */
class session extends users { // open the class definition

    /**
     * string file path
     *
     * @var string
     * @access private
     */
    var $_sFilePath;

    /**
     * PEAR::DB object
     *
     * @var object
     * @access private
     */
    var $_oConn;
```

The constructor method instantiates any default member properties as well as any inherited objects:

```php
    // CONSTRUCTOR

    /**
     * class constructor
     *
     * @access public
     */
    function session() {

        // implement db object
        $this->_oConn =& DB::connect(DSN);

        if( DB::isError($this->_oConn) ) {

            catchExc($this->_oConn->getMessage());
        }

        // assign file path variable
        $this->_sFilePath = str_replace($_SERVER["DOCUMENT_ROOT"], "",
                                        $_SERVER["SCRIPT_FILENAME"]);
    }
```

Once again, the constructor instantiates and assigns any base PEAR objects that we'll need within this class.

This time we do have a setter, but it's a private member that sets the session cookie for use throughout the application:

```
/**
 * set session
 *
 * @param array $aArgs session data
 * @access private
 */
function _setSession($aArgs) {

    // start session
    session_start();

    // check session state
    if( !session_is_registered("sUSER") ) {

        // register session
        session_register("sUSER");
        $_SESSION["sUSER"] = array();
    }

    // assign session value
    $sVal = implode("|", $aArgs);
    $_SESSION["sUSER"] = $sVal;

}
```

Next we'll write the core class member which is the _authenticate function. This function provides as much information as possible to the web master in the event that we cannot authenticate properly. There are several reasons as to why authentication can fail and we should not leave the web master confused or frustrated. Some of those reasons might be that the password is incorrect, the web master account has been deactivated, or the web master account cannot be found.

Here's the code for the function:

```
/**
 * authenticate user
 *
 * @param array $aArgs user login
 * @return boolean
 * @access private
 */
function _authenticate($aArgs) {

    $sql = "SELECT
                admin_user_id,
                admin_user_pass,
                admin_user_email,
```

```
                    status
            FROM
                    ".PREFIX."_admin_users
            WHERE
                    admin_user_name='".$aArgs["User Name"]."' AND
                    deleted=0";
```

If the web master account isn't found, then an appropriate error message would be returned:

```
    if( DB::isError($rsTmp = $this->_oConn->query($sql)) ) {

        catchExc($rsTmp->getMessage());
        return FALSE;
    }

    // assign result to array
    $aRow = $rsTmp->fetchRow(DB_FETCHMODE_ASSOC);

    // check row count
    if( $rsTmp->numRows() < 1 ) {

        catchErr("User does not exist");
        return FALSE;

    // check record status
    } elseif ( $aRow["status"] < 1 ) {

        catchErr("Account inactive");
        return FALSE;

    // check password string
    } elseif ( !empty($aRow["admin_user_pass"]) ) {

        // match passwords
        if( strcmp(substr(md5($aArgs["Password"]), 3, 8),
                        $aRow["admin_user_pass"]) ) {

            catchErr("Invalid password");
            return FALSE;
        }

        // assign user session array
        $aUser = array($aRow["admin_user_id"], $aArgs["User Name"],
                    $aRow["admin_user_pass"],
                    $aRow["admin_user_email"]);

        // set user session
        settype($aRow["admin_user_id"], "integer");
        $this->setUserId($aRow["admin_user_id"]);
        $this->_setSession($aUser);
        return TRUE;
    }
}
```

Once the web master has successfully logged in to the site, his/her login information needs to be updated as we may need to refer to them at some point:

```php
/**
 * update user login values
 *
 * @return boolean
 * @access private
 */
function _updateLogin() {

    // get user IP address
    $sAddress = $_SERVER["REMOTE_ADDR"];

    // get user host name
    $sHost = gethostbyaddr($sAddress);

    $sql = "UPDATE ".PREFIX."_admin_users
        SET
            last_login_dt=(NOW()),
            last_login_ip='".$sAddress."',
            last_login_host='".$sHost."'
        WHERE
            admin_user_id=".$this->_iUserId;

    if( DB::isError($rsTmp = $this->_oConn->query($sql)) ) {

        catchExc($rsTmp->getMessage());
        return FALSE;
    }
}
```

Now that all of the foundational code is in place, let's create the login() function, which is called from the login page upon successful form data submission:

```php
/**
 * login user
 *
 * @param array $aArgs user data
 * @return string
 * @access public
 */
function login($aArgs) {

    // authenticate user
    if( !$this->_authenticate($aArgs) ) {

        catchErr("Could not authenticate user");
        return FALSE;
    }

    $sql = "SELECT
```

```
                            app.admin_app_path
                    FROM
                            ".PREFIX."_admin_apps app,
                            ".PREFIX."_admin_perms perm
                    WHERE
                            app.admin_app_id=perm.admin_app_id AND
                            perm.admin_user_id=".$this->_iUserId." AND
                            perm.admin_perm > 0
                    ORDER BY
                            app.admin_app_id
                    LIMIT 0, 1";

        if( DB::isError($sPath = $this->_oConn->getOne($sql)) ) {

            catchExc($sPath->getMessage());
            return FALSE;
        }

        // verify path value
        if( empty($sPath) ) {

            catchErr("No acceptable application permissions");
            return FALSE;
        }

        // update login and return path
        $this->_updateLogin();
        return $sPath;
    }
```

The getPerms() function is very important. It's run on each and every secure page to ensure that web masters have proper access to the page that they have requested. It verifies that they are logged in and also returns the level of permission that they have for the page level:

```
/**
 * get user permissions
 *
 * @param array user$aArgs session data
 * @return array
 * @access public
 */
function getPerms($aArgs) {

    // apply path parts to array
    $sFile = array_pop(explode("/", $this->_sFilePath));

    // reformat path value
    $sApp = str_replace($sFile, "", $this->_sFilePath);


    $sql = "SELECT
                perm.admin_perm
```

```
                    FROM
                            ".PREFIX."_admin_perms perm,
                            ".PREFIX."_admin_apps app,
                            ".PREFIX."_admin_users user
                    WHERE
                            user.admin_user_name='".$aArgs[1]."' AND
                            user.admin_user_pass='".$aArgs[2]."' AND
                            user.admin_user_id=".$aArgs[0]." AND
                            perm.admin_app_id=app.admin_app_id AND
                            perm.admin_user_id=user.admin_user_id AND
                            app.admin_app_path='".$sApp."'";

        if( DB::isError($iPerm = $this->_oConn->getOne($sql)) ) {

            catchExc($iPerm->getMessage());
            return FALSE;
        }

        // if permitted, set session and return permission
        if( $iPerm > 0 ) {

            $this->_setSession($aArgs);
            return $iPerm;
        }

        return FALSE;
    }
```

All that is left now is our menu – since we are storing the applications as well as related permissions for specific web masters in the database, we can dynamically query our menu items and return them to the page so that we display only the accessible applications as navigation choices to the web master:

```
/**
 * get application menu
 *
 * @return array
 * @access public
 */
function getMenu() {

    $sql = "SELECT
                    app.admin_app_name,
                    app.admin_app_path,
                    perm.admin_perm
            FROM
                    ".PREFIX."_admin_apps app,
                    ".PREFIX."_admin_perms perm
            WHERE
                    app.admin_app_id=perm.admin_app_id AND
                    perm.admin_user_id=".$this->_iUserId." AND
                    perm.admin_perm > 0
            ORDER BY
```

```
                            app.admin_app_id";

        if( DB::isError($rsTmp = $this->_oConn->query($sql)) ) {

            catchExc($rsTmp->getMessage());
            return FALSE;
        }

        // loop result and build return array
        $i = 0;
        while( $aRow = $rsTmp->fetchRow(DB_FETCHMODE_ASSOC) ) {
            $return[$i]["App Name"] = $aRow["admin_app_name"];
            $return[$i]["App Path"] = $aRow["admin_app_path"];
            $return[$i]["App Perm"] = $aRow["admin_app_perm"];
            ++$i;
        }
        return $return;
    }
} // close the class definition

?>
```

Data Object Error Handling

The catchExc() and catchErr() functions are defined in the funcs.php file to pass an error string and populate an array, which is then used to return errors or exceptions to the web master in a clean, intuitive manner:

```
<?php

function catchExc($sMsg) {

    global $EXCEPTS;
    array_push($EXCEPTS, $sMsg);
}

function catchErr($sMsg) {

    global $ERRORS;
    array_push($ERRORS, $sMsg);
}
?>
```

PEAR provides a very useful error handling system that allows us to assign any PEAR function call to a variable, which upon error, becomes an object that stores the error message. We can take that error message and handle it similarly to our literal text errors and exceptions.

Presentation Layer

We'll be applying pages to this code in practice, so we'll also have to consider some of the page state control that exists during a user session. Any standard HTTP request is done via the GET method, and the POST method is used to post the login credentials to the server for authentication – we can take advantage of both these methods and create the notion of states within our pages, therefore utilizing each page to its fullest extent.

Before we dive into the pages and their supporting codebase, let's briefly look at the realm in which we are trying to develop and how that realm and its content relate to our base architecture:

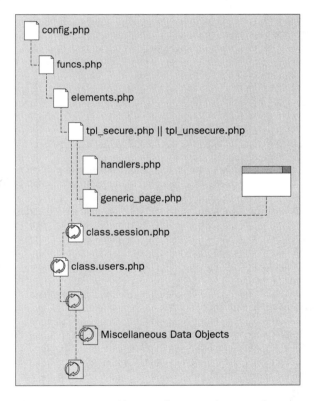

As seen in the diagram, the configuration files are the root of our application, and their hierarchy is linear, based on the nature and use of the files therein. Now that we have a reference of our application environment, let's look at some of the details that are used to build and render pages.

CMS Login Page

The following is the login page:

The login page displays two form fields – one for the web master name and one for the web master password. These two values are passed on POST to the same page where we can then run the login code.

Our inline PHP simply determines the state of the HTTP request and handles the content accordingly:

```php
<?php

// File Location: /site/login/index.php

// template framework file for pages inside the CMS application
require_once("tpl_unsecure.php");

// data input validation functions
require_once("handlers.php");

require_once("class.session.php");

if( $_POST ) { // check for HTTP POST variables

    // assign post variables
    $sUser = $_POST["user"];
    $sPass = $_POST["pass"];

    // validate web master name
    if( !validUser($sUser) ) {
```

```
            catchErr("Enter a valid user name");
            $FORMOK = FALSE;
        }

        // validate web master password
        if( !validPass($sPass) ) {

            catchErr("Enter a valid password");
            $FORMOK = FALSE;
        }

        // if forms variables are validated
        if( $FORMOK ) {

            // assign array values
            $aArgs["User Name"] = $sUser;
            $aArgs["Password"] = $sPass;

            $oSess = new session;

            // try login and redirect
            if( $sPath = $oSess->login($aArgs) ) {
                header("Location: ".$sPath);
            }
        }
```

If the page request is not made via the POST method, we assign our variables to NULL. This ensures that when we call the variables to print in the form fields, they will not cause a system error:

```
} else { // POST variables not sent

    // initialize page variables
    $sUser = null;
}
```

We'll call the generic `setHeader()` and `openPage()` functions that render the appropriate HTML framework for our page. These functions can be reviewed in their defining file `/core/tpl_unsecure.php` – the template framework file inside the CMS application:

```
// generate the header information
setHeader();

// start a new page with a banner advertisement
openPage();
?>
```

The script includes some HTML too:

```
<tr>
        <td><div class="formlabel">User Name:</div></td>

        <td><input type="text" name="user"
                value="<?php print clean($sUser) ?>"
                class="textfield" /></td>
</tr>
```

In the actual POST processing, we validate our POST variables, and if they are valid we proceed to authenticate the web master session via the login function. After validation, we can redirect the web master to the page application path, which is returned by the login function. If there are errors during the login process, we capture them, set our $FORMOK variable to FALSE, and then display them to the web master, like this:

Once inside the CMS application interface, with a valid user session, the menus change to match those of the applications stored in the apress_admin_apps table:

Only those applications to which the web master has access will be visible in the menu list on the left side of the screen.

CMS Web Master Listing

This page displays a generic list that contains a general set of information about the web masters – the permissions (that we have assigned to the web master) for a particular application will determine whether he/she can add, edit, delete, or change the status of an item.

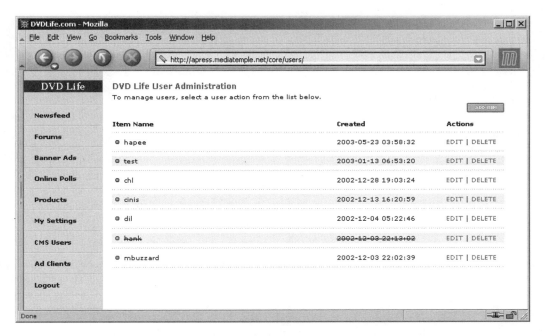

All of our applications will use a templated set of elements to display common content. Our content listing for each section is a primary example of that element:

Before we go through the display code, let's step back for a moment and look at some of the security aspects of the application that are included by our active page within the **tpl_secure.php** file. This file sets all of the web master information and validates the web master session on each and every secure page request. It also assigns some generic variables that are commonly passed, like the following:

❑ $id – A unique identifier

❑ $op – An operation string that tells us what operation to perform on a specified item ID

The opening of our template page contains the following code, where the initial task on every page call is the session verification:

```php
<?php

// File Location: /core/tpl_secure.php

// reusable generic elements such as error display functions
require_once("elements.php");

require_once("class.session.php");

// instantiate session class
$oSess = new session();

// start the session
session_start();

// get and set session information (DO NOT RENAME VARIABLES)
$aSess = explode("|", $_SESSION["sUSER"]);
$iUserId = (int) $aSess[0];
$oSess->setUserId($iUserId);

// get and set permission setting (DO NOT RENAME VARIABLES)
if( !$iPerm = $oSess->getPerms($aSess) ) {
    header("Location: ../../site/login/");
}

// get and set action variables
$op = $_GET["op"];
$id = (int) $_GET["id"];
$_GET["cursor"] ? $iCursor = $_GET["cursor"] : $iCursor = 0;
.......
```

Now we'll look at the script that delivers the CMS web master content to the page:

```php
<?php

// File Location: /core/users/index.php

require_once("tpl_secure.php");

// the session class is instantiated in the tpl_secure.php file

// get web masters and web master count
$aUsers = $oSess->getUsers("created_dt DESC", $iCursor);
$iCnt = $oSess->getUsersCount();

// check for users
if( count($aUsers) ) {

    // build page data array
```

```
    $i = 0;
    while( $i < count($aUsers) ) {
        $aData[$i]["Id"] = $aUsers[$i]["User Id"];
        $aData[$i]["Name"] = $aUsers[$i]["User Name"];
        $aData[$i]["Status"] = $aUsers[$i]["Status"];
        $aData[$i]["Created"] =$aUsers[$i]["Created Date"];
        ++$i;
    }
}

// check for ID
if( $id ) {

    // assign user ID
    $oSess->setUserId($id);

    // check operation type
    if( !strcmp($op, "del") ) {

        // try delete user and redirect
        $oSess->deleteUser();
        header("Location: ".SELF);

    } elseif ( !strcmp($op, "act") ) {

        // try activate user and redirect
        $oSess->activateUser();
        header("Location: ".SELF);

    } elseif ( !strcmp($op, "deact") ) {

        // try deactivate user and redirect
        $oSess->deactivateUser();
        header("Location: ".SELF);
    }
}
setHeader();
openPage();
?>
```

We are retrieving our user list data, but we are not displaying it yet – we have abstracted the code to render a list with pagination so that it can be used generically throughout the CMS. Let's take a brief look at that element located in /_lib/_base/elements.php. Inside the page body, we call the following function:

```
<?php renderList($iCnt, $aData) ?>
```

When the renderList() function is called from the elements.php library, the code loops through an associative array and renders each line of our list. The different actions available to the user interface are determined by the web master's permissions for that application. This value is referenced inside the renderList() function by globalizing the known variable name as seen on the next page:

```
// renders a paginated list for the site admin
function renderList($iCnt=0, $aData='') {

    global $iCursor, $iPerm;
```

CMS Web Master Form Page

Now that we see how we can render lists in the CMS application, let's look at the actual form page that is used to add and edit content:

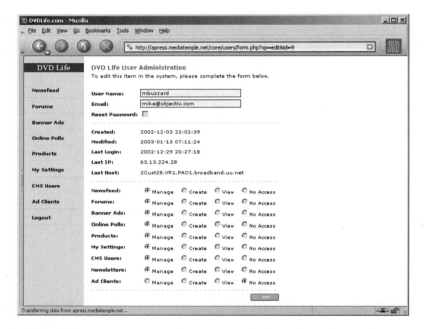

This page displays all the pertinent user information as well as the application's content displayed inside of an HTML form. Here is the code that generates this page:

```php
<?php

// File Location: /core/users/form.php

// template framework file for pages inside the CMS application
require_once("tpl_secure.php");

// data input validation functions
require_once("handlers.php");

require_once("class.users.php");

// instantiate users class
$oUsers = new users;
```

```php
// check for ID
if( $id ) {

    // assign user id
    $oUsers->setUserId($id);
}

if( $_POST ) { // check for HTTP POST variables

    // assign post variables
    $sUser = $_POST["user"];
    $sEmail = $_POST["email"];
    $iReset = $_POST["reset"];
    $aPerms = $_POST["perms"];

    // validate user name
    if( !validUser($sUser) ) {

        catchErr("Enter a valid user name");
        $FORMOK = FALSE;
    }

    // validate user e-mail
    if( !validEmail($sEmail) ) {

        catchErr("Enter a valid email address");
        $FORMOK = FALSE;
    }

    // validate permissions array
    if( !array_sum($aPerms) ) {

        catchErr("Select at least one permission");
        $FORMOK = FALSE;
    }
```

The following section of code is executed if the form variables are validated:

```php
if( $FORMOK ) {

    // assign array values
    $aArgs["User Name"] = $sUser;
    $aArgs["Email"] = $sEmail;
    $aArgs["Reset"] = $iReset;
    $aArgs["Perms"] = $aPerms;

    // check operation type
    if( !strcmp("edit", $op) ) {

        // try edit user
        $FORMOK = $oUsers->editUser($aArgs);
```

```
        } elseif ( !strcmp("add", $op) ) {

            // try add user
            $FORMOK = $oUsers->addUser($aArgs);
        }

        // redirect if successful
        if( $FORMOK ) {

            header("Location: index.php");
        }
    }
```

And this bit of the loop is executed if the POST variables are not sent:

```
    } else {

        // initialize page variables
        $sUser = null;
        $sEmail = null;
        $iReset = 0;

        if( !strcmp("edit", $op) ) {

            $aUser = $oUsers->getUser();
            $aPerms = $aUser["Perms"];
            $sUser = $aUser["User Name"];
            $sEmail = $aUser["Email"];
        }

    }

    $aApps = $oSess->getApps();

    // generate the header information
    setHeader();

    // start a new page with a banner advertisement
    openPage();
    ?>
```

We handle this form in the same manner that we handled our login form, and retrieve and display initial content based on the operation that was passed.

We also assign our data to an array that will be used to populate the form:

```
    <?php

    if( count($aApps) ) {
        $i = 0;
        while( $i < count($aApps) ) {
```

```
            $iAppId = $aApps[$i]["App Id"];
    ?>


    <tr>
        <td><div class="formlabel"><?php print $aApps[$i]["App Name"]
            ?>:</div></td>
        <td>

        <table border="0" cellpadding="3" cellspacing="0">
            <tr>
                <td><input type="radio" name="perms[<?= $iAppId ?>]
                <?= $iAppId ?>" value="3"
                <? !strcmp(3, $aPerms[$iAppId]) ?
                 print "checked" : print ""; ?>>Manage </td>
                <td><input type="radio" name="perms[<?= $iAppId ?>]
                <?= $iAppId ?>" value="2"<? !strcmp(2, $aPerms[$iAppId]) ?
                 print "checked" : print ""; ?>>Create </td>
                <td><input type="radio" name="perms[<?= $iAppId ?>]
                <?= $iAppId ?>" value="1"<? !strcmp(1, $aPerms[$iAppId]) ?
                 print "checked" : print ""; ?>>View </td>
                <td><input type="radio" name="perms[<?= $iAppId ?>]
                <?= $iAppId ?>" value="0"<? !$aPerms[$iAppId] ?
                 print "checked" : print ""; ?>>No Access </td>
            </tr>
        </table>
        </td>
    </tr>

    <?php
            ++$i;
        }
    }
    ?>
```

Since our data is stored in an array, we can loop through the array and populate our form accordingly. By assigning our form values to an array, we also know that our posted variable will come across as such. Thus by using the functions defined within our classes, we can easily manage all of the site content for a web master and a session.

Summary

This chapter started off by looking at the real world problems that developers face when trying to develop a secure environment for CMS applications.

We discussed our base requirements and definitions of the features and functions that we would like to implement. Based on this information, we proposed a design to accommodate these requirements. Our design looked at all of the potential structures and definitions of data and functions that we wanted to have, and then organized them based on our coding standards and practices defined in Chapter 2.

Hopefully, you have found this chapter useful, and developed a sound understanding of the different considerations and practices that are used in building a security architecture. Now you can use the following concepts when developing your own CMS administration application:

❑ The issues and concerns surrounding web master authentication

❑ Managing web masters and content in a streamlined yet secure fashion

❑ Considerations for page-level and access-level security features

❑ Designing and implementing reusable code based on your assumed application requirements

❑ A simplified approach to handling forms, and intuitive web master interaction with those forms

Now that we have defined the CMS security architecture, we shall look into developing a solution for managing our site visitors by providing visitor accounts, in the next chapter. Thereafter, we can begin to look at the applications that are dependent on this architecture for managing secure content. Understanding the involvement of users and session management will enable us to implement secure applications for content management into our system.

5

Visitor Accounts

Now that a secure and extensible means of managing content has been established, we need to develop a solution for managing our site visitors by providing visitor accounts. An effective way to enhance and deliver dynamic content is by encouraging visitors to publish complementary content of their own. By allowing site visitors to create unique identities for accessing the web site, we can add personalization features to the entire site experience. These personalization features will ensure an enhanced, tailored user experience in the site, thus creating a 'stickiness' or encouragement for the user to return frequently.

Once we establish a structure for managing user data and activity within the web site, we need to consider how to provide a non-intrusive means for encouraging users to participate. Often web site registration systems are introduced to users by requiring the completion of lengthy informational forms to gain access to the simplest content. This approach seems both obvious and ridiculous to a visitor and can easily deter rather than encourage membership. Although this is more of a design consideration, it'll greatly affect how we handle our data input and error reporting to the user. Thus it also gives us an idea of how we should manage our data to simplify the intended display uses.

In this chapter, we will:

❑ Define the problems of visitor account management

❑ Design the accounts management system to gather information while still providing a fluid and non-intrusive experience

❑ Write the code necessary to build our accounts management solution into the web site

The Problem

Our site visitors should have the option of registering a unique user identity within the web site, which will enable them to contribute content to the DVD discussion forums as well as any DVD news articles.

In Chapter 4, we discussed user authentication for the CMS system. This chapter will use similar authentication practices although we have a much smaller set of access permissions. The site visitors will either be logged in or not logged in to the web site. A simple TRUE or FALSE condition will determine the characteristics of the user interface (UI) and the visitor's ability to contribute supplemental content within the site. Without some sort of authentication system we would likely run the risk of spamming or defacing from anonymous visitors.

Since our web site is also a storefront for DVD products, we need to obtain information about our visitors' shipping address and newsletter preferences to streamline their e-commerce experience and enable a means of bi-directional communication. The user account preferences should store information regarding a visitor's willingness to receive the newsletters and the preferred format of each newsletter. Having the preferences as a subset of the user accounts enables us to easily extend the personalization settings and allows us to add new preferences for any new applications or offerings.

We don't want to discourage our visitors from registering an account by requiring long forms and seemingly private information. Therefore, our registration process should be quick and simple, requiring only the information necessary for gaining access. Any other information that we may require can be obtained later at the user's option. For example, the visitors shouldn't be prompted to enter their shipping address when they may just want to contribute to the site forums, but we should provide them the option to add/update their shipping address at their own discretion. This information will be necessary only during a purchase check out, so if they haven't entered it before they can always be prompted to add it then.

The Design

Since our visitor accounts are similar to the web master accounts, we can manage the sessions and authentication similarly. As mentioned earlier, the visitor access permission consists of TRUE/FALSE values.

We also know that we need to store our visitor entity information throughout the site. Like the administrative user accounts, we'll store our visitor account information in a session cookie with a timeout value. This design is lightweight and reliable enough to apply for site access authentication. We could consider using PHP sessions here; however, if our site popularity grows to a large number of unique daily visitors, we do not want to manage the overhead of sessions on the server. This design allows the users to manage their own session tokens and relieves the burden of pooling these sessions on the server.

Besides the basic visitor account information (consisting of the user name and an encrypted copy of the password), we'll also store the visitor's billing address and preferences to personalize and streamline user involvement for all site activities. We'll design our tables to extend the personalization boundaries and allow for multiple addresses and account preferences, although we'll only store the basic information that is needed for deploying the web site.

Feature Functionality Aspects

Here are some of the key functionality and features that we will provide:

❑ Visitor login and password reminder functionality

❑ Access-level login authentication with intuitive error handling

❑ Page-level authentication verification

❑ Visitor preferences for account information management

❑ Streamlined registration process to encourage greater numbers of membership

The following is a diagrammatic representation of the authentication process:

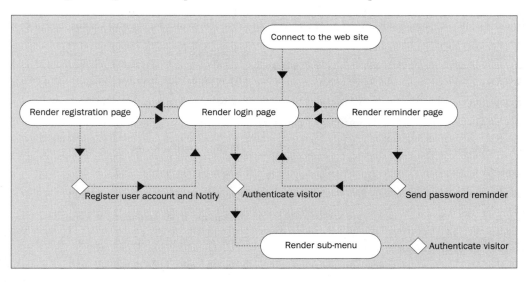

As detailed in the diagram, the process is similar to the web master login process; however, this model includes the user-centric account registration functionality.

Designing the Data Layer

Our database needs a simplified set of tables to store visitor account information as generically as possible so that we can easily extend the level of functionality on our site.

We'll use the following three tables for managing the account content:

❑ `apress_accounts` – The core accounts table that stores the visitor account identity.

❑ `apress_account_addr` – The generic addresses table, which can store visitor account shipping address information. If we wanted to, we could easily allow for multiple shipping addresses to third-party recipients or alternate primary addresses. This table can be reused for storing consumer billing address information or any other type of generic mailing address.

❏ `apress_account_prefs` – The user preferences table, which stores any visitor account personalization preferences that we wish to implement. For the time being, we're only storing information about the newsletter preferences. The preferences table could easily be extended to store a preferred address, a DVD genre, or any type of attribute that could personalize a user account and site experience.

We could easily store all of the base information in one table and then modify that table when we want to make scale adjustments, but planning ahead will also ensure better reuse of data collections that'll help to increase the performance and avoid implementing a bad relational design.

Let's look at our tables in detail to get a better understanding of the relative data.

The Accounts Table

The `apress_accounts` table is the core of the visitor account security model. It's a simplified reference of all basic account information, such as the user's e-mail address and recent login activity:

Field	Type	Description
account_id	INT(10)	The unique identifier for each account record
account_pass	VARCHAR(32)	Password value with MD5 encryption
account_remind	VARCHAR(100)	Password value as plaintext
account_email	VARCHAR(100)	Unique e-mail address
account_screenname	VARCHAR(100)	Unique screen name
last_login_ip	VARCHAR(15)	IP address from last account login
last_login_host	VARCHAR(100)	Host name from last account login
last_login_dt	DATETIME	Date/time value from last account login
status	INT(1)	Boolean value for account status
deleted	INT(1)	Boolean value for deleted account
deleted_dt	DATETIME	Date/time value when account was deleted
created_dt	DATETIME	Date/time value when account was created
modified_dt	DATETIME	Date/time value when account was last modified

The `account_id` primary key is referenced by both the `apress_account_addr` and `apress_account_prefs` tables. We also place an index on both the `account_email` and `account_screenname` fields since we'll be doing a significant amount of queries on those fields during repetitive authentication and/or search lookups and display references.

The Account Addresses Table

The `apress_account_addr` table provides a generic model for addresses, with an `account_id` reference for simplifying referenced lookups. Since all addresses are comprised of the same definable properties, we can abstract this data and reference it by ID:

Field	Type	Description
account_addr_id	INT(10)	The unique identifier for each account address record
account_id	INT(10)	Account reference ID
account_addr_name	VARCHAR(100)	Recipient name for the address which will allow accounts to have nicknames for each address in the system
account_addr_company	VARCHAR(100)	Recipient company name for the address
account_addr_street	VARCHAR(100)	Street address
account_addr_street_ext	VARCHAR(100)	Additional street address information
account_addr_city	VARCHAR(100)	Address city
account_addr_state	VARCHAR(100)	Address state
account_addr_country	VARCHAR(100)	Address country
account_addr_postal	VARCHAR(15)	Address postal code
account_addr_phone	VARCHAR(20)	Address phone number
deleted	INT(1)	Date time value when address was deleted
created_dt	DATETIME	Date/time value when address was created
modified_dt	DATETIME	Date/time value when address was last modified
deleted_dt	DATETIME	Date/time value when address was deleted

The Account Preferences Table

The apress_account_prefs table is a simple set of values that are associated to an account and can be easily expanded to allow for additional preferences. It stores a set of account personalization preferences and uses the account_id reference for simplifying referenced lookups:

Field	Type	Description
account_pref_id	INT(10)	The unique identifier for each account preferences record
account_id	INT(10)	Account reference ID
newsletter_recipient	INT(1)	Boolean flag for newsletter recipients

Table continued on following page

Field	Type	Description
created_dt	DATETIME	Date/time value when the address record was created in the database table
modified_dt	DATETIME	Date/time value when address was last modified

Designing the Data Object

The accounts data object will handle all of the data collection and manipulation functionality for our site visitor accounts. Since the visitor accounts act as autonomous entities within the application framework we can simplify the design by encapsulating all of the account functionality inside a single class.

The Accounts Class

Let's look at the different class variables needed to provide the functionality desired from our accounts data object:

accounts Class Variable	Description
_iAccountId	Property containing the accounts unique identifier
_oMail	Property containing a reference to the PEAR::Mail object
_oConn	Property containing a reference to the PEAR::DB connection handle object

We'll also need some class methods that'll manipulate these variables and ultimately manage the accounts:

accounts Class Method	Description
accounts($iAccountId = '')	Constructor method that instantiates the _oConn and _oMail objects. This member also optionally assigns the _iAccountId property if passed.
_setSession($aArgs)	Sets a session cookie containing the values stored in the $aArgs array.
_screenNameExists ($sScreenName)	Verifies if a visitor-entered screen name, $sScreenName, is unique.
_accountEmailExists($sEmail)	Verifies if a visitor-entered e-mail address, $sEmail, is unique.
_notifyAccount($sBody)	Sends an e-mail containing the content stored in the $sBody argument passed.
_authenticate($aArgs)	Verifies an account session based on the values stored in the $aArgs array argument passed.

accounts Class Method	Description
_updateLogin()	Updates the account login information upon successful authentication.
setAccountId($iAcountId)	Assigns the class member _iAccountId to the value passed in the $iAccountId argument for the class instance.
getSession()	Builds an associative array of values from the client-stored session cookie.
validateSession()	Validates an account session. This method is used while accessing information or functionality that is intended to be secure.
sendReminder($aArgs)	Sends a password reminder to a user based on the validation of values passed in the $aArgs array.
login($aArgs)	Calls the _authenticate() and _updateLogin() methods based on the values passed in the $aArgs array.
getAccount()	Returns an associate array of account data.
getPreferences()	Returns an associative array of account preferences.
getAccountAddress()	Returns an associative array of account shipping address values.
addAccount($aArgs)	Creates a new account based on the values that are passed in the $aArgs array.
updateAccount($aArgs)	Updates an account based on the values that are passed in the $aArgs array.
updatePreferences($aArgs)	Updates an account preferences record based on values that are passed in the $aArgs array.
updateAccountAddress($aArgs)	Updates an account address record based on values that are passed in the $aArgs array.

The Solution

Now that we've reviewed the problems and considerations that need to be addressed when building the accounts management modules, let's look at the base files used in the application framework. Having already written the code for many of these files that constitute our application framework, we can simply plug our new functionality into that framework.

The following diagram shows the different relationships and dependencies of files within our application framework that are necessary to implement the accounts management module:

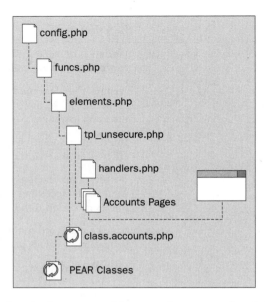

The following table describes the location and functional purpose of each file:

File Name	File Path	Description
config.php	/_lib/_base/	Configuration values for the application.
funcs.php	/_lib/_base/	Utility functions for the application.
elements.php	/_lib/_base/	Reusable generic elements such as error display functions. This file also assigns the common GET variables – $op and $id.
tpl_unsecure.php	/site/	Template framework file for pages outside the CMS application.
handlers.php	/_lib/_base/	Data input validation functions.
index.php	/site/accounts/	Account login page.
reminder.php	/site/accounts/	Account login reminder page.
register.php	/site/accounts/	Account registration page.
manage.php	/site/accounts/	Account management page.
logout.php	/site/accounts/	Account logout page.
prefs.php	/site/accounts/	Account preferences management page.
shipping.php	/site/accounts/	Shipping address management page.
class.accounts.php	/_lib/_classes/	Data object for accounts logic.

Implementing the Data Layer

As mentioned earlier, we need three tables to store all of the relative data for the visitor accounts:

❑   apress_accounts to store the visitor account identity

❑   apress_account_addr to store consumer billing address information or any other type of generic mailing address

❑   apress_account_prefs to store any visitor account personalization preferences that we wish to implement

Next we'll look at the SQL scripts used to build the three tables.

apress_accounts

This table uses an account_id as the primary key for each record. We've added an index for the account_email column, the account_pass, and the account_screenname column since we'll be executing queries against these columns.

Here is the script to create the apress_accounts table:

```
CREATE TABLE apress_accounts (
    account_id         INT(10)        NOT NULL auto_increment,
    account_pass       VARCHAR(32)    NOT NULL default '',
    account_remind     VARCHAR (100)  NOT NULL default '',
    account_email      VARCHAR (100)  NOT NULL default '',
    account_screenname VARCHAR (100)  NOT NULL default '',
    last_login_ip      VARCHAR (15)   default NULL,
    last_login_host    VARCHAR (100)  default NULL,
    last_login_dt      VARCHAR        default NULL,
    status             INT(1)         NOT NULL default '1',
    deleted            INT(1)         default '0',
    deleted_dt         DATETIME       default NULL,
    created_dt         DATETIME       NOT NULL default '0000-00-00 00:00:00',
    modified_dt        DATETIME       NOT NULL default '0000-00-00 00:00:00',
                       PRIMARY KEY  (account_id),
                       KEY account_email_ref (account_email),
                       KEY account_pass_ref (account_pass),
                       KEY account_screenname_ref (account_screenname)
) TYPE=MyISAM;
```

apress_account_addr

This table stores generic address information with a relationship reference to an account ID. Multiple address references can be stored in this table if we decide to extend our user preferences at a later time. Again, we've added an additional index, this time to the account_id column, for improving the performance of queries that are executed against that column.

Here is the script to create the `apress_account_addr` table:

```
CREATE TABLE apress_account_addr (
    account_addr_id        INT(10)        NOT NULL auto_increment,
    account_id             INT (10)       NOT NULL default '0',
    account_addr_name      VARCHAR(100)   NULL default NULL,
    account_addr_company   VARCHAR (100)  NULL default NULL,
    account_addr_street    VARCHAR (100)  NOT NULL default '',
    account_addr_street_ext VARCHAR (100) NULL default NULL,
    account_addr_city      VARCHAR (100)  NOT NULL default '',
    account_addr_state     VARCHAR (100)  NOT NULL default '',
    account_addr_country   VARCHAR (100)  NOT NULL default '',
    account_addr_postal    VARCHAR (15)   NOT NULL default '',
    account_addr_phone     VARCHAR (20)   NULL default NULL,
    deleted                INT(1)         default '0',
    deleted_dt             DATETIME       default NULL,
    created_dt             DATETIME       NOT NULL default '0000-00-00 00:00:00',
    modified_dt            DATETIME       NOT NULL default '0000-00-00 00:00:00',
                           PRIMARY KEY   (account_addr_id),
                           KEY account_id_ref (account_id)
) TYPE=MyISAM;
```

apress_account_prefs

The `apress_account_prefs` table stores account preferences with a relationship to an account ID. We can easily add new personalization preferences to this table by adding a new column for each preference. Again, the additional index on the `account_id` column improves the performance of queries executed against that column.

Here is the script to create the `apress_account_prefs` table:

```
CREATE TABLE apress_account_prefs (
    account_pref_id      INT(10)      NOT NULL auto_increment,
    account_id           INT(10)      NOT NULL default '0',
    newsletter_recipient INT(1)       NOT NULL default '1',
    created_dt           DATETIME     NOT NULL default '0000-00-00 00:00:00',
    modified_dt          DATETIME     default NULL,
                         PRIMARY KEY  (account_pref_id),
                         KEY account_id_ref (account_id)
) TYPE=MyISAM;
```

Implementing the Data Object

Our database tables are now ready to work with, so we'll move on to constructing and implementing our proposed solution. Let's start by looking at the code that comprises the `accounts` class. Then we'll integrate the data objects into the application framework, which we've already constructed.

class.accounts.php

We begin writing the `class.accounts.php` by including all the files upon which our class is dependent:

```php
<?php

// File Location: /_lib/_classes/class.accounts.php

// the Mail.php, and DB.php scripts are in the PEAR library, and
// they'll include and extend the PEAR.php class object automatically
require_once("Mail.php");
require_once("DB.php");

/**
 * handles account functions
 */
class accounts { // open the class definition

    /**
     * unique identifier for an account
     *
     * @var integer
     * @access private
     * @see setAccountId()
     */
    var $_iAccountId;

    /**
     * PEAR mail object
     *
     * @var object
     * @access private
     */
    var $_oMail;

    /**
     * PEAR::DB object
     *
     * @var object
     * @access private
     */
    var $_oConn;
```

The constructor method instantiates any default member properties and inherited objects:

```php
    // CONSTRUCTOR
    /**
     * class constructor
     *
     * @param integer $iAccountId [optional] account identifier
     * @access public
     */
    function accounts($iAccountId = '') {

        // implement PEAR::Mail object
        $this->_oMail =& Mail::factory("mail");
```

```
        if( Mail::isError($this->_oMail) ) {

            catchExc($this->_oMail->getMessage());
        }

        // implement PEAR::DB object
        $this->_oConn =& DB::connect(DSN);

        if( DB::isError($this->_oConn) ) {

            catchExc($this->_oConn->getMessage());
        }

        // set account ID
        if( is_int($iAccountId) ) {

            $this->setAccountId($iAccountId);
        }
    }
```

Here we used two PEAR objects:

❑ The PEAR::DB object for database connectivity

❑ The PEAR::Mail object for all of its SMTP communications

The following method assigns the unique identifier value to be used during an instance of the class and will be used throughout the class as well as inside the pages of our site:

```
/**
 * set the unique identifier variable for the class
 *
 * @param integer $iAccountId unique identifier
 * @access public
 */
function setAccountId($iAccountId) {
    // Note: If the value passed to this method isn't an integer, the
    // ID wouldn't get set and any dependent query would fail

    // assign unique identifier
    if( is_int($iAccountId) ) {

        $this->_iAccountId = $iAccountId;
    }
}
```

The following method sets a cookie with account authentication values – this is the key that is passed back and forth between the client and server to verify authentication during a session:

```
/**
 * sets session values for a user
 *
```

```
 * @param array $aArgs session data
 * @access private
 */
function _setSession($aArgs) {

    // create string from account array values
    $sVal = implode("|", $aArgs);

    // set account session cookie
    setcookie("cACCOUNT", $sVal, time()+(TIMEOUT / 2), "/", "", "");
}
```

The next two methods are used to verify unique values for an account based on data entered by the user in the registration form:

```
/**
 * verify unique screen name
 *
 * @param string $sScreenName screen name
 * @return integer
 * @access private
 */
function _screenNameExists($sScreenName) {

    // check for matching screen name
    $sql = "SELECT
                    account_id
            FROM
                    ".PREFIX."_accounts
            WHERE
                    account_screenname='".$sScreenName."' AND
                    deleted=0";

    if( DB::isError($rsTmp = $this->_oConn->query($sql)) ) {

        catchExc($rsTmp->getMessage());
        return FALSE;
    }

    // return matching number of rows
    $return = $rsTmp->numRows();
    return $return;
}

/**
 * verify unique e-mail address
 *
 * @param string $sEmail e-mail address
 * @return integer
 * @access private
 */
function _accountEmailExists($sEmail) {

    // check for valid _iAccountId member value
    if( is_int($this->_iAccountId) ) {

        $sFilter = " AND account_id != ". $this->_iAccountId;
```

```
        }

        // get matching e-mail address
        $sql = "SELECT
                    account_id
                FROM
                    ".PREFIX."_accounts
                WHERE
                    account_email='".$sEmail."'".$sFilter." AND
                    deleted=0";

        if( DB::isError($rsTmp = $this->_oConn->query($sql)) ) {

            catchExc($rsTmp->getMessage());
            return FALSE;
        }

        // return matching number of rows
        $return = $rsTmp->numRows();
        return $return;
    }
```

We don't want multiple visitor accounts that share e-mail addresses or screen names. To prevent this, we could set a unique key on these table columns in the database; however, it's better to handle these errors in a more delicate manner by displaying an informative message to the user regarding the data expectations.

After the account is created, we need to notify the users of the access information so that they have a soft copy of their credentials:

```
/**
 * send mail notification to user
 *
 * @param string $sBody e-mail body to send
 * @return boolean
 * @access private
 */
function _notifyAccount($sBody) {

    // get account information and assign mail members
    $aAccount = $this->getAccount();
    $aHeaders["To"] = $sRecipients = $aAccount["Email"];
    $aHeaders["From"] = ENTITY." <".EMAIL.">";
    $aHeaders["Subject"] = ENTITY." User Account Notification";
    $aHeaders["Priority"] = "3";

    // try to send mail
    if( Mail::isError($mailTmp = $this->_oMail->
                    send($sRecipients, $aHeaders, $sBody)) ) {
        catchExc($mailTmp->getMessage());
        return FALSE;
    }

    return TRUE;
}
```

Here, the notification method implements the PEAR::Mail object for sending e-mail. Notifying a user is the first line of defense to prevent user error. Should a user forget or lose the account creation e-mail, the password reminder acts as a second line of defense. We'll look at the password reminder functionality in the *Presentation Layer* section.

The following class method is used to authenticate a visitor account session. This method is called during the login process and verifies several aspects of the data entered by the user:

```php
/**
 * authenticate user account
 *
 * @param array $aArgs user login values
 * @return boolean
 * @access private
 */
function _authenticate($aArgs) {

    // get account information
    $sql = "SELECT
                account_id,
                account_pass,
                account_email,
                account_screenname,
                status
            FROM
                ".PREFIX."_accounts
            WHERE
                account_email='".$aArgs["Email"]."' AND
                deleted=0";

    if( DB::isError($rsTmp = $this->_oConn->query($sql)) ) {

        catchExc($rsTmp->getMessage());
        return FALSE;
    }

    // capture query results
    $aRow = $rsTmp->fetchRow(DB_FETCHMODE_ASSOC);

    // check if account exists
    if( $rsTmp->numRows() < 1 ) {

        catchErr("User Account does not exist");
        return FALSE;

    // check account status
    } elseif ( $aRow["status"] < 1 ) {

        catchErr("Account inactive");
        return FALSE;

    // make sure the password exists
    } elseif ( !empty($aRow["account_pass"]) ) {
```

```
            // check acocunt password value against
            // the user-entered password
            if( strcmp(substr(md5($aArgs["Password"]), 3, 8),
                              $aRow["account_pass"]) ) {

                catchErr("Invalid password");
                return FALSE;
            }

            // assign account array values
            $aAccount = array($aRow["account_id"],
                              $aRow["account_screenname"],
                              $aRow["account_email"],
                              $aRow["account_pass"]);

            // update account session
            settype($aRow["account_id"], "integer");
            $this->setAccountId($iAccountId);
            $this->_setSession($aAccount);
            return TRUE;
        }
    }
```

We are capturing errors to be displayed to the visitor within the page constructs rather than delivering a standard cryptic message that might confuse the visitor.

After successfully authenticating a visitor, we need to update the account access information for further reference:

```
/**
 * update user login values
 *
 * @return boolean
 * @access private
 */
function _updateLogin() {

    // get remote user IP address
    $sAddress = $_SERVER["REMOTE_ADDR"];

    // look up hostname if available
    $sHost = gethostbyaddr($sAddress);

    // update login records
    $sql = "UPDATE ".PREFIX."_accounts
            SET
                last_login_dt=(NOW()),
                last_login_ip='".$sAddress."',
                last_login_host='".$sHost."'
            WHERE
                account_id=".$this->_iAccountId;
```

```
            if( DB::isError($rsTmp = $this->_oConn->query($sql)) ) {

                catchExc($rsTmp->getMessage());
                return FALSE;
            }
        }
```

Since we'll require our user session values in several methods throughout the class, we'll create a simple method to return an associative array of the visitor session values:

```
    /**
     * get the user account session values
     *
     * @return array session data
     * @access public
     */
    function getSession() {

        // check for account session cookie
        if( isset($_COOKIE["cACCOUNT"]) ) {

            // apply account session values to an array
            $aSess = explode("|", $_COOKIE["cACCOUNT"]);
            $return["Account Id"] = $aSess[0];
            $return["Screen Name"] = $aSess[1];
            $return["Email"] = $aSess[2];
            $return["Password"] = $aSess[3];
            return $return;
        }

        return FALSE;
    }
```

We need to verify the visitor account session in several places throughout the site. The following method provides a quick and simple means of doing so – it'll automatically assign the _iAccountId member variable for the specific instance of the class:

```
    /**
     * validate the user account session
     *
     * @return boolean
     * @access public
     */
    function validateSession() {

        // if the session array is active
        if( $aUser = $this->getSession() ) {

            // validate account credentials
            $sql = "SELECT
```

```
                        account_id
                FROM
                        ".PREFIX."_accounts
                WHERE
                        account_id=".$aUser["Account Id"]." AND
                        account_pass='".$aUser["Password"]."' AND
                        account_email='".$aUser["Email"]."' AND
                        account_screenname='".$aUser["Screen Name"]."' AND
                        status=1 AND
                        deleted=0";

        if( DB::isError($rsTmp = $this->_oConn->query($sql)) ) {

                catchExc($rsTmp->getMessage());
                return FALSE;
        }

        // verify single record for account
        if( !strcmp(1, $rsTmp->numRows()) ) {

                // update session
                $this->_setSession($aUser);
                $iAccountId = (int) $aUser["Account Id"];
                $this->setAccountId($iAccountId);
                return TRUE;
        }

        return FALSE;
    }
    return FALSE;
}
```

In the event that a visitor forgets the account login information and also lost the account creation e-mail, we provide a method for sending a login reminder to the user once we have verified that the visitor account does exist:

```
/**
 * send an account password reminder to the associated user
 *
 * @param array $aArgs user login data
 * @return boolean
 * @access public
 */
function sendReminder($aArgs) {

    // get account information from screen name
    $sql = "SELECT
                account_id,
                account_email
            FROM
                ".PREFIX."_accounts
            WHERE
                account_screenname='".$aArgs["Screen Name"]."' AND
                status=1 AND
                deleted=0";

    if( DB::isError($rsTmp = $this->_oConn->query($sql)) ) {
```

```
            catchExc($rsTmp->getMessage());
            return FALSE;
        }

        // verify single record
        if( $rsTmp->numRows() < 1 ) {

            catchErr("Cannot find user account information");
            return FALSE;
        }

        // assign result values
        $aRow = $rsTmp->fetchRow(DB_FETCHMODE_ASSOC);

        // compare e-mail addresses
        if( strcmp($aRow["account_email"], $aArgs["Email"]) ) {

            catchErr("Account email does not match account information");
            return FALSE;
        }

        // get account information
        settype($aRow["account_id"], "integer");
        $this->setAccountId($aRow["account_id"]);
        $aAccount = $this->getAccount();

        $sBody = "Your ".ENTITY." account login information is:\r\n\r\n";
        $sBody .= "Email: ".$aAccount["Email"]."\r\n";
        $sBody .= "Password: ".$aAccount["Password Reminder"];

        // send e-mail
        return $this->_notifyAccount($sBody);
    }
```

Our login method calls some of our more complicated methods (previously defined). This type of reuse is exactly what we are trying to achieve by using an object-oriented (OO) approach to our design:

```
/**
 * login to a user account
 *
 * @param array $aArgs user login data
 * @return boolean
 * @access public
 */
function login($aArgs) {

    // try authentication
    if( $this->_authenticate($aArgs) ) {

        // update login information
        $this->_updateLogin();
        return TRUE;
    }
}
```

We'll need to retrieve visitor account information for a commercial transaction, interaction with the news or forum applications, or managing visitor account preferences. The getAccount() method collects all the core account information as well as the dependent data that's collected through calls to other class members:

```php
/**
 * get a single account by account ID
 *
 * @return array account data
 * @access public
 */
function getAccount() {

    // get account values
    $sql = "SELECT
                account_id,
                account_pass,
                account_remind,
                account_email,
                account_screenname,
                last_login_ip,
                last_login_host,
                last_login_dt,
                status,
                created_dt,
                modified_dt
          FROM
                ".PREFIX."_accounts
          WHERE
                account_id=".$this->_iAccountId;

    if( DB::isError($rsTmp = $this->_oConn->query($sql)) ) {

        catchExc($rsTmp->getMessage());
        return FALSE;
    }

    // assign account values
    $aRow = $rsTmp->fetchRow(DB_FETCHMODE_ASSOC);

    // build associative array of account data
    $return["Account Id"] = $aRow["account_id"];
    $return["Password"] = $aRow["account_pass"];
    $return["Password Reminder"] = $aRow["account_remind"];
    $return["Email"] = $aRow["account_email"];
    $return["Screen Name"] = $aRow["account_screenname"];
    $return["Account Address"] = $this->getAccountAddress();
    $return["Account Preferences"] = $this->getPreferences();
    $return["Login Address"] = $aRow["last_login_ip"];
    $return["Login Host"] = $aRow["last_login_host"];
    $return["Login Date"] = strtotime($aRow["last_login_dt"]);
    $return["Status"] = $aRow["status"];
    $return["Created Date"] = strtotime($aRow["created_dt"]);
    $return["Modified Date"] = strtotime($aRow["modified_dt"]);
    return $return;

}
```

We've abstracted our preferences method from the base `getAccount` method to modify and extend our account preferences. This method can be called independently or the data can be referenced from the account data set return seen above:

```
/**
 * get account preferences for a user account
 *
 * @return array
 * @access public
 */
function getPreferences() {

    // get account preferences
    $sql = "SELECT
                newsletter_recipient,
            FROM
                ".PREFIX."_account_prefs
            WHERE
                account_id=".$this->_iAccountId;

    if( DB::isError($rsTmp = $this->_oConn->query($sql)) ) {

        catchExc($rsTmp->getMessage());
        return FALSE;
    }

    // if preferences exist
    if( $rsTmp->numRows() ) {

        // assign preferences to variables
        $aRow = $rsTmp->fetchRow(DB_FETCHMODE_ASSOC);

        // build associative array of preferences
        $return["Newsletter Recipient"] = $aRow["newsletter_recipient"];
        return $return;
    }
}
```

The address method works similarly to the preferences method seen above. We can also provide multiple addresses for a specific account by making minor modifications to the preferences method by enabling an incrementing array index:

```
/**
 * get account address for a user account
 *
 * @return array
 * @access public
 */
function getAccountAddress() {
```

```
            // get account address information
            $sql = "SELECT
                        account_addr_id,
                        account_addr_name,
                        account_addr_company,
                        account_addr_street,
                        account_addr_street_ext,
                        account_addr_city,
                        account_addr_state,
                        account_addr_country,
                        account_addr_postal,
                        account_addr_phone
                    FROM
                        ".PREFIX."_account_addr
                    WHERE
                        deleted=0
                        AND account_id=".$this->_iAccountId;

            if( DB::isError($rsTmp = $this->_oConn->query($sql)) ) {

                catchExc($rsTmp->getMessage());
                return FALSE;
            }

            // if address exists
            if( $rsTmp->numRows() ) {

                // assign address values
                $aRow = $rsTmp->fetchRow(DB_FETCHMODE_ASSOC);

                // build associative array of address values
                $return["Address Id"] = $aRow["account_addr_id"];
                $return["Address Name"] = $aRow["account_addr_name"];
                $return["Address Company"] = $aRow["account_addr_company"];
                $return["Address Street"] = $aRow["account_addr_street"];
                $return["Address Street Ext"] =
                                        $aRow["account_addr_street_ext"];
                $return["Address City"] = $aRow["account_addr_city"];
                $return["Address State"] = $aRow["account_addr_state"];
                $return["Address Country"] = $aRow["account_addr_country"];
                $return["Address Postal"] = $aRow["account_addr_postal"];
                $return["Address Phone"] = $aRow["account_addr_phone"];
                return $return;
            }
        }
```

Adding a new account to the system is a lengthy process with many decision points. First we'll verify the unique values for the account e-mail address and account screen name. Then we'll assign the account credentials and set the default account preferences. We should also lock the apress_accounts table during the INSERT query until after we've selected the unique identifier, to ensure that we get the correct unique identifier for the newly added account record.

We'll go through this function step by step:

```
/**
 * add a new account record
 *
 * @param array $aArgs user account data
 * @return boolean
 * @access public
 */
function addAccount($aArgs) {
```

First we assign the password values:

```
$sPasswordRemind = $aArgs["Password"];
$sPassword = substr(md5($sPasswordRemind), 3 , 8);
```

Next we verify the account e-mail address and account screen name:

```
// check for screen name
if( $this->_screenNameExists($aArgs["Screen Name"]) ) {

    catchErr("This screen name already exists");
    return FALSE;

// check for e-mail
} else if( $this->_accountEmailExists($aArgs["Email"]) ) {

    catchErr("This email address already exists");
    return FALSE;
} else {
```

Before going any further, we need lock the table in order to capture the unique ID accurately:

```
$sql = "LOCK TABLES ".PREFIX."_accounts WRITE";

if( DB::isError($rsTmp = $this->_oConn->query($sql)) ) {

    catchExc($rsTmp->getMessage());
    return FALSE;
}

// insert new account record
$sql = "INSERT INTO ".PREFIX."_accounts (
                account_pass,
                account_remind,
                account_email,
                account_screenname,
                status,
                created_dt,
                modified_dt
```

```
                   ) VALUES (
                           '".$sPassword."',
                           '".$sPasswordRemind."',
                           '".$aArgs["Email"]."',
                           '".$aArgs["Screen Name"]."',
                           1,
                           (NOW()),
                           (NOW())
                   )";

if( DB::isError($rsTmp = $this->_oConn->query($sql)) ) {

    catchExc($rsTmp->getMessage());
    return FALSE;
}

// get newest account identifier from the added record
$sql = "SELECT MAX(account_id)
        FROM ".PREFIX."_accounts";

if( DB::isError($iAccountId = $this->_oConn->getOne($sql)) ) {

    catchExc($iAccountId->getMessage());
    return FALSE;
}

// set unique identifier member variable
settype($iAccountId, "integer");
$this->setAccountId($iAccountId);

// unlock tables
$sql = "UNLOCK TABLES";

if( DB::isError($rsTmp = $this->_oConn->query($sql)) ) {

    catchExc($rsTmp->getMessage());
    return FALSE;
}
```

Next we add a new record for account preferences:

```
$sql = "INSERT INTO ".PREFIX."_account_prefs (
                   account_id,
                   created_dt
        ) VALUES (
                   ".$this->_iAccountId.",
                   (NOW())
        )";

if( DB::isError($rsTmp = $this->_oConn->query($sql)) ) {

    catchExc($rsTmp->getMessage());
    return FALSE;
```

```
        }

        // build e-mail body
        $sBody = "Your ".ENTITY." account has been created.\r\n";
        $sBody .= "Your login information is:\r\n\r\n";
        $sBody .= "Email: ".$aArgs["Email"]."\r\n";
        $sBody .= "Password: ".$sPasswordRemind;

        return $this->_notifyAccount($sBody);
    }
}
```

Editing an account is a much simpler process than adding an account:

```
/**
 * update an existing account record by account ID
 *
 * @param array $aArgs user account data
 * @return boolean
 * @access public
 */
function updateAccount($aArgs) {

    // initialize SQL filter
    $sFilter = "";

    // check for e-mail address
    if( $this->_accountEmailExists($aArgs["Email"]) ) {

        catchErr("This email address already exists");
        return FALSE;
    }

    // verify password value
    if( strcmp("", $aArgs["Password"]) ) {

        // create password variables
        $sPasswordRemind = $aArgs["Password"];
        $sPassword = substr(md5($sPasswordRemind), 3 , 8);

        // add SQL filter
        $sFilter = " account_pass='".$sPassword."',
        account_remind='".$sPasswordRemind."',";
    }

    // update account record
    $sql = "UPDATE ".PREFIX."_accounts
        SET
            account_email='".$aArgs["Email"]."',
            ".$sFilter."
            modified_dt=(NOW())
        WHERE
            account_id=".$this->_iAccountId;
```

```
        if( DB::isError($rsTmp = $this->_oConn->query($sql)) ) {

            catchExc($rsTmp->getMessage());
            return FALSE;
        }

        return TRUE;
    }
```

In the page construction, we've separated the various features involved in account information management from each other – this design allows us to update these different features (account information, account address information, account preferences) independently.

The next two class methods are similar to the method above. They cover the other two child references of an account – the addresses and the preferences. Since we don't require the visitor's account address information to be entered during the registration process and we can't assign default values for an address, we must determine if the query should be an update or an insert based on the operation type passed by the client web form.

```
    /**
     * update account preferences by account ID
     *
     * @param array $aArgs account preferences data
     * @return boolean
     * @access public
     */
    function updatePreferences($aArgs) {

        // update account preferences
        $sql = "UPDATE ".PREFIX."_account_prefs
            SET
                newsletter_recipient=".$aArgs["Newsletter Recipient"].",
                modified_dt=(NOW())
            WHERE
                account_id=".$this->_iAccountId;

        if( DB::isError($rsTmp = $this->_oConn->query($sql)) ) {

            catchErr("This email address already exists");
            return FALSE;
        }

        return TRUE;
    }
```

The following function will update an account address by account ID, and insert a new record if one does not exist:

```
    /**
     * @param array $aArgs account billing address data
     * @return boolean
     * @access public
```

```
    */
    function updateAccountAddress($aArgs) {

        // update account address, check operation for add or edit
        if( !strcmp("add", $aArgs["Operation"]) ) {

            // insert new record
            $sql = "INSERT INTO ".PREFIX."_account_addr (
                            account_id,
                            account_addr_name,
                            account_addr_company,
                            account_addr_street,
                            account_addr_street_ext,
                            account_addr_city,
                            account_addr_state,
                            account_addr_country,
                            account_addr_postal,
                            account_addr_phone,
                            created_dt
                    ) VALUES (
                            ".$this->_iAccountId.",
                            '".$aArgs["Name"]."',
                            '".$aArgs["Company"]."',
                            '".$aArgs["Street"]."',
                            '".$aArgs["Street Ext"]."',
                            '".$aArgs["City"]."',
                            '".$aArgs["State"]."',
                            '".$aArgs["Country"]."',
                            '".$aArgs["Postal"]."',
                            '".$aArgs["Phone"]."',
                            (NOW())
                    )";
```

If the operation type is 'edit' then update the account address by account ID:

```
    } elseif ( !strcmp("edit", $aArgs["Operation"]) ) {

        // update existing record
        $sql = "UPDATE ".PREFIX."_account_addr
                SET
                    account_addr_name='".$aArgs["Name"]."',
                    account_addr_company='".$aArgs["Company"]."',
                    account_addr_street='".$aArgs["Street"]."',
                    account_addr_street_ext='".$aArgs["Street Ext"]."',
                    account_addr_city='".$aArgs["City"]."',
                    account_addr_state='".$aArgs["State"]."',
                    account_addr_country='".$aArgs["Country"]."',
                    account_addr_postal='".$aArgs["Postal"]."',
                    account_addr_phone='".$aArgs["Phone"]."',
                    modified_dt=(NOW())
                WHERE
                    account_id=".$this->_iAccountId;
    }
```

133

```
        if( DB::isError($rsTmp = $this->_oConn->query($sql)) ) {

            catchExc($rsTmp->getMessage());
            return FALSE;
        }

        return TRUE;
    }
} // close the class definition
?>
```

That completes the code required for deploying the class.accounts.php file. If you wanted to add accounts to the CMS application in order to manage account data and status, you could easily add the methods needed for doing so. We've not included those members in this class since it's a common practice that can be referenced throughout several of our other data objects including the news class (Chapter 6), the advertisements class (Chapter 8), and the polls class (Chapter 9).

Presentation Layer

Now that we've constructed the accounts data object, let's look at implementing this object in our web site. All of our account pages will be stored inside of the /site/accounts/ directory on the server.

We'll need to accommodate the following six main views:

- ❑ Account login page (**index.php**)
- ❑ Account registration page (**register.php**)
- ❑ Password reminder page (**reminder.php**)
- ❑ Account management page (**manage.php**)
- ❑ Newsletter preferences page (**prefs.php**)
- ❑ Shipping information page (**shipping.php**)

Account Login Page

The following screenshot shows the default index page in the accounts directory:

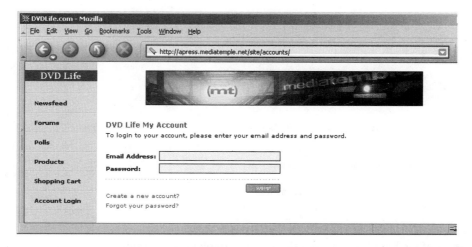

This page controls the login to the accounts management for a single visitor. All of the page processing is handled in the top of this page, depending on the HTTP method variables sent to the server:

```php
<?php

// File Location: /site/accounts/index.php

// template framework file for pages outside of the CMS application
require_once("tpl_unsecure.php");

require_once("class.accounts.php");

// data input validation functions
require_once("handlers.php");

if( $_POST ) { // check for HTTP POST variables

    // assign POST variables
    $sEmail = $_POST["email"];
    $sPass = $_POST["pass"];

    // validate user e-mail
    if( !validEmail($sEmail) ) {

        catchErr("Enter a valid email address");
        $FORMOK = FALSE;
    }

    // validate user password
    if( !validPass($sPass) ) {

        catchErr("Enter a valid password");
        $FORMOK = FALSE;
    }
```

The next bit of code is executed if the form variables are validated:

```
if( $FORMOK ) {

    // assign array values
    $aArgs["Email"] = $sEmail;
    $aArgs["Password"] = $sPass;

    $oAccounts = new accounts;

    // try login and redirect
    if( $oAccounts->login($aArgs) ) {

        header("Location: manage.php");
    }
}
```

And this bit of the loop is executed if the POST variables are not sent:

```
} else {

    // initialize page variables
    $sEmail = null;
}
```

Finally we call the generic setHeader() and openPage() functions that render the appropriate HTML framework for our page. These functions can be reviewed in their defining file (/core/tpl_unsecure.php):

```
setHeader();
openPage(TRUE);
?>
```

Account Registration Page

If a visitor has not yet registered an account, he or she can click the link to the accounts registration page. The form processing is relatively simple. Since we abstracted all of our processing into the accounts class, all we need to do is perform some simple error handling on the user-entered data, construct the arguments array, and call the class method.

Let's look at the code that drives the registration page and how we implement it:

```
<?php

// File Location: /site/accounts/register.php

// template framework file for pages outside of the CMS application
require_once("tpl_unsecure.php");

require_once("class.accounts.php");
```

```
    // data input validation functions
    require_once("handlers.php");

    if( $_POST ) { // check for HTTP POST variables

        // assign POST variables
        $sScreenName = $_POST["screenname"];
        $sEmail = $_POST["email"];
        $sPass = $_POST["pass"];
        $sConfirm = $_POST["confirm"];

        // validate user name
        if( !validUser($sScreenName) ) {

            catchErr("Enter a valid screen name");
            $FORMOK = FALSE;

        }
```

The following error is displayed if the visitor tries to create an account with an already-existing screen name:

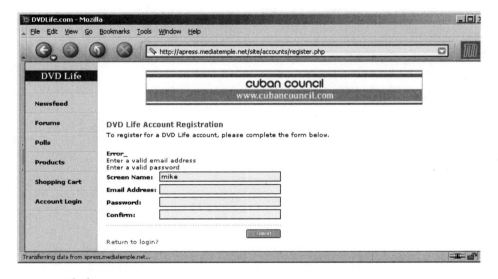

Let's continue with the script:

```
    // validate e-mail address
    if( !validEmail($sEmail) ) {

        catchErr("Enter a valid email address");
        $FORMOK = FALSE;

    }
```

```
    // validate user password
    if( !validPass($sPass) ) {

        catchErr("Enter a valid password");
        $FORMOK = FALSE;

    } else {

        if( strcmp($sPass, $sConfirm) ) {

            catchErr("Your password and password confirmation do not
                    match");
            $FORMOK = FALSE;
        }
    }
```

First we captured and validated the data entered by the user with the validation functions pre-defined in the `handlers.php` file. Once the data is validated and structured we can pass the array as an argument to the class method:

```
    // if forms variables validated
    if( $FORMOK ) {

        // assign array values
        $aArgs["Screen Name"] = $sScreenName;
        $aArgs["Email"] = $sEmail;
        $aArgs["Password"] = $sPass;

        $oAccounts = new accounts;

        // try account add and redirect
        if( $FORMOK = $oAccounts->addAccount($aArgs) ) {

            header("Location: manage.php");
        }
    }

} else { // POST variables not sent

    // initialize page variables
    $sScreenName = null;
    $sEmail = null;
}

// generate the header information
setHeader();

// start a new page with a banner advertisement
openPage(TRUE);
?>
```

Password Reminder Page

We'll provide a password reminder page for visitors who forget their account login information. This page is small and simple since it only requires two values to be passed for verification:

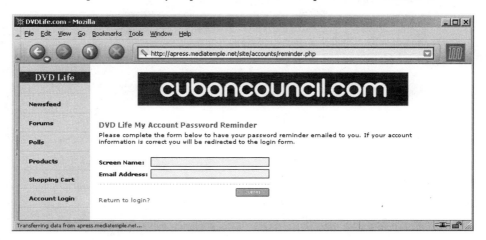

```php
<?php

// File Location: /site/accounts/reminder.php

// template framework file for pages outside the CMS application
require_once("tpl_unsecure.php");

require_once("class.accounts.php");

// data input validation functions
require_once("handlers.php");
```

The `if` loop checks for HTTP POST variables:

```php
if( $_POST ) {

    // assign POST variables
    $sScreenName = $_POST["screenname"];
    $sEmail = $_POST["email"];

    // validate user name
    if( !validUser($sScreenName) ) {

        catchErr("Enter a valid screen name");
        $FORMOK = FALSE;
    }
```

```
    // validate user e-mail
    if( !validEmail($sEmail) ) {

        catchErr("Enter a valid email address");
        $FORMOK = FALSE;
    }
```

The following `if` loop is executed if the form variables are validated:

```
    if( $FORMOK ) {

        // assign array values
        $aArgs["Screen Name"] = $sScreenName;
        $aArgs["Email"] = $sEmail;

        $oAccounts = new accounts;

        // try login and redirect
        if( $oAccounts->sendReminder($aArgs) ) {

            header("Location: index.php");
        }
    }

} else { // POST variables not sent

    // initialize page variables
    $sScreenName = null;
    $sEmail = null;
}

// generate the header information
setHeader();

// start a new page with a banner advertisement
openPage(TRUE);
?>
```

Account Management Page

Now that we've looked at all of the account pages that do not require authentication, let's look at the pages for managing a visitor's account after he or she has logged in:

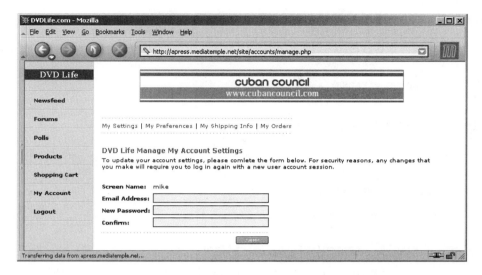

Remember that our session information is contained within the session cookie, and that the session is validated for each page within the secured sections of the site. If any of the credentials in this section are changed, they'll no longer match the session values and the session will be invalid, requiring re-authentication:

```php
<?php

// File Location: /site/accounts/manage.php

// template framework file for pages outside the CMS application
require_once("tpl_unsecure.php");

require_once("class.accounts.php");

// data input validation functions
require_once("handlers.php");

// instantiate accounts class
$oAccounts = new accounts;

// validate account session
$oAccounts->validateSession() ? $aSess = $oAccounts->getSession() :
header("Location: index.php");
```

The `if` loop checks for HTTP POST variables:

```php
if( $_POST ) {

    // assign POST variables
    $sEmail = $_POST["email"];
    $sPass = $_POST["pass"];
    $sConfirm = $_POST["confirm"];
```

This `if` loop validates the user's e-mail address:

```
if( !validEmail($sEmail) ) {

    catchErr("Enter a valid email address");
    $FORMOK = FALSE;
}
```

This `if` loop validates the user's password:

```
if( strcmp("", $sPass) ) {

    // validate password
    if( !validPass($sPass) ) {

        catchErr("Enter a valid password");
        $FORMOK = FALSE;

    } elseif ( strcmp($sPass, $sConfirm) ) {

        catchErr("Your password and confirmation do not match");
        $FORMOK = FALSE;
    }
}
```

Then this loop is executed if the form variables are validated:

```
if( $FORMOK ) {

    // assign array values
    $aArgs["Email"] = $sEmail;
    $aArgs["Password"] = $sPass;

    // try account update and redirect
    if( $FORMOK = $oAccounts->updateAccount($aArgs) ) {

        header("Location: ".SELF);
    }
}

} else { // POST variables not sent

    // initialize page variables
    $sScreenName = $aSess["Screen Name"];
    $sEmail = $aSess["Email"];
}
```

All of the work for the header, navigation, and footer is handled by the `setHeader()` and `openPage()` functions:

```
setHeader();
openPage(TRUE);
?>
```

Now that the user has created an account and successfully logged in, we can offer more account settings to be managed. It's not required that these items be changed or added; however, it'll provide additional information and simplify other processes within the web site, such as the check out process of our shopping cart.

Account Newsletter Preferences Page

The following is the accounts preferences page that currently stores personalization values regarding the newsletter:

Here is the code for the preferences page:

```php
<?php

// File Location: /site/accounts/prefs.php

// template framework file for pages outside the CMS application
require_once("tpl_unsecure.php");

require_once("class.accounts.php");

// data input validation functions
require_once("handlers.php");

// instantiate account class
$oAccounts = new accounts;
```

```php
// validate account session
$oAccounts->validateSession() ? $aSess = $oAccounts->getSession() :
header("Location: index.php");

// set account ID
$iAccountId = (int) $aSess["Account Id"];
$oAccounts->setAccountId($iAccountId);

if( $_POST ) { // check for HTTP POST variables

    // assign POST variables
    $iRecipient = $_POST["recipient"];

    // assign array values
    $aArgs["Newsletter Recipient"] = $iRecipient;

    // try account preferences update
    $FORMOK = $oAccounts->updatePreferences($aArgs);

} else { // POST variables not sent

    // initialize page variables
    $aPrefs = $oAccounts->getPreferences();

    // check for values
    if( is_array($aPrefs) ) {

        // assign page values
        $iRecipient = $aPrefs["Newsletter Recipient"];

    } else {

        // assign page values
        $iRecipient = 1;
    }
}

// generate the header information
setHeader();

// start a new page with a banner advertisement
openPage(TRUE);
?>
```

Account Shipping Information Page

The account shipping address is only pertinent when a visitor is purchasing a DVD within the site. Users can opt to insert the address information into the account settings once they're logged in; otherwise they'll be prompted to do so during the check out process.

This is the My Shipping Info page:

This page functions somewhat differently from the other pages. Since we don't know for certain whether an address has been assigned to a visitor account, we need to set an operation variable to determine whether to add or edit the form submission.

Here's the code for this page:

```php
<?php

// File Location: /site/accounts/shipping.php

// template framework file for pages outside the CMS application
require_once("tpl_unsecure.php");

require_once("class.accounts.php");

// data input validation functions
require_once("handlers.php");

// instantiate accounts class
$oAccounts = new accounts;

// validate accounts session
$oAccounts->validateSession() ? $aSess = $oAccounts->getSession() :
header("Location: index.php");

// set account ID
```

```
$iAccountId = (int) $aSess["Account Id"];
$oAccounts->setAccountId($iAccountId);

if( $_POST ) { // check for HTTP POST variables

    // assign POST variables
    $op = $_POST["op"];
    $sName = $_POST["name"];
    $sCompany = $_POST["company"];
    $sStreet = $_POST["street"];
    $sExt = $_POST["ext"];
    $sCity = $_POST["city"];
    $sState = $_POST["state"];
    $sCountry = $_POST["country"];
    $sPostal = $_POST["postal"];
    $sPhone = $_POST["phone"];

    // validate name
    if( !validInput($sName, 1, 100) ) {

        catchErr("Enter a valid name");
        $FORMOK = FALSE;
    }

    // validate street
    if( !validInput($sStreet, 1, 100) ) {

        catchErr("Enter a valid street address");
        $FORMOK = FALSE;
    }

    // validate city, state, country, postal code, and phone number
    ......
```

The if loop is executed if the POST variables are validated:

```
if( $FORMOK ) {

    // assign array values
    $aArgs["Operation"] = $op;
    $aArgs["Name"] = $sName;
    $aArgs["Company"] = $sCompany;
    $aArgs["Street"] = $sStreet;
    $aArgs["Street Ext"] = $sExt;
    $aArgs["City"] = $sCity;
    $aArgs["State"] = $sState;
    $aArgs["Country"] = $sCountry;
    $aArgs["Postal"] = $sPostal;
    $aArgs["Phone"] = $sPhone;

    // try account address update
    $FORMOK = $oAccounts->updateAccountAddress($aArgs);
}
```

This part of the loop is executed if the POST variables aren't sent:

```
} else {

    // initialize page variables
    $aAddress = $oAccounts->getAccountAddress();

    if( is_array($aAddress) ) {

        $op = "edit";
        $sName = $aAddress["Address Name"];
        $sCompany = $aAddress["Address Company"];
        $sStreet = $aAddress["Address Street"];
        $sExt = $aAddress["Address Street Ext"];
        $sCity = $aAddress["Address City"];
        $sState = $aAddress["Address State"];
        $sCountry = $aAddress["Address Country"];
        $sPostal = $aAddress["Address Postal"];
        $sPhone = $aAddress["Address Phone"];

    } else {

        $op = "add";
        $sName = null;
        $sCompany = null;
        $sStreet = null;
        $sExt = null;
        $sCity = null;
        $sState = null;
        $sCountry = null;
        $sPostal = null;
        $sPhone = null;

    }
}
```

The setHeader() and openPage() functions render the appropriate HTML framework for our page. These functions can be reviewed in their defining file (/core/tpl_unsecure.php):

```
setHeader();
openPage(TRUE);
?>
```

In this section we looked at most of the pages that comprise the accounts section of the web site. The only page we did not look at is the My Orders page in the account management section. This page will be covered in Chapter 12, which details the building of a shopping cart.

Summary

The purpose of this chapter was to provide an understanding of site visitor accounts. We covered several problems that need to be considered when building an account-based visitor community. We covered the differences and similarities between the visitor accounts and the CMS administration user accounts, and decided to segregate these user types.

This chapter illustrated the following key points:

- ❑ The issues and concerns surrounding visitor identity and authentication
- ❑ How to manage visitor properties and preferences within a secured environment
- ❑ How to design and implement reusable code based on the application requirements
- ❑ A simplified approach for handling forms and intuitive user interaction with those forms

Now that we've implemented the foundation for registering and managing unique visitor entities into the web site, we can look at the applications that'll be dependent on those accounts. We'll see how this framework allows us to easily extend application functionality for registered users, and how they can contribute to the content of our web site. In the next chapter, we'll see how the visitors' accounts enable these visitors to share comments to news publications in the web site.

6

Dynamic News Content

Extra! Extra! Read all about it! The days of the newsboy standing on corners hollering headlines have long passed, but reaching a targeted community to share news and information is more widespread than ever. Using a web site delivery system, we can share information about industry and community updates to the site's visitors.

In Chapters 4 and 5 we looked at laying the foundation for our application by implementing a user management system for the Content Management System (CMS) as well as the web site's visitor accounts. Now we are going to look at building on to that framework by implementing vertical applications. A vertical application for our implementation practice is an application that extends the foundation of our application environment. These vertical applications will be used to manage and deliver the content of our web site by plugging into that foundation, inheriting or adhering to all of the rules and dependent constructs defined therein.

For DVD Life, we are going to be sharing news about the DVD community and the industry with our visitors. These news articles may simply be referencing new releases or possibly DVD reviews from news authors within the CMS system. In order to build on top of our dynamic content and influence the community presence that we are aiming for, we could allow our visitors to post their own comments about the news article. This functionality will create an added interest for the site's visitors to become more involved with the endlessly progressing delivery of news and information.

Using the CMS, we can also distribute the editorial tasks to several web masters to ensure that our newsfeed maintains a constantly updated content stream. Furthermore, once we have the web standards in place for syndicating distributed content, we can build an RSS newsfeed for online advocates to re-purpose and re-distribute the content.

In this chapter we'll look at how to build a simple news management and delivery system. We'll also lay the groundwork for our RSS news syndication, which we'll cover in Chapter 7.

In this chapter, we will:

❑ Define the different problems associated with the data elements that we wish to provide in our newsfeed

❑ Organize a database table structure that accommodates the content

❑ Create data objects for handling all of the news

❑ Implement the newsfeed application into the CMS and the web site

To extend the level of interactivity in our newsfeeds, we are going to enable site visitors with registered accounts (users) to publish their own associated content to news articles in the form of comments. The commenting will enable the users to post their opinions about a news article and offer a community presence. We'll look at how the accounts management is easily (and elegantly) implemented into the newsfeed application to provide a seamless authentication and contribution process.

> *Remember that we have three different user types: Users who are not logged in are known as 'visitors', users who are logged in, but do not have any administrator privileges, are known as 'users', and users who are logged in with administrator privileges are known as 'web masters'.*

The Problem

Now that we have both a CMS (Chapter 4) and a visitor accounts (Chapter 5) registration system, we have to look at plugging a newsfeed application into these respective environments. The news content should be chronological as well as categorized for delivery and visibility. We also need to implement a standard, flexible structure that allows us to easily extend our newsfeed for syndication and possible expansion. It's important to keep our content relatively flexible by organizing our tables in a way that allows for stable growth and relative association. We want the freedom to expand our newsfeed as we see fit, which means that we'll need to consider different expansion possibilities during our design. So the newsfeed module should include the potential to extend the initial content to allow for additional materials or properties, such as images or other forms of file references. In the same vein, we could also quite possibly decide to add links to a movie site or something that we would want to normalize for ease of management and delivery.

Since our DVD community is focused on an extensive commodity, we should organize our news content into categories to allow a more associated means of displaying news. These categories should rarely change so we can treat them as static from the CMS side of the application; however, we still do want some flexibility, which means that we'll want them dynamically accessed.

Since our users have an identity on the web site, we should implement and encourage as much interaction as possible. This concept ensures that the site content will be self-updating. When we post a news article and enable our users to share their thoughts and feelings about each article, we can begin to effectively grow a community of personalities in an organised manner.

So let's take a look at the problem by isolating its high-level requirements:

- ❑ CMS application plug-in – The application files that will be used for managing the news content

- ❑ Flexible database design – A simple, yet easily extended data framework for the news

- ❑ Front-end display integration with visitor accounts, to enable comments functionality – Using accounts to authenticate the ability to offer news comment contributions

- ❑ Transparent visitor authentication – Provide additional display elements for authenticated accounts versus non-authenticated accounts without inhibiting the user experience

The Design

Now that we've identified the primary problems that need to be addressed, let's proceed by considering some design options. We have decided that **modularity** and **extensibility** are the primary design principles for effectively developing the newsfeed application. The foundation of that design lies within our database tables. We want strict associations that provide as much flexibility as possible, though we must be careful to not abstract too much content in our database design as this would make for awkward accessibility of the news data. The data objects should accommodate the different data sets that we may wish to return for display.

Let's look at the basic flow of our newsfeed application and see how the different pieces of our news application and accounts authentication play into the design:

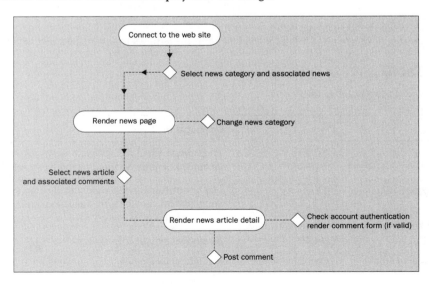

Note that there is less user interaction involved for rendering pages than the accounts application has. We can perform these functions in a transparent manner since we have an underlying architecture to support the application.

Now that we have planned the desired functionality, let's move on and begin designing the database tables for the newsfeed application.

Designing the Data Layer

As discussed earlier, our tables should provide as much flexibility as possible, to ensure smooth and transitional growth in case we wish to implement such changes down the road. We also need to construct a set of tables and relationships that will allow for the greatest performance beneath this flexibility.

The three tables will be named as follows:

❏   apress_news_types to define different news types

❏   apress_news to store news articles

❏   apress_news_comments to store comments entered by the users

The News Types Table

This table defines our news types for associated news:

Field	Type	Description
news_type_id	INT(2)	The unique identifier for each news type record. This primary key contains our presumed news types.
news_type	VARCHAR(50)	The descriptive name for the news type.

The index on the news_type_id field is used to map these news types to the news articles.

The News Table

This table stores our actual news items:

Field	Type	Description
news_id	INT(10)	The unique identifier for each news record. This primary key indexes each of the news articles uniquely.
news_type_id	INT(2)	The identifier for the associated news type. There is an index on this column for maximizing the performance of grouped associative queries.
news_title	VARCHAR(255)	The news article title string.
news_article	TEXT	The news article copy.
news_release_dt	DATE	A date value representing the news release date.
news_expire_dt	DATE	A date value representing the news expiration date.

Field	Type	Description
status	INT(1)	A Boolean flag to determine the news article status. *Note that status values are bit values, either TRUE/FALSE or 1/0, which flag an item visible to the public web site.*
deleted	INT(1)	A Boolean flag to set a 'deleted' status to the news record.
created_dt	DATETIME	Date time value when the article was created.
modified_dt	DATETIME	Date time value when the article was last modified.
deleted_dt	DATETIME	Date time value when the article was deleted.

The index on the news_id field acts as a unique identifier, while the index on the news_type_id field allows us to associate our articles with a particular news type.

The News Comments Table

This table stores all of our news comments referenced by the news_id column:

Field	Type	Description
news_comment_id	INT(10)	The unique comment ID for each news comment record. This primary key is where the indexed records can be referenced if we wish to provide a moderator tool in our CMS at a later date.
news_id	INT(10)	The unique identifier of the article that this comment relates to.
account_id	INT(10)	The unique identifier of the account that this comment relates to, which means that it holds the comment poster's account ID.
news_comment	TEXT	The news comment.
created_dt	DATETIME	Date time value when the comment was created.

This table has an index on the news_comment_id field that serves as the unique identifier for each record. There is also an index on the news_id field to map each comment to a news article.

Designing the Data Object

The news data object will handle all of our data collection and manipulation functionality within the CMS and the web site. Additionally, the commenting functions will be implemented into the news data object since its only purpose is directly related to news items.

The News Class

We'll need the following member variables to provide the functionality desired from the news data object:

news Class Variable	Description
_iNewsId	Property containing the news item unique identifier
_oConn	Property containing a reference to the PEAR::DB object

Naturally, we'll need some class methods that will manipulate these variables and ultimately generate our newsfeed for us. The following set will be employed:

news Class Method	Description
news($iNewsId='')	Constructor method that instantiates the _oConn object. This member also optionally assigns the _iNewsId property if passed.
setNewsId($iNewsId)	Assigns the _iNewsId class member to the value passed in the $iNewsId argument for the class instance.
getNewsCount($iStatus=FALSE, $iType=0)	Returns a count of news items. These are the optional arguments for the method: ❏ $iStatus – Boolean value to return only the active items ❏ $iType – Integer value representing the news type ID
getNewsItems($sSort, $iPage=0)	Returns an associative array of news items. These are the optional arguments for the method: ❏ $sSort – String value representing the sort column name ❏ $iPage – Integer value representing the cursor position for the limit call
getActiveNewsItems($iPage=0, $iType=0)	Returns an associative array of active news articles only. These are the optional arguments for the method: ❏ $iPage – Integer value representing the cursor position for the limit call ❏ $iType – Integer value representing the news type ID
getNewsTypes()	Returns an associative array of news types in the system.

news Class Method	Description
getNewsItem()	Returns an associative array containing information for a single news article.
getNewsComments()	Returns an associative array of news comments ordered by their created date.
addNews($aArgs)	Adds a new news article to the system. The $aArgs argument passes all of the news article data for the new item.
addComment($aArgs)	Adds a comment to a news item. The $aArgs argument passes all of the comment data for the news item.
editNews($aArgs)	Updates a news item with the data contained in the $aArgs array argument passed.
deleteNews()	Deletes a news item from the system.
activateNews()	Activates a news item in the system.
deactivateNews()	Deactivates a news item in the system.

The Solution

Now that we have discussed the problems that need to be considered when building the news management and delivery modules, we'll look at the base files used in the application framework. Having already written the code for many of the files that constitute our application framework, we can simply plug this new functionality into that framework.

This table describes the location and functional purpose of each file:

> As detailed in Chapter 2, the _lib directory contains files like the shared function libraries and custom classes. Further, it contains a _base subdirectory that includes the common function libraries and the global configuration file, and a _classes subdirectory that includes the custom classes that are written through the book. All our application modules fall into the site directory, and its news subdirectory houses the files that define the news content for the site. The core directory includes the admin tools used to control the site, and web masters will be able to post new news stories to the site from its news subdirectory.

File Name	File Path	Description
config.php	/_lib/_base/	Configuration values for the application.
funcs.php	/_lib/_base/	Utility functions for the application.

Table continued on following page

File Name	File Path	Description
elements.php	/_lib/_base/	Reusable generic elements such as error display functions. This file also assigns the common GET variables of $op and $id.
tpl_secure.php	/site	Template framework file for pages inside the CMS application.
tpl_unsecure.php	/site/	Template framework file for pages outside of the CMS application.
handlers.php	/_lib/_base/	Data input validation functions.
index.php	/core/news/	The article listing within the CMS.
form.php	/core/news/	The article management form within the CMS.
index.php	/site/news/	The article listing in the web site.
detail.php	/site/news/	The detailed view of an article in the web site that also allows for user commenting.
class.news.php	/_lib/_classes/	Data object for news logic.

All these scripts are available, as part of the code download for the book, from http://www.apress.com.

This diagram shows the different relationships and dependencies of the files within our application framework that are necessary to implement the news management modules:

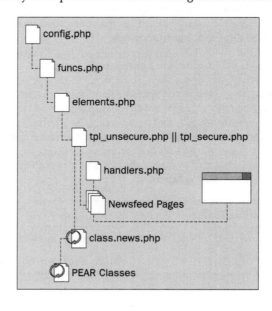

Implementing the Data Layer

As proposed, the news database will consist of three tables, which store relative data records for each news item in the system. Using the normalized design of our database (defined earlier), we'll be able to efficiently manage the different tasks needed to be implemented later with our data objects.

Next we'll write the MySQL commands to create the three tables needed for this module.

apress_news_types

The news types table uses a `news_type_id` as the primary key index for each record. This table does not need the common fields for state and management information since it's simply a container for semi-static information:

```
CREATE TABLE apress_news_types (
   news_type_id INT(2)      NOT NULL auto_increment,
   news_type    VARCHAR(50) NOT NULL default '',
                PRIMARY KEY (news_type_id)
) TYPE=MyISAM;
```

> *You may elect to use an InnoDB table type to implement foreign keys and transactional support. However, MySQL supports foreign keys only with InnoDB tables, which are not always available in the shared server ISP environments that we are supporting in this book. We will use MyISAM tables in this book, since it allows support for generic shared server environments. Refer to Chapter 2 for more information on why we support shared server ISP environments.*

Since we know that the data values for the news types are relatively static, we can insert them along with our create script:

```
INSERT INTO apress_news_types(news_type) VALUES ('New Releases');
INSERT INTO apress_news_types(news_type) VALUES ('Product Release');
INSERT INTO apress_news_types(news_type) VALUES ('General News');
INSERT INTO apress_news_types(news_type) VALUES ('DVD Reports');
```

apress_news

The news table stores our core news content with a relationship reference to a `news_type_id`. In this table we have added an additional index on the `news_type_id` column to improve the performance of the queries that are executed against that column:

```
CREATE TABLE apress_news (
   news_id         INT(10)      NOT NULL auto_increment,
   news_type_id    INT(2)       NOT NULL default '0',
   news_title      VARCHAR(255) NOT NULL default '',
   news_article    TEXT         NOT NULL,
   news_release_dt DATE         NOT NULL default '0000-00-00',
   news_expire_dt  DATE         NULL default NULL,
   status          INT(1)       NOT NULL default '1',
   deleted         INT(1)       NOT NULL default '0',
   deleted_dt      DATETIME     NULL default NULL,
```

```
    created_dt        DATETIME      NOT NULL default '0000-00-00 00:00:00',
    modified_dt       DATETIME      NOT NULL default '0000-00-00 00:00:00',
                                    PRIMARY KEY  (news_id),
                                    KEY news_type_rel (news_type_id)
) TYPE=MyISAM;
```

apress_news_comments

The comments table stores news comments posted by authenticated visitors who have a valid account ID. We have also added an index on the `news_id` column, which lets us improve the performance of the queries executed against that column:

```
CREATE TABLE apress_news_comments (
    news_comment_id INT(10)  NOT NULL auto_increment,
    news_id         INT(10)  NOT NULL default '0',
    account_id      INT(10)  NOT NULL default '0',
    news_comment    TEXT NOT NULL,
    created_dt      DATETIME NOT NULL default '0000-00-00 00:00:00',
                    PRIMARY KEY (news_comment_id),
                    KEY news_id_rel (news_id)
) TYPE=MyISAM;
```

Implementing the Data Object

Now that we have clearly defined our data object design as well as our database, let's begin constructing and implementing our proposed solution, by looking at the code that comprises the news class. Then we'll look at implementing the data objects into the CMS framework and the web site.

class.news.php

We will open our class with includes for all the files that our class is dependent on. Then, we'll write a constructor method to instantiate any default member properties as well as any inherited objects:

```php
<?php

// File Location: /_lib/_classes/class.news.php

// import the PEAR::DB class
require_once("DB.php");

class news { // open the class definition

    /**
     * unique identifier for a news item
     *
     * @var integer
     * @access private
     * @see setNewsId()
     */
    var $_iNewsId;
```

```
/**
 * PEAR::DB  object
 *
 * @var object
 * @access private
 */
var $_oConn;

// CONSTRUCTOR

/**
 * class constructor
 *
 * @param integer $iNewsId [optional] unique news identifier
 * @access public
 */
function news($iNewsId = '') {

    // implement PEAR::DB object
    $this->_oConn =& DB::connect(DSN);

    if( DB::isError($this->_oConn) ) {

        catchExc($this->_oConn->getMessage());
    }

    // assign member variable
    if( is_int($iNewsId) ) {

        $this->setNewsId($iNewsId);
    }
}
```

The next method assigns the unique identifier value to be used within an instance of the class and will be used throughout the class as well as inside the pages in our site to select or target a specific article for action:

```
/**
 * set the _iNewsId variable for the class
 *
 * @param integer $iNewsId news identifier
 * @access public
 */
function setNewsId($iNewsId) {

    if( is_int($iNewsId) ) {

        $this->_iNewsId = $iNewsId;
    }
}
```

The following method gets a row count of all the applicable items in the database. We can optionally pass two different arguments to this method depending on the type of data we wish to return. The first argument tells the method whether or not we want published (active) articles – this is used in the web site implementation. The second argument optionally requires items of a specific news type – again, we'll use this in our web site implementation.

The 'status' variable is a Boolean flag that indicates whether an item is published (active) or unpublished (staged). Published items are viewable on the public web site and unpublished items are only visible in the CMS. Each index page of a CMS application will have an icon that indicates its 'status' – the icon will be either gray or green, gray being staged and green being active. The icon is clickable to quickly toggle published and staged states for an item, and this enables CMS users (web masters) to manage what is visible/not visible on the public web site. The idea is that a web master can stage an item until it's reviewed or edited for readiness. Also, the different user types dictate who can and can't toggle the status of an item.

Here is the `getNewsCount()` method:

```
/**
 * get news count for paging
 *
 * @param boolean $iStatus status
 * @param integer $iType news type identifier
 * @return boolean
 * @access private
 */
function getNewsCount($iStatus=FALSE, $iType=0) {

    // set SQL filter values
    $sFilter = "";
    if( $iStatus ) $sFilter .= " AND status=1";
    if( $iType ) $sFilter .= " AND news_type_id=".$iType;

    $sql = "SELECT
                count(news_id) AS news_cnt
            FROM
                ".PREFIX."_news
            WHERE
                deleted=0".$sFilter;

    if( DB::isError($iCnt = $this->_oConn->getOne($sql)) ) {

        catchExc($iCnt->getMessage());
        return FALSE;
    }

    return $iCnt;
}
```

The next method is used to return an array of news items in the database. It accepts two optional arguments much like the previous method, though the purpose for these arguments is different. The first argument is the default sort column name and the second argument is the paging cursor to assign to the limit call in MySQL. This method will return an associative array that is specific to the CMS system:

```
/**
 * get news items list
 *
 * @param string $sSort sort key
 * @param integer $iPage [optional] cursor
 * @return array news data
 * @access public
 */
function getNewsItems($sSort, $iPage=0) {

    // get news items from db
    $sql = "SELECT
                news_id,
                news_type_id,
                news_title,
                news_article,
                news_release_dt,
                news_expire_dt,
                status,
                created_dt,
                modified_dt
            FROM
                ".PREFIX."_news
            WHERE
                deleted=0
            ORDER BY
                ".$sSort."
            LIMIT ".$iPage.", ".ROWCOUNT;

    if( DB::isError($rsTmp = $this->_oConn->query($sql)) ) {

        catchExc($rsTmp->getMessage());
        return FALSE;
    }
```

Next, build a return array:

```
    // build return array
    $i = 0;
    while( $aRow = $rsTmp->fetchRow(DB_FETCHMODE_ASSOC) ) {

        $return[$i]["News Id"] = $aRow["news_id"];
        $return[$i]["News Type Id"] = $aRow["news_type_id"];
        $return[$i]["Title"] = $aRow["news_title"];
        $return[$i]["Article"] = $aRow["news_article"];
        $return[$i]["Release Date"] =
                                    strtotime($aRow["news_release_dt"]);
        $return[$i]["Expire Date"] = strtotime($aRow["news_expire_dt"]);
        $return[$i]["Status"] = $aRow["status"];
        $return[$i]["Created Date"] = strtotime($aRow["created_dt"]);
        $return[$i]["Modified Date"] = strtotime($aRow["modified_dt"]);
        ++$i;
    }
    return $return;
}
```

Similar to the above method, we need a method to retrieve an associative array for published content to be displayed on the web site. This method also accepts a page cursor argument as well as an optional news type identifier argument:

```php
/**
 * get active news items list
 *
 * @param integer $iPage [optional] cursor
 * @param integer $iType [optional] news type ID
 * @return array active news data
 * @access public
 */
function getActiveNewsItems($iPage=0, $iType=0) {

    // set SQL filter
    $sFilter = "";
    if( $iType ) $sFilter = " AND news_type_id=".$iType;

    $sDate = date("Y-m-d");

    $sql = "SELECT
                n.news_id,
                n.news_title,
                n.news_article,
                n.news_release_dt,
                COUNT(c.news_comment_id) AS cmt_cnt
            FROM
                ".PREFIX."_news n
                LEFT JOIN ".PREFIX."_news_comments c ON
                    (c.news_id=n.news_id)
            WHERE
                deleted=0 AND
                status=1 AND
                news_release_dt <= '".$sDate."' AND
                news_expire_dt > '".$sDate."'".$sFilter."
            GROUP BY
                n.news_id
            ORDER BY
                news_release_dt DESC
            LIMIT ".$iPage.", ".ROWCOUNT;

    if( DB::isError($rsTmp = $this->_oConn->query($sql)) ) {

        catchExc($rsTmp->getMessage());
        return FALSE;
    }

    // build return array
    $i = 0;
    while( $aRow = $rsTmp->fetchRow(DB_FETCHMODE_ASSOC) ) {

        $return[$i]["News Id"] = $aRow["news_id"];
        $return[$i]["Title"] = $aRow["news_title"];
```

```
        $return[$i]["Article"] = $aRow["news_article"];
        $return[$i]["Comment Count"] = $aRow["cmt_cnt"];
        $return[$i]["Release Date"] =
                                strtotime($aRow["news_release_dt"]);
        ++$i;
    }
    return $return;
}
```

Since we are only using our news types for the newsfeed application, we can include any news type methods within the news class rather than creating an independent class to allow for more generic accessibility. This function returns an associative array of news types to be used in select lists both in the CMS and the web site:

```
/**
 * get news types list
 *
 * @return array news types
 * @access public
 */
function getNewsTypes() {

    $sql = "SELECT
                news_type_id,
                news_type
            FROM
                ".PREFIX."_news_types";

    if( DB::isError($rsTmp = $this->_oConn->query($sql)) ) {

        catchExc($rsTmp->getMessage());
        return FALSE;
    }

    // build return array
    $i = 0;
    while( $aRow = $rsTmp->fetchRow(DB_FETCHMODE_ASSOC) ) {

        $return[$i]["News Type Id"] = $aRow["news_type_id"];
        $return[$i]["News Type"] = $aRow["news_type"];
        ++$i;
    }
    return $return;
}
```

The next method is used to retrieve a single news article from the database. It depends on the _iNewsId class member being set in order to operate correctly:

```
/**
 * get a single news item
 *
```

```
     * @return array
     * @access public
     */
    function getNewsItem() {

        $sql = "SELECT
                    news_type_id,
                    news_title,
                    news_article,
                    news_release_dt,
                    news_expire_dt,
                    status,
                    deleted,
                    created_dt,
                    modified_dt
                FROM
                    ".PREFIX."_news
                WHERE
                    news_id=".$this->_iNewsId;

        if( DB::isError($rsTmp = $this->_oConn->query($sql)) ) {

            catchExc($rsTmp->getMessage());
            return FALSE;
        }

        // assign result to array
        $aRow = $rsTmp->fetchRow(DB_FETCHMODE_ASSOC);

        // build data return array
        $return["News Type Id"] = $aRow["news_type_id"];
        $return["Title"] = $aRow["news_title"];
        $return["Article"] = $aRow["news_article"];
        $return["Release Date"] = strtotime($aRow["news_release_dt"]);
        $return["Expire Date"] = strtotime($aRow["news_expire_dt"]);
        $return["Status"] = $aRow["status"];
        $return["Deleted"] = $aRow["deleted"];
        $return["Created Date"] = strtotime($aRow["created_dt"]);
        $return["Modified Date"] = strtotime($aRow["modified_dt"]);
        return $return;

    }
```

We mentioned that new comments can be entered by users. Here is the method that returns those comments associated to a specific news article. This method is also dependent on the _iNewsId member variable:

```
    /**
     * get news item comments by news ID
     *
     * @return array
     * @access public
     */
```

```
function getNewsComments() {

    $sql = "SELECT
                c.news_comment,
                c.created_dt,
                a.account_screenname
            FROM
                ".PREFIX."_news_comments c,
                ".PREFIX."_accounts a
            WHERE
                news_id=".$this->_iNewsId."
                AND c.account_id=a.account_id
            ORDER BY
                created_dt DESC";

    if( DB::isError($rsTmp = $this->_oConn->query($sql)) ) {

        catchExc($rsTmp->getMessage());
        return FALSE;
    }

    // loop through result and build return array
    $i = 0;
    while( $aRow = $rsTmp->fetchRow(DB_FETCHMODE_ASSOC) ) {

        $return[$i]["Comment"] = $aRow["news_comment"];
        $return[$i]["Screen Name"] = $aRow["account_screenname"];
        $return[$i]["Comment Date"] = strtotime($aRow["created_dt"]);
        ++$i;
    }
    return $return;
}
```

Our 'add' method for the news class is similar to how we have been adding content in our other applications. It's a simple function that accepts an associative array argument containing the new record data:

```
/**
 * add a news record
 *
 * @param array $aArgs news item values
 * @return boolean
 * @access public
 */
function addNews($aArgs) {

    // create new news record
    $sql = "INSERT INTO ".PREFIX."_news (
                    news_type_id,
                    news_title,
                    news_article,
                    news_release_dt,
                    news_expire_dt,
```

```
                          status,
                          created_dt,
                          modified_dt
            ) VALUES (
                          ".$aArgs["Type Id"].",
                          '".$aArgs["Title"]."',
                          '".$aArgs["Article"]."',
                          '".date("Y-m-d", $aArgs["Release Date"])."',
                          '".date("Y-m-d", $aArgs["Expire Date"])."',
                          1,
                          NOW(),
                          NOW()
            )";

      if( DB::isError($rsTmp = $this->_oConn->query($sql)) ) {

          catchExc($rsTmp->getMessage());
          return FALSE;
      }

      return TRUE;
}
```

You'll notice that we aren't locking tables and capturing the unique ID in this instance. The reason for skipping that step is that we don't need the unique identifier for any additional functionality during this process. We simply return a Boolean value upon success.

> *If we need the ID in the class method, however, we should lock the tables to ensure that someone else doesn't add a row behind ours and return the wrong ID.*

Adding a news comment is similar to adding a news item, except in this case we are dependent on the _iNewsId member variable that represents the dependent news article to successfully complete the process:

```
/**
 * add a comment by news ID
 *
 * @param array $aArgs news comment values
 * @return boolean
 * @access public
 */
function addComment($aArgs) {

    $sql = "INSERT INTO ".PREFIX."_news_comments (
                    news_id,
                    account_id,
                    news_comment,
                    created_dt
            ) VALUES (
                    ".$this->_iNewsId.",
                    ".$aArgs["Account Id"].",
                    '".$aArgs["Comment"]."',
                    (NOW())
```

```
                )";

        if( DB::isError($rsTmp = $this->_oConn->query($sql)) ) {

            catchExc($rsTmp->getMessage());
            return FALSE;
        }

        return TRUE;
    }
```

Next we'll write the 'edit' method that updates a news record in the database. The pre-assigned _iNewsId member variable is used to target the record and the array values passed since the function argument contains the updated information:

```
/**
 * edit a news record
 *
 * @param array $aArgs news values
 * @return boolean
 * @access public
 */
function editNews($aArgs) {

    // update news record
    $sql = "UPDATE ".PREFIX."_news
            SET
                news_type_id=".$aArgs["Type Id"].",
                news_title='".$aArgs["Title"]."',
                news_article='".$aArgs["Article"]."',
                news_release_dt='".date("Y-m-d",
                                $aArgs["Release Date"])."',
                news_expire_dt='".date("Y-m-d",
                                    $aArgs["Expire Date"])."',
                modified_dt=(NOW())
            WHERE
                news_id=".$this->_iNewsId;

    if( DB::isError($rsTmp = $this->_oConn->query($sql)) ) {

        catchExc($rsTmp->getMessage());
        return FALSE;
    }

    return TRUE;
}
```

Here is our somewhat generic 'delete' method that sets a soft delete on the record:

A soft delete does not actually remove the record from the database; instead it flags the record as deleted so that it's not displayed on the public web site.

```
/**
 * delete a news record
 *
 * @return boolean
 * @access public
 */
function deleteNews() {

    $sql = "UPDATE ".PREFIX."_news
        SET
            deleted=1,
            deleted_dt=(NOW())
        WHERE
            news_id=".$this->_iNewsId;

    if( DB::isError($rsTmp = $this->_oConn->query($sql)) ) {

        catchExc($rsTmp->getMessage());
        return FALSE;
    }

    $this->deactivateNews();
    return TRUE;
}
```

The last two class methods are used to activate and deactivate the news items. These are also quite generic as we have seen the same functionality used throughout the CMS application:

These are good candidates for global functions; however, doing so might disallow for any additional functions that we may wish to call during a process. Therefore, we will stick to defining them separately.

```
/**
 * activate a news record
 *
 * @return boolean
 * @access public
 */
function activateNews() {

    $sql = "UPDATE ".PREFIX."_news
        SET
            status=1
        WHERE
            news_id=".$this->_iNewsId;

    if( DB::isError($rsTmp = $this->_oConn->query($sql)) ) {

        catchExc($rsTmp->getMessage());
        return FALSE;
    }
}
```

```
/**
 * deactivate a news record
 *
 * @return boolean
 * @access public
 */
function deactivateNews() {

    $sql = "UPDATE ".PREFIX."_news SET
                status=0
            WHERE
                news_id=".$this->_iNewsId;

    if( DB::isError($rsTmp = $this->_oConn->query($sql)) ) {

        catchExc($rsTmp->getMessage());
        return FALSE;
    }
}

} // close the class definition
?>
```

That's all there is to it. You can see that our news class is much smaller and more self-contained than the security classes we looked at previously. The concept is very simple. We needed to implement a data layer that handles our news content for both the CMS and the web site, so we employed our standard practices and built class methods tailored to the intended usage of the class. Now let's take a look at the pages, involved in both the CMS and the web site, that will use this class.

Presentation Layer

We know that there are four main views that we need to accommodate. Let's make a short list to define those uses:

❏ CMS news item listing – **index.php**

❏ CMS news item form – **form.php**

❏ Site active news item listing – **index.php**

❏ Site active news item detail (optional commenting form) – **detail.php**

We'll be including /site/tpl_unsecure.php on our public pages and using it to generate menus, banner advertisements, and the footer for the page. Similarly we will use the tpl_secure.php file to render the page framework for pages inside the CMS application. With this in mind, let's start with the /core/news/index.php file.

171

CMS News Item Listing

Our first page is the CMS listing of news items:

Now let's take a look at the code used to generate this page:

```php
<?php

// File Location: /core/news/index.php

require_once("tpl_secure.php");
require_once("class.news.php");

// instantiate news class
$oNews = new news;

// get users and user count
$aNews = $oNews->getNewsItems("created_dt DESC", $iCursor);
$iCnt = $oNews->getNewsCount();

// check for users
if( count($aNews) ) {

    // build page data array
    $i = 0;
    while( $i < count($aNews) ) {
        $aData[$i]["Id"] = $aNews[$i]["News Id"];
        $aData[$i]["Name"] = $aNews[$i]["Title"];
        $aData[$i]["Status"] = $aNews[$i]["Status"];
        $aData[$i]["Created"] =$aNews[$i]["Created Date"];
        ++$i;
    }
}
```

You might recognize the generic data array construction from the user's implementation. Our basic page lists elements located in the `elements.php` file will take this array and render a paginated list from the content passed.

Now let's look at the page logic for handling the available list actions:

```php
// check for ID
if( $id ) {

    // assign News ID
    $oNews->setNewsId($id);

    // check operation type
    if( !strcmp($op, "del") ) {

        // try delete news and redirect
        $oNews->deleteNews();
        header("Location: ".SELF);

    } elseif ( !strcmp($op, "act") ) {

        // try activate news and redirect
        $oNews->activateNews();
        header("Location: ".SELF);

    } elseif ( !strcmp($op, "deact") ) {

        // try deactivate news and redirect
        $oNews->deactivateNews();
        header("Location: ".SELF);
    }
}

setHeader();
openPage();
?>
```

Again, the above code is somewhat of a generic implementation across our CMS applications. The remainder of the page is the simple HTML for page errors and notices, instructions, and the generic list rendering call that is passed from the array above:

```php
<?php renderList($iCnt, $aData) ?>
```

CMS News Item Form

The following is the forms page that handles the user-entered form data for adding and editing news articles:

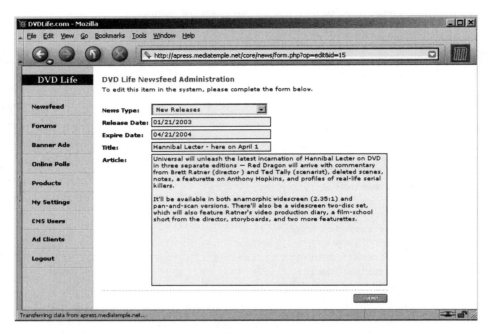

Now let's look at the code used to generate this page. First include the required files:

```php
<?php

// File Location: /core/news/form.php

require_once("tpl_secure.php");
require_once("handlers.php");
require_once("class.news.php");

// instantiate news class
$oNews = new news;
```

Next we'll check for a value assigned to the $id variable – this variable is assigned (by default) in the tpl_secure.php file that renders the page framework. If the value does exist it'll be assigned to the class identifier:

```php
// check for ID
if( $id ) { // if a value doesn't exist, a matching record isn't returned,
            // and it fails to get one.
```

```
        // assign user ID
        $oNews->setNewsId($id);
}
```

The next block of code is designed to handle several potential states of the browser request. We immediately check for POST variables to determine if we should validate form input or assign the default page values. Inside each of these conditionals we'll also check for the operation type, which (if captured) is also assigned in the tpl_secure.php file. Finally, we'll perform either data assignments or class member calls based on the results of $id, $op, and the form input validation:

```
if( $_POST ) { // check for HTTP POST variables

    // assign POST variables
    $iType = $_POST["type"];
    $sReleaseDt = $_POST["reldate"];
    $sExpireDt = $_POST["expdate"];
    $sTitle = $_POST["title"];
    $sArticle = $_POST["article"];

    // check news type
    if( !validInput($iType, 1, 2) ) {

        catchErr("Select a news type");
        $FORMOK = FALSE;
    }

    // check release date
    if( !validDate($sReleaseDt) ) {

        catchErr("Invalid release date");
        $FORMOK = FALSE;
    }

    // check expiration date
    if( !validDate($sExpireDt) ) {

        catchErr("Invalid expiration date");
        $FORMOK = FALSE;
    }

    // compare dates
    if( strtotime($sExpireDt) <= strtotime($sReleaseDt) ) {

        catchErr("Article cannot expire before or during release");
        $FORMOK = FALSE;
    }

    // check title
    if( !validInput($sTitle, 1, 255) ) {

        catchErr("Enter a news title");
        $FORMOK = FALSE;
    }

    // check article
    if( !strcmp("", $sArticle) ) {
```

```
            catchErr("Enter a news article");
            $FORMOK = FALSE;
    }
```

The following section of code is executed if the form variables are validated:

```
    if( $FORMOK ) {

        $aArgs["Type Id"] = $iType;
        $aArgs["Title"] = $sTitle;
        $aArgs["Article"] = $sArticle;
        $aArgs["Release Date"] = strtotime($sReleaseDt);
        $aArgs["Expire Date"] = strtotime($sExpireDt);

        // check operation type
        if( !strcmp("edit", $op) ) {

            // try edit news
            $FORMOK = $oNews->editNews($aArgs);

        } elseif ( !strcmp("add", $op) ) {

            // try add news
            $FORMOK = $oNews->addNews($aArgs);
        }

        // redirect if successful
        if( $FORMOK ) {

            // redirect if successful
            header("Location: index.php");
        }
    }
```

And this bit of the loop is executed if the POST variables are not sent:

```
    } else { // POST variables not sent

        // initialize page variables
        if( !strcmp("edit", $op) ) {

            $aNews = $oNews->getNewsItem();
            $iType = $aNews["News Type Id"];
            $sTitle = $aNews["Title"];
            $sArticle = $aNews["Article"];
            $sReleaseDt = date("m/d/Y", $aNews["Release Date"]);
            $sExpireDt = date("m/d/Y", $aNews["Expire Date"]);

        } elseif ( !strcmp("add", $op) ) {
```

```
            $iType = 0;
            $sReleaseDt = date("m/d/Y");
            $sExpireDt = date("m/d/Y", strtotime("+3 month"));
        }
    }
    setHeader();
    openPage();
```

All that's left to do now is to collect the news types that are used to render the select list within the form:

```
// get news types
$aTypes = $oNews->getNewsTypes();


?>
```

Once we have the news types array we can render the list:

```
<select name="type" class="textfield">
  <option value="">Select a news type</option>
  <?php
  if( count($aTypes) ) {

      $i = 0;
      while( $i < count($aTypes) ) {

          // write form options for news types
          !strcmp($aTypes[$i]["News Type Id"],
                  $iType) ? $sSelected = " selected" : $sSelected = "";
          print "<option value=\"".$aTypes[$i]["News Type Id"].
                "\"".$sSelected.">".
                clean($aTypes[$i]["News Type"])."</option>\n";
          ++$i;
      }

  }
  ?>
</select>
```

That covers the CMS section of the news application. Now let's take a look at the actual content delivered to the web site and how visitors can interact with that content.

Public News Item Listing

This is the initial page that a visitor is redirected to upon connecting to the web site. It lists all the active news articles organized by type:

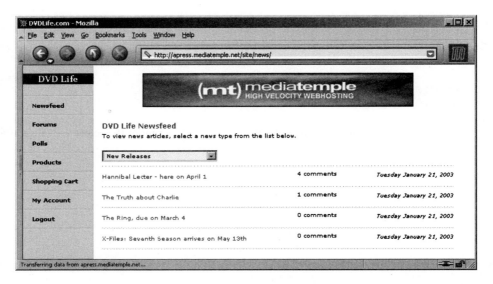

As usual, we have a generic pagination element that we can call, as well as a customized display of the returned data list:

```php
<?php

// File Location: /site/news/index.php

require_once("tpl_unsecure.php");
require_once("class.news.php");

// instantiate news class
$oNews = new news;

// get news types
$aTypes = $oNews->getNewsTypes();

// get and set news type
$iType = $_GET["type"];
$iType ? $iType = $iType : $iType = $aTypes[0]["News Type Id"];

// get users and user count
$aNews = $oNews->getActiveNewsItems($iCursor, $iType);
$iCnt = $oNews->getNewsCount(TRUE, $iType);

// generate the header information
setHeader();

// start a new page with a banner advertisement
openPage(TRUE);
?>
```

The first element on the page is the news type list. If the news type list is empty, we don't want to return an error, but rather a list of all the available news items regardless of type:

```php
<?php if( count($aTypes) ) { ?>
    <tr>
        <td colspan="3"><select name="type" class="textfield"
        onchange="document.forms[0].submit();">

        <option value="">Select a news type</option>

        <?php

        // loop through news types and build select list
        $i = 0;
        while( $i < count($aTypes) ) {

            // write form options for news types
            !strcmp($aTypes[$i]["News Type Id"],
                $iType) ? $sSelected = " selected" : $sSelected = "";
            print "<option value=\"".$aTypes[$i]["News Type Id"].
                "\"".$sSelected.">".
                clean($aTypes[$i]["News Type"])."</option>\n";
            ++$i;
        }
        ?>

        </select></td>
    </tr>


    <tr>
        <td colspan="3" class="dotrule"><img src="../../_img/spc.gif"
        width="1" height="15" alt="" border="0" /></td>
    </tr>

<?php } // end type count check ?>
```

Now all that's left is writing the news items into the page with our pagination:

```php
<?php

// loop through news items and display information
if( count($aNews) ) {

    $i = 0;
    while( $i < count($aNews) ) {

        ?>

        <tr>
            <td><div class="section"><a href="detail.php?id=
            <?php print $aNews[$i]["News Id"] ?>">
            <?php print format($aNews[$i]["Title"]) ?></a>
            </div></td>

            <td valign="top"><div class="copy"><?php print
            format($aNews[$i]["Comment Count"]) ?> comments
            </div></td>
```

```
              <td align="right"><div class="copy"><i><?php print
                format(date("l F j, Y", $aNews[$i]["Release Date"])) ?>
                </i></div></td>
          </tr>

          <tr>
            <td colspan="3" class="dotrule"><img src="../../_img/spc.gif"
              width="1" height="15" alt="" border="0" /></td>
          </tr>

          <?php
          ++$i;

      } //end while loop

      ?>
      <tr>
        <td colspan="3">
          <?php renderPaging($iCursor, $iCnt, "&type=".$iType) ?>
        </td>
      </tr>

      <?php

  } else {

      ?>
      <tr>
        <td><div class="copy">I am sorry, there are no articles available
        in this section.</div></td>
      </tr>

      <?php
  } ?>
```

Since all of our data logic as well as reusable elements have been extracted out of the page, this was just a matter of calling a few simple functions and formatting some content.

Public News Item Detail Page

The screenshot on the next page shows a news article detail page with a non-authenticated visitor session:

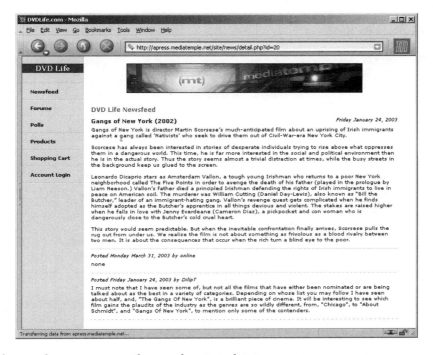

And here is the same page with an authenticated visitor session:

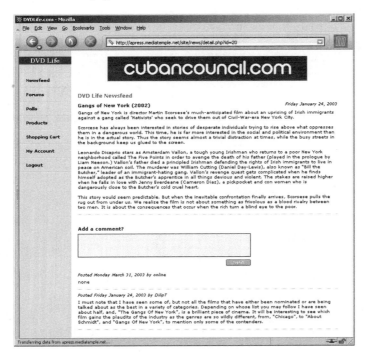

You can see that the menu has changed and we now have the option to add a comment to the news article. Let's go ahead and do so:

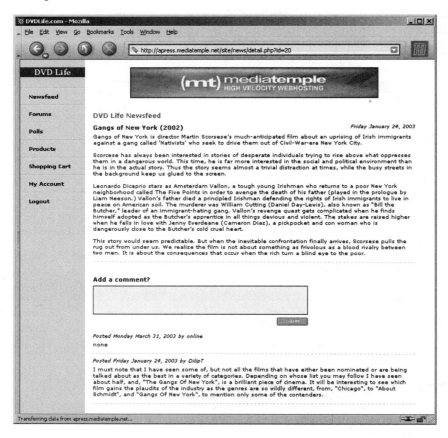

And there you see the comment. Now let's look at the code that renders this page, the conditions for displaying the comment form, and the listing of existing comments:

```php
<?php

// File Location: /site/news/detail.php

require_once("tpl_unsecure.php");
require_once("class.news.php");
require_once("class.accounts.php");
require_once("handlers.php");

$oNews = new news;
$oAccounts = new accounts;

// validate session get account information
if( isset($_COOKIE["cACCOUNT"]) && $oAccounts->validateSession() ) {
```

```php
        $aSess = $oAccounts->getSession();
    }

    // set news ID
    $oNews->setNewsId($id);

    // get users and user count
    $aNews = $oNews->getNewsItem();
    $aComm = $oNews->getNewsComments();

    if( $_POST ) {

        $sComment = $_POST["comment"];

        if( !strcmp("", $sComment) ) {

            catchErr("Enter a valid comment<br />");
            $FORMOK = FALSE;
        }

        if( $FORMOK ) {

            $aArgs["Account Id"] = $aSess["Account Id"];
            $aArgs["Comment"] = $sComment;

            if( $FORMOK = $oNews->addComment($aArgs) ) {

                header("Location: ".SELF."?id=".$id);
            }
        }

    } else {

        $sComment = "";
    }

    // generate the header information
    setHeader();

    // start a new page with a banner advertisement
    openPage(TRUE);
?>
```

Here we implemented the accounts class to validate the visitor session. If the session validates we can assign our visitor session array and thus capture the unique identifier associated with the account. We can then use this unique identifier to associate the visitor comment with the news article if the form has been successfully posted.

Let's take a brief look at the comments display code, to see how we render the comment list:

```php
<?php
    if( count($aComm) ) {

        $i = 0;
        while( $i < count($aComm) ) {
            ?>

            <tr>
              <td colspan="2"><div class="copy"><i>Posted
               <?php print format(date("l F j, Y",
                 $aComm[$i]["Comment Date"])) ?> by
               <?php print format($aComm[$i]["Screen Name"]) ?>
              </i></div></td>
            </tr>

            <tr>
             <td colspan="2"><div class="copy">
              <?php print format($aComm[$i]["Comment"]) ?></div></td>
            </tr>

            <tr>
             <td colspan="2" class="dotrule"><img src="../../_img/spc.gif"
              width="1" height="15" alt="" border="0" /></td>
            </tr>

            <?php
            ++$i;

        } // end while loop
    } // end if loop
?>
```

That concludes the code for our news application. The application we built is small and limited to a few attributes, but this code can easily be extended to provide greater detail and more content by amending the different aspects of the design and implementation.

One consideration for extending the content could be adding the ability to rate each article or the comment about the article. By using a rating system we could then order the comments based on their highest rating score so that what would seemingly be the most useful information would be displayed first.

Summary

In this chapter we covered the simple process of plugging a new application into both our CMS framework and web site framework. Hopefully, you have found this chapter useful, and have learned how to plan and deploy an efficient, functional application solution with the foundation that we built in the previous two chapters. The management of data for this application is common and generic, which makes for easy management and growth of the application layer itself, resulting in truly dynamic content and content management.

This chapter provided insights by exploring the following aspects:

❑   The issues and considerations involved in building vertical applications

❑   The importance and ease of implementing interactive content delivery

❑   How to build shared objects that serve multiple purposes in both of our application layers

❑   How to organize data more effectively by introducing associative types

Now that we have begun to write our vertical applications into the system, let's take a look at some ways to extend the existing content for syndication. In the next chapter we'll cover the use of RSS to provide a standard distribution of our newsfeed via XML.

7

Syndication

We spent Chapter 6 in developing a newsfeed system. This provides us with a great deal of flexibility when it comes to the task of publishing content and delivering it to our users dynamically. News is a critical focal point of DVD Life – it's the first section that users see when they come to the site, and is one of the primary features offered.

We could take this a step further though. The only 'problem' with the newsfeed right now is that users have to come to our site to get any of the content. In an increasingly networked world, it's useful to make our content more easily available to other network-aware devices. The technical name for doing this is **syndication**, which will be the focus of this chapter.

Syndicated content is fast becoming a popular and convenient way for people to provide easy access to news and important information about ongoing events on the World Wide Web. Simply put, when somebody syndicates a piece of content, that person makes it available to some, or possibly any, network resource that can read and parse the content. The resource is then able to incorporate that data into its own operations.

In practice this is generally used to provide information and links to data that is updated on a fairly regular basis. News story headlines, financial data such as stock quotes, sports scores, and weather immediately come to mind, since the data describing these events is constantly changing. As one would imagine, Extensible Markup Language (**XML**) is a terrific way to provide syndicated content. It's easy for network-enabled programs to read/parse XML data, and XML is designed to be a flexible format that can describe different types of events. Also the files are portable since XML is essentially a flat text format. Furthermore, RDF Site Summary (**RSS**) is a lightweight metadata description format that uses XML, and one of the common ways to syndicate content is within RSS files.

In this chapter, we will:

- ❑ Develop an understanding of the RSS XML format used for this type of content publishing
- ❑ Use new and existing data objects to dynamically generate, well-formed and valid, XML for the DVD Life news
- ❑ Publish our syndicated content
- ❑ Look at a simple example of parsing and displaying the syndicated content to ensure that our syndicated feed is constructed properly and can be used by others

The Problem

As it stands, we provide news to our users with the newsfeed module (created in Chapter 6). This is a great feature of our site, but we could take things a step further. Specifically, we want to provide an easily accessible file, published to a set URL, which contains information that we wish to provide to other devices on the network. These devices will most likely be other computers, but could include user agents like cellular phones as well.

Requirements

Now keep in mind that we aren't attempting to provide any sort of presentation here. What we do want is to provide data in a structured way, which makes it easy for whoever is looking at the file to get the desired information. This requirement seems perfectly tailored towards some kind of XML format. After all, this is exactly what XML was designed to do – provide data in a structured, self-descriptive way.

> For more information on using XML with PHP, refer to *Professional PHP4 XML* from *Apress (ISBN 1-861007-21-3)*.

Of course, we aren't the first people to have considered this and come to the conclusion that XML is the way to go. In fact, **RDF Site Summary** (RSS) was designed to solve the exact problem that we are facing. This format was first introduced by Netscape in 1999, originally at version 0.9. It was then used as a description framework for their My Netscape Network web portal. At the time, there were no widely used lightweight standards for this type of publication, so RSS found a following quickly. Version 0.91 followed and was at the time named Rich Site Summary. This introduced the item level <description> element that firmly planted RSS into the lightweight syndication format arena. Currently, the RSS format is at version 1.0, and is so widely used that it has become the de facto standard for this type of publishing.

> The RSS specification is currently available at **http://www.purl.org/rss/**.

Taking this into consideration, our design must accommodate the following features:

❑ It should provide a file that is easily accessible on the network, for example, a URI

❑ The file should use the common RSS 1.0 format to provide the most useful possible implementation, since this is very widely used and understood

❑ Since the newsfeed itself can view different news stories based on categories, the RSS feed should allow this type of selection too

The Design

Now that our problem is both well-defined and well-understood, let's get down to the job of getting our newsfeed data and using it to generate an RSS file. Looking at this, half of our job has already been done – we have an existing news `class.news.php`, created in Chapter 6 that will take care of getting the data we need. So most of our work will go into creating a class that generates a well-formed RSS file. Before doing that, however, it's a good idea to take a look at the RSS file format.

The RSS Format

One of the things that makes XML such a wonderful technology is that it remains simple enough to be human readable, which was in fact one of its design goals from the outset. Therefore, the fastest way to get our feet wet with the RSS format is to look at an example and dissect it. What follows is a file that is easy to understand, though it's not related to DVD Life.

The first few lines just define this as an XML file and import the appropriate namespaces. An RSS document should begin with an XML declaration. Though RSS 1.0 doesn't require this (as RSS files are XML-compliant), RSS 0.9 did and backward compatibility should be maintained:

```
<?xml version="1.0" encoding="ISO-8859-1"?>
```

The root element of every RSS file is the `<rdf>` element. It associates the `rdf` namespace prefix with the RDF Schema and makes this Schema the default for this document:

```
<rdf:RDF
  xmlns:rdf="http://www.w3.org/1999/02/22-rdf-syntax-ns#"
  xmlns="http://purl.org/rss/1.0/"
>
```

Note that the root element of the document is in the RDF namespace. RDF stands for Resource Description Framework and is a recommendation published by the World Wide Web Consortium (W3C). It provides a foundation for processing **metadata**, which is data that describes some other data. For example, say we have two files – a `.jpg` file of a tree and a text file that contains information about the picture such as its name, size in kilobytes, dimensions in pixels, and a short description of what the picture is of. That file might look like this:

```
Filename: tree.jpg
Size: 56k
Dimensions: 380px by 500px
Descriptoin: A photograph of a tree
```

This would all be considered metadata describing the `tree.jpg` file. Of course, we must ask why this matters to us. But if we think about it, the syndication that we're doing does deal with metadata. For example, we want to provide short descriptions of the articles in our syndication, and these descriptions are in fact metadata about the articles.

The next thing we need to understand is the relationship between RSS and RDF. From the description above, you might be wondering why we don't syndicate everything using just RDF. The answer is that the RDF format is much bigger and more complex than what we need for our purposes. We want our syndication to be lightweight, easy to implement, and easy to use by others, and this is exactly what the RSS format strives to do.

However, there are parts of RDF that are very useful for our RSS feed. Those parts are made use of by including the desired RDF parts via XML namespaces. If this sounds confusing, don't worry; it's not. It will make much more sense once we see a little more of this example.

Next is the `<channel>` element. It contains a sort of top-level summary of the rest of the file. The first three required elements are `<title>`, `<link>`, and `<description>`:

```
<channel rdf:about="http://apress.mediatemple.net">
  <title>DVD Life</title>
  <link>http://apress.mediatemple.net</link>
  <description>The DVD Life Web Site.</description>
```

Each of these provides base information about the content that we're syndicating. The next element, which is still nested under `<channel>`, is `<items>`. It's used to catalogue the links that will appear later in the file. After `<items>`, we can close the `<channel>` element:

```
<items>
  <rdf:Seq>
    <rdf:li resource="http://apress.mediatemple.net/site/news/" />
    <rdf:li resource="http://apress.mediatemple.net/site/forums/" />
  </rdf:Seq>
</items>

</channel>
```

Now, to finish, we'll put in the `<item>` elements, which are typically the parts that most people are interested in. Each `<item>` must have a `<title>`, `<link>`, and `<description>` that is specific to the item in question. Also, note that the `<link>` content must match the value of the about attribute for the corresponding `<item>` element:

```
<item rdf:about="http://apress.mediatemple.net/site/news/">
  <title>The DVD Life Newsfeed</title>
  <link> http://apress.mediatemple.net/site/news/</link>
  <description>The most recent news from DVD Life.</description>
</item>

<item rdf:about="http://apress.mediatemple.net/site/forums/">
  <title>The DVD Life Discussion Forums </title>
  <link>http://apress.mediatemple.net/site/forums/</link>
  <description>A place to discuss DVD related topics.</description>
</item>

</rdf:RDF>
```

For completeness, we should mention that there are other things in the RSS specification that aren't included here, specifically, elements corresponding to text inputs and images. There is no need for our syndication users to type anything in, so the text inputs aren't necessary. Likewise, we aren't publishing images with our news stories, so the image elements aren't needed. Their syntax, however, is very similar to what is shown above.

For more information about the RSS specification refer to Chapter 11 in Professional PHP4 XML from Apress (ISBN 1-861007-21-3), which deals with syndicated content.

Designing the Data Object

Let's now construct an object that will help us generate an RSS file that conforms to the specification. Before we start with this data object, we should note that we aren't going to discuss a data or presentation layer in this section. The reason for this is clear – the data layer already exists since the data for the news is already stored in the database tables defined in Chapter 6, and we do not need a presentation layer for this module. Note that XML is wholly unconcerned with presentation and is entirely concerned with data and structure.

The RSS Feed Class

Let's begin thinking about our RSS class. The following member variables will be needed to generate the sort of example file that we saw earlier:

`rssfeed` Class Variable	Description
_aChannel	An associative array that contains the title, link, and description values for the channel
_aChannelItems	An array that holds the link values for the `<items>` element for the channel
_aItems	A compound array that holds the link, title, and description for the individual items
_sEncoding	A string that sets the encoding for the XML file
_iCurrentItem	A counter integer used to keep track of which `<item>` element we are working on

Naturally, we'll need some class methods that will manipulate these variables and ultimately will generate our XML for us. The following set will be employed:

`rssfeed` Class Method	Description
rssfeed()	Constructor that sets up default values for the member variables
setEncoding($sEncoding)	Sets the encoding for the resulting XML document to the value of $sEncoding

Table continued on following page

`rssfeed` Class Method	Description
`_writeHeader()`	Private method that generates the opening XML needed for the document
`_writeClose()`	Private method that generates the closing XML needed for the document
`_fixEntities($sVar)`	Replaces characters that aren't allowed in XML with their entity counterparts
`setChannelTitle($sVar)`	Sets the channel's title element to the value of $sVar
`setChannelLink($sVar)`	Sets the channel's link element to the value of $sVar
`setChannelDescription($sVar)`	Sets the channel's description element to the value of $sVar
`startItem()`	Tells the object that we'll begin putting in data for a new <item> element
`setItemTitle($sVar)`	Sets the value of the title element for the current item to the value of $sVar
`setItemLink($sVar)`	Sets the value of the link element for the current item to the value of $sVar
`setItemDescription($sVar)`	Sets the value of the description element for the current item to the value of $sVar
`_addChannelItem($sVar)`	Adds the value of $sVar to the links reported in the channel's items element
`endItem()`	Tells the object that we have finished putting in data for the current item
`getRssFeed()`	Returns the RSS file generated from the data that we have entered

These variables and methods should, if properly implemented, allow us to generate the data that we want.

The Application Flow

Of course, having the ability to create an RSS file is different from actually having a useful piece of data. We'll also need a way to put our news into this RSS object to achieve the desired end result. As noted, this will largely be accomplished by using the news objects that were created in Chapter 6.

Therefore, our final implementation will perform the following sequence of steps:

1. Instantiate RSS feed and news objects to use

2. Set up any variables needed by these objects

3. Get the news data using methods from our news data object

4. Loop through our stores assigning the data stored to individual <item> elements in our RSS feed

5. Print out the resulting file

The Solution

We now have a good design that will help us accomplish our goal of providing syndicated news content via an RSS feed. Our job in this chapter is comparatively simple to the others because we don't really need to worry about the data layer, since that has already been handled, or a presentation layer which is not needed.

Implementing the Data Object

The bulk of the work lies in creating our RSS feed class, so let's start with that.

class.rssfeed.php

Create a class.rssfeed.php file in /_lib/_classes/. This will define the class that generates our XML file for us.

We'll start by defining the member variables that were outlined in the design section:

```php
<?php

// File Location: /_lib/_classes/class.rssfeed.php

class rssfeed { // open the class definition

    /**
     * @var array
     */
    var $_aChannel;

     /**
      * @var array
      */
     var $_aChannelItems;

    /**
     * @var array
     */
    var $_aItems;

    /**
     * @var string
     */
    var $_sEncoding;

    /**
     * @var integer
     */
    var $_iCurrentItem;
```

This is more or less standard fare. The next thing to do is write our constructor function that assigns default values to the variables:

```
// {{{ CONSTRUCTOR

/**
 * @access public
 */
function rssfeed() {

    $this->_aChannel = array();
    $this->_aChannelItems = array();
    $this->_aItems = array();
    $this->_sEncoding = "ISO-8859-1";
    $this->_iCurrentItem = 0;
}

// }}}
```

Although it's not required for valid XML, it's always a good idea to assign an encoding value for the document. And if we are going to assign it, we may as well be able to set it to different values. The two that are normally used are ISO-8859-1 (the default) and UTF-8.

Here is the setEncoding() method:

```
// {{{ setEncoding()

/**
 * sets the value of the _sEncoding variable
 *
 * @access public
 */
function setEncoding($sEncoding) {

    $this->_sEncoding = $sEncoding;
}

// }}}
```

The next two functions are private methods that generate the beginning and end bits of our XML document, which is all static data with the exception of the encoding value:

```
// {{{ _writeHeader()

/**
 * generates the beginning XML needed for the RSS feed
 *
 * @access private
 * @return string
 */
function _writeHeader() {

    $sHeader .= "<?xml version=\"1.0\" encoding=\"" . $this->_sEncoding .
            "\"?>\n";
    $sHeader .= "<rdf:RDF\n";
```

```
        $sHeader .= "  xmlns:rdf=\"http://www.w3.org/1999/02/22-rdf-syntax-
                       ns#\"\n";
        $sHeader .= "  xmlns=\"http://purl.org/rss/1.0/\"\n";
        $sHeader .= ">\n";

        return $sHeader;
    }

// }}}
// {{{ _writeClose()

/**
 * generates the closing XML needed for the RSS feed
 *
 * @access private
 * @return string
 */
function _writeClose() {

    return "</rdf:RDF>\n";
}

// }}}
```

Use of the <, >, and & characters will cause an XML document to be poorly formed, which is an issue that we need to talk about. For an XML file to be 'correct' it must be **well-formed** and **valid**. The first of these requirements – well-formed – means that the file must obey the rules of XML syntax. The second requirement – valid – means that if there are any rules defined, such as in a DOCTYPE declaration, about what kinds of elements should be in the file and where they should go, the file must adhere to them.

For a more thorough treatment of these topics, refer to Beginning XML from Wiley (ISBN 1-861003-41-2).

In well-formed XML files, the <, >, and & characters aren't allowed since they are in conflict with the naming conventions in other XML structures. We must always be careful to replace these with the proper SGML entities. Failure to do so will result in an XML file that is not considered valid. If an XML file is not valid, then there are a large number of parsers in use that will simply choke on the file and not process it, which basically makes our file useless. This happens often enough that it's best to define a private method to do the job for us:

```
// {{{ _fixEntities()

/**
 * replace bad XML characters with XML entities
 *
 * @param string string to be fixed
 * @return string
 * @access private
 */
function _fixEntities($sVar) {

    $sVar = str_replace("<" , "&lt;" , $sVar);
    $sVar = str_replace(">" , "&gt;" , $sVar);
```

```
    $sVar = str_replace("&" , "&amp;" , $sVar);

    return $sVar;
}

// }}}
```

The **channel element** has several elements that must be nested beneath it, and the next three methods set the values for the title, link, and description elements that we'll need. Note that we should use the `_fixEntities()` method to ensure that we don't introduce any bad characters into our result file:

```
// {{{ setChannelTitle()

/**
 * sets the title for the RSS channel
 *
 * @param string channel title
 * @access public
 */
function setChannelTitle($sVar) {

    $this->_aChannel["title"] = $this->_fixEntities($sVar);
}

// }}}
// {{{ setChannelLink()

/**
 * sets the link for the RSS channel
 *
 * @param string channel link
 * @access public
 */
function setChannelLink($sVar) {

    $this->_aChannel["link"] = $this->_fixEntities($sVar);
}

// }}}
// {{{ setChannelDescription()

/**
 * sets the description for the RSS channel
 *
 * @param string description
 * @access public
 */
function setChannelDescription($sVar) {

    $this->_aChannel["description"] = $this->_fixEntities($sVar);
}

// }}}
```

The `<channel>` element itself has an `about` attribute, and we would like to be able to set this as well. Note that this is going to be used as an attribute (and not an element) later on:

```php
// {{{ setChannelAbout()

/**
 * sets the about attribute for the RSS channel
 *
 * @param string about attribute
 * @access public
 */
function setChannelAbout($sVar) {

    $this->_aChannel["about"] = $this->_fixEntities($sVar);
}

// }}}
```

The past few functions handled the `<channel>` element of the file. The next major part is the `<item>` elements that come after the `<channel>` element.

We'll handle the use of multiple elements with the same name by keeping track of the current element using a counter. When we start working on a new item, we'll call the `startItem()` method. This simply returns the ID of the current item in case we need it for some reason, for example, if we were keeping track of how many we had:

```php
// {{{ startItem()

/**
 * just returns the current item ID
 *
 * @access public
 * @return integer
 */

function startItem() {

    return $this->_iCurrentItem;
}

// }}}
```

Each `<item>` element has its own title, link, and description elements that are required by the RSS specification. The next three methods set the values for these. Here we use the `_iCurrentItem` member variable to keep track of which item we are working on, and the `_fixEntities()` method to keep bad characters out of our markup:

```php
// {{{ setItemTitle()

/**
 * sets the item title for the current item
 *
 * @param string title value
 * @access public
```

```php
    */
    function setItemTitle($sVar) {

        $this->_aItems[$this->_iCurrentItem]["title"] =
                $this->_fixEntities($sVar);
    }

    // }}}

    // {{{ setItemLink()

    /**
     * sets the item link for the current item
     *
     * @param string link value
     * @access public
     */
    function setItemLink($sVar) {

        $this->_aItems[$this->_iCurrentItem]["link"] =
                        $this->_fixEntities($sVar);
        $this->_addChannelItem($sVar);
    }

    // }}}

    // {{{ setItemDescription()

    /**
     * sets the description for the current item
     *
     * @param string description value
     * @param boolean whether description value is XML CDATA
     * @access public
     */
    function setItemDescription($sVar,$bCdata = FALSE) {

        if( $bCdata ) {
            $this->_aItems[$this->_iCurrentItem]["description"] =
                    "<![CDATA[$sVar]]>";
        } else {
            $this->_aItems[$this->_iCurrentItem]["description"] =
                    $this->_fixEntities($sVar);
        }
    }

    // }}}
```

This last method – setItemDescription() – needs a little more explanation. At times, if there are a lot of HTML links, for example, it can get a little ugly to always replace characters like < with <. In this case, we can tell the XML parser that the information is CDATA by enclosing it in <![CDATA[and]]> tags, thereby making it legal to leave in characters like <. It's nice to have this option, so for this method we have defined a second, optional argument called $bCdata, which defaults to FALSE, meaning that we use _fixEntities() to take care of bad characters. But if set to TRUE, it would generate the necessary CDATA tags.

Moving on, you may have noticed that whenever `setItemLink()` is called, it in turn calls the `_addChannelItem()` private method that is used to populate the `<items>` element that belongs to the channel:

```
// {{{ _addChannelItem()

/**
 * adds this item to the <items> element in the channel
 *
 * @param string resource link
 * @access private
 */
function _addChannelItem($sVar) {
    $this->_aChannelItems[$this->_iCurrentItem] =
            $this->_fixEntities($sVar);
}

// }}}
```

The `endItem()` method tells the object that we are done with the current item, by incrementing the `$_iCurrentItem` member variable:

```
// {{{ endItem()

/**
 * increments the current item ID
 *
 * @access public
 */
function endItem() {
    $this->_iCurrentItem++;
}

// }}}
```

The final method in the `rssfeed` class is the most complex. It takes the data that we've put in so far and uses it to generate the RSS XML file that will be used for syndication. We start out by calling the `_writeHeader()` method:

```
// {{{ getRssFeed()

/**
 * returns a string with the RSS XML file
 *
 * @access public
 */
function getRssFeed() {

    // get the header info
    $sRssFeed .= $this->_writeHeader();
```

Start the `<channel>` element and put in the value of the `about` attribute:

```
        // write out channel information
        $sRssFeed .= "  <channel rdf:about=\"" . $this->_aChannel["about"] .
            "\">\n";
```

Now loop through the values of the $_aChannel array to create the title, link, and description elements. Note that we skip the about key since it was used for the attribute above:

```
foreach ( $this->_aChannel as $sKey => $sValue ) {

    // "about" is an attribute, not an element
    if( 0 != strcmp($sKey , "about") ) {

        $sRssFeed .= "      <$sKey>$sValue</$sKey>\n";
    }
}
```

Now we have to create the <items> element for this channel. This is accomplished by looping through the $_aChannelItems array and getting the values stored:

```
// generate the <items> element nested in the <channel> element
$sRssFeed .= "      <items>\n";
$sRssFeed .= "         <rdf:Seq>\n";

foreach( $this->_aChannelItems as $sResource ) {

    $sRssFeed .= "            <rdf:li resource=\"$sResource\" />\n";
}

$sRssFeed .= "         </rdf:Seq>\n";
$sRssFeed .= "      </items>\n";
$sRssFeed .= "   </channel>\n";
```

We've finished with the <channel> element, and now it's time to generate the <item> elements. One last loop through the $_aItems array does this:

```
//write out all of our items
for( $i = 0 ; $i < count($this->_aItems) ; ++$i ) {

    $sRssFeed .= "  <item rdf:about=\"" . $this->_aItems[$i]["link"] .
                "\">\n";

    foreach( $this->_aItems[$i] as $sKey => $sValue ) {

        $sRssFeed .= "     <$sKey>$sValue</$sKey>\n";
    }

    $sRssFeed .= "  </item>\n";
}
```

All that's left is to write out the closing and return the resultant file:

```
// get close
$sRssFeed .= $this->_writeClose();

    return $sRssFeed;
}

// }}}
```

```
} // end class rssfeed
?>
```

This brings us to the end of the `class.rssfeed.php` file, which means that we have already accomplished most of the 'heavy lifting' that was needed in this chapter. What's left is to use this class, along with the news class, to syndicate something useful.

rss.php

Create an `rss.php` file in `/site/news/`. This will be the main implementation of the `rssfeed` class. In *The Design* section, we had outlined the basic steps that we'll need to take here, and the first thing was to include the necessary class definition files:

```php
<?php

// File Location: /site/news/rss.php

require_once("class.news.php");
require_once("class.rssfeed.php");

// /_lib/_base/funcs.php contains utility functions for the application
require_once("funcs.php");
```

Note that we also include `funcs.php` explicitly here, since we don't have another include file that picks it up for us.

We'll use the `header()` function to tell the user agent that it will be getting XML data:

```php
header("Content-type: text/xml");
```

> **The header information must always be sent before anything else is printed out by PHP. This includes blank lines and other kinds of whitespace. If you are going to use the `header()` function, it must be the first thing to send any output to the browser.**

We'll want the location of our own server to reference links later on, so let's go ahead and get that now:

```php
// string variable we'll need here
$sServer = "http://" . $_ENV["HOSTNAME"];
```

We'll need one news object to get our news data, and one `rssfeed` object to generate an RSS file from that data:

```php
// instantiate news and RSS objects
$oNews = new news;
$oRssFeed = new rssfeed;
```

Since the news is split into different categories, we want to be able to show just the headlines for a specific category in our syndicated feed that mirrors the functionality of the actual newsfeed. This is accomplished by looking at the type GET variable. If that doesn't exist, just use the default that we can get from the getNewsTypes() news class method:

```
// get news types
$aTypes = $oNews->getNewsTypes();

// set the $iType and $iCursor variables that we'll need
// for the getActiveNewsItems() method
$_GET["type"] ? $iType = $_GET["type"] : $iType = $aTypes[0]["News Type Id"];
```

The news object also has a method that will conveniently get the active news items for a particular type. However, it needs a cursor variable to tell where to start pulling news items in the database. If a cursor value has been set, we'll use that. Otherwise we'll just default to 0:

```
$_GET["cursor"] ? $iCursor = $_GET["cursor"] : $iCursor = 0;
```

Now we can use getActiveNewsItems() to get an associative array with all the news data that we are interested in. This really highlights the benefits of creating well-designed, reusable objects. We have accomplished the task of getting our news data using an existing data object without having to write any SQL code:

```
// get an associative array with the active news items
$aNews = $oNews->getActiveNewsItems($iCursor,$iType);
```

We can now turn our attention to generating the RSS file itself. We'll first use the setChannel*() methods to set up the basic information:

```
// base information for this RSS channel
$oRssFeed->setChannelTitle("DVD Life News");
$oRssFeed->setChannelLink($sServer);
$oRssFeed->setChannelDescription("News for DVD Enthusiasts!");
$oRssFeed->setChannelAbout($sServer);
```

Next loop through each of the headlines and handle their data:

```
// loop through news items and add information to the RSS feed
for( $i=0 ; $i < count($aNews) ; ++$i ) {
```

Looking ahead, it makes sense to use the first 80 or so characters (nicely formatted) of the article itself as the description for a specific item. So we'll grab and format those 80 characters here:

```
    // just show the first 80 characters of any given article
    if( strlen($aNews[$i]["Article"]) > 80 ) {

        $sArticle = format(substr($aNews[$i]["Article"] , 0 , 77) . "...");

    } else {

        $sArticle = format($aNews[$i]["Article"]);

    }
```

Now, we'll start a new item, put in the data for the title, link, and description, and end the current item. The `for` loop ensures that all of the data is represented in the final files:

```
    // start a new item
    $oRssFeed->startItem();

    // set item title
    $oRssFeed->setItemTitle(format($aNews[$i]["Title"]));

    // set item link
    $oRssFeed->setItemLink($sServer . dirname(SELF) . "/detail.php?id=" .
            $aNews[$i]["News Id"]);

    // set item description
    $oRssFeed->setItemDescription($sArticle);

    // end the item
    $oRssFeed->endItem();
}
```

With all of this done, we can print out the file, like this:

```
    // print out the RSS feed
    print $oRssFeed->getRssFeed();
    ?>
```

Checking the Data

Of course, it's always a good idea to ensure that things are working properly. In other parts of this book, this was a little easier to do – there was a graphical interface and we could just use to try out our new application to make sure it was working. Here, we've only generated data, so there's not really anything to 'click on' to make sure that our job was done correctly.

The first thing we should do is to ensure that we did produce a useful XML document. XML is a strict format, so if anything is out of place then we will be in trouble. Fortunately, current versions of Mozilla and Internet Explorer (IE) will let us know right away if this is the case.

Here is the RSS file displayed on a Mozilla browser:

Some older versions of Mozilla do not display XML this way. If you do not see something similar on your screen, try changing `Content-type` *to* `text/plain` *(instead of* `text/xml`*) in the* `header()` *function so that the browser doesn't try to interpret it. Any recent version of IE should give a readable display.*

Since the Mozilla parser was able to parse the file into a document tree, we can be sure that the XML file is well-formed, especially because Mozilla generates a hard-to-miss error message if the file isn't well-formed.

The next thing to do is to ensure that we have generated an RSS file that can be used and parsed by other people. Fortunately, there is a very easy way for us to do this. The PEAR class libraries provide an RSS class (`RSS.php`) that makes it easy to parse a networked RSS file, so building a quick viewer and checking our file will just take a minute.

> **The PEAR RSS parser class documentation is available at the PEAR web site (http://pear.php.net), and the class itself is available at http://pear.php.net/package-info.php?pacid=22.**

Create a file called `dvdlifenews.php` in the web server's root directory. It starts by including the necessary class definition:

```php
<?php

//File Name: dvdlifenews.php

require_once("RSS.php");
```

The `RSS.php` file provides our application with an **XML_RSS class** that makes parsing and displaying data from RSS files very easy. It's an extension of the base `XML_Parser` class that is part of the standard PEAR installation, so we automatically have all of the methods available from `XML_Parser` as well. The `XML_Parser` class provides functionality to set up a SAX style parser for an XML document. That is to say, it sets up the needed callback functions for all the elements for us. It also provides a `parse()` method that parses the document.

> *One caveat is that this class does not degrade gracefully if* `error_reporting` *is set to E_ALL in* `php.ini`*. The correct line to have in* `php.ini` *is:* `error_reporting = E_ALL & ~E_NOTICE`*, which is the typical setup.*

Now assign the location of the networked RSS file:

```php
// the location of the RSS file
$sRssFeed = "http://apress.mediatemple.net/site/news/rss.php";
```

We instantiate our RSS object with this location, and have our object parse the file:

```php
// instantiate new RSS object
$oRss =& new XML_RSS($sRssFeed);

// parse the RSS file
$oRss->parse();
?>
```

Note that we assigned the `$oRss` variable with the `=&` operator. This is because, to use the `parse()` method that the `XML_RSS` class inherits, we need the `$oRss` object (that is created in the code bit above) and not a copy of the object created (that would have been passed if we had used = as the assignment operator).

> *The use of references in PHP constructors can be a little confusing. To make things easy, the PHP authors have a short tutorial-style document that explains how things work at* http://www.php.net/manual/en/language.oop.newref.php.

We don't need anything fancy in terms of presentation here. After all, we're just checking to make sure that things are working properly:

```html
<html>
  <head>
    <title>DVD Life NewsFeed</title>
    <style type="text/css">

    body {
```

```
        background: #ffffff;
        margin: 50px 0px 0px 40px;
    }

    </style>
  </head>
<body>

<h2>DVD Life NewsFeed</h2>

<ul>
```

The XML_RSS class provides a getItems() method. This returns an associative array where the keys are the element names of the next <item> element, and the values are the data for those elements. Since getItem() will always get the next available item (until there are none left) it's very easy to loop through all the items in the file:

```php
<?php

// loop through items and print out links
foreach( $oRss->getItems() as $aItem ) {

    print "<li><a href=\"" . $aItem["link"] . "\">" . $aItem["title"] .
            "</a></li>\n";
}
?>
```

Now we close out the list and HTML:

```
</ul>

</html>
```

This file generates the following output in a Mozilla browser:

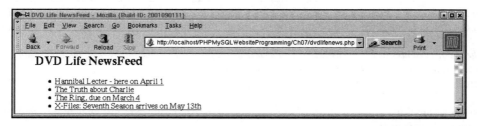

The code works just as we expected it to – each link takes us to the page on the DVD Life web site where the full article can be viewed.

A free RSS validator is available at **http://feeds.archive.org/validator/**.

This brings us to the end of the development, but we can imagine further uses for the kinds of things we have developed.

To begin with, our RSS feed will do us little good unless we get other people to use it. There are sites available (http://www.syndicat8.com and the slashbox at http://www.slashdot.org, for example) where we can submit our site's feed. If accepted, it will be catalogued and made available to those who visit the site. We have also seen how to easily use RSS feeds located just about anywhere. So it might be advisable to include news from other relevant, but non-competing sites, to augment our own content. For example, a site providing news about movies that are currently in theaters might make a nice complement to the after-market news provided on our site.

Summary

This chapter has taken us through the process of building a syndication module for our web site. It was a little simpler than the other modules we have talked about in this book. This was primarily because our data layer and data objects were already defined and ready to use, and also because we did not really need to concern ourselves with a presentation layer.

Our syndication application is a nice addition to the site, though, because it provides the following:

- ❑ A feed that allows other network devices to display and link to our news content
- ❑ A convenient format that ensures people will have no trouble implementing interfaces to our content
- ❑ The ability to get syndicated feeds for specific categories of news, mirroring the functionality in the actual newsfeed on the site

Along the way, we learned something about the industry standard RSS format that is in wide use today. And when we were done, we checked to ensure that the RSS file was working correctly. With all this in place, the DVD Life news will become easily available to all.

However, we are far from done with developing DVD Life. In the next chapter, we'll dive back in and create a system for displaying banner advertisements. After that, we'll tackle topics such as online polls, newsletters, discussion forums, and shopping carts.

8

Advertising

For many web sites, advertising is a supplementary source of income and an additional means of sustaining revenue that keeps them online. They use banner advertisements to promote products, and content from their own web sites as well as other web sites and in turn earn a profit for this service. This is the most common form of browser-based advertising on the Web today. The benefit for the owner of the advertisement, or the client, is the probability of a site visitor clicking their banner and proceeding to their web site for more information. Ideally, this will result in a purchase of some sort which directly or indirectly benefits the client. It's important to note that advertising is rapidly moving in the direction of Flash media and popups, which we aren't going to discuss in this chapter, but could feasibly be implemented in the same manner as our banner advertisements.

There are several means of handling banner advertisements and their activity. One of these is to audit the number of views or impressions that an advertisement receives, and another would be to capture the actual click-throughs of an advertisement. Regardless of which revenue and management design we decide to use, the key is to organize our advertising mechanisms to efficiently manage the banners and accurately report their activity.

In this chapter, we will:

- ❑ Review potential design options
- ❑ Discuss common advertising practices
- ❑ Construct an application design based on our problem discovery
- ❑ Implement the design into our existing CMS and web site architecture

The Problem

Having decided that we want to use banner advertising to support our revenue model, we need to consider which features we wish to include in our advertising system, and what considerations we need to take into account to do so efficiently and accurately.

Let's look at some of the different options we have to choose from:

❑ Impression monitoring and reporting

❑ Click-through monitoring and reporting

❑ Scheduled display

❑ Syndicated advertising

These four different types of advertising are common practices in today's web market. They are all based on banner advertisements and provide different means of revenue. Let's look at a more detailed overview of these four different options to help us decide which ones we should use.

Impressions

Impressions are merely single viewings or browser downloads of a banner advertisement. Any time we request a web page that has a banner advertisement on it, we have made an impression or received a viewing of that advertisement.

Keeping a log of these viewings is a simple process of incrementing visitor activity about that advertisement and then charging our clients based on the number of impressions that their advertisement has received. This is a fast and effective means of implementing a more-technical advertising system. Once we capture the impressions into a log of some sort, we can bill our clients for each viewing/impression based on an agreed upon rate. Some advertising models will work based on a pre-pay model that requires the advertiser to purchase their advertising up front for a guaranteed number of impressions. This approach would seem more reliable for billings, as at times customers don't feel that their advertising efforts have done 'enough' and are therefore reluctant to pay after the fact.

Click-Throughs

Click-throughs occur when a site visitor not only views an advertisement, but also clicks that advertisement, thus redirecting the visitor to whatever URL is associated with that advertisement. Capturing a click-through relies on the same type of system that an impression mechanism would use, however, it's an entirely different activity since it requires user interaction.

Now, if the site visitor clicks on a banner, then surely the advertisement somehow captured his or her interest. This is an attractive means of providing a banner advertisement system since we can assume that a click-through would be of higher value than a mere impression. Again, the click-through system can be a more technically challenging implementation since it requires a means of redirecting the client browser as well as auditing the visitor's activity.

Scheduled Display

Knowing when a specific demographic uses the web site, or when a higher volume of traffic can be expected creates an opportunity for us to offer our clients a targeted marketing campaign by displaying their banner advertisement during a scheduled period and prioritizing it too. This can be done using the impression and the click-through mechanisms.

Syndication

The simplest means of generating revenue from advertising would be to implement a syndication plan. This could be considered as a traffic sharing service or even a referral service. The way these systems work is that you agree to provide third-party advertising on your web site and in return receive compensation for the impressions and click-throughs that are tracked and reported by the syndicating company. Since we are trying to actually build something here, we'll skip the syndication option for now.

Requirements

Now that we have covered the different types of advertising that we may wish to implement, let's organize a set of requirements to guide the design and development of the banner advertisements module:

- ❑ **Database design** – The database needs to store information about the visitor impressions and possible interaction with the advertisements. Also needed is a flexible table structure to ensure that we can easily extend our feature set, thus enabling us to offer specialized, targeted advertising services should we elect to do so. Some consideration of these additional features may be a scheduled delivery of advertising or organizing the advertising priorities of banners in the system.

- ❑ **Auditing and reporting** – Since our income is based on the auditing of banner advertisement activity, we need to ensure that our system for logging impressions and/or click-throughs is accurate. We also need to build a reporting tool that is clear and concise since the content of these reports will determine our income.

- ❑ **Content management** – To get our client's banners into a profitable rotation, quickly, we need to build onto our CMS framework to simplify the management of banners and their associated information.

The Design

Now that we've discussed several options for implementing advertisements on our web site, let's pick the features needed to get an initial system up and running. We are going to rule out the syndicated advertising option for our solution since there's no fun in doing it, if we don't get to build it ourselves. Another reason to rule out the syndication option is that the revenue is typically lower since we are using someone else's service versus implementing our own. That leaves us with the impressions feature, the click-throughs feature and the scheduling feature. Since the collective focus of these three options is the auditing activity, we need to build our advertising system based on both the impression logging and the click-through tracking.

The flow for our front-end interaction is fairly simple – all we need to do is load a page, insert an advertisement, and redirect visitors to the URL associated with that advertisement (if they click on it):

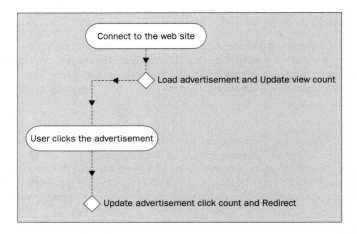

Next we'll detail the database tables that are used to manage our banner advertisements, their respective clients, and the auditing logs.

Designing the Data Layer

Since we need to extend our feature set in the future, we shall design the database tables so that we can easily add fields without disrupting the existing architecture. To do this, we need to abstract our associative information into the different understood entities – advertisements, clients, and activity.

The three tables will be named as follows:

❑   apress_ads to hold the banner advertisement information

❑   apress_ads_clients to store the client information

❑   apress_ads_activity that will be the logging index for all of the banner advertisement activity

We'll discuss each table in a little more detail to see the different parts that will make up our advertising content.

The Advertisement Table

The apress_ads table defines the banner advertisement, associates a client by the client ID (client_id), and stores the general link and path parameters of the advertisement:

Field	Type	Description
ad_id	INT(10)	The unique identifier for each advertisement record. The apress_ads_activity dependent table references this primary key.
ad_client_id	INT(10)	The unique identifier reference for our relative client.

Field	Type	Description
ad_title	VARCHAR(200)	The title or name of our advertisement used for reference in the CMS.
ad_url	VARCHAR(255)	The redirect URL to be called on a click-through.
ad_path	VARCHAR(255)	The path where the advertisement banner is located.
status	INT(1)	Flag to determine the advertisement's status.
deleted	INT(1)	Flag to determine if the advertisement is deleted.
created_dt	DATETIME	Date time value when the advertisement was created.
modified_dt	DATETIME	Date time value when the advertisement was last modified.
deleted_dt	DATETIME	Date time value when the advertisement was deleted.

The Client Table

The apress_ads_clients table stores all of our client information, like contact methods, the company name, and so on:

Field	Type	Description
ad_client_id	INT(10)	The unique identifier for each advertisement client record. This primary key indexes each of the clients uniquely.
ad_client_name	VARCHAR(100)	The company name for each client.
ad_client_contact	VARCHAR(100)	The contact name for each client.
ad_client_email	VARCHAR(100)	The contact e-mail address for each client.
ad_client_phone	VARCHAR(20)	The contact phone number for each client.
status	INT(1)	Flag to determine the client's status.
deleted	INT(1)	Flag to determine if the client is deleted.
created_dt	DATETIME	Date time value when the client was created.
modified_dt	DATETIME	Date time value when the client was last modified.
deleted_dt	DATETIME	Date time value when the client was deleted.

The Activity Table

The apress_ads_activity table is the logging index for all our banner advertisement activity, where we store the month and year for each instance of the advertisement, as well as manually increment the value for the actual activity.

It's worth mentioning that we could easily store each instance of activity in its own record. This would allow us to capture more information about the activity such as a client IP address, potential referrer information, and even specific times of activity. This information could prove very useful while marketing our advertising services, since we can dissimilate more information about primary advertising times, interests, and even geographic interests. Doing so would require that our database be prepared to handle the immediate and continual growth.

Our design contains less information but remains very small and efficient:

Field	Type	Description
`ad_activity_id`	INT(10)	The unique identifier for each advertisement activity record.
`ad_id`	INT(10)	The unique identifier for the relative advertisement. The index on this column helps to improve the performance of our queries.
`ad_view_cnt`	INT(15)	The incrementing count of impressions or views.
`ad_click_cnt`	INT(15)	The incrementing count of click-throughs or clicks.
`ad_activity_month`	INT(2)	The month of activity.
`ad_activity_year`	INT(4)	The year of activity

That concludes the design of our database tables. As you can see, we have separated the different types of content to allow for an easily extensible framework.

Designing the Data Object

The advertisement data object will manage all of the activity and data used for the banner advertisements, as well as the auditing and reporting functionality.

The Ads Data Object

Before writing the code let's define the functionality that our data object needs to perform. We want to keep our class self-contained as we have in our other objects. Since we don't need to extend any of the existing data objects to obtain the desired implementation, we can write the ads class as a self-contained data object.

Our data object needs to be able to satisfy the following requirements:

- Implement the PEAR::DB object
- Assign a member variable with a unique identifier
- Return a count of advertisements from the apress_ads table for pagination
- Return a limited collection of advertisements from the apress_ads table for the CMS listing
- Return a single advertisement from the apress_ads table with all of its relative information
- Get a list of the client's active advertisements from the apress_ads_clients table

❏ Get a collection of data to render an activity report from the `apress_ads_activity` table

❏ Add a new advertisement record

❏ Edit an existing advertisement record

❏ Get a single random advertisement from the `apress_ads` table and increment the activity in the `apress_ads_activity` table

❏ Increment the activity in the `apress_ads_activity` table and return a Boolean value to conditionally redirect a browser

❏ Delete an advertisement from the `apress_ads` table

❏ Activate an advertisement in the `apress_ads` table

❏ Deactivate an advertisement in the `apress_ads` table

Now that we've defined the functionality that our data object requires, let's look at the different class variables that we'll create to provide the desired functionality:

ads Class Variable	Description
`_id`	Property containing the unique identifier for an item
`_oConn`	Property containing a reference to the PEAR::DB object

Naturally, we need some class methods that will manipulate these variables and ultimately generate the advertisements. The following set will be employed:

ads Class Method	Description
`ads($id='')`	Constructor method that instantiates the _oConn object. This member also optionally assigns the _id property, if passed.
`setId($id)`	Assigns the _id class member to the value passed in the $id argument for the class instance.
`getAdsCount()`	Returns a count of the advertisement items.
`getClientsCount()`	Returns a count of the advertising client items.
`getAds($sSort, $iPage=0)`	Returns an associative array of advertisement items. These are the optional arguments for the method: ❏ $sSort – String value representing the sort column name ❏ $iPage – Integer value representing the cursor position for the limit call

Table continued on following page

ads Class Method	Description
getClients($sSort, $ipage=0)	Returns an associative array of advertising client items. The optional arguments passed perform the following: ❑ $sSort – String value representing the sort column name ❑ $iPage – Integer value representing the cursor position for the limit call
getAd()	Returns an associative array of a single advertisement, which is indexed by the _id class member.
getClient()	Returns an associative array of a single advertising client, which is indexed by the _id class member.
getClientsList()	Returns an associative array of clients that have active advertisements within the system.
getAdsReport()	Returns an associative array of collective advertisement activity.
addAd($aArgs)	Adds a new advertisement to the system. The $aArgs argument passes all of the advertisement data for the new item.
addClient($aArgs)	Adds a new advertising client to the system. The $aArgs argument passes all of the client data for the new item.
editAd($aArgs)	Updates an advertisement record with the data contained in the $aArgs array argument passed.
editClient($aArgs)	Updates an advertising client record with the data contained in the $aArgs array argument passed.
getRandomAd()	Returns an associative array containing information for a single random advertisement. This method also increments the advertisement activity.
redirectAd()	Increments the advertisement activity and returns a Boolean value that triggers a redirect.
deleteAd()	Deletes an advertisement record from the system.
deleteClient()	Deletes an advertising client from the system.
activateAd()	Activates an advertisement record in the system.
activateClient()	Activates an advertising client in the system.
deactivateAd()	Deactivates an advertisement record in the system.
deactivateClient()	Deactivates an advertising client record in the system.

We'll place the banner files inside a /_img/_banners/ directory within our common images directory (_img), so they can be easily accessed.

> Note that an underscore character precedes our directory name. We use this notation to
> identify files and directories that should only be accessed by the application or from
> within the web pages and not directly from a browser address.

Now that we have planned the design of our data layer, let's begin to build our advertisement mechanism
and content management tools.

The Solution

Before we dive into the code it would be a good idea to look at the files that are being used for this chapter
and their inter-relatedness.

This diagram outlines the general page hierarchy used within the web site and the CMS. It shows the
different relationships and dependencies of the files within our application framework that are necessary to
implement the advertisements module:

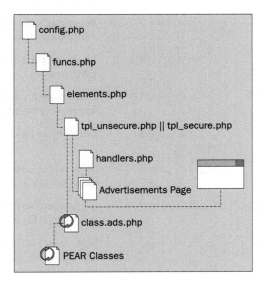

The following table details the file location and functional purpose of all the files used in this chapter:

File Name	File Path	Description
config.php	/_lib/_base/	Configuration values for the application.
funcs.php	/_lib/_base/	Utility functions for the application.
elements.php	/_lib/_base/	Reusable generic elements such as error display functions. This file also assigns the common GET variables – $op and $id.

Table continued on following page

File Name	File Path	Description
tpl_unsecure.php	/site/	Template framework file for pages outside the CMS application. It implements banner advertisements into the page framework.
tpl_secure.php	/core/	Template framework file for pages inside the CMS application.
handlers.php	/_lib/_base/	Data input validation functions.
redirect.php	/site/	Page used to capture click-throughs and redirect the browser.
index.php	/site/report/	Page that generates a real-time report of statistics and logging of the advertisement activity.
index.php	/core/ads/	List page for advertisements in the CMS system.
form.php	/core/ads/	Form page for adding and editing advertisements.
index.php	/core/clients/	List page for advertising clients in the CMS system.
form.php	/core/clients/	Form page for adding and editing advertising clients.
class.ads.php	/_lib/_classes/	Data object for advertisements logic.
apress_ads.sql	/_lib/_sql	SQL create script for the apress_ads database table.
apress_ads_clients.sql	/_lib/_sql/	SQL create script for the apress_ads_clients database table.
apress_ads_activity.sql	/_lib/_sql/	SQL create script for the apress_ads_activity database table.

Implementing the Data Layer

Having already defined our tables in the design phase, we can now write the conforming SQL scripts that will create them in the database.

apress_ads

Since we need to store a direct reference to a client record for each advertisement, we can store the `ad_client_id` in the advertisements table. Note that we're storing a string path to the advertisement file rather than storing the binary object in the database as a BLOB type. The reason for this is that 'pathing' the file is far more efficient than retrieving the object from the database, especially since these files will be called on every public page. The primary benefit of storing binary objects in the database would be the portability advantage if we wished to move or redistribute our existing application. However, our design already makes this possible, without having to use BLOBs, by using configuration assignments.

Here is the table creation script:

```
CREATE TABLE apress_ads (
   ad_id         INT(10)      NOT NULL auto_increment,
   ad_client_id  INT(10)      NOT NULL default '0',
   ad_title      VARCHAR(200) NOT NULL default '',
   ad_url        VARCHAR(255) NOT NULL default '',
   ad_path       VARCHAR(255) NOT NULL default '',
   status        INT(1)       NOT NULL default '1',
   deleted       INT(1)       NOT NULL default '0',
   deleted_dt    DATETIME     default NULL,
   created_dt    DATETIME     NOT NULL default '0000-00-00 00:00:00',
   modified_dt   DATETIME     NOT NULL default '0000-00-00 00:00:00',
                 PRIMARY KEY  (ad_id)
) TYPE=MyISAM;
```

apress_clients

The client table is a generic associated collection of client information that shares a direct relationship with one or many advertisements:

```
CREATE TABLE apress_ads_clients (
   ad_client_id      INT(10)      NOT NULL auto_increment,
   ad_client_name    VARCHAR(100) NOT NULL default '',
   ad_client_contact VARCHAR(100) NOT NULL default '',
   ad_client_email   VARCHAR(100) NOT NULL default '',
   ad_client_phone   VARCHAR(20)  NULL default NULL,
   status            INT(1)       NOT NULL default '1',
   deleted           INT(1)       NOT NULL default '0',
   deleted_dt        DATETIME     default NULL,
   created_dt        DATETIME     NOT NULL default '0000-00-00 00:00:00',
   modified_dt       DATETIME     NOT NULL default '0000-00-00 00:00:00',
                     PRIMARY KEY  (ad_client_id)
) TYPE=MyISAM;
```

apress_ads_activity

The activity table will store a one-to-one relationship with our advertisements referenced on the `ad_id` column:

```
CREATE TABLE apress_ads_activity (
   ad_activity_id  INT(10) NOT NULL auto_increment,
   ad_id           INT(10) NOT NULL default '0',
```

```
    ad_view_cnt        INT(15)  NOT NULL default '0',
    ad_click_cnt       INT(15)  NOT NULL default '0',
    ad_activity_month INT(2)   NOT NULL default '0',
    ad_activity_year  INT(4)   NOT NULL default '0',
                       PRIMARY KEY  (ad_activity_id),
                       KEY ad_id_rel (ad_id)
) TYPE=MyISAM;
```

Implementing the Data Object

At this point, we've defined our problem and designed a solution. We have also created the foundation of our advertising system by creating the database tables that will store all of the necessary information. Now it's time to begin writing the code. Let us start by building our data object since it's the link between the data layer, and the presentation layer.

class.ads.php

The first thing we need to do in our class is to include any dependent files, and define all the class member variables:

```php
<?php

// File Location: /_lib/_classes/class.ads.php

// import the PEAR::DB class
require_once("DB.php");

class ads { // open the class definition

    /**
     * unique identifier for an advertisement
     *
     * @var integer
     * @access private
     * @see setId()
     */
    var $_id;

    /**
     * PEAR::DB object
     *
     * @var object
     * @access private
     */
    var $_oConn;
```

Next, we'll build the constructor, which will run upon instantiating the class from our web pages:

```php
    // CONSTRUCTOR
    /**
     * class constructor
     *
     * @param integer $id [optional] advertisement identifier
     * @access public
```

```
    */
    function ads($id = '') {

        // implement PEAR::DB object
        $this->_oConn =& DB::connect(DSN);

        if( DB::isError($this->_oConn) ) {

            catchExc($this->_oConn->getMessage());
        }

        // set ad ID
        if( is_int($id) ) {

            $this->setId($id);
        }
    }
```

The next function assigns the _id class member, which is used to pass a unique identifier from a web page to the data object:

```
/**
 * set the _id member variable for the class
 *
 * @param integer $id unique identifier
 * @access public
 */
function setId($id) {

    if( is_int($id) ) {

        $this->_id = $id;
    }
}
```

Next let's get into the data. Earlier we mentioned the need for a record count function that will be used for our pagination elements within the pages – here are the getAdsCount() and getClientsCount() methods that meet our requirements:

```
/**
 * get advertisements count for paging
 *
 * @return boolean
 * @access private
 */
function getAdsCount() {

    $sql = "SELECT
                count(ad_id) AS cnt
            FROM
                ".PREFIX."_ads
            WHERE
```

```
                        deleted=0";

        if( DB::isError($iCnt = $this->_oConn->getOne($sql)) ) {

            catchExc($iCnt->getMessage());
            return FALSE;
        }

        return $iCnt;
    }

/**
 * get clients count for paging
 *
 * @return boolean
 * @access private
 */
function getClientsCount() {

    $sql = "SELECT
                count(ad_client_id) AS cnt
            FROM
                ".PREFIX."_ads_clients
            WHERE
                deleted=0";

    if( DB::isError($iCnt = $this->_oConn->getOne($sql)) ) {

        catchExc($iCnt->getMessage());
        return FALSE;
    }

    return $iCnt;
}
```

The main functions for returning lists of advertisements and clients in the CMS are fairly complex functions, which only return a limited array to reduce the overhead of our query:

```
/**
 * get advertisements list
 *
 * @param string $sSort sort key
 * @param integer $iPage [optional] cursor
 * @return array advertisements data
 * @access public
 */
function getAds($sSort, $iPage=0) {

    $sql = "SELECT
                ad_id,
                ad_title,
                status,
                created_dt,
```

```
                    modified_dt
          FROM
              ".PREFIX."_ads
          WHERE
              deleted=0
          ORDER BY
              ".$sSort."
          LIMIT
              ".$iPage.", ".ROWCOUNT;

    if( DB::isError($rsTmp = $this->_oConn->query($sql)) ) {

        catchExc($rsTmp->getMessage());
        return FALSE;
    }
```

This `while` loop, loops through the result and returns the data collection:

```
        $i = 0;
        while( $aRow = $rsTmp->fetchRow(DB_FETCHMODE_ASSOC) ) {

            $return[$i]["Ad Id"] = $aRow["ad_id"];
            $return[$i]["Title"] = $aRow["ad_title"];
            $return[$i]["Status"] = $aRow["status"];
            $return[$i]["Created Date"] = strtotime($aRow["created_dt"]);
            $return[$i]["Modified Date"] = strtotime($aRow["modified_dt"]);
            ++$i;
        }
        return $return;
    }
```

This method returns the list of clients in the CMS:

```
    /**
     * get clients list
     *
     * @param string $sSort sort key
     * @param integer $iPage [optional] cursor
     * @return array clients data
     * @access public
     */
    function getClients($sSort, $iPage=0) {

        $sql = "SELECT
                    ad_client_id,
                    ad_client_name,
                    status,
                    created_dt,
                    modified_dt
                FROM
                    ".PREFIX."_ads_clients
                WHERE
                    deleted=0
                ORDER BY
                    ".$sSort."
                LIMIT
                    ".$iPage.", ".ROWCOUNT;
```

```
            if( DB::isError($rsTmp = $this->_oConn->query($sql)) ) {

                catchExc($rsTmp->getMessage());
                return FALSE;
            }

            // loop through result and return data collection
            $i = 0;
            while( $aRow = $rsTmp->fetchRow(DB_FETCHMODE_ASSOC) ) {

                $return[$i]["Client Id"] = $aRow["ad_client_id"];
                $return[$i]["Client"] = $aRow["ad_client_name"];
                $return[$i]["Status"] = $aRow["status"];
                $return[$i]["Created Date"] = strtotime($aRow["created_dt"]);
                $return[$i]["Modified Date"] = strtotime($aRow["modified_dt"]);
                ++$i;
            }
            return $return;
    }
```

The next two functions are used to return all information about a single advertisement or advertising client. The queries identify the records by conditionally querying against the _id member variable, which we can assume has been assigned already from within the web page. Since we have made the identifier generic in the setter method, we can use this member for either an advertisement or a client, depending on which instance we are using:

```
/**
 * get single advertisement by ID
 *
 * @return array
 * @access public
 */
function getAd() {

    // get advertisement record
    $sql = "SELECT
                a.ad_id,
                a.ad_client_id,
                a.ad_url,
                a.ad_title,
                a.ad_path,
                c.ad_client_name,
                c.ad_client_contact,
                c.ad_client_email,
                c.ad_client_phone,
                a.status,
                a.deleted,
                a.deleted_dt,
                a.created_dt,
                a.modified_dt
            FROM
                ".PREFIX."_ads a,
```

```
                            ".PREFIX."_ads_clients c
                    WHERE
                        c.ad_client_id=a.ad_client_id
                        AND a.ad_id=".$this->_id;

        if( DB::isError($rsTmp = $this->_oConn->query($sql)) ) {

            catchExc($rsTmp->getMessage());
            return FALSE;
        }

        // capture results row in an array
        $aRow = $rsTmp->fetchRow(DB_FETCHMODE_ASSOC);

        // build return array
        $return["Ad Id"] = $aRow["ad_id"];
        $return["Client Id"] = $aRow["ad_client_id"];
        $return["URL"] = $aRow["ad_url"];
        $return["Title"] = $aRow["ad_title"];
        $return["Path"] = $aRow["ad_path"];
        $return["Client"]["Name"] = $aRow["ad_client_name"];
        $return["Client"]["Contact"] = $aRow["ad_client_contact"];
        $return["Client"]["Email"] = $aRow["ad_client_email"];
        $return["Client"]["Phone"] = $aRow["ad_client_phone"];
        $return["Status"] = $aRow["status"];
        $return["Deleted"] = $aRow["deleted"];
        $return["Deleted Date"] = strtotime($aRow["deleted_dt"]);
        $return["Created Date"] = strtotime($aRow["created_dt"]);
        $return["Modified Date"] = strtotime($aRow["modified_dt"]);
        return $return;
    }
```

This method returns information about an advertising client:

```
/**
 * get single client by ID
 *
 * @return array
 * @access public
 */
function getClient() {

    // get advertisement record
    $sql = "SELECT
                ad_client_name,
                ad_client_contact,
                ad_client_email,
                ad_client_phone,
                status,
                deleted,
                deleted_dt,
                created_dt,
                modified_dt
            FROM
                ".PREFIX."_ads_clients
            WHERE
```

```
                                ad_client_id=".$this->_id;

            if( DB::isError($rsTmp = $this->_oConn->query($sql)) ) {

                catchExc($rsTmp->getMessage());
                return FALSE;
            }

            // capture results row in an array
            $aRow = $rsTmp->fetchRow(DB_FETCHMODE_ASSOC);

            // build return array
            $return["Name"] = $aRow["ad_client_name"];
            $return["Contact"] = $aRow["ad_client_contact"];
            $return["Email"] = $aRow["ad_client_email"];
            $return["Phone"] = $aRow["ad_client_phone"];
            $return["Status"] = $aRow["status"];
            $return["Deleted"] = $aRow["deleted"];
            $return["Deleted Date"] = strtotime($aRow["deleted_dt"]);
            $return["Created Date"] = strtotime($aRow["created_dt"]);
            $return["Modified Date"] = strtotime($aRow["modified_dt"]);
            return $return;
    }
```

The following function is used to return an associative array of client information for populating a client list in our advertisement forms:

```
    /**
     * get actively associated clients list
     *
     * @return array
     * @access public
     */
    function getClientsList() {

        // get clients from db
        $sql = "SELECT
                    ad_client_id,
                    ad_client_name
                FROM
                    ".PREFIX."_ads_clients
                WHERE
                    deleted=0 AND
                    status=1
                ORDER BY
                    ad_client_name";

        if( DB::isError($rsTmp = $this->_oConn->query($sql)) ) {

            catchExc($rsTmp->getMessage());
            return FALSE;
        }
```

```
      // loop through results and build return array
      $i = 0;
      while( $aRow = $rsTmp->fetchRow(DB_FETCHMODE_ASSOC) ) {

          $return[$i]["Client Id"] = $aRow["ad_client_id"];
          $return[$i]["Client"] = $aRow["ad_client_name"];
          ++$i;
      }
      return $return;
}
```

We will need to display a detailed report of activity for our advertisements, as below:

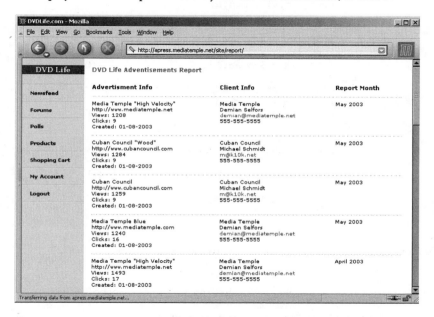

Such clear and concise activity information (as listed in the above screenshot) will certainly help in calculating our billing. The following function will return such a list by querying all of the tables in our advertising system, conditionally matching keys to relative indexes, and finally building a large associative array that will be returned to the web page:

```
/**
 * get advertisements activity report data
 *
 * @return array
 * @access public
 */
```

```
function getAdsReport() {

    // get report data
    $sql = "SELECT
                a.ad_title,
                a.ad_url,
                a.created_dt,
                c.ad_client_name,
                c.ad_client_contact,
                c.ad_client_email,
                c.ad_client_phone,
                r.ad_view_cnt,
                r.ad_click_cnt,
                r.ad_activity_month,
                r.ad_activity_year
            FROM
                ".PREFIX."_ads a,
                ".PREFIX."_ads_clients c,
                ".PREFIX."_ads_activity r
            WHERE
                a.ad_client_id=c.ad_client_id
                AND r.ad_id=a.ad_id
                AND a.deleted=0
            ORDER BY
                r.ad_activity_year DESC,
                r.ad_activity_month DESC";

    if( DB::isError($rsTmp = $this->_oConn->query($sql)) ) {

        catchExc($rsTmp->getMessage());
        return FALSE;
    }
```

The while loop, loops through the result and builds the return array:

```
    $i = 0;
    while( $aRow = $rsTmp->fetchRow(DB_FETCHMODE_ASSOC) ) {

        $return[$i]["Title"] = $aRow["ad_title"];
        $return[$i]["URL"] = $aRow["ad_url"];
        $return[$i]["Client"]["Name"] = $aRow["ad_client_name"];
        $return[$i]["Client"]["Contact"] = $aRow["ad_client_contact"];
        $return[$i]["Client"]["Email"] = $aRow["ad_client_email"];
        $return[$i]["Client"]["Phone"] = $aRow["ad_client_phone"];
        $return[$i]["View Count"] = $aRow["ad_view_cnt"];
        $return[$i]["Click Count"] = $aRow["ad_click_cnt"];
        $return[$i]["Month"] = $aRow["ad_activity_month"];
        $return[$i]["Year"] = $aRow["ad_activity_year"];
        $return[$i]["Created Date"] = strtotime($aRow["created_dt"]);
        ++$i;
    }
    return $return;
}
```

The 'add' methods are some of the most complex methods in the advertisement data object. This method is called when a new advertising client or a new advertisement is added to the system. So we need to ensure that the following actions take place:

❑ Lock tables until the INSERT query has been completed successfully and the unique identifier can be retrieved. This ensures that another item is not added later resulting in an inaccurately returned identifier.

❑ Add a client record if a client identifier was not passed in the add arguments. This would indicate that a client was not selected from the client list and that we must add one.

Here are the addAd() and addClient() methods:

```php
/**
 * add new advertisement record
 *
 * @param array $aArgs advertisement data
 * @return boolean
 * @access public
 */
function addAd($aArgs) {

    // if no client ID was passed
    if( empty($aArgs["Client Id"]) ) {

        $aArgs["Client Id"] = $this->addClient($aArgs);
    }

    // insert new advertisement record
    $sql = "INSERT INTO ".PREFIX."_ads (
                    ad_client_id,
                    ad_url,
                    ad_title,
                    ad_path,
                    status,
                    created_dt,
                    modified_dt
            ) VALUES (
                    ".$aArgs["Client Id"].",
                    '".$aArgs["URL"]."',
                    '".$aArgs["Title"]."',
                    '".$aArgs["Path"]."',
                    1,
                    (NOW()),
                    (NOW())
            )";

    if( DB::isError($rsTmp = $this->_oConn->query($sql)) ) {

        catchExc($rsTmp->getMessage());
        return FALSE;
    }

    return TRUE;
}

/**
 * add new client record
```

```
 *
 * @param array $aArgs client data
 * @return boolean
 * @access public
 */
function addClient($aArgs) {

    // lock tables to capture unique identifier
    $sql = "LOCK TABLES ".PREFIX."_ads_clients WRITE";

    if( DB::isError($rsTmp = $this->_oConn->query($sql)) ) {

        catchExc($rsTmp->getMessage());
        return FALSE;
    }

    // insert new client record
    $sql = "INSERT INTO ".PREFIX."_ads_clients (
                    ad_client_name,
                    ad_client_contact,
                    ad_client_email,
                    ad_client_phone
            ) VALUES (
                    '".$aArgs["Client"]["Name"]."',
                    '".$aArgs["Client"]["Contact"]."',
                    '".$aArgs["Client"]["Email"]."',
                    '".$aArgs["Client"]["Phone"]."'
            )";

    if( DB::isError($rsTmp = $this->_oConn->query($sql)) ) {

        catchExc($rsTmp->getMessage());
        return FALSE;
    }

    // get unique client ID
    $sql = "SELECT MAX(ad_client_id)
            FROM ".PREFIX."_ads_clients";

    if( DB::isError($iClientId = $this->_oConn->getOne($sql)) ) {

        catchExc($iClientId->getMessage());
        return FALSE;
    }

    // unlock tables
    $sql = "UNLOCK TABLES";

    if( DB::isError($rsTmp = $this->_oConn->query($sql)) ) {

        catchExc($rsTmp->getMessage());
        return FALSE;
    }

    return $iClientId;
}
```

Contrary to the `addClient()` method, the 'edit' method is quite simple. We don't check to see if the image path has changed in order to delete the old image and replace the new one; however, this is a recommended procedure if the storage directory is becoming inundated with legacy content. You may wish to archive this file into a BLOB column, or perhaps move the file to an archived or soft delete directory on the web server. Our edit client method is a simple updation of string data into the table.

A soft delete does not actually remove the record from the database; instead it flags the record as deleted so that it's not displayed on the public web site.

Here are the `editAd()` and `editClient()` methods:

```php
/**
 * edit a advertisement record
 *
 * @param array $aArgs advertisement data
 * @return boolean
 * @access public
 */
function editAd($aArgs) {

    // initialize SQL filter
    $sFilter = "";

    // if a file was uploaded, ad path value to SQL filter
    if( !empty($aArgs["Path"]) )
        $sFilter = "ad_path='".$aArgs["Path"]."', ";

    // update advertisement record
    $sql = "UPDATE ".PREFIX."_ads
            SET
                ad_client_id=".$aArgs["Client Id"].",
                ad_url='".$aArgs["URL"]."',
                ad_title='".$aArgs["Title"]."',
                ".$sFilter."
                modified_dt=(NOW())
            WHERE
                ad_id=".$this->_id;

    if( DB::isError($rsTmp = $this->_oConn->query($sql)) ) {

        catchExc($rsTmp->getMessage());
        return FALSE;
    }

    return TRUE;
}

/**
 * edit a client record
 *
 * @param array $aArgs client data
 * @return boolean
```

```
     * @access public
     */
    function editClient($aArgs) {

        // update client record
        $sql = "UPDATE ".PREFIX."_ads_clients
                SET
                    ad_client_name='".$aArgs["Client"]["Name"]."',
                    ad_client_contact='".$aArgs["Client"]["Contact"]."',
                    ad_client_email='".$aArgs["Client"]["Email"]."',
                    ad_client_phone='".$aArgs["Client"]["Phone"]."',
                    modified_dt=(NOW())
                WHERE
                    ad_client_id=".$this->_id;

        if( DB::isError($rsTmp = $this->_oConn->query($sql)) ) {

            catchExc($rsTmp->getMessage());
            return FALSE;
        }

        return TRUE;
    }
```

Whenever a web page is rendered, we need to display an advertisement if the page template calls for it. To do so requires us to increment our view count to record the impression made by the browser. Before we can update the count, we need to make sure that an activity record exists for the particular advertisement. If it does not exist then we need to create a new one.

The REPLACE INTO query in MySQL gives the same result as this method emulates by first attempting an update, and adding the record (if no rows are affected). This would seemingly be more efficient; however, note that REPLACE INTO will always delete the matching record and re-create it each time resulting in a new unique identifier value and two transactions. Since the UPDATE query will only affect any row once per month, per impression, it's more efficient to use this practice.

The next method gets a random advertisement:

```
    /**
     * get a random advertisement
     *
     * @return array
     * @access public
     */
    function getRandomAd() {

        $sql = "SELECT
                    ad_id,
                    ad_client_id,
                    ad_title,
                    ad_url,
                    ad_path
                FROM
                    ".PREFIX."_ads
                WHERE
```

```
                    status=1 AND
                    deleted=0
              ORDER BY
                    rand()
              LIMIT 0, 1";

if( DB::isError($rsTmp = $this->_oConn->query($sql)) ) {

    catchExc($rsTmp->getMessage());
    return FALSE;
}

// assign result to array
$aRow = $rsTmp->fetchRow(DB_FETCHMODE_ASSOC);

// assign return array values
$return["Ad Id"] = $aRow["ad_id"];
$return["Client Id"] = $aRow["ad_client_id"];
$return["Title"] = $aRow["ad_title"];
$return["URL"] = $aRow["ad_url"];
$return["Path"] = $aRow["ad_path"];
```

Next, update the advertisement activity:

```
$sql = "UPDATE ".PREFIX."_ads_activity
        SET
            ad_view_cnt=ad_view_cnt+1,
            ad_activity_month=".date("m").",
            ad_activity_year=".date("Y")."
        WHERE
            ad_id=".$aRow["ad_id"]." AND
            ad_activity_month=".date("m")." AND
            ad_activity_year=".date("Y");

if( DB::isError($rsTmp = $this->_oConn->query($sql)) ) {

    catchExc($rsTmp->getMessage());
    return FALSE;
}
```

The if loop checks if the update affected any rows:

```
if( $this->_oConn->affectedRows() < 1 ) {

    // add new record for auditing
    $sql = "INSERT INTO ".PREFIX."_ads_activity (
                        ad_id,
                        ad_view_cnt,
                        ad_activity_month,
                        ad_activity_year
                ) VALUES (
                        ".$aRow["ad_id"].",
                        1,
                        ".date("m").",
                        ".date("Y")."
                )";
```

```
            if( DB::isError($rsTmp = $this->_oConn->query($sql)) ) {

                catchExc($rsTmp->getMessage());
                return FALSE;
            }
        }

    return $return;
}
```

The 'redirect' method works similar to the activity logging; though it's a simpler method, since we don't have to capture an advertisement:

```
/**
 * redirect advertisement on user click
 *
 * @return boolean
 * @access public
 */
function redirectAd() {

    // update activity logs
    $sql = "UPDATE ".PREFIX."_ads_activity SET
                ad_click_cnt=ad_click_cnt+1,
                ad_activity_month=".date("m").",
                ad_activity_year=".date("Y")."
            WHERE
                ad_id=".$this->_id." AND
                ad_activity_month=".date("m")." AND
                ad_activity_year=".date("Y");

    if( DB::isError($rsTmp = $this->_oConn->query($sql)) ) {

        catchExc($rsTmp->getMessage());
        return FALSE;
    }

    // check if any rows were updated
    if( $this->_oConn->affectedRows() < 1 ) {

        // add new activity record
        $sql = "INSERT INTO ".PREFIX."_ads_activity (
                    ad_id,
                    ad_click_cnt,
                    ad_activity_month,
                    ad_activity_year
                ) VALUES (
                    ".$iAdId.",
                    1,
                    ".date("m").",
                    ".date("Y")."
                )";

        if( DB::isError($rsTmp = $this->_oConn->query($sql)) ) {

            catchExc($rsTmp->getMessage());
            return FALSE;
```

```
        }
    }
    return TRUE;
}
```

The last six class methods are used to delete, activate, and deactivate the advertisement and advertising client items. These are generic functions that are used similarly throughout the application data objects:

```
/**
 * delete an advertisement record
 *
 * @return boolean
 * @access public
 */
function deleteAd() {

    $sql = "UPDATE ".PREFIX."_ads
        SET
            deleted=1,
            deleted_dt=(NOW())
        WHERE
            ad_id=".$this->_id;

    if( DB::isError($rsTmp = $this->_oConn->query($sql)) ) {

        catchExc($rsTmp->getMessage());
        return FALSE;
    }

    $this->deactivateAd();
    return TRUE;
}
```

This method deletes a client record:

```
/**
 * delete a client record
 *
 * @return boolean
 * @access public
 */
function deleteClient() {

    $sql = "UPDATE ".PREFIX."_ads_clients
        SET
            status=0,
            deleted=1,
            deleted_dt=(NOW())
        WHERE
            ad_client_id=".$this->_id;

    if( DB::isError($rsTmp = $this->_oConn->query($sql)) ) {

        catchExc($rsTmp->getMessage());
        return FALSE;
    }
```

```
        $sql = "UPDATE ".PREFIX."_ads
                SET
                    status=0,
                    deleted=1,
                    deleted_dt=(NOW() )
                WHERE
                    ad_client_id=".$this->_id;

        if( DB::isError($rsTmp = $this->_oConn->query($sql)) ) {

            catchExc($rsTmp->getMessage());
            return FALSE;
        }
    }
```

This method activates an advertisement record:

```
    /**
     * activate an advertisement record
     *
     * @return boolean
     * @access public
     */
    function activateAd() {

        $sql = "UPDATE ".PREFIX."_ads
                SET
                    status=1
                WHERE
                    ad_id=".$this->_id;

        if( DB::isError($rsTmp = $this->_oConn->query($sql)) ) {

            catchExc($rsTmp->getMessage());
            return FALSE;
        }
    }
```

And this method activates a client record:

```
    /**
     * activate a client record
     *
     * @return boolean
     * @access public
     */
    function activateClient() {

        $sql = "UPDATE ".PREFIX."_ads_clients
                SET
                    status=1
                WHERE
                    ad_client_id=".$this->_id;

        if( DB::isError($rsTmp = $this->_oConn->query($sql)) ) {

            catchExc($rsTmp->getMessage());
            return FALSE;
```

```
            }
        }
```

This method deactivates an advertisement record:

```
    /**
     * deactivate an advertisement record
     *
     * @return boolean
     * @access public
     */
    function deactivateAd() {

        $sql = "UPDATE ".PREFIX."_ads
                SET
                    status=0
                WHERE
                    ad_id=".$this->_id;

        if( DB::isError($rsTmp = $this->_oConn->query($sql)) ) {

            catchExc($rsTmp->getMessage());
            return FALSE;
        }
    }
```

And this method deactivates a client record:

```
    /**
     * deactivate a client record
     *
     * @return boolean
     * @access public
     */
    function deactivateClient() {

        $sql = "UPDATE ".PREFIX."_ads_clients
                SET
                    status=0
                WHERE
                    ad_client_id=".$this->_id;

        if( DB::isError($rsTmp = $this->_oConn->query($sql)) ) {

            catchExc($rsTmp->getMessage());
            return FALSE;
        }
    }
} // close the class definition
?>
```

That's all there is to it – at this point we should have a fully functioning data object. Now let's take a look at the pages involved in both the CMS and the web site, which will use this class.

Presentation Layer

Now that all of our application logic has been implemented, we need to tie its functionality into the web pages. Since we are only dealing with banner advertisements, this is a relatively small process. We'll start with the CMS system to see how we can allow for easy management of the banners.

We know that there are four main views that need to be accommodated. Let's make a short list to define those uses:

- ❏ CMS advertisement listing (`/core/ads/index.php`)
- ❏ CMS advertisement management form (`/core/ads/form.php`)
- ❏ CMS client listing page (`/core/clients/index.php`)
- ❏ CMS client management form (`/core/clients/form.php`)

We also need some PHP scripts to:

- ❏ Implement the advertisement on the public web site (`/site/tpl_unsecure.php`)
- ❏ Redirect the page upon click-through (`/site/redirect.php`)
- ❏ Display the auditing report page (`/site/report/index.php`)

We'll be including `/site/tpl_unsecure.php` on our public pages and using it to generate menus, banner advertisements, and the footer for the page. Similarly we will use the `tpl_secure.php` file to render the page framework for pages inside the CMS application. With this in mind, let's start with the `/core/ads/index.php` file.

CMS Advertisement Listing

As we've seen in our other applications, we need a listing page to show us all of the advertisements in the system, like this:

Now, let's take a look at the code used to generate this page:

```php
<?php

// File Location: /core/ads/index.php

// template framework file for pages inside CMS
require_once("tpl_secure.php");

// data object for advertisements logic
require_once("class.ads.php");

// instantiate ads class
$oAds = new ads;

// get users and user count
$aAds = $oAds->getAds("created_dt DESC", $iCursor);
$iCnt = $oAds->getAdsCount();

// check for users
if( count($aAds) ) {

    // build page data array
    $i = 0;
```

```
    while( $i < count($aAds) ) {
        $aData[$i]["Id"] = $aAds[$i]["Ad Id"];
        $aData[$i]["Name"] = $aAds[$i]["Title"];
        $aData[$i]["Status"] = $aAds[$i]["Status"];
        $aData[$i]["Created"] =$aAds[$i]["Created Date"];
        ++$i;
    }
}

// check for ID
if( $id ) {

    // assign News ID
    $oAds->setId($id);

    // check operation type
    if( !strcmp($op, "del") ) {

        // try deleting the advertisement and redirect
        $oAds->deleteAd();
        header("Location: ".SELF);

    } elseif ( !strcmp($op, "act") ) {

        // try activating the advertisement and redirect
        $oAds->activateAd();
        header("Location: ".SELF);

    } elseif ( !strcmp($op, "deact") ) {

        // try deactivating the advertisement and redirect
        $oAds->deactivateAd();
        header("Location: ".SELF);
    }
}
```

We'll call the generic setHeader() and openPage() functions that render the appropriate HTML framework for our page. These functions can be reviewed in their defining file (/core/tpl_secure.php):

```
setHeader();
openPage();
?>
```

Again, the above code is somewhat of a generic implementation across our CMS applications. The remainder of the page is the simple HTML for page errors and notices, instructions, and the generic list rendering call that is passed from the array above:

```
<?php renderList($iCnt, $aData) ?>
```

CMS Advertisement Management Form

The next page we shall look at is the forms page that will handle both the 'add' and 'edit' activity in the CMS.

During the 'add' mode, the client list appears as a select box in the top of the page, like so:

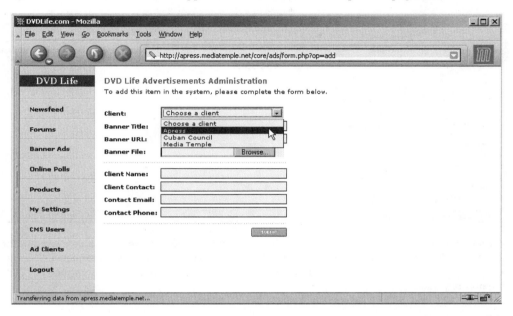

If the user does not select a client, they will be forced to enter a new client by using the additional fields below the advertisement fields.

The following is the same page in the 'edit' mode, where the client information is not editable (as seen in the following screenshot). However, if we select a new associative client for our advertisement, and the current client is left un-associated, then it will no longer appear in the client list due to the nature of our client list function:

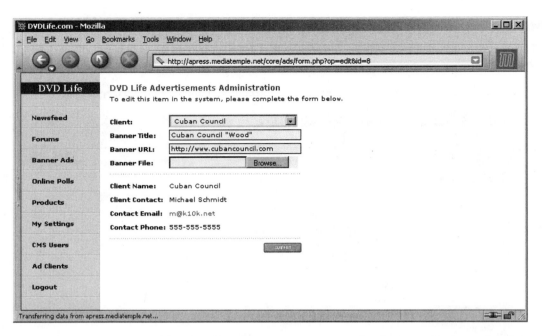

The differentiation between the 'add' and 'edit' functionality is made by the $op value passed in the $_GET variables, which is an operation identifier that tells the form page which mode to render. Let's now look at the code that renders the form pages and how it handles the user-entered data to complete a submission request:

```php
<?php

// File Location: /core/ads/form.php

// template framework file for pages inside CMS
require_once("tpl_secure.php");

// data input validation functions
require_once("handlers.php");

// data object for advertisements logic
require_once("class.ads.php");

// instantiate ads class
$oAds = new ads;

// check for ID
if( $id ) {
```

```
        // assign unique ID
        $oAds->setId($id);
    }
```

The `if` loop is executed if the form was posted:

```
if( $_POST ) {

    // assign page variables
    $iClientId = $_POST["clientid"];
    $sTitle = $_POST["title"];
    $sUrl = $_POST["url"];
    $sPath = "";
    $sClient = $_POST["client"];
    $sContact = $_POST["contact"];
    $sEmail = $_POST["email"];
    $sPhone = $_POST["phone"];
```

Then the advertisement title and advertisement URL are validated:

```
    if( !validInput($sTitle, 1, 200) ) {

        catchErr("Enter a valid advertisement title");
        $FORMOK = FALSE;
    }

    if( !validUrl($sUrl) ) {

        catchErr("Enter a advertisement URL");
        $FORMOK = FALSE;
    }
```

Next we check for the uploaded file:

```
    if( is_uploaded_file($_FILES["banner"]["tmp_name"]) ) {

        // get file extension
        if( !$sExt = validFile("banner") ) {

            $FORMOK = FALSE;

        } else {

            // generate random unique file name
            $iRand = rand(100001, 999999);
            $sImgName = md5(strtotime(date("Y-m-d
                         H:i:s")).$iRand).".".$sExt;
            $sPath = SITE_URL."/_img/_banners/".$sImgName;
        }

    } else { // file not uploaded
```

```
        // if the operation is add, then catch an error
        if( !strcmp("add", $op) ) {

            catchErr("Upload a banner image file");
            $FORMOK = FALSE;
        }
    }
```

Once the client ID is validated the rest of the client information is checked, like the client name, contact e-mail address, and so on:

```
    // validate client ID
    if( $iClientId < 1 && !strcmp("add", $op) ) {

        // validate client name
        if( !validInput($_POST["client"], 1, 100) ) {

            catchErr("Enter a client name");
            $FORMOK = FALSE;
        }

        // validate client contact
        if( !validInput($sContact, 1, 100) ) {

            catchErr("Enter a client contact name");
            $FORMOK = FALSE;
        }

        // validate client contact e-mail
        if( !validEmail($sEmail) ) {

            catchErr("Enter a client contact email address");
            $FORMOK = FALSE;
        }

        // validate client contact phone
        if( !validInput($sPhone, 1, 20) ) {

            catchErr("Enter a client contact phone number");
            $FORMOK = FALSE;
        }

    } elseif ( $iClientId < 1 && !strcmp("edit", $op) ) {

        catchErr("Select a client");
        $FORMOK = FALSE;
    }
```

The following loop is executed if the form variables validated correctly:

```
    if( $FORMOK ) {

        // assign item values
        $aArgs["Client Id"] = $iClientId;
        $aArgs["Title"] = $sTitle;
        $aArgs["URL"] = $sUrl;
```

```
            $aArgs["Path"] = $sPath;
            $aArgs["Client"]["Name"] = $sClient;
            $aArgs["Client"]["Contact"] = $sContact;
            $aArgs["Client"]["Email"] = $sEmail;
            $aArgs["Client"]["Phone"] = $sPhone;

            // check operation type
            if( !strcmp("edit", $op) ) {

                // try edit advertisement
                $FORMOK = $oAds->editAd($aArgs);

            } elseif ( !strcmp("add", $op) ) {

                // try adding an advertisement
                $FORMOK = $oAds->addAd($aArgs);
            }

            // redirect if successful
            if( $FORMOK ) {

                // copy file
                copy($_FILES["banner"]["tmp_name"],
                    "../../_img/_banners/".$sImgName);

                // redirect if successful
                header("Location: index.php");
            }
        }
```

This part of the main `if` loop is executed if the POST variables aren't send:

```
    } else {

        // initialize page variables
        if( !strcmp("edit", $op) ) {

            // get advertisement
            $aAd = $oAds->getAd();

            // initialize page variables
            $iClientId = $aAd["Client Id"];
            $sTitle = $aAd["Title"];
            $sUrl = $aAd["URL"];
            $sClient = $aAd["Client"]["Name"];
            $sContact = $aAd["Client"]["Contact"];
            $sEmail = $aAd["Client"]["Email"];
            $sPhone = $aAd["Client"]["Phone"];
        }
    }

    setHeader();
    openPage();
    ?>
```

Note that the switch, used in several pages throughout the page processing, determines how to render the page, as well as how to handle the data submitted from the client form.

Let's briefly look at the code inside the HTML to see how we switch display options based on the operation type:

```php
<?php if( !strcmp("add", $op) ) { ?>

    <tr>
        <td><div class="formlabel">Client Name:</div></td>
        <td><input type="text" name="client"
         value="<?php print clean($sClient) ?>" class="textfield" /></td>
    </tr>

    <tr>
        <td><div class="formlabel">Client Contact:</div></td>
        <td><input type="text" name="contact"
         value="<?php print clean($sContact) ?>" class="textfield" /></td>
    </tr>

    <tr>
        <td><div class="formlabel">Contact Email:</div></td>
        <td><input type="text" name="email"
         value="<?php print clean($sEmail) ?>" class="textfield" /></td>
    </tr>

    <tr>
        <td><div class="formlabel">Contact Phone:</div></td>
        <td><input type="text" name="phone"
         value="<?php print clean($sPhone) ?>" class="textfield" /></td>
    </tr>

    <tr>
        <td class="dotrule" colspan="2"><img src="../../_img/spc.gif"
         width="1" height="15" alt="" border="0" /></td>
    </tr>

<?php } else { ?>

    <tr>
        <td><div class="formlabel">Client Name:</div></td>
        <td><?php print format($sClient) ?></td>
    </tr>

    <tr>
        <td><div class="formlabel">Client Contact:</div></td>
        <td><?php print format($sContact) ?></td>
    </tr>

    <tr>
        <td><div class="formlabel">Contact Email:</div></td>
        <td><?php print format($sEmail) ?></td>
    </tr>

    <tr>
        <td><div class="formlabel">Contact Phone:</div></td>
        <td><?php print format($sPhone) ?></td>
    </tr>

    <tr>
        <td class="dotrule" colspan="2"><img src="../../_img/spc.gif"
         width="1" height="15" alt="" border="0" /></td>
```

```
        </tr>

<?php } ?>
```

CMS Client Listing Page

Now let's look at the same practices being applied to manage the advertising clients within our CMS application.

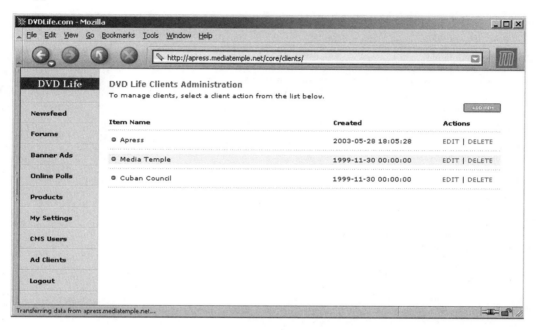

Here is the code that creates the client listing page:

```php
<?php

// File Location: /core/clients/index.php

// template framework file for pages inside CMS
require_once("tpl_secure.php");

// data object for advertisements logic
require_once("class.ads.php");

// instantiate ads class
$oAds = new ads;
```

```
// get users and user count
$aClients = $oAds->getClients("created_dt DESC", $iCursor);
$iCnt = $oAds->getClientsCount();
```

The `if` loop checks for users:

```
if( count($aClients) ) {

    // build page data array
    $i = 0;
    while( $i < count($aClients) ) {
        $aData[$i]["Id"] = $aClients[$i]["Client Id"];
        $aData[$i]["Name"] = $aClients[$i]["Client"];
        $aData[$i]["Status"] = $aClients[$i]["Status"];
        $aData[$i]["Created"] =$aClients[$i]["Created Date"];
        ++$i;
    }
}

// check for ID
if( $id ) {

    // assign unique ID
    $oAds->setId($id);

    // check operation type
    if( !strcmp($op, "del") ) {

        // try delete client and redirect
        $oAds->deleteClient();
        header("Location: ".SELF);

    } elseif ( !strcmp($op, "act") ) {

        // try activate client and redirect
        $oAds->activateClient();
        header("Location: ".SELF);

    } elseif ( !strcmp($op, "deact") ) {

        // try deactivate client and redirect
        $oAds->deactivateClient();
        header("Location: ".SELF);
    }
}

setHeader();
openPage();
?>
```

CMS Client Management Form

This is the form page that's used to manage our client's information:

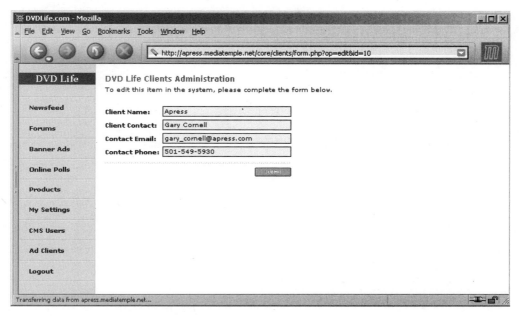

Here is the code for the client's form page:

```php
<?php

// File Location: /core/clients/form.php

// template framework file for pages inside CMS
require_once("tpl_secure.php");

// data input validation functions
require_once("handlers.php");

// data object for advertisements logic
require_once("class.ads.php");

// instantiate ads class
$oAds = new ads;

// check for ID
if( $id ) {

    // assign unique ID
    $oAds->setId($id);
}
```

The following `if` loop checks for HTTP POST variables and tries to validate the form:

```php
if( $_POST ) {

    // assign page variables
    $sClient = $_POST["client"];
    $sContact = $_POST["contact"];
    $sEmail = $_POST["email"];
    $sPhone = $_POST["phone"];

    // validate client name
    if( !validInput($_POST["client"], 1, 100) ) {

        catchErr("Enter a client name");
        $FORMOK = FALSE;
    }

    // validate client contact
    if( !validInput($sContact, 1, 100) ) {

        catchErr("Enter a client contact name");
        $FORMOK = FALSE;
    }

    // validate client contact e-mail
    if( !validEmail($sEmail) ) {

        catchErr("Enter a client contact email address");
        $FORMOK = FALSE;
    }

    // validate client contact phone
    if( !validInput($sPhone, 1, 20) ) {

        catchErr("Enter a client contact phone number");
        $FORMOK = FALSE;
    }
```

The next bit of code is executed if the form variables are validated:

```php
if( $FORMOK ) {

    // assign item values
    $aArgs["Client"]["Name"] = $sClient;
    $aArgs["Client"]["Contact"] = $sContact;
    $aArgs["Client"]["Email"] = $sEmail;
    $aArgs["Client"]["Phone"] = $sPhone;

    // check operation type
    if( !strcmp("edit", $op) ) {

        // try editing an advertising client record
        // with the data contained in the $aArgs array argument passed.
```

```
            $FORMOK = $oAds->editClient($aArgs);

     } elseif ( !strcmp("add", $op) ) {

          // try add a new advertising client to the system, where
          // $aArgs passes all of the client data for the new item.
          $FORMOK = $oAds->addClient($aArgs);
     }

     // redirect if successful
     if( $FORMOK ) {

          // redirect if successful
          header("Location: index.php");
     }
  }
```

And this bit of the loop is executed if the POST variables are not sent:

```
} else {

     // initialize page variables
     if( !strcmp("edit", $op) ) {

          // get advertisement
          $aClient = $oAds->getClient();

          // initialize page variables
          $sClient = $aClient["Name"];
          $sContact = $aClient["Contact"];
          $sEmail = $aClient["Email"];
          $sPhone = $aClient["Phone"];
     }
}

setHeader();
openPage();
?>
```

Front-End Implementation of the Advertisement

Here is the front-end implementation of a banner advertisement in the public web site:

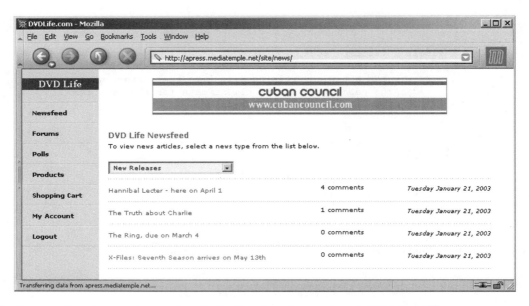

The banner advertisement is prominently displayed on the top center of the page. This is consistent on all of our front-end pages unless otherwise specified in the template construction calls. The banner will change, randomly, on each page load and will also update our activity table each time an impression is made.

Now we'll look at the code that is used to call the banner into the page template. First we'll include the ads class in the page:

```php
<?php

// File Location: /site/tpl_unsecure.php

// data object for advertisements logic
require_once("class.ads.php");
```

This is followed by some almost static HTML and consists of a few simple functions that are quite like subroutines, since they don't display any values – they just write the needed HTML for the page framework.

Let's continue with the script further down the page where it would be embedded:

```php
<?php
if( $bBanner ) {

    $oAds = new ads;
    $aAd = $oAds->getRandomAd();
?>
```

The `$bBanner` variable is an argument that is defined in our function construct for the template call that renders the relevant portion of the page.

We first instantiated the `ads` object, and grabbed a random advertisement that triggers the view or impression update. Now we print the contents of the advertisement array appropriately to inline our banner advertisement:

```html
<tr>
    <td align="center"><div class="banner">
        <a href="../redirect.php?id=<?php print $aAd["Ad Id"] ?>
        &url=<?php print $aAd["URL"] ?>" target="_blank">
        <img src="<?php print $aAd["Path"] ?>"
        width="468" height="60" alt="" border="0" /></a></div></td>
</tr>

<?php } ?>
```

Redirect Page via Click-Through

When the banner is clicked-through by a site visitor it will call the `redirect.php` page. This page has a very simple purpose – update the click count and re-route the browser to the associated link passed in the `$_GET` variables.

Let's look at this script to see how the second type of revenue can be generated:

```php
<?php

// File Location: /site/redirect.php
```

The `funcs.php` file is being included here since we aren't dependent on a template for this page. Otherwise the `funcs.php` file would have already been included for us:

```php
// utility functions for the application
require_once("funcs.php");

// data object for advertisements logic
require_once("class.ads.php");

// instantiate ads class
$oAd = new ads;

// check the $id GET variable
if( $_GET["id"] > 1 ) {

    // get advertisement
    $id = (int) $_GET["id"];
    $oAd->setId($id);

    // redirect
    if( $oAd->redirectAd() ) {

        // send location header
        header("Location: ".$_GET["url"]);
```

```
    }

} else { // if the advertisement was not valid

    // then send to the referrer instead of hanging on a dead page
    header("Location: ".$_SERVER["HTTP_REFERER"]);
}
?>
```

Note that we haven't URL encoded the redirect value, since we are certain that our value is valid as we did a preg_match check on it in the form handler inside the CMS.

Auditing Reports Page

Finally, here is the auditing reports page, which issues our billing statement (the real-time invoice):

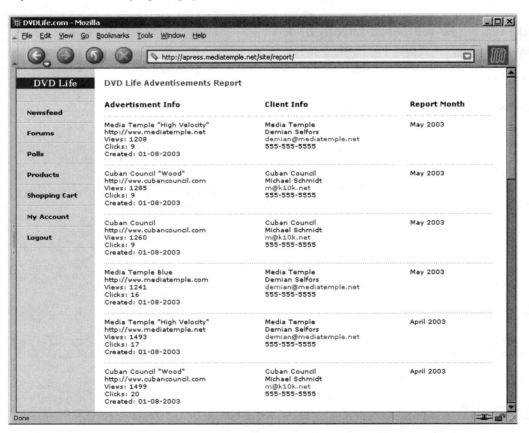

Let's take a look at the code used to render this page. Remember that we created a function to return an organized data set containing the report information, so our page needs to do little more than display that information.

First we'll need to include our dependent files and then open the page:

```php
<?php

// File Location: /site/report/index.php

// template file for pages outside CMS
require_once("tpl_unsecure.php");

// data object for advertisements logic
require_once("class.ads.php");

$oAds = new ads;

$aReport = $oAds->getAdsReport();

// generate the header information
setHeader();

// start a new page with a banner advertisement
openPage();
?>
```

Next we can loop through the data contained in the $aReport array and organize it on the page:

```php
<?php if( count($aReport) ) { ?>

    <tr>
        <td><div class="section">Advertisment Info</div></td>
        <td><div class="section">Client Info</div></td>
        <td><div class="section">Report Month</div></td>
    </tr>

    <tr>
        <td colspan="3" class="dotrule"><img src="../../_img/spc.gif"
         width="1" height="15" alt="" border="0" /></td>
    </tr>

    <?php
        $i = 0;
        while( $i < count($aReport) ) {

            $sDate = mktime(0, 0, 0, $aReport[$i]["Month"], 1,
                            $aReport[$i]["Year"]);
        ?>

        <tr>
            <td valign="top"><div class="copy">
            <?php print format($aReport[$i]["Title"]) ?><br />
            <?php print format($aReport[$i]["URL"]) ?><br />
            Views: <?php print format($aReport[$i]["View Count"]) ?><br />
            Clicks: <?php print format($aReport[$i]["Click Count"]) ?><br />
```

```
            Created: <?php print date("m-d-Y", $aReport[$i]["Created Date"])
            ?></div></td>

            <td valign="top"><div class="copy">
            <?php print format($aReport[$i]["Client"]["Name"]) ?><br />
            <?php print format($aReport[$i]["Client"]["Contact"]) ?><br />
            <?php print format($aReport[$i]["Client"]["Email"]) ?><br />
            <?php print format($aReport[$i]["Client"]["Phone"]) ?>
            </div></td>

            <td valign="top"><div class="copy">
            <?php print date("F Y", $sDate) ?></div></td>
        </tr>

        <tr>
            <td colspan="3" class="dotrule"><img src="../../_img/spc.gif"
            width="1" height="15" alt="" border="0" /></td>
        </tr>

        <?php
            ++$i;
        } // end while loop
    ?>

<?php } else { ?>

    <tr>
        <td><div class="copy">Sorry, there are no statistics to report
                        at this time.</div></td>
    </tr>

    <?php } ?>
```

Now that we have our reports, a working system for delivering advertising solutions, and a flexible framework for extending the features and functionality of our mechanism we can begin to earn revenues with our web site.

Summary

Throughout the course of this chapter, we discussed different options for implementing reliable, practical, and effective advertising systems into a web site. Hopefully you have learned how to build a similar system that is tailored to the type of advertising model that best suits your needs. Obviously, we could have taken a simpler route requiring less involvement and control to complete this task, however, managing your own profit center often seems like a comfortable approach when beginning an online advertising venture.

At this stage, the following key points should be clear to you when deciding to build an online advertising system:

❑ How to choose a design that is efficient, effective, and practical for your web site needs

❑ Provide a scaleable database design that allows for growth and expansion of both features and functionality

❑ Design an extensible data object to suit your calculated needs

❑ Build the necessary CMS tools for managing advertising content

❑ Implement an advertising mechanism into a public web site

❑ Create a simple, detailed form of reporting the logged advertising activity

In the next chapter we'll look at how to find out what our readers think, by creating an online poll, and how the poll activity can be an effective marketing tool for a web site.

9

Online Polls

How do we solicit feedback from our site visitors without being so formal as to require surveys or unexpected forms during their visit? As you know, polls are not by any means a new web site feature, but they are an effective one. While simple to create and deploy, the benefits of regular usage can uncover minute details about our site that even marketing/content professionals could not gather with such a simple method.

Online polls can prove to be a means of gathering marketing information as well as general demographic information about the target audience. By creating polls that have some correlation to our content we can determine valuable information about our visitors. For instance, we could run a poll where visitors need to choose their favorite movies from a list that consists of different genres of films. From the results of the poll, we can identify which genre is a favorite among our site visitors. Thus we can use the polls to gain insight into the types of DVDs our visitors prefer, how and when they watch DVDs, where they buy them, and so on. This visitor feedback also provides insight into our marketing potential as we now can organize marketing efforts and attract sponsors to advertise on the site.

It's also interesting to maintain a poll archive on our site so we can go back and look through the different polls and their results to see the change in visitor preferences or feedback. Over time we can see how our community is diversifying and expanding based on the ever-changing feedback received in our polls. This archive is also interesting to the visitor in order to see how other poll results are totaled.

Visitors also like to know what their peers think and how they vote so as to know which the most popular response is. This is a reason why polls are usually well-accepted, and why visitors generally vote willingly.

In this chapter, we will:

- ❑ Define the problems that need to be addressed to implement a poll facility, to gauge the opinions of our users, and to generate a sense of community
- ❑ Design and write the code for the polls application
- ❑ Deploy the application into the CMS and the web site

The Problem

To effectively create and apply polls to our web site we need to focus on the poll's ease of use. We want to encourage as much interaction with our polls as possible while not discouraging our visitors from participating, which could produce an inaccurate result. We also don't want our visitors to easily be able to alter the results of our poll by voting excessively for a single item.

Our poll should be user-friendly, yet non-intrusive. It needs to be fast and efficient since we can assume that it'll receive heavy traffic. It should also maintain a visitor's state of interaction for the life of a single poll so that visitors cannot sway the results. We also know that we don't want to restrict user interaction with our poll to just authenticated visitors, but to everyone who visits the web site, although it might be worthwhile to require account authentication.

The polls should allow for multiple answer options to allow for flexibility with the poll questions. In some cases we might only want two possible answers in a TRUE/FALSE type of question. In other cases we may want to allow for several answers for a 'preferred choice' type of poll. This means that we need to allow for a dynamic assignment of poll options in our admin (CMS) system.

We don't want our visitors to be able to easily favor a specific answer by voting repeatedly on a single answer multiple times. Therefore, we need to manage visitor interaction with the poll to try and ensure that each visitor only votes once on a single poll.

We'll also provide some impetus for voting by using the results of the poll as an incentive. Visitors will take the time to vote in order to see how their vote compared with others' votes. By allowing voters to see the results of the current/past poll only after they vote, we can encourage a more widespread voterbase. This also addresses our concern for maintaining the visitors' vote state with the poll so we know how and when to display the poll content.

The lifetime of a poll, or how long you should run the poll before introducing a new one and archiving the present one, is completely a preference of the content manger (web master). Once you have an understanding of the base traffic that your site attracts, you can easily gauge how much time a poll would require to gain responses from the majority of the visitor base. If your site tends to have 10,000 unique visits per week, then we can assume that running your poll for 3 weeks would yield roughly 30,000 responses. However, there is no guarantee that everyone is going to vote and that all of these visitors aren't going to vote more than once. So again, the preference for when to change the poll is completely at the discretion of the content manger.

Let's isolate some of the primary concerns that we have addressed above:

❑ Dynamic poll options

❑ Maintain visitor interaction state for accuracy and incentive

❑ Create a lightweight, high-performance polling system that can easily be managed in our CMS

❑ Incorporate poll archival and retrieval

In the next section, we'll think through a design that allows these features to be implemented.

The Design

Having identified the problems that we need to consider while designing our polls application, we can now begin the design process. As with our previous applications, we'll build the polls application into our CMS and web site framework. The foundation of our application is in the database where our tables define and contain the data that will be used. Our data object will be responsible for handling the business logic for our polls, and the pages are simply an interface to the user input processing and data object retrieval/display of the polls and results.

To gain a better understanding of our application functionality, let's take a look at the intended flow of our polls application:

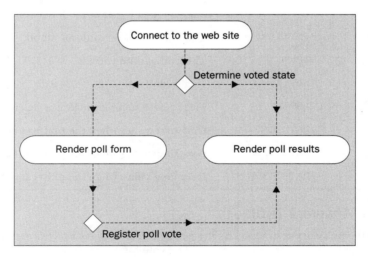

As detailed in the diagram, there are two states in which to render the poll. The first is a form if the visitor does not have a cookie record of the active current poll. The second is the poll results for when the visitor has voted and is paging through the archived polls.

Now that we have taken a glance at the desired functionality of our poll, let's look at the database tables, which will store the poll content.

Designing the Data Layer

We have a one-to-many relationship of poll questions and answers, where each poll consists of a single question with as few as two and as many as six answer options. We can easily store all of our poll data in two tables that relate to one another on the highest common identifier. In this case, that identifier is the poll ID (poll_id).

The two tables will be named as follows:

❑   apress_polls to hold the poll question and the total vote count for the poll

❑   apress_poll_answers to store the poll answers and their vote totals

Let's look at our tables in a little more detail to get a better understanding of the relative data and the proposed design of our polls application.

The Apress Polls Table

This table defines the poll questions to be used as well as the vote count for each poll:

Field	Type	Description
poll_id	INT(10)	The unique identifier for each poll record. This primary key is referenced by the apress_poll_answers dependent table.
poll_vote_cnt	INT(10)	The total count of votes for a poll.
poll_question	TEXT	The poll question string.
Status	INT(1)	Flag to determine the poll status.
Deleted	INT(1)	Flag to determine if the poll is deleted.
created_dt	DATETIME	Date time value when the poll was created.
modified_dt	DATETIME	Date time value when the poll was last modified.
deleted_dt	DATETIME	Date time value when the poll was deleted.

The Apress Poll Answers Table

This table stores the poll answer mapped by the poll_id column. It has a primary key on the poll_answer_id column as a unique identifier. The vote totals are stored in this table and incremented as the votes are cast.

Field	Type	Description
poll_answer_id	INT(10)	The unique identifier for each poll answer option record. This primary key indexes each of the poll answer options uniquely.

Field	Type	Description
poll_id	INT(10)	The identifier for the associative poll. There is an index on this column, to maximize the performance of grouped associative queries.
poll_answer	TEXT	The poll's answer option string.
poll_answer_cnt	INT(10)	The count of votes for the answer option.

Designing the Data Object

The polls data object will handle all of the functionality for managing and using data/content, both in the CMS application as well as in the web site. Note that this data object is relatively small compared to most of our other applications since online polls are comparatively quite simple. Some of the common methods in this class are the setter for the unique identifier, the data collection methods, and the management methods that allow us to change the state and/or delete items in the CMS.

The Polls Class

Let's look at the different class variables needed to provide the functionality desired from our polls data object:

polls Class Variable	Description
_iPollId	Property containing the poll item's unique identifier
_iAnswerId	Property containing the poll answer option's unique identifier
_oConn	Property containing a reference to the PEAR::DB object

We'll also need some class methods that will manipulate these variables and ultimately generate the polls for us. Again, you'll notice common practices used in this class:

polls Class Method	Description
polls($iPollId='')	Constructor method that instantiates the _oConn object. This member also optionally assigns the _iPollId property if passed.
setPollId($iPollId)	Assigns the _iPollId class member to the value passed in the $iPollId argument for the class instance.
setAnswerId($iAnswerId)	Assigns the _iAnswerId class member to the value passed in the $iAnswerId argument for the class instance.

Table continued on following page

polls Class Method	Description
getPollsCount($iStatus=FALSE)	Returns a count of polls within the system. The $iStatus (optional) argument is a Boolean value that returns only active items.
getPolls($sSort, $iPage=0)	Returns an associative array containing the base information for the polls (does not include answer options).
	These are the optional arguments for the method:
	❏ $sSort – String value representing the sort column name.
	❏ $iPage – Integer value representing the cursor position for the limit call.
getActivePolls($iPage=0)	Returns an associative array of active poll data only. The $iPage (optional) argument is an integer value representing the cursor position for the limit call.
	By active, we mean polls that are published in the CMS system.
getPoll()	Returns an associative array containing all of the data elements for a single poll.
getPollAnswers($iPollId)	Returns an associative array containing the answer options for a specific poll.
	The required $iPollId argument is a unique identifier for a specific poll_id field (apress_polls) to return any relative data against.
addPoll($aArgs)	Adds a new poll to the system. The $aArgs argument passes all of the poll data for the new item.
editPoll($aArgs)	Updates a poll record with the data contained in the $aArgs array argument passed.
addVote()	Adds a new vote to the specific poll and increments the poll vote count as well as the answer vote count.
deletePoll()	Deletes a poll record from the system.
activatePoll()	Activates a poll record in the system.
deactivatePoll()	Deactivates a poll record in the system.

The Solution

Now that we have provided a design proposal for building the polls application, let's look at some of the dependent files and the basic architecture of our CMS and web site.

The following diagram shows the different relationships and dependencies of the files within our application framework that are necessary to implement the polls application:

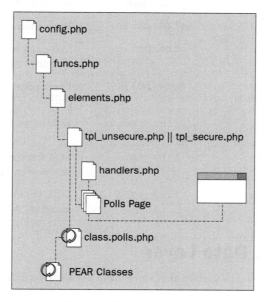

This table describes the location and functional purpose of each file:

As detailed in Chapter 2, the _lib directory contains files like the shared function libraries and custom classes. It includes a _base subdirectory that includes the common function libraries and the global configuration file, a _sql subdirectory that includes the MySQL creation files, and a classes subdirectory that includes the custom classes that are written through the book. All our application modules fall into the site directory, and its polls subdirectory houses the files that define the poll content for the site. The core directory includes the admin tools used to control the site, and new polls will be created in its polls subdirectory.

File Name	File Path	Description
config.php	/_lib/_base/	Configuration values for the application.
funcs.php	/_lib/_base/	Utility functions for the application.
elements.php	/_lib/_base/	Reusable generic elements such as error display functions. This file also assigns the common GET variables of $op and $id.

Table continued on following page

File Name	File Path	Description
tpl_unsecure.php	/site/	Template framework file for pages outside the CMS application.
tpl_secure.php	/core/	Template framework file for pages inside the CMS application.
handlers.php	/_lib/_base/	Data input validation functions.
index.php	/site/polls/	Web site page for polls.
index.php	/core/polls/	List page for polls in the CMS system.
form.php	/core/polls/	Form page for adding and editing polls.
class.polls.php	/_lib/_classes/	Data object for polls logic.
apress_polls.sql	/_lib/_sql/	SQL create script for the apress_polls table.
apress_polls_answers.sql	/_lib/_sql/	SQL create script for the apress_polls_answers table.

Implementing the Data Layer

As mentioned earlier, we need two tables that store all of the relative data for our polls application:

❑ The apress_polls parent table that stores the actual poll question and a count of the poll votes

❑ The apress_polls_answers child table that stores the unique answer options for each poll record as well as the vote count for each option value

apress_polls

Since our poll answer options are dependent on the poll data, we can store the generic application columns of status, deleted, deleted_dt, created_dt, and modified_dt in the parent table:

```
CREATE TABLE apress_polls (
  poll_id       INT(10)  NOT NULL auto_increment,
  poll_vote_cnt INT(10)  NOT NULL default '0',
  poll_question TEXT     NOT NULL,
  status        INT(1)   NOT NULL default '1',
  deleted       INT(1)   NOT NULL default '0',
  deleted_dt    DATETIME NULL default NULL,
  created_dt    DATETIME NOT NULL default '0000-00-00 00:00:00',
  modified_dt   DATETIME NOT NULL default '0000-00-00 00:00:00',
                PRIMARY KEY (poll_id)
) TYPE=MyISAM;
```

apress_polls_answers

The poll answer options table is a simple reference to unique polls with multiple options for each poll:

```
CREATE TABLE apress_polls_answers (
  poll_answer_id  INT(10) NOT NULL auto_increment,
  poll_id         INT(10) NOT NULL default '0',
  poll_answer     TEXT    NOT NULL,
  poll_answer_cnt INT(10) NOT NULL default '0',
                  PRIMARY KEY (poll_answer_id),
                  KEY poll_id_rel (poll_id)
) TYPE=MyISAM;
```

There is no need to store any status information for these records since they are strictly dependent on the `apress_polls` table. We should, however, store the individual vote count for each answer option to ensure an easy means for calculating vote percentages while displaying the poll results.

Implementing the Data Object

Now that we have created the foundation of the polls data, let's look into the data object that will be managing this data and interacting with the presentation layer to deliver the poll for both the CMS and the web site. Our data object is a simple processor that will return data collection sets for our polls.

This object needs to adhere to the following principles:

- ❏ No member variables will be directly exposed. Instead, we'll use get() and set() methods to change them from the outside, if necessary.

- ❏ Method names will be clear and meaningful.

- ❏ The objects will handle and manipulate data, and not concern themselves with the display of this data. This will help to reduce code bloat and will make them more reusable.

class.polls.php

First let's include any files that our class is dependent on so that we can access them easily inside of our object:

```php
<?php

// File Location: /_lib/_classes/class.polls.php

// import the PEAR::DB class
require_once("DB.php");

/*
 * handles poll functions
 */
class polls { // open the class definition

    /**
```

```
    * unique identifier for a poll
    *
    * @var integer
    * @access private
    * @see setPollId()
    */
   var $_iPollId;

   /**
    * unique identifier for a poll answer
    *
    * @var integer
    * @access private
    * @see setAnswerId()
    */
   var $_iAnswerId;

   /**
    * PEAR::DB object
    *
    * @var object
    * @access private
    */
   var $_oConn;
```

Next we'll define our constructor and instantiate any members that may be needed throughout our class usage:

```
   // CONSTRUCTOR

   /**
    * class constructor
    *
    * @param integer $iPollId [optional] poll ID
    * @access public
    */
   function polls($iPollId = '') {

       // implement db object
       $this->_oConn =& DB::connect(DSN);

       if( DB::isError($this->_oConn) ) {

           catchExc($this->_oConn->getMessage());
       }

       // set unique identifier
       if( is_int($iPollId) ) {

           $this->setPollId($iPollId);
       }
   }
```

The following two methods are setters for the optional identifiers used throughout the class:

```
/*
 * set the _iPollId variable for the class
 *
 * @param integer $iPollId unique poll identifier
 * @access public
 */
function setPollId($iPollId) {

    if(is_int($iPollId) ) {

        $this->_iPollId = $iPollId;
    }
}

/**
 * set the _iAnswerId variable for the class
 *
 * @param integer $iAnswerId unique answer identifier
 * @access public
 */
function setAnswerId($iAnswerId) {

    if( is_int($iAnswerId) ) {

        $this->_iAnswerId = $iAnswerId;
    }
}
```

The next method returns a total count of polls in the system. The optional status parameter ($iStatus) can be passed if it's necessary that our count returns published (active) poll items only. This is necessary to determine the row count for a specific state of the poll item depending on where we are using them:

```
/**
 * get polls count for paging
 *
 * @param boolean $iStatus status of poll
 * @return boolean
 * @access private
 */
function getPollsCount($iStatus=FALSE) {

    // set SQL filter
    $iStatus ? $sFilter .= " AND status=1" : $sFilter .= "";

    $sql = "SELECT
                count(poll_id) AS poll_cnt
            FROM
                ".PREFIX."_polls
            WHERE
                deleted=0".$sFilter;

    if( DB::isError($iCnt = $this->_oConn->getOne($sql)) ) {

        catchExc($iCnt->getMessage());
        return FALSE;
```

```
            }

        return $iCnt;
    }
```

Now let's look at the method that returns the collection of polls from within the system. This method is to be used only in the CMS, since it does not distinguish between published and unpublished polls:

```
    /**
     * get polls list
     *
     * @param string $sSort sort key
     * @param integer $iPage [optional] cursor
     * @return array poll data
     * @access public
     */
    function getPolls($sSort, $iPage=0) {

        $sql = "SELECT
                    poll_id,
                    poll_vote_cnt,
                    poll_question,
                    status,
                    created_dt,
                    modified_dt
                FROM
                    ".PREFIX."_polls
                WHERE
                    deleted=0
                ORDER BY
                    ".$sSort."
                LIMIT
                    ".$iPage.", ".ROWCOUNT;

        if( DB::isError($rsTmp = $this->_oConn->query($sql)) ) {

            catchExc($rsTmp->getMessage());
            return FALSE;
        }

        // loop result and build return array
        $i = 0;
        while( $aRow = $rsTmp->fetchRow(DB_FETCHMODE_ASSOC) ) {

            $return[$i]["Poll Id"] = $aRow["poll_id"];
            $return[$i]["Vote Count"] = $aRow["poll_vote_cnt"];
            $return[$i]["Question"] = $aRow["poll_question"];
            $return[$i]["Status"] = $aRow["status"];
            $return[$i]["Created Date"] = strtotime($aRow["created_dt"]);
            $return[$i]["Modified Date"] = strtotime($aRow["modified_dt"]);
            ++$i;
        }
        return $return;
    }
```

Similar to the above method (to return the collection of polls from within the system), the next method returns a list of poll data. This method, however, requires data that is published in the system, and its usage is intended for the public web site only:

```php
/**
 * get active polls list
 *
 * @param integer $iPage [optional] cursor
 * @return array active poll data
 * @access public
 */
function getActivePolls($iPage=0) {

    $sql = "SELECT
                poll_id,
                poll_vote_cnt,
                poll_question
            FROM
                ".PREFIX."_polls
            WHERE
                status=1
                AND deleted=0
            ORDER BY
                created_dt DESC
            LIMIT ".$iPage.", 1";

    if( DB::isError($rsTmp = $this->_oConn->query($sql)) ) {

        catchExc($rsTmp->getMessage());
        return FALSE;
    }

    // check for results
    if( $rsTmp->numRows() > 0 ) {

        // assign result to array
        $aRow = $rsTmp->fetchRow(DB_FETCHMODE_ASSOC);

        $return["Poll Id"] = $aRow["poll_id"];
        $return["Vote Count"] = $aRow["poll_vote_cnt"];
        $return["Question"] = $aRow["poll_question"];
        $return["Answers"] = $this->getPollAnswers($aRow["poll_id"]);
        return $return;
    }
}
```

Now that we have looked at the methods used to return sets of polls, let's detail the method that returns a single poll item and its relative answer data. This method uses the _iPollId member to capture a specific poll record:

```php
/**
 * get a single poll
 *
 * @return array
 * @access public
 */
```

```
function getPoll() {

    $sql = "SELECT
                poll_id,
                poll_vote_cnt,
                poll_question,
                status,
                created_dt,
                modified_dt
            FROM
                ".PREFIX."_polls
            WHERE
                poll_id=".$this->_iPollId;

    if( DB::isError($rsTmp = $this->_oConn->query($sql)) ) {

        catchExc($rsTmp->getMessage());
        return FALSE;
    }

    // assign result to array
    $aRow = $rsTmp->fetchRow(DB_FETCHMODE_ASSOC);

    // build return array
    $return["Poll Id"] = $aRow["poll_id"];
    $return["Vote Count"] = $aRow["poll_vote_cnt"];
    $return["Question"] = $aRow["poll_question"];
    $return["Answers"] = $this->getPollAnswers($aRow["poll_id"]);
    $return["Status"] = $aRow["status"];
    $return["Created Date"] = strtotime($aRow["created_dt"]);
    $return["Modified Date"] = strtotime($aRow["modified_dt"]);

    return $return;
}
```

The next method is used to capture relative answer options for a poll. It builds an associative array that can be further passed along or used by a calling method to combine with a larger return:

```
/**
 * get poll answers or options
 *
 * @param integer $iPollId poll ID
 * @return array
 * @access public
 */
function getPollAnswers($iPollId) {

    $sql = "SELECT
                poll_answer_id,
                poll_answer,
                poll_answer_cnt
            FROM
```

```
                        ".PREFIX."_polls_answers
                WHERE
                    poll_id=".$iPollId;

        if( DB::isError($rsTmp = $this->_oConn->query($sql)) ) {

            catchExc($rsTmp->getMessage());
            return FALSE;
        }

        // loop through result and build return array
        $i = 0;
        while( $aRow = $rsTmp->fetchRow(DB_FETCHMODE_ASSOC) ) {

            $return[$i]["Answer Id"] = $aRow["poll_answer_id"];
            $return[$i]["Answer"] = $aRow["poll_answer"];
            $return[$i]["Answer Count"] = $aRow["poll_answer_cnt"];
            ++$i;
        }
        return $return;
    }
```

The following method is the largest class member in our `polls` data object. It's used to add a new poll to the system.

Here we lock the `apress_polls` table during the INSERT query, to capture the unique identifier prior to unlocking. This practice ensures that our unique identifier will be the proper associative value for the record added. We then use this value to loop through the passed answer options and insert them into the `apress_polls_answers` table.

Here is the script for the `addPoll()` method:

```
/**
 * add a poll record
 *
 * @param array $aArgs poll data
 * @return boolean
 * @access public
 */
function addPoll($aArgs) {

    // lock tables to capture unique identifier
    $sql = "LOCK TABLES ".PREFIX."_polls WRITE";

    if( DB::isError($rsTmp = $this->_oConn->query($sql)) ) {

        catchExc($rsTmp->getMessage());
        return FALSE;
    }

    // add new record
```

```
$sql = "INSERT INTO ".PREFIX."_polls (
                poll_question,
                status,
                created_dt,
                modified_dt
        ) VALUES (
                '".$aArgs["Question"]."',
                1,
                (NOW()),
                (NOW())
        )";

if( DB::isError($rsTmp = $this->_oConn->query($sql)) ) {

    catchExc($rsTmp->getMessage());
    return FALSE;
}

// get last unique identifier from entry
$sql = "SELECT MAX(poll_id)
        FROM ".PREFIX."_polls";

if( DB::isError($iPollId = $this->_oConn->getOne($sql)) ) {

    catchExc($iPollId->getMessage());
    return FALSE;
}

$sql = "UNLOCK TABLES";

if( DB::isError($rsTmp = $this->_oConn->query($sql)) ) {

    catchExc($rsTmp->getMessage());
    return FALSE;
}

// set unique identifier member variable
settype($iPollId, "integer");
$this->setPollId($iPollId);

// loop through answers and add records
$i = 0;
while( list($key, $val) = each($aArgs["Answers"]) ) {

    if( strcmp("", $val) ) {

        // add records
        $sql = "INSERT INTO ".PREFIX."_polls_answers (
                        poll_id,
                        poll_answer
                ) VALUES (
                        ".$this->_iPollId.",
                        '".$aArgs["Answers"][$i]."'
```

```
                )";

            if( DB::isError($rsTmp = $this->_oConn->query($sql)) ) {

                catchExc($rsTmp->getMessage());
                return FALSE;
            }
        }
        ++$i;
    }
    return TRUE;
}
```

For more information about locking and unlocking tables, refer to
http://www.mysql.com/doc/en/LOCK_TABLES.html.

The 'edit' method is similar to the 'add' method, though we no longer need to lock tables since we aren't writing to them. We can update the poll record by its unique identifier, which has been assigned via the setPollId() method from within the calling page. Do note a similar practice of looping through the passed answer option values to update their records in the system. The passed argument contains a sub-array of the answer options with their unique identifier as the array key values:

```
/**
 * edit a poll record
 *
 * @param array $aArgs poll data
 * @return boolean
 * @access public
 */
function editPoll($aArgs) {

    $sql = "UPDATE ".PREFIX."_polls
        SET
            poll_question='".$aArgs["Question"]."',
            modified_dt=(NOW())
        WHERE
            poll_id=".$this->_iPollId;

    if( DB::isError($rsTmp = $this->_oConn->query($sql)) ) {

        catchExc($rsTmp->getMessage());
        return FALSE;
    }

    // loop through answers and update records
    $i = 0;
    while( list($key, $val) = each($aArgs["Answers"]) ) {

        if( strcmp("", $val) ) {

            $sql = "UPDATE ".PREFIX."_polls_answers
                SET
```

```
                             poll_answer='".$val."'
                    WHERE
                        poll_answer_id=".$key;

            if( DB::isError($rsTmp = $this->_oConn->query($sql)) ) {

                catchExc($rsTmp->getMessage());
                return FALSE;
            }
        }
    }
    return TRUE;
}
```

The following method records votes in our system. This method is quite simple based on the design we have chosen to use – incrementing the vote counts for both the poll total and the answer option total. Then we set a cookie to make sure that the visitor doesn't vote again until the poll has changed, the cookie has been deleted, or the cookie has expired (in 56 days/8 weeks). We are setting our cookie expiration based on the assumption that polls will change within an 8 week period. Using cookies to store our vote state will allow users to delete their cookie and vote again if they are so inclined to do so. This can be seen as a security issue; however, we are looking for a general consensus and not a strict, factual number. If we did want to add more security to this function, we could require that an authenticated account be established before allowing a vote, thus tying our vote state to the account.

Let's now write the addVote() script that adds a poll vote:

```
/**
 * add a poll vote
 *
 * @return boolean
 * @access public
 */
function addVote() {

    // increment poll count
    $sql = "UPDATE ".PREFIX."_polls
        SET
            poll_vote_cnt=poll_vote_cnt+1
        WHERE
            poll_id=".$this->_iPollId;

    if( DB::isError($rsTmp = $this->_oConn->query($sql)) ) {

        catchExc($rsTmp->getMessage());
        return FALSE;
    }

    // increment poll answer count
    $sql = "UPDATE ".PREFIX."_polls_answers
        SET
            poll_answer_cnt=poll_answer_cnt+1
        WHERE
```

```
                    poll_answer_id=".$this->_iAnswerId;

        if( DB::isError($rsTmp = $this->_oConn->query($sql)) ) {

            catchExc($rsTmp->getMessage());
            return FALSE;
        }

        // set poll vote cookie
        setcookie("cPOLL", $this->_iPollId, time()+3600*24*56, "/", "", "");
    }
```

Here the generic delete method sets a soft delete on the record:

```
/**
 * delete a poll record
 *
 * @return boolean
 * @access public
 */
function deletePoll() {

    $sql = "UPDATE ".PREFIX."_polls
        SET
            deleted=1,
            deleted_dt=(NOW())
        WHERE
            poll_id=".$this->_iPollId;

    if( DB::isError($rsTmp = $this->_oConn->query($sql)) ) {

        catchExc($rsTmp->getMessage());
        return FALSE;
    }

    $this->deactivatePoll();
    return TRUE;
}
```

The last two class methods are used to activate and deactivate the poll items. These are generic methods, and we have seen similar functionality used throughout the CMS application:

```
/**
 * activate a poll record
 *
 * @return boolean
 * @access public
 */
function activatePoll() {
```

```
            $sql = "UPDATE ".PREFIX."_polls
                SET
                    status=1
                WHERE
                    poll_id=".$this->_iPollId;

        if( DB::isError($rsTmp = $this->_oConn->query($sql)) ) {

            catchExc($rsTmp->getMessage());
            return FALSE;
        }
    }

    /**
     * deactivate a poll record
     *
     * @return boolean
     * @access public
     */
    function deactivatePoll() {

        $sql = "UPDATE ".PREFIX."_polls
                SET
                    status=0
                WHERE
                    poll_id=".$this->_iPollId;

        if( DB::isError($rsTmp = $this->_oConn->query($sql)) ) {

            catchExc($rsTmp->getMessage());
            return FALSE;
        }
    }
} // close the class definition
?>
```

That concludes the code for our `polls` data object. This class has been designed to be efficient in managing, recording, updating, and displaying polls. The class methods are fairly generic when they apply to our CMS applications, whereas the other methods are very specific to their usage within the web site. Now let's take a look at implementing the polls data object into the CMS and web site.

Presentation Layer

Our design diagrams illustrated some conditional page views based on the state of our visitors' poll vote activity. Let's review those states and the conditions that dictate those views as well as the pages that we'll need to apply to the CMS framework:

❑ CMS poll listings page

❑ CMS poll management forms page

❑ Web site poll form – This page is rendered if the visitor has not voted or if the last poll vote is from a different poll

❑ Web site poll results and archives page – This page is rendered if the visitor has voted on the current poll and/or has selected an archived poll

CMS Poll Listings Page

Our first page is the CMS listing of poll items:

Let's take a look at the code used to generate this page. First, we need to include all the dependent files, and then instantiate our data object and gather some general data from the object:

As mentioned in Chapter 2, our .htaccess file was used to set the value of PHP's include_path, which is the listing of directories that PHP will go through when it's looking for a file that has been included in a piece of code. Our web server's root directory is /var/www/html, but you may need to adjust this to comply with your setup.

```php
<?php

// File Location: /core/polls/index.php

// template framework file for pages inside of the CMS application
require_once("tpl_secure.php");
require_once("class.polls.php");

// instantiate polls class
$oPolls = new polls;

// get polls and polls count
$aPolls = $oPolls->getPolls("created_dt DESC", $iCursor);
$iCnt = $oPolls->getPollsCount();

// check for polls
```

```
if( count($aPolls) ) {

    // build page data array
    $i = 0;
    while( $i < count($aPolls) ) {
        $aData[$i]["Id"] = $aPolls[$i]["Poll Id"];
        $aData[$i]["Name"] = $aPolls[$i]["Question"];
        $aData[$i]["Status"] = $aPolls[$i]["Status"];
        $aData[$i]["Created"] =$aPolls[$i]["Created Date"];
        ++$i;
    }
}

// check for ID
if( $id ) {

    // assign poll ID
    $oPolls->setPollId($id);

    // check operation type
    if( !strcmp($op, "del") ) {

        // try delete poll and redirect
        $oPolls->deletePoll();
        header("Location: ".SELF);

    } elseif ( !strcmp($op, "act") ) {

        // try activate poll and redirect
        $oPolls->activatePoll();
        header("Location: ".SELF);

    } elseif ( !strcmp($op, "deact") ) {

        // try deactivate poll and redirect
        $oPolls->deactivatePoll();
        header("Location: ".SELF);
    }
}
```

We'll call the generic setHeader() and openPage() functions that render the appropriate HTML framework for our page. These functions can be reviewed in their defining file (/core/tpl_secure.php):

```
setHeader();
openPage();
?>
```

Again, the above code is somewhat of a generic implementation across our CMS applications. The remainder of the page is the simple HTML for page errors and notices, instructions, and the generic list rendering call that is passed from the array in the earlier bit of the script:

```
<?php renderList($iCnt, $aData) ?>
```

The abstracted elements being used here can be found in the elements.php file located in the /_lib/_base/ directory.

CMS Poll Management Form

Let's now look over the forms page that handles the user-entered form data for adding and editing polls in the system. This implementation is a bit different. Remember that we are using a shared page for forms; however, for the polls we only want to edit existing content, and not add to the content, which would alter the vote results.

In the poll item (displayed on the following screen), we need to include the option to add a question with up to six answers and set a requirement that at least two answers be provided:

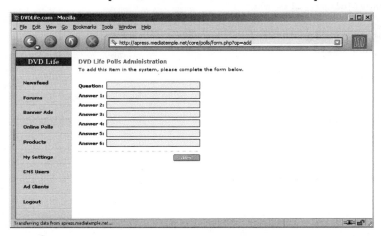

In the sample poll item we entered five answers and submitted the form. Following is the edit screen for the poll item that only allows editing of the existing content – there is no longer the ability to add any answers since we don't want to alter the results:

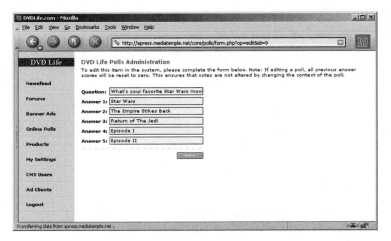

Here is the code that renders the poll CMS forms page:

```php
<?php

// File Location: /core/polls/form.php

require_once("tpl_secure.php");
require_once("handlers.php");
require_once("class.polls.php");

// instantiate polls class
$oPolls = new polls;

// check for ID
if( $id ) {

    // assign poll ID
    $oPolls->setPollId($id);
}
```

The `if` loop checks for the HTTP POST variables:

```php
if( $_POST ) {

    // assign post variables
    $sQuestion = $_POST["question"];
    $aAnswer = $_POST["answer"];

    // check question value
    if( !strcmp("", $sQuestion) ) {

        catchErr("Enter a poll question");
        $FORMOK = FALSE;
    }

    // check answers
    $i = 0;
    while( list($key, $val) = each($aAnswer) ) {

        $aAnswers[$i]["Answer Id"] = $key;
        $aAnswers[$i]["Answer"] = $val;

        if( !strcmp("", $val) && $i < 2 ) {
            catchErr("Enter a value for answer ".($i + 1));
            $FORMOK = FALSE;
        }
        ++$i;
    }
```

The next bit of code is executed if the form variables are validated:

```
if( $FORMOK ) {

    $aArgs["Question"] = $sQuestion;
    $aArgs["Answers"] = $aAnswer;

    // check operation type
    if( !strcmp("edit", $op) ) {

        // try edit poll
        $FORMOK = $oPolls->editPoll($aArgs);

    } elseif ( !strcmp("add", $op) ) {

        // try add poll
        $FORMOK = $oPolls->addPoll($aArgs);
    }

    // redirect if successful
    if( $FORMOK ) {

        // redirect if successful
        header("Location: index.php");
    }
}
```

And this bit of the loop is executed if the POST variables are not sent:

```
} else {

    // assign page variables
    if( !strcmp("edit", $op) ) {

        $aPoll = $oPolls->getPoll();
        $sQuestion = $aPoll["Question"];
        $aAnswers = $aPoll["Answers"];

        $i = 0;
        while( $i < count($aAnswers) ) {

            $aAnswer[$i] = $aAnswers[$i]["Answer"];
            ++$i;
        }
    }
}

setHeader();
openPage();
?>
```

In this portion of the script we wrote the form processing logic and any data assignments that may take place prior to building the page per the operation type – add or edit.

Next we render the different form fields and the conditions upon which they are dependent:

```
<tr>
        <td><div class="formlabel">Question:</div></td>
        <td><input type="text" name="question"
                        value="<?php print clean($sQuestion) ?>"
                        class="textfield" /></td>
</tr>

<?php
if( !strcmp("add", $op) ) {

    for( $i = 0; $i < 6; ++$i ) {

        ?>
        <tr>
            <td><div class="formlabel">Answer
             <?php print $i + 1 ?>:</div></td>
            <td><input type="text"
                name="answer[<?php print $aAnswers[$i]["Answer Id"] ?>]"
                value="<?php print clean($aAnswers[$i]["Answer"]) ?>"
                class="textfield" /></td>
        </tr>
    <?php } ?>

    <?php

} elseif ( !strcmp("edit", $op) ) {

    $i = 0;
    while( $i < count($aAnswers) ) {
        ?>
        <tr>
            <td><div class="formlabel">Answer
             <?php print $i + 1 ?>:</div></td>
            <td><input type="text"
                name="answer[<?php print $aAnswers[$i]["Answer Id"] ?>]"
                value="<?php print clean($aAnswers[$i]["Answer"]) ?>"
                class="textfield" /></td>
        </tr>

        <?php
        ++$i;
    }
    ?>
<?php } ?>
```

There we have it – the pages are now implemented into our CMS to begin managing and publishing poll content.

Web Site Poll Page

This page displays the polls, capture the votes, and render the poll results:

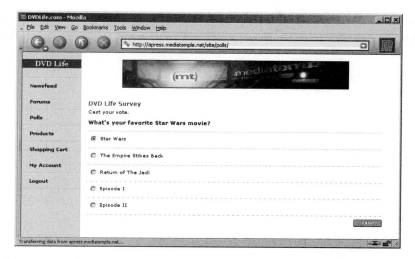

Note that this page is rendered when we have not voted for the current poll or if our last poll vote is from a different poll. Here we are unable to page (previous and next) between the current poll and any archived polls, which empowers our notion of providing an incentive for visitors to vote.

The following page is rendered when a visitor casts his or her vote:

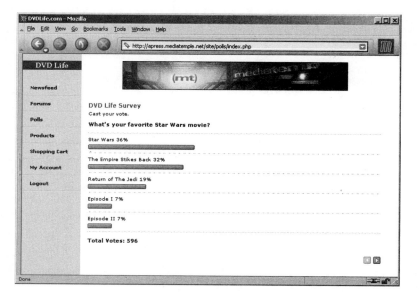

On the above page we can see the poll results and we also have the ability to view the archived polls. From now on when we visit the polls page we'll only see the results unless the poll changes, the cookie expires, or the cookie is deleted.

Let's now look at the code used to render this page in its different states. First, we need to include all the dependent files, and then instantiate the data object and gather some general data from the object:

```php
<?php

// Page Location: /site/polls/index.php

require_once("tpl_unsecure.php");
require_once("class.polls.php");

// instantiate polls class
$oPolls = new polls;

// get poll data
$aPoll = $oPolls->getActivePolls($iCursor);
$iCnt = $oPolls->getPollsCount(TRUE);
```

Note that we assign (conditionally) class member values if the form has been posted; these member variables are then used to update our poll values by calling the `addVote()` method. We'll then redirect the user to the same page via the 'get' method so that a page refresh by the user will not duplicate the form post:

```php
if( $_POST ) {

    // assign poll member variables and add vote
    $iPollId = (int) $_POST["pollid"];
    $oPolls->setPollId($iPollId);
    $iVote = (int) $_POST["vote"];
    $oPolls->setAnswerId($iVote);
    $oPolls->addVote();
    header("Location: ".SELF);
}

setHeader();
openPage(TRUE);
?>
```

The rest of the script renders the page content HTML form or the poll results, conditionally:

```php
<?php if( $iCnt ) { // check poll count value ?>

    <tr>
        <td><div class="section"><?php print format($aPoll["Question"])
            ?></div></td>
    </tr>

    <tr>
```

```
            <td class="dotrule"><img src="../../_img/spc.gif"
             width="1" height="15" alt="" border="0" /></td>
        </tr>

        <tr>
            <td>
            <table width="608" border="0" cellpadding="0" cellspacing="0">

            <?php
            $i = 0;
            $sChecked = " checked";
            strcmp($_COOKIE["cPOLL"], $aPoll["Poll Id"]) ? $iVoted = FALSE :
                    $iVoted = TRUE;
```

This bit loops through the poll answers:

```
            while( $i < count($aPoll["Answers"]) ) { // loop poll answers
                ?>
                <?php if( !$iVoted && $iCursor < 1 ) { // poll vote check ?>

                    <tr>
                        <td width="25"><div class="copy">
                         <input type="radio" name="vote"
                          value="<?php print $aPoll["Answers"][$i]["Answer Id"]
                          ?>"<?php print $sChecked ?>></div></td>

                        <td width="583"><div class="copy">
                         <?php print format($aPoll["Answers"][$i]["Answer"]) ?>
                         </div></td>
                    </tr>

                    <tr>
                        <td colspan="2" class="dotrule">
                         <img src="../../_img/spc.gif"
                          width="1" height="15" alt="" border="0" /></td>
                    </tr>

                    <?php
                } else { // display results

                    // assign calculation defaults
                    $iPerc = 0;
                    $iWidth = 0;

                    // if the poll total vote count is greater than 0
                    if( $aPoll["Vote Count"] ) {
                        // find the percentage
                        $iPerc = round($aPoll["Answers"][$i]["Answer Count"] /
                                $aPoll["Vote Count"] * 100, 0);
                    }

                    // multiply the percentage by 5.9
                    // to get a scaled image length
```

```
            $iWidth = round(($iPerc * 5.9) - 1, 0);
        ?>

        <tr>
            <td><div class="copy">
            <?php print format($aPoll["Answers"][$i]["Answer"])
              ." ".$iPerc ?>%</div></td>
        </tr>

        <tr>
            <td><img src="../../_img/meter_left.gif"
             width="5" height="10" alt="" border="0">
            <img src="../../_img/meter.gif"
             width="<?php print $iWidth ?>" height="10"
             alt="" border="0">
            <img src="../../_img/meter_right.gif"
             width="5" height="10" alt="" border="0"></td>
        </tr>

        <tr>
            <td class="dotrule"><img src="../../_img/spc.gif"
             width="1" height="15" alt="" border="0" /></td>
        </tr>

    <?php } // end answers display check ?>

    <?php
    // check default state for radio buttons
    if( !strcmp(" checked", $sChecked) ) {
        $sChecked = "";
    }

    ++$i;
    } // end poll answers loop

    ?>
    </table>
    </td>
</tr>
```

This portion of the script checks for the poll votes, and the totals of the poll will be rendered if a vote has been recorded:

```
<?php if( !$iVoted && $iCursor < 1 ) { // poll vote check ?>

    <tr>
        <td align="right">
         <input type="image" src="../../_img/buttons/btn_submit.gif"
          width="58" height="15" alt="" border="0"
          onfocus="this.blur();" />
        </td>
    </tr>
```

```
        <tr>
            <td><img src="../../_img/spc.gif"
             width="1" height="15" alt="" border="0" /></td>
        </tr>

    <? } else { // poll vote has been recorded, render totals ?>

        <tr>
            <td><div class="section">
             Total Votes: <?php print $aPoll["Vote Count"] ?></div></td>
        </tr>

        <tr>
            <td><img src="../../_img/spc.gif"
             width="1" height="15" alt="" border="0" /></td>
        </tr>

    <?php  } // end poll vote check ?>

    <tr>
        <td>
```

Next the paginated display is verified:

```
// // verify pagination display
    <?php if( $iCnt > 1 && ($iVoted || $iCursor > 0) ) {?>
        <table width="100%" border="0" cellpadding="0" cellspacing="0">
            <tr>
                <td align="right"><div class="paging">
                <!--| paging |-->

                <table border="0" cellpadding="0" cellspacing="0">
                    <tr>
                        <td width="15">
                         <?php if( $iCursor > 0 ) { ?>
                         <a href="<?php print SELF ?>?cursor=
                          <?php print $iCursor - 1 ?>
                          <?php print $sVar ?>">
                         <img src="../../_img/buttons/btn_prev.gif"
                          width="15" height="15" alt="" border="0" />
                        <?php } else { ?>
                          <img src=
                           "../../_img/buttons/btn_prev_null.gif"
                           width="15" height="15" alt="" border="0" />
                        <?php } ?></a></td>

                    <td width="5"><img src="../../_img/spc.gif"
                     width="5" height="1" alt="" border="0" /></td>

                    <td width="15">
                     <?php if( $iCursor + 1 < $iCnt ) { ?>
```

```
                                <a href="<?php print SELF ?>?cursor=
                                <?php print $iCursor + 1 ?>
                                <?php print $sVar ?>">
                                <img src="../../_img/buttons/btn_next.gif"
                                 width="15" height="15" alt="" border="0" />
                            <?php } else { ?>
                                <img src=
                                 "../../_img/buttons/btn_next_null.gif"
                                 width="15" height="15" alt="" border="0" />
                            <?php } ?></a></td>
                    </tr>
                </table>

                <!--| paging |-->
                </div></td>
            </tr>
        </table>
        <br />
    <?php } // end pagination display verification ?>
    </td>
</tr>
```

Finally, if there are no polls to be displayed, an appropriate message is displayed:

```
<?php } else { // there are no polls ?>
    <tr>
        <td><div class="copy">I am sorry, there are no polls available
                            at this time.</div></td>
    </tr>
<?php } // end poll count value check ?>
```

This concludes the code for our web site implementation of polls. As you can see, it's a fairly simple application that demands greater emphasis on the user interaction state rather than the data processing.

All of the web site implementation code that we have looked at here can easily be put inside a reusable module and then placed anywhere on the site. Since the pages are built from a templating system and the content pages are all confined within a bounding framework table, we can reorganize the elements as we see fit.

Summary

In this chapter we defined the problems associated with implementing a visitor poll into our web site. We then produced a logical design concept to adhere to the intended functionality that we decided upon, and then proceeded to code our design solution into a functional application that seamlessly plugged into the CMS architecture for easy management.

Hopefully, you are now aware of the following aspects and are comfortable with implementing them in your application:

- The problems, considerations, and benefits to be evaluated when building an online polls application

- The importance of designing an efficient and performance-focused application data layer

- Building an application to plug into the existing architecture

- Managing and referencing user interaction states to determine the display content

In the next chapter we'll look at how to create discussion forums to provide a nice community-building aspect to the site. These forums allow users to interact and communicate with one another on our web site, and encourage visitors to register with the site so that they can interact with the forum beyond the read-only access offered to anonymous users.

10

User Discussion Forums

The concept of a site's user community is becoming increasingly important in modern web development. Some well-known sites, such as Slashdot (http://slashdot.org/) and Kuro5hin (http://www.kuro5hin.org/), are almost completely defined by the culture that is evident in their userbase. This is not entirely surprising because the best known sites often cater to a specific interest group that clearly defines their target audience. Since the users, almost by definition, have some common ground (the common interest that brought them to the site), it makes sense that they might have other similarities that could provide the foundations for a community.

Our site clearly falls into this sort of category. We're targeting DVD enthusiasts and providing them with different means to get the DVD-centric information that they're interested in. We could go a step further though, and encourage more community development if we allow the site's visitors to interact with each other. This is best accomplished through the use of discussion forums, where visitors can browse the messages in the forums, ask questions and reply to those of others, and share ideas and tips.

Apart from the encouragement of community growth, these discussion forums present certain other advantages too. For instance, since the forums provide an ideal place for users to discuss the products that are being sold on the site, they might return often to meet the other people that they have chatted with, or to find comments and opinions about their interests. This would likely lead to more sales as the word gets spread about different titles. Also, it would increase the 'stickiness' of the site – it gives the users a reason to stay longer than they normally would.

In this chapter we will:

- Outline the advantages of implementing a forum
- Identify the goals for our web site community
- Produce an initial design concept for how to achieve those goals
- Implement the module for setting up and managing the discussion forum

The Problem

We want to allow and encourage the development of a virtual community comprised of our site's userbase. To accomplish this, it's necessary to develop the discussion forum functionality.

Ideally, the inclusion of a forum provides the following benefits:

- A way for site users to interact with each other.
- An increase in the average time that users spent at the site.
- More opportunities for the users to use different modules, like the shopping cart facility, of the site. Basically, the longer they are on the site, the more page views (with appropriate links) they'll see, which is to say that they'll more likely explore the available functionality and make use of it.
- Additional space on the site to provide banner advertising.
- Increased repeat visitors.
- Increased user registration.

The marketing advantages of a properly implemented forum are obvious. First, the availability of forums should have the effect of causing more users to register at the site. This is desirable since we'll have more user information to be used for other applications such as the newsletter detailed in Chapter 11. Second, if a user is an active participant in a discussion, he or she is going to have more page views, which corresponds to more banner advertisements being served, and hence more clickthroughs, generating increased site revenues. Furthermore, if a user is at the site for longer periods, it increases the chances that he/she will use other modules such as the shopping cart. Finally, if users feel that they are a part of the discussion community, they'll certainly have an increased desire to come back and revisit the site in the future. All of these things are desirable for our site's popularity and success.

Of course we must work hard to ensure that the forum is intuitive to use. This part of the site is, by definition, very interactive, and the primary reason we are creating this is to get users involved with the site in a continuous way. We want users to come back to our site repeatedly to see other replies and to post more of their own. If the user interface makes this hard to do in any way, then very few users are going to make more than a few posts before they get discouraged. If that happens, then we have lost a lot of the potential benefits of this application.

The Problem Statement

Our problem statement is simple – we need to design and implement a discussion forum for DVD Life. It should strive to provide whatever functionality is necessary to achieve the desirable points mentioned in *The Problem* section. And, of course, it should follow the general design guidelines for our application modules that were outlined in Chapter 2.

Listed below is some of the basic functionality that our forum should include:

❑   Users can create and reply to topics.

❑   Visitors cannot create or reply to topics – they will have read-only access.

❑   Users can store topics they are interested in as 'favorites'. Furthermore, they should be able to choose between display modes that show all the topics or just their favorites.

❑   The forum should be easy to navigate and use.

In the next section, we'll think through a design that allows these features to be implemented.

The Design

As with each of our application modules, we need to think about the aspects of this discussion forum in terms of the data layer, the application logic, and the presentation layer. We'll talk about each of these in this section. Before we start, though, it'll be useful to quickly walk through what we would like a typical user experience with our forum to be.

Application Flow

Looking at our requirements, it's clear that our forum will effectively operate in two different states. One state will be invoked if the user is logged in, and the other will be used for users who are not logged in.

> **People who are not logged in will be referred to as 'visitors', and those who are logged in will be referred to as 'users'.**

Users

When a user comes to the forum, he or she will have a variety of options in terms of what to do next. For starters, the user should see a list of forum topics, with the most recently replied to first, like this:

If the user is viewing in the Favorites mode, then the topics listed will be those the user has designated as favorites. Otherwise, all the topics will be available. Note that we are referring to this 'all topics' listing as the Recent Topics view, since the list will be ordered with the most recently replied to topic first, the next most recently replied to topic second, and so on.

> **Since we are allowing users to start their own topics, there could potentially be a great many to choose from. Therefore, we'll have to provide a paging functionality, so that the user is presented with a manageable number of topics on any given page.**

The following actions should be allowable:

- ❏ The user should have links that, when clicked, set the viewing mode to Recent Topics or Favorites.

- ❏ Users should have a link (Start a Topic) that takes them to a page where they can start a new topic.

- ❏ Each topic should have a corresponding checkbox. Clicking these checkboxes and submitting the associated form should add the selected topics to the favorites list if the viewer is seeing the page in the 'most recent' mode. Furthermore, the user should be able to remove favorites from the selected list if he or she is in the Favorites mode.

- ❏ Clicking on a topic itself should take the user to a page where the replies can be viewed.

Since reading topics and replying to them is the basis of any forum, let's elaborate this last point. Clearly, clicking on a topic link should take us to a page where the replies can be viewed, with the first reply being at the top of the page and other replies beneath it according to when they were posted. Since users are logged in, they'll need a link that allows them to post their own reply

Of course, there may be many replies to any given topic, so we should provide the same paging functionality that we used on the page where we saw the topics themselves. We should, however, show the corresponding topic on every page of replies so that people can easily remember what they are replying to.

Visitors

The application flow for a visitor is substantially simpler than that for a user. This makes sense, as we are not exposing all of the forum functionality to visitors. So the visitor page of the forums module would look like this:

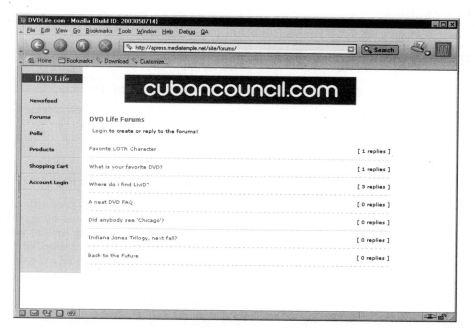

When visitors get to the forums, they have the following available options:

- ❏ Click on a topic to view replies
- ❏ Click on a link that takes them to the login page

Visitors are not allowed to post new topics, so we won't expose this option to them. The same is true for the ability to put topics into the favorites list. Naturally, since viewing favorites is not possible, the page should always go into the 'view recent' mode if the user is not logged in.

The same methodology is applied to the 'view replies' page. The visitors can see the replies but will be unable to post any of their own. On all pages, we should make sure that there is a link to the login/register page (http://apress.mediatemple.net/site/accounts/). This will encourage visitors to sign in or to register with the site if they have not yet created an account.

Designing the Data Layer

There are two kinds of data objects in this application. We can think of a forum topic as one kind of data, and a topic reply as another kind of data. Therefore, it makes sense that we should start out with two tables in our database for topics and replies. We'll also need a third table to handle the user's favorites.

The three tables will be named as follows:

- ❏ apress_forums to hold the different topics
- ❏ apress_forums_replies to hold topic replies
- ❏ apress_forums_prefs to hold user favorites

The Topics Table

The apress_forums table will house various fields related to topics:

Field	Type	Description
forum_id	INT(10)	Unique identifier for this forum topic.
account_id	INT(10)	Identifier of the person who created this topic.
forum_name	VARCHAR(100)	The title for this topic.
forum_topic	TEXT	The text for this topic.
forum_reply_cnt	INT(10)	The number of replies for this topic.
		This will be automatically updated whenever we create or delete replies. It would be nice if we could assign a database trigger here to take care of things automatically. However, since MySQL does not support triggers we will code the functionality ourselves.
deleted	INT(1)	Flag to tell if this topic is to be shown.
deleted_dt	DATETIME	Date that the deleted flag was last set.
created_dt	DATETIME	Date that this topic was created.
modified_dt	DATETIME	Date that this topic was last modified.
		As mentioned earlier, forum topics will be displayed with the most recently replied to topic at the top. This is a useful way to make sure that the 'hot topics' are the ones seen most often. Therefore, the modified_dt field will be set whenever someone replies to this topic. Again, it would be nice to have triggers available, but we'll make do with PHP.

It should be obvious from their names where these fields are used.

We mention triggers because they would be useful for setting the modified_dt *field. Specifically, it would be useful to set up a trigger so that whenever a reply is created, the field for the corresponding topic is updated automatically. However, since triggers aren't available with MySQL, we'll update this field using PHP.*

The Replies Table

The data for replies will be stored in the apress_forums_replies table:

Field	Type	Description
forum_reply_id	INT(10)	Unique identifier for this reply
forum_topic_id	INT(10)	The identifier of the topic with which this reply is associated
account_id	INT(10)	Identifier of the person who created this reply
forum_reply	TEXT	The text for this reply
deleted	INT(1)	Flag to tell if this topic is to be shown
deleted_dt	DATETIME	Date that the deleted flag was last set
created_dt	DATETIME	Date that this reply was created
modified_dt	DATETIME	Date that this reply was last modified

The forum_topic_id field is linked to the forum_id field from the apress_forums table. If MySQL always supported foreign keys, then we could use them here to make sure that the system maintained referential integrity. However, MySQL supports foreign keys only with InnoDB tables, which are not always available in the shared server ISP environments that we are supporting in this book.

We will use MyISAM tables in this book, since it allows support for generic shared server environments. Refer to Chapter 2 for more information on why we're supporting shared server ISP environments.

The Favorites Table

The third table, apress_forums_prefs, is simpler than the other two, and is used to contain data about a user's favorite topics. This is not hard to do – all we need is a lookup table:

Field	Type	Description
forum_pref_id	INT(10)	Unique identifier for the favorite topic
forum_topic_id	INT(10)	The identifier of the topic with which this favorite is associated
account_id	INT(10)	Identifier of the user who created this favorite

For a thorough discussion of issues like foreign keys, triggers, and referential integrity, refer to Beginning PHP4 Databases from Wiley Press (ISBN 1-861007-82-5). For more MySQL information, refer to Beginning Databases with MySQL from Apress (ISBN 1-904344-54-2), or SQL in a Nutshell from O'Reilly & Associates (ISBN 1-56592-744-3).

Designing the Data Objects

Now that we have our database tables figured out, it's time to turn our attention to the task of creating objects to handle the data we'll store. These objects need to adhere to the following principles:

❑ No member variables will be directly exposed. Instead, we'll use get() and set() methods to change them from the outside, if necessary.

❑ Method names will be clear and meaningful.

❑ The objects will handle and manipulate data, and not concern themselves with the display of this data. This will help to reduce code bloat and will make them more reusable.

Of course we'll use the coding standards outlined in Chapter 2, to ensure that things are consistent in our web application.

Since we like to think of our data objects as models of real world things, we should examine our data structures to identify the best way to represent and manipulate the data. Earlier we saw that there are two things that we are dealing with – topics and replies. Therefore, it makes sense to have two distinct data objects, one to handle topics and another to handle the replies.

As it turns out though, we are actually going to create three objects in this chapter because there are certain variables and methods that are useful when manipulating both topics and replies. To avoid duplication of the code needed to do this, we will consolidate that functionality into a **helper class**. Our topic and reply classes will then extend this class to inherit the desired code. The helper class will never be instantiated directly, but it'll make the development of the other two classes easier.

You may be wondering how we can tell in advance that a helper class will be needed. The honest answer is that a lot of the time we don't. For example, the author of this module initially started writing the two classes mentioned earlier without the helper class. Along the way, he realized that he was duplicating a lot of code, so he went back and created an auxiliary class to avoid this. We should always try to plan ahead, but in any real life development project there will likely be some reorganizing of the code as we go along.

With this in mind, let's start with the helper class that we'll be using.

The Helper Class

To reiterate, the forumhelp class will provide some properties and methods that are useful to both the topic and reply classes that we'll create afterwards. The helper class is not really designed to do anything by itself, and is never instantiated directly from within the code.

Here is a listing of the members of the class:

`forumhelp` Class Member	Description
`_bStripHtml`	A Boolean variable that indicates whether or not HTML tags should be stripped.
`_sAllowTags`	A string of tags that will be allowed if HTML stripping is enabled.
`_oConn`	A PEAR database object.
`forumhelp()`	Constructor function that creates the database object and sets default values for the HTML stripping variables.
`_stripHtml($sString)`	Strips HTML from the `$sString` argument according to the set variables. This is basically a smart wrapper for PHP's `strip_tags()` function.
`setAllowTags($sString)`	Sets the `_sAllowTags` variable to the value of the `$sString` argument.
`setStripHtml($bAllow)`	Sets the `_bStripHtml` variable to the value of the `$bAllow` argument.
`getScreennameFromId($iUserId)`	Retrieves the screen name for the user with `user_id` equal to `$iUserId`.
`getEmailFromId($iUserId)`	Retrieves the e-mail address for the user with `user_id` equal to `$iUserId`.

The Topic Class

As the name suggests, the `forumtopic` class will be used to create, delete, and manipulate data relevant to the forum topics. It'll extend the helper class and therefore will inherit all of its properties and methods also.

Here is a listing of the members of the class:

`forumtopic` Class Member	Description
`_iTopicId`	The topic ID value for this topic
`_sTopicName`	The name of this topic
`_sTopicText`	The text of the entry for this topic
`_iAccountId`	The account ID of the person who created this topic

Table continued on following page

forumtopic Class Member	Description
_iReplyCount	The number of replies to this topic
forumtopic()	Constructor function
setAccountId($iAccountId)	Sets the _iAccountId variable to the value of $iAccountId
getAccountId()	Retrieves the _iAccountId variable
setTopicName($sTopicName)	Sets the _sTopicName variable to the value of $sTopicName
getTopicName()	Retrieves the _sTopicName variable
setTopicText($sTopicText)	Sets the _sTopicText variable to the value of $sTopicText
getTopicText()	Retrieves the _sTopicText variable
createTopic()	Creates a new topic entry in the database
getTopicFromDb($iTopicId)	Populates the object variables with values from the database corresponding to the topic with the $iTopicId value
deleteTopic($iTopicId)	Sets the deleted flag for the topic with $iTopicId to 1
undeleteTopic($iTopicId)	Sets the deleted flag for the topic with $iTopicId to 0
getReplyCount($iTopicId [optional])	Gets the reply count, from the database, for the topic with a $iTopicId ID
addFavorites($aFavorite,$aSess)	Adds the indicated topics to the favorites list for the user identified by $aSess
delFavorites($aFavorite,$aSess)	Deletes the indicated topic from the favorites list for the user identified by $aSess
getTopicDisplay($iCursor,$sView,$aSess)	Returns an array of data needed to display titles for a group of topics
getTotalTopics($sView,$aSess)	Gets the total number of topics available for a particular view, which is needed for paging

The Reply Class

Finally, we'll describe the reply class. Like the topic class, this will extend our helper class to make use of the functionality contained therein. It'll also include properties and methods that we'll use to create, delete, and manipulate replies.

Here is a listing of the members of the class:

`forumreply` Class Member	Description
`_iTopicId`	The ID of the topic with which this reply is associated
`_sReply`	The text of this reply
`_iAccountId`	The account ID of the user who posted this reply
`forumreply($iAccountId [optional], $iTopicId [optional])`	Constructor function that sets the values of _iAccountId and _iTopicId, if they are supplied as arguments
`setTopicId($iTopicId)`	Sets the _iTopicId variable to the value of $iTopicId
`setAccountId($iAccountId)`	Sets the _iAccountId variable to the value of $iAccountId
`setReply($sReply)`	Sets the _sReply variable to the value of $sReply
`getReplyFromDB($iReplyId)`	Returns an array with the different data fields needed for display, corresponding to the reply identified by $iReplyId
`createReply()`	Inserts a new reply into the database, based on the values of the private member variables
`deleteReply($iReplyId)`	Sets the deleted flag for the reply identified by $iReplyId to 1
`undeleteReply($iReplyId)`	Sets the deleted flag for the reply identified by $iReplyId to 0
`getReplyIds($iCursor, $iTopicId)`	Returns an array of data needed to display a selection of replies

Administrative Functionality

There is some administrative functionality associated with this module. Although we would like to believe that everyone who comes to our site will have nothing but good intentions, there is no way to guarantee that. As a consequence somebody could potentially post things to the discussion forum that are off-topic or inappropriate, such as where to download the latest Warez version of Microsoft Office.

With this in mind, administrators need the ability to go in and delete certain topics or specific replies. We're not really going to remove anything from the database (we might want or need it later) but as you can see, we've talked about defining methods to manipulate the `deleted` flags for both forums and replies.

Having said this, we aren't going to detail the construction of the administrative functionality in this chapter. There are two reasons for this. First, we would like to keep this chapter to a size that is readable. Second, the construction of the admin is almost identical to the construction of the actual forums. They have almost the exact same interface and they make use of the same classes. The difference is that instead of calling methods to put new data into the database, in the admin we call methods to set the `deleted` flags in the database tables. As a consequence, a detailed description of this section would be a bit redundant.

Since actually building something is a lot more fun (and instructive) than just making minor data modifications, we are going to forge ahead with the implementation of the forums. Once you understand how they work, figuring out the administration module from the book's code download (available at the Apress web site) will be a trivial task. The complete admin functionality is available there and will pose no problems for you to figure out how it works.

The Solution

Now that we have designed our database tables and data objects, it's time to create the database and start doing some real PHP coding. First we'll detail the creation of the database tables and the classes that will manipulate the data. After these data-centric layers are done, we'll get to the presentation layer where we can see the fruits of our labor.

Implementing the Data Layer

This section will detail the MySQL commands needed to create the three tables needed for this module.

apress_forums

The following script will create the forums table with the correct structure:

```
CREATE TABLE apress_forums (
    forum_id          INT(10)       NOT NULL auto_increment,
    account_id        INT(10)       NOT NULL default '0',
    forum_name        VARCHAR(100)  NOT NULL default '',
    forum_topic       TEXT          NOT NULL,
    forum_reply_cnt   INT(10)       NOT NULL default '0',
    deleted           INT(1)        NOT NULL default '0',
    deleted_dt        DATETIME      default NULL,
    created_dt        DATETIME      NOT NULL default '0000-00-00 00:00:00',
    modified_dt       DATETIME      NOT NULL default '0000-00-00 00:00:00',
                      PRIMARY KEY (forum_id)
) TYPE=MyISAM;
```

apress_forums_replies

This table will hold the information about the replies that are posted:

```
CREATE TABLE apress_forums_replies (
    forum_reply_id INT(10)  NOT NULL  auto_increment,
    forum_topic_id INT(10)  NOT NULL  default '0',
    account_id     INT(10)  NOT NULL  default '0',
```

```
    forum_reply    TEXT     NOT NULL,
    deleted        INT(1)   NOT NULL   default '0',
    deleted_dt     DATETIME default  NULL,
    created_dt     DATETIME NOT NULL default '0000-00-00 00:00:00',
    modified_dt    DATETIME NOT NULL default '0000-00-00 00:00:00',
                   PRIMARY KEY (forum_reply_id)
) TYPE=MyISAM;
```

apress_forums_prefs

Finally, we need the table to house the lookup table for the users' favorite threads:

```
CREATE TABLE apress_forums_prefs (
    forum_pref_id  INT(10) NOT NULL auto_increment,
    account_id     INT(10) NOT NULL default '0',
    forum_topic_id INT(10) NOT NULL default '0',
                   PRIMARY KEY (forum_pref_id)
) TYPE=MyISAM;
```

Implementing the Data Objects

Our database tables are now created and ready to work with, so we'll move on to creating our data objects. We have clearly defined coding standards and we know what properties and methods are to be employed. Therefore, all that's left to us now is the creation of conforming code.

class.forumhelp.php

The first on the list is our helper class. Create the file /_lib/_classes/class.forumhelp.php under the web server's root directory. The first thing to do is include the necessary files:

```php
<?php

// File Location: /_lib/_classes/class.forumhelp.php

/*
 * class that provides some helper functions to
 * other forum classes for our application
 */

// import the PEAR::DB class
require_once("DB.php");

// funcs.php is located in /_lib/_base/ and
// contains some utility functions, such as our error trapping functions
require_once("funcs.php");
```

These files provide some functions and objects that we'll need throughout this development.

Now, we'll define the class and its private member variables:

```php
class forumhelp { //open the class definition

    /**
     * @var boolean
```

```
 */
var $_bStripHtml;

/**
 * @var string
 */
var $_sAllowTags;

/**
 * @var object
 */
var $_oConn;
```

The next part of the class is the constructor. It provides the standard functionality of creating default values for our private member variables:

```
// {{{ CONSTRUCTOR

/**
 * @access public
 */
function forumhelp() {
```

The following connection code is added to every class, instead of creating a general connection management and database tools class, since this makes the class more self-contained. Besides, it doesn't add any overhead since PEAR::DB will try reusing existing connections instead of calling new ones wherever possible:

```
    $this->_oConn = DB::connect(DSN);

    if( DB::isError($this->_oConn) ) {

        // getMessage() is inherited from the PEAR::ERROR object
        catchExc($this->_oConn->getMessage());

    }

    $this->_bStripHtml = TRUE;
    $this->_sAllowTags = '';
}
// }}}
```

The `forumhelp` class has a member variable, which is a `PEAR::DB` object. This means that any class that extends this one (as the topic and reply classes do) will automatically have a database object to make use of. As we progress, this will prove very useful indeed.

The first method that we'll code up is `stripHtml()` – all it does is look at the `$_bStripHtml` variable, and depending on its value apply the `strip_tags()` PHP function on the argument string (if necessary):

```
// {{{ _stripHtml

/**
 * conditionally strips HTML tags
```

```
 *
 * @access private
 * @return string
 */
function _stripHtml($sString) {

    if( !$this->_bStripHtml ) {
        return $sString;
    }

    if( !strcmp($this->_sAllowTags,'') ) {
        return strip_tags($sString);
    } else {
        return strip_tags($sString , $this->_sAllowTags);
    }
}
// }}}
```

Of course, the `strip_tags()` method can allow certain tags (it can bypass tags that we want to allow to remain or allow desired tags to remain, that is), and we've made provisions for this with the `$_sAllowTags` variable. So we'll need to have a `setAllowTags()` method to make use of this fact:

```
// {{{ setAllowTags

/**
 * specify the allowable HTML tags
 *
 * @param string allowable tags
 */
function setAllowTags($sAllowTags) {

    if( is_string($sAllowTags) ) {
        $this->_sAllowTags = $sAllowTags;

    } else {
        catchExc("Tried to set allowable HTML tags to non-string in " .
                __FILE__);
    }
}
// }}}
```

All of this HTML stripping ability is dependent on the value of the `$_bStripHtml` variable, so we must code a `set()` method for it as well:

```
// {{{ setStripHtml

/**
 * set the allow HTML variable
 *
 * @param boolean allow HTML value
 */

function setStripHtml($bAllow) {
```

```
            if( is_boolean($bAllow) ) {

                $this->_bStripHtml = $bAllow;

            } else {

                catchExc("Tried to set _bStripHtml to non-bool value in " .
                        __FILE__);
            }
    }
    // }}}
```

Now we'll turn our attention to methods that require some database interaction. It's easy to imagine that we'll want a simple way to extract just the user's screen name from the apress_accounts table. The following method takes care of this for us:

```
    // {{{ getScreennameFromID

    /**
     * get a username from a user ID
     *
     * @param integer user ID
     * @access public
     * @return string
     */
    function getScreennameFromId($iUserId) {

        // ensure that the user supplied a number for the user ID
        if( !is_integer($iUserId) ) {

            catchExc("Tried to get user name with non-int user ID in " .
                    __FILE__);
            return FALSE;
        }

        $sql = "SELECT
                    account_screenname
                FROM
                    ".PREFIX."_accounts
                WHERE
                    account_id = $iUserId";

        // run the query and check for errors.
        $rsTmp = $this->_oConn->getOne($sql);

        if( DB::isError($rsTmp) ) {

            catchExc($rsTmp->getMessage());
            return FALSE;
        } else {

            return $rsTmp;
        }
    }
    // }}}
```

In an analogous fashion, we may want to get a user's e-mail address from the same database table:

```php
    // {{{ getEmailFromId

/**
 * get a email from a user ID
 *
 * @param integer user ID
 * @access public
 * @return string
 */
function getEmailFromId($iUserId) {

    // make sure the user has supplied a number for the user ID
    if( !is_integer($iUserId) ) {

        catchExc("Tried to get email with non-int user ID in " .
                __FILE__);
        return FALSE;
    }

    $sql = "SELECT account_email
            FROM ".PREFIX."_accounts
            WHERE account_id = $iUserId";

    // run query and check for errors
    $rsTmp = $this->_oConn->getOne($sql);

    if( DB::isError($rsTmp) ) {

        catchExc($rsTmp->getMessage());
        return FALSE;

    } else {
        return $rsTmp;
    }
}
    // }}}

} // end class forumhelp
?>
```

Here we use the `DB::isError()` method. Since the PEAR::DB class extends the base PEAR class, we have access to the `PEAR::isError()` function. We use this, and then wrap the PEAR `getMessage()` function in our own error handling `catchExc()` function so that we can deal with it in a standard way for our site.

This completes our helper class. Next, let's write the code for the topic class.

class.forumtopic.php

Create a `/_lib/_classes/class.forumtopic.php` file under the web server's root directory. This will contain the topic class, which will extend the helper class to inherit the abilities that we have just created. As before, we'll start by including the necessary class to be extended and opening the class definition:

```php
<?php

// File Location: /_lib/_classes/class.forumtopic.php

require_once("class.forumhelp.php");

class forumtopic extends forumhelp { // open the class definition
```

Next, we'll define the member variables that are used in this class:

```php
/**
 * @var integer
 */
var $_iTopicId;

/**
 * @var string
 */
var $_sTopicName;

/**
 * @var string
 */
var $_sTopicText;

/**
 * @var integer
 */
var $_iAccountId;

/**
 * @var integer
 */
var $_iReplyCount;
```

These are all self-explanatory. Note that we're being careful to use the naming conventions we agreed upon earlier in the book.

The constructor comes next. It does nothing except to invoke the constructor of its parent class. This will make sure that the DB object, which we talked about earlier, is created and ready for us to use later on:

```php
// {{{ CONSTRUCTOR

/*
 * constructor
 *
 * @access public
 */
function forumtopic() {

    parent::forumhelp();
}
// }}}
```

The next two methods are very straightforward. They are the get() and set() methods for the $_iAccountId member variable:

```
// {{{ setAccountId()

/*
 * Set the Creator ID variable
 *
 * @param integer account ID
 * @access public
 */
function setAccountId($iAccountId) {

    if( is_numeric($iAccountId) ) {

        $this->_iAccountId = $iAccountId;

    } else {

        catchExc("Tried to set topic creator ID to non-int value in " .
                __FILE__);

        return FALSE;
    }
}
// }}}

// {{{ getAccountId()

/*
 * Get the Creator ID variable
 *
 * @access public
 * @return integer
 */
function getAccountId() {

    return $this->_iAccountId;
}
// }}}
```

Next are the analogous methods for the $_sTopicName variable:

```
// {{{ setTopicName()

/*
 * Set the Topic Name variable
 *
 * @param string topic name
 * @access public
 */
function setTopicName($sTopicName) {

    if( is_string($sTopicName) ) {

        $this->_sTopicName = $this->_stripHtml($sTopicName);

    } else {
```

```
                catchExc("Tried to set topic name to non-string value in " .
                        __FILE__);

            return FALSE;
        }
    }

// }}}
// {{{ getTopicName()

/*
 * Get the Topic Name variable
 *
 * @access public
 * @return string
 */
function getTopicName() {

    return $this->_sTopicName;
}
// }}}
```

The last get() and set() methods we'll create in this class are for the $_sTopicText variable:

```
// {{{ setTopicText()

/*
 * Set the Topic Text variable
 *
 * @param string topic text
 * @access public
 */
function setTopicText($sTopicText) {

    if( is_string($sTopicText) ) {

        $this->_sTopicText = $this->_stripHtml($sTopicText);

    } else {

        catchExc("Tried to set topic text to non-string value in " .
                __FILE__);

        return FALSE;
    }
}

// }}}

// {{{ getTopicText()

/*
 * Get the Topic Text variable
 *
 * @access public
 * @return string
 */
```

```
    function getTopicText() {

        return $this->_sTopicText;
}
// }}}
```

Now we have all the methods that we need to get and/or set the member variables. This means that it's time to produce the code that'll put these values into our database. The createTopic() method offers no surprises. First, validity checks are done on the inputs:

```
// {{{ createTopic()

/*
 * Create new Topic in database
 *
 * @access public
 */
function createTopic() {
    // first, we'll do some checks to ensure that the data is the right
    // type
    if( !is_numeric($this->_iAccountId) ) {

        catchExc("Tried to create new topic without valid creator id in
                " . __FILE__);
        return FALSE;
    }

    if( !is_string($this->_sTopicName) ) {

        catchExc("Tried to create new topic without valid topic name in
                " . __FILE__);
        return FALSE;
    }

    if( !is_string($this->_sTopicText) ) {

        catchExc("Tried to create new topic without valid topic text in
                " . __FILE__);
        return FALSE;
    }
```

Next we create the SQL INSERT statement to create a new row in the apress_forums table:

```
// create new row in apress_forums table. Note that we're using the
// DB::quote() method to quote the strings properly before insertion
$sql = "INSERT INTO ".PREFIX."_forums(
            account_id , forum_name , forum_topic ,
            created_dt , modified_dt)
    VALUES (
            '" . $this->_iAccountId . "' ,
            " . $this->_oConn->quote($this->_sTopicName) . " ,
            " . $this->_oConn->quote($this->_sTopicText) . " ,
            NOW() ,
            NOW()
            )";
```

Finally, we'll run the query and check for errors. If things go as they should, we'll return true:

```
        // run the query and check for errors
        $rsTmp = $this->_oConn->query($sql);

        if( DB::isError($rsTmp) ) {

            catchExc($rsTmp->getMessage());
            return FALSE;
        }

        // return true if everything worked
        return TRUE;
    }
    // }}}
```

Note that we use $this->_oConn->quote() in the method. PEAR::DB objects have a quote() method that'll quote a string appropriately for database queries.

Now we have created the ability to put a topic into the database. The flip side of the coin, of course, is getting a topic out of the database. The next method will pull the data for a specific topic out of the database tables and return it to us in an array that we can use as we wish.

As usual, we'll start by checking to ensure that we got the correct inputs:

```
    // {{{ getTopicFromDb()

    /*
     * Set member variables based on values in db
     *
     * @param integer topic ID
     * @access public
     * @return array
     */
    function getTopicFromDb($iTopicId) {

        if( !is_numeric($iTopicId) ) {

            catchExc("Tried to get topic info without valid topic id in " .
                    __FILE__);
            return FALSE;
        }
```

We're going to use a MySQL function to get a formatted date in our result set, and this will require a formatting string:

```
        // date format string for MySQL
        // form of Sun Dec 22nd, 2002 at HH:MM:SS
        $sDateFormat = "%a %b %D, %Y at %r";
```

Our SQL query involves using a LEFT JOIN operation between the tables:

```
        // LEFT JOIN apress_forums and apress_accounts tables since we need
        // the account screen name from the accounts table
```

```
$sql = "SELECT
            account_screenname,forum_name,forum_topic,
            forum_reply_cnt,
            DATE_FORMAT(forums.created_dt,\"$sDateFormat\") AS date
        FROM
            ".PREFIX."_forums forums
        LEFT JOIN
            ".PREFIX."_accounts accounts
        ON
            (forums.account_id=accounts.account_id)
        WHERE
            forums.deleted = 0 AND
            forum_id = $iTopicId";
```

Next we'll run the query. If any errors occur we'll catch them and return false:

```
// run query and catch any errors
$rsTmp = $this->_oConn->getRow($sql);

if( DB::isError($rsTmp) ) {

    catchExc($rsTmp->getMessage());
    return FALSE;

}
```

Finally, we'll return an array with the data that we're interested in:

```
// return associative array with the desired information
$aReturn["TopicId"] = $iTopicId;
$aReturn["ScreenName"] = $rsTmp[0];
$aReturn["TopicName"] = $rsTmp[1];
$aReturn["TopicText"] = $rsTmp[2];
$aReturn["ReplyCount"] = $rsTmp[3];
$aReturn["CreatedDate"] = $rsTmp[4];

return $aReturn;
}
// }}}
```

Here we used the DATE_FORMAT() MySQL function to get a nicely formatted date string. You may be wondering why this was done with a MySQL function as opposed to using PHP to do the same job. It is mostly a matter of preference, since either method would work and is easy to implement. This route was chosen so the formatted date string could be retrieved from the database in one step, as opposed to getting it out and then reformatting it with PHP.

For more information on the available MySQL functions, refer to the official documentation at http://www.mysql.com/doc/en/. The DATE_FORMAT() function is described at: http://www.mysql.com/doc/en/Date_and_time_functions.html.

Now, we'll program the method that sets the deleted flag for a particular topic to 1. This is used in the administration side of things, to remove undesired topics from display on the site:

```
// {{{ deleteTopic()

/*
 * Set deleted field in DB to 1 for this topic
 *
 * @param integer forum ID to delete
 * @access public
 */
function deleteTopic($iTopicId) {
```

We check the input data to make sure the user has supplied us with a number for the topic ID:

```
if( !is_numeric($iTopicId) ) {

    catchExc("Tried to delete Forum with non-int forum id in " .
            __FILE__);
    return FALSE;
}
```

The SQL is simple and updates three fields in the apress_forums table:

```
$sql = "UPDATE
        ".PREFIX."_forums
    SET
        deleted = 1 ,
        deleted_dt = NOW() ,
        modified_dt = NOW()
    WHERE
        forum_id = " . $iTopicId;
```

Execute the query and check for errors:

```
$rsTmp = $this->_oConn->query($sql);

if( DB::isError($rsTmp) ) {

    catchExc($rsTmp->getMessage());
    return FALSE;
}
}
// }}}
```

There is an analogous undeleteTopic() method as well:

```
// {{{ undeleteTopic()

/*
 * Set deleted field in DB to 0 for this forum
```

```
 *
 * @param integer forum ID to reactivate
 * @access public
 */
function undeleteTopic($iTopicId) {

    if( !is_numeric($iTopicId) ) {

        catchExc("Tried to reinstate Forum with non-int forum id in " .
                __FILE__);
        return FALSE;
    }

    $sql = "UPDATE
                ".PREFIX."_forums
            SET
                deleted = 0 ,
                deleted_dt = NOW() ,
                modified_dt = NOW()
            WHERE
                forum_id = " . $iTopicId;

    $rsTmp = $this->_oConn->query($sql);

    if( DB::isError($rsTmp) ) {

        catchExc($rsTmp->getMessage());
        return FALSE;
    }
}
// }}}
```

It may be useful to have a method that tells us the reply count for a particular topic. This method does just that. If no argument is supplied, the method assumes that we want the reply count for the topic represented by the object that the method is being called on, which is the sensible thing to try:

```
// {{{ getReplyCount()

/**
 * Get the number of replies for a topic
 *
 * @access public
 * @param integer Forum ID [optional]
 * @return integer
 */
function getReplyCount($iTopicId = '') {

    // use the supplied topic ID if available, and the member variable
    // if not.
    if( !strcmp($iTopicId,'') && !strcmp($this->_iTopicId , '') ) {
```

```
            catchExc("Tried to get count for forum without ID in " .
                    __FILE__);
            return;
        }

        if( !strcmp($iTopicId,'') && isset($this->_iTopicId) ) {
            $iTopicId = $this->_iTopicId;
        }

        $sql = "SELECT forum_reply_cnt
                FROM ".PREFIX."_forums
                WHERE forum_id = $iTopicId";

        $rsTmp = $this->_oConn->getOne($sql);

        if( DB::isError($rsTmp) ) {

            catchExc($rsTmp->getMessage());
            return FALSE;
        }

        return $rsTmp;
    }
    // }}}
```

Now, one of the features that we're building into our forum is the ability for a user to put topics, in which they are interested, into a favorites list. When they look at the forum topics, they can choose to see everything that's available or just their favorites.

The addFavorites() method takes care of adding a selected group of topic IDs to the apress_forums_prefs table so that they can be referenced later, if the user wants to see his or her favorite topics. It takes two arguments that are used to associate topics with specific users; the first argument is an array of the IDs to add, and the second is the account ID for the user. The first thing is the customary data validation:

```
    // {{{ addFavorites()

    /**
     * add indicated topics to favorites
     *
     * @param array favorites IDs
     * @param integer account ID
     * @return boolean
     */
    function addFavorites($aFavorite,$iAccountId) {

        if( !is_array($aFavorite) ) {

            catchExc("Passed non-array value for favorites.");
            return FALSE;
        }
```

```
    if( !is_numeric($iAccountId) ) {

        catchExc("Passed numeric value for account id.");
        return FALSE;
    }
```

Now, we'll loop through the values in the `$aFavorite` array:

```
    for( $i=0 ; $i < count($aFavorite) ; ++$i ) {
```

Next, we need to address an issue that will affect the UI later on. If there are a group of topics in the user's favorites, and the user is looking at a view that shows all the topics, then a topic could be added to the favorites that already exist there. If we're not careful, then the same topic could show up in the favorites list twice. Therefore, we need to check each potential new favorite to make sure it doesn't already exist in the favorites list for the same user, before we add it. The following SQL does this check for us:

```
        // only want to add this if it's not already in the database
        $sql = "SELECT
                    COUNT(forum_pref_id)
                FROM
                    ".PREFIX."_forums_prefs
                WHERE
                    forum_topic_id = " . $aFavorite[$i] . " AND
                    account_id = $iAccountId";
```

We can use this query to conditionally add the topic in question to the favorites list:

```
        if( $this->_oConn->getOne($sql) == 0 ) {
            $sql = "INSERT INTO ".PREFIX."_forums_prefs (
                        forum_topic_id , account_id)
                    VALUES (
                        '" . $aFavorite[$i] . "' ,
                        '$iAccountId'
                        )";

            $rsTmp = $this->_oConn->query($sql);

            if( DB::isError($rsTmp) ) {

                catchExc($rsTmp->getMessage());
                return FALSE;
            }
        }
    }
    return TRUE;
}
// }}}
```

We can add favorites, but we want to be able to remove them also. The following method is very similar to addFavorites(), except that it handles deletion. The SQL is a little simpler here since we don't have to worry about 'double deletion' happening. That is to say, users can't take one of the topics in their favorites list out twice in the way that they could add a topic to the list twice.

Here is the delFavorites() script:

```
// {{{ delFavorites

/**
 * delete indicated topics from favorites
 *
 * @param array favorites IDs
 * @param integer account ID
 * @return boolean
 */
function delFavorites($aFavorite,$iAccountId) {

    if( !is_array($aFavorite) ) {

        catchExc("Passed non-array value for favorites.");
        return FALSE;
    }

    if( !is_numeric($iAccountId) ) {

        catchExc("Passed non-numeric value for account id.");
        return FALSE;
    }
```

Again, we'll loop through the topic IDs contained in the $aFavorite array. For each topic ID, we'll perform a simple SQL query to remove the corresponding row from the database:

```
    for( $i=0 ; $i < count($aFavorite) ; ++$i ) {

        $sql = "DELETE FROM
                    ".PREFIX."_forums_prefs
                WHERE
                    forum_topic_id = " . $aFavorite[$i] . " AND
                    account_id = $iAccountId";

        $rsTmp = $this->_oConn->query($sql);

        if( DB::isError($rsTmp) ) {

            catchExc($rsTmp->getMessage());
            return FALSE;
        }
    }
    return TRUE;
}
// }}}
```

Next, we'll define the `getTopicDisplay()` method. This gets the topic ID, name, and reply count for a grouping of topics.

There is some conditional logic related to the `$sView` argument passed. Basically, we're looking to see if the users are looking at all the topics, or just their favorites, since the list of things to be displayed is most likely different for those two cases. Naturally, we only want information for topics that have not been deleted. The data is returned to us in a convenient associative array so that we may do what we like with it. As mentioned earlier, note that the class is only used to handle data, and does not in any way deal with how the data is to be displayed.

Here is the class listing:

```
// {{{ getTopicDisplay

/**
 * get the data to be displayed
 *
 * @param integer cursor position
 * @param string view mode
 * @param integer account ID
 * @return array
 */
function getTopicDisplay($iCursor,$sView,$iAccountId) {
```

The SQL for the case where the user's view is 'recent' is simple, since we're just getting all the recent topics posted:

```
if( !strcmp($sView,"recent") ) {

    $sql = "SELECT
                forum_id,
                forum_name,
                forum_reply_cnt
            FROM
                ".PREFIX."_forums
            WHERE
                deleted = 0
            ORDER BY
                modified_dt DESC
            LIMIT
                $iCursor,".ROWCOUNT;
} else {
```

If the view is not 'recent', meaning that the user is in the 'favorites' view mode, the SQL is a little more complex. We have to do a `JOIN` operation with the `apress_forums_prefs` table to get the topics that the user has in his/her favorites list, like this:

```
    $sql = "SELECT
                forum_id,
                forum_name,
                forum_reply_cnt
```

```
                        FROM
                            ".PREFIX."_forums forums,
                            ".PREFIX."_forums_prefs prefs
                        WHERE
                            deleted = 0 AND
                            forums.forum_id = prefs.forum_topic_id AND
                            prefs.account_id = $iAccountId
                        ORDER BY
                            modified_dt DESC
                        LIMIT
                            $iCursor,".ROWCOUNT;
        }
```

The execution of the query is independent of the SQL statement used:

```
        $rsTmp = $this->_oConn->query($sql);
        if( DB::isError($rsTmp) ) {

            catchExc($rsTmp->getMessage());
        } else {
```

If there are no errors, the function loops through the result set and populates the array that it will return, as follows:

```
            // counter for $topic array
            $i=0;

            while( list($id,$name,$replyCount) =
                    $rsTmp->fetchRow(DB_FETCHMODE_ORDERED) ) {
                $aTopic[$i]["Id"] = $id;
                $aTopic[$i]["Name"] = $name;
                $aTopic[$i]["ReplyCount"] = $replyCount;
                ++$i;
            }
        }
        return $aTopic;
    }
    // }}}
```

There is one last method that we'll define in this class. At times, for the pager functionality, we'll want to know the total number of topics that can be displayed. Again, this will depend on whether the user is looking at the full list or just his or her favorites, so we'll see the $sView variable being used again:

```
    // {{{ getTotalTopics

    /**
     * get total number of undeleted topics
     *
     * @param string view
     * @param integer account ID
     * @return integer
     */
    function getTotalTopics($sView,$iAccountId) {
        // need to know total number of topics for paging
```

Again, if the user is simply looking at all the topics, the SQL used to get the number available is very simple:

```
            if( !strcmp($sView,"recent") ) {

                $sql = "SELECT COUNT(forum_id)
                        FROM ".PREFIX."_forums
                        WHERE deleted = 0";
            } else {
```

If the user is in the 'favorites' mode, then we'll again use a JOIN (a LEFT JOIN this time) to make use of the apress_forums_prefs table, like this:

```
                $sql = "SELECT
                            COUNT(forum_topic_id)
                        FROM
                            ".PREFIX."_forums_prefs prefs
                        LEFT JOIN
                            ".PREFIX."_forums forums
                        ON
                            (prefs.forum_topic_id=forums.forum_id)
                        WHERE
                            deleted = 0 AND
                            prefs.account_id = $iAccountId";
            }
            return $this->_oConn->getOne($sql);
        }

    // }}}
}

} // end class forumtopic
?>
```

This brings us to the end of the forumtopic class, which is the largest one we'll be creating for this module. The only class left to write is the forumreply class, which is detailed next.

class.forumreply.php

The file for this class is /_lib/_classes/class.forumreply.php. The methods and variables that we'll be creating here are in some cases similar to those of the topic class, so if you understood that, then this shouldn't be any trouble at all.

We'll begin in the usual fashion by defining the member variables that the class needs:

```
    <?php

    // File Location: /_lib/_classes/class.forumreply.php

    require_once("class.forumhelp.php");

    class forumreply extends forumhelp {

        /**
         * @var integer
         */
        var $_iTopicId;
```

```
/**
 * @var string
 */
var $_sReply;

/**
 * @var integer
 */
var $_iAccountId;
```

The constructor is a little more involved than it was for the previous class. Again it calls the constructor for its parent class, but we are allowing the user the option of passing values for two of its member variables. We check for these and set the variables if that's the appropriate thing to do:

```
// {{{ Constructor

/**
 * constructor
 *
 * @access public
 * @param integer forum ID [optional]
 */
function forumreply($iAccountId = '', $iTopicId = '') {
```

As with the `forumtopic` class, we want to inherit all the functionality of the helper class. So we call `parent::forumhelp()`:

```
// ensure that we have everything from the parent class
parent::forumhelp();
```

If account or topic IDs were supplied, initialize the member variables:

```
// set account ID if supplied
if( strcmp($iAccountId,'') ) {

    if( is_numeric($iAccountId) ){
        $this->_iAccountId = $iAccountId;
    } else {
        catchExc("Tried to set poster id to non-int value in " .
                __FILE__);
    }
}

// set topic ID if supplied
if( strcmp($iTopicId,'') ) {

    if( is_numeric($iTopicId) ) {
        $this->_iTopicId = $iTopicId;
    } else {
        catchExc("Tried to set forum id to non-int value in " .
                __FILE__);
    }
}
}
// }}}
```

Since we've been through this a few times now, let's just take a quick look at the set methods for the three member variables at the top of the class file:

```
// {{{ setTopicId

/**
 * Set the Forum ID variable
 *
 * @param integer forum ID
 */
function setTopicId($iTopicId) {

    if( is_numeric($iTopicId) ) {

        $this->_iTopicId = $iTopicId;

    } else {

        catchExc("Tried to set forum id to non-int value in " .
                __FILE__);
        return FALSE;
    }
}

// }}}
// {{{ setAccountId

/**
 * Set the Poster ID variable
 *
 * @param integer poster ID
 */
function setAccountId($iAccountId) {

    if( is_numeric($iAccountId) ) {

        $this->_iAccountId = $iAccountId;

    } else {

        catchExc("Tried to set poster id to non-int value in " .
                __FILE__);
        return FALSE;
    }
}

// }}}
// {{{ setReply

/**
 * Set the reply
 *
 * @param string the reply
 */
function setReply($sReply) {

    if( !is_string($sReply) ) {
```

```
            catchExc("Tried to set post reply to non-string value in " .
                 __FILE__);
            return FALSE;
        }

        if( $this->_bStripHtml ) {
            $this->_sReply = $this->_stripHtml($sReply);
        } else {
            $this->_sReply = $sReply;
        }
    }
// }}}
```

The first interesting method we come to is getReplyFromDB(). For a given reply, the pieces of information we'll need for the display are the account_id, the reply itself, and the screen name of the poster. This method will query the necessary tables and return this information to us, for use as an associative array:

```
// {{{ getReplyFromDB

/**
 * get the relevant post information for a given ID
 *
 * @param integer the post ID
 * @return array associative array with data
 */
function getReplyFromDB($iReplyId) {

    if( !is_numeric($iReplyId) ) {
        catchExc("Tried to get post info with non-int post id in " .
                 __FILE__);
        return FALSE;
    }
```

As before, we'll be using the MySQL DATE_FORMAT() function to get a formatted string, so we need to define that format:

```
    // date format string for MySQL
    // form of Sun Dec 22nd, 2002 at HH:MM:SS
    $sDateFormat = "%a %b %D, %Y at %r";

    $sql = "SELECT
                r.account_id,forum_reply,
                DATE_FORMAT(r.created_dt,\"$sDateFormat\")
                        AS postdate,
                a.account_screenname
            FROM
                ".PREFIX."_forums_replies r
            LEFT JOIN
                ".PREFIX."_accounts a
            ON
                (r.account_id=a.account_id)
            WHERE
                r.forum_reply_id = $iReplyId";

    $rsTmp = $this->_oConn->query($sql);
```

```
              if( DB::isError($rsTmp) ) {
                  catchExc($rsTmp->getMessage());
              }

              list($id, $reply, $postDate, $screenName) = $rsTmp->fetchRow();

              $aReturn["Id"] = $id;
              $aReturn["Reply"] = $reply;
              $aReturn["PostDate"] = $postDate;
              $aReturn["ScreenName"] = $screenName;

              return $aReturn;
          }
      // }}}
```

Here we used a LEFT JOIN to get all the information we want in one query.

So far, we don't have a method to help us create a new reply in the database, so let's do that now. This method is quite similar to the corresponding method for the creation of topics. There is, however, one important difference. When somebody posts a reply, we need to update the replies table, but we must also update the reply count and the modified date for that topic in the apress_forums table. So, we'll perform an extra query to take care of that:

```
// {{{ createReply

/**
 * put a new reply into the db
 *
 * @access public
 */
function createReply() {

    if( !is_numeric($this->_iTopicId) ) {
        catchErr("Tried to use non-int forum id for post in " .
                 __FILE__);
        return FALSE;
    }

    if( !is_numeric($this->_iAccountId) ) {
        catchExc("Tried to use non-int poster id for post in " .
                 __FILE__);
        return FALSE;
    }

    if( !is_string($this->_sReply) ) {
        catchExc("Tried to use non-string reply for post in " .
                 __FILE__);
        return FALSE;
    }
```

In the INSERT statement, we make use of the PEAR::DB quote() method to ensure that our reply text is escaped correctly for insertion:

```
        $sql = "INSERT INTO ".PREFIX."_forums_replies(
                    forum_topic_id ,
                    account_id ,
                    forum_reply ,
                    created_dt ,
                    modified_dt)
            VALUES (
                    '" . $this->_iTopicId . "' ,
                    '" . $this->_iAccountId . "' ,
                    " . $this->_oConn->quote($this->_sReply) . " ,
                    NOW() ,
                    NOW()
                    )";

        $rsTmp = $this->_oConn->query($sql);

        if( DB::isError($rsTmp) ) {

            catchExc($rsTmp->getMessage());
            return FALSE;
        }
```

Now we'll update the reply count in the apress_forums table for this topic:

```
        $sql = "UPDATE ".PREFIX."_forums
            SET
                forum_reply_cnt = forum_reply_cnt + 1,
                modified_dt = NOW()
            WHERE
                forum_id = " . $this->_iTopicId;

        $rsTmp = $this->_oConn->query($sql);

        if( DB::isError($rsTmp) ) {

            catchExc($rsTmp->getMessage());
            return FALSE;
        }
        return TRUE;
    }
    // }}}
```

At this point, we can create replies and grab them out of the database, but our admin functionality requires that we have methods to set the deleted flag for a specific reply. This is fairly simple to do, and again, would look almost exactly like the deletion methods for the topics. However, we need to take into account the reply count in the apress_forums table. If a certain reply is deleted, then the reply count for the corresponding topic should be decreased.

The following two methods will handle the deletion and reinstatement of the replies. Note that the reinstatement process is exactly the reverse of the deletion process. We set the deleted flag back to 0, and re-increment the reply count for the corresponding topic in the forums table:

```
// {{{ deleteReply

/**
 * Set deleted flag for a reply to 1
 *
 * @param integer reply ID
 */
function deleteReply($iReplyId) {

    if( !is_numeric($iReplyId) ) {

        catchExc("Tried to delete reply with non-int reply id in " .
                __FILE__);
        return FALSE;
    }
```

We'll have to get the topic ID so that we can update the reply count for this topic:

```
// we need the topic ID, because we'll need to update the
// reply count for this topic once we delete the reply
$sql = "SELECT forum_topic_id
        FROM ".PREFIX."_forums_replies
        WHERE forum_reply_id = " . $iReplyId;

$iTopicId = $this->_oConn->getOne($sql);

if( DB::isError($iTopicId) ) {

    catchExc($iTopicId->getMessage());
    return FALSE;
}
```

Set the indicated ID as deleted, and set the deleted and modified dates:

```
$sql = "UPDATE ".PREFIX."_forums_replies
        SET
            deleted = 1,
            deleted_dt = NOW() ,
            modified_dt = NOW()
        WHERE
            forum_reply_id = " . $iReplyId;

$rsTmp = $this->_oConn->query($sql);
if( DB::isError($rsTmp) ) {

    catchExc($rsTmp->getMessage());
    return FALSE;
}
```

Now, update the forums table to fix the reply count:

```
$sql = "UPDATE ".PREFIX."_forums
        SET forum_reply_cnt = forum_reply_cnt - 1
        WHERE forum_id = " . $iTopicId;
```

```
            $rsTmp = $this->_oConn->query($sql);
            if( DB::isError($rsTmp) ) {

                catchExc($rsTmp->getMessage());
                return FALSE;
            }
    }
    // }}}
```

Contained below is the code to later reinstate a reply that was deleted:

```
    // {{{ undeleteReply

    /**
     * Set deleted flag for a reply to 0
     *
     * @param integer reply ID
     */
    function undeleteReply($iReplyId) {

        if( !is_numeric($iReplyId) ) {

            catchExc("Tried to undelete reply with non numeric reply id in "
                    __FILE__);
            return FALSE;
        }

        // we'll need the forum topic ID so that we can update the reply
        // count
        $sql = "SELECT forum_topic_id
                FROM ".PREFIX."_forums_replies
                WHERE forum_reply_id = $iReplyId";

        $iTopicId = $this->_oConn->getOne($sql);
        if( DB::isError($iTopicId) ) {

            catchExc($iTopicId->getMessage());
            return FALSE;
        }

        // set the deleted flag for the indicated reply to 0
        $sql = "UPDATE ".PREFIX."_forums_replies
                SET
                    deleted = 0,
                    modified_dt = NOW()
                WHERE
                    forum_reply_id = " . $iReplyId;

        $rsTmp = $this->_oConn->query($sql);
        if( DB::isError($rsTmp) ) {

            catchExc($rsTmp->getMessage());
            return FALSE;
        }

        // increment the reply count for this forum
        $sql = "UPDATE ".PREFIX."_forums
```

```
                    SET forum_reply_cnt = forum_reply_cnt + 1
                    WHERE forum_id = " . $iTopicId;

        $rsTmp = $this->_oConn->query($sql);
        if( DB::isError($rsTmp) ) {

            catchExc($rsTmp->getMessage());
            return FALSE;
        }
    }
    // }}}
```

There is one last method that we need, and its job is to get an array of the IDs of the replies that we'll display on a certain page. We don't have to worry about the 'view status' in this case, since that only affects a view where the user sees a collection of topics. Once the user is browsing through a specific topic, the display is the same regardless:

```
    // {{{ getReplyIds

    /**
     * get the IDs of the replies we want to show
     *
     * @param integer cursor position
     * @param integer forum ID
     * @return array
     */
    function getReplyIds($iCursor,$iTopicId) {

        // we will return the $aReplyId array
        $aReplyId = array();

        $sql = "SELECT
                    forum_reply_id
                FROM
                    ".PREFIX."_forums_replies
                WHERE
                    forum_topic_id = $iTopicId AND
                    deleted = 0
                ORDER BY
                    created_dt
                LIMIT
                    $iCursor, " . ROWCOUNT;

        $rsTmp = $this->_oConn->query($sql);
        if( DB::isError($rsTmp) ) {

            catchExc($rsTmp->getMessage());
            return FALSE;
        }

        // loop through our results
        while( list($id) = $rsTmp->fetchRow() ) {
            $aReplyId[] = $id;
        }
        return $aReplyId;
    }
```

```
    // }}}

} // end class forumreply

?>
```

We have now, finally, created the data objects. In the next section, we'll put together the UIs for the forums.

There are just four distinct pages that we'll need, and two of those are very similar. Each page will have a little procedural PHP code that will serve to ascertain the appropriate action and invoke the proper object methods. Fortunately, we have developed feature-complete classes so the amount of procedural code needed on each page is quite small.

Implementing the Forum's UI

Finishing this module will involve the creation of the UI, and the integration of the data objects created to provide content to the user. In addition to the classes written so far, we'll be implementing the session functionality that was discussed in Chapter 4. This will allow the code to handle users and visitors appropriately.

The Required UI Files

There will be a total of four interface files for the forums, and each will reside in the /site/forums directory. A brief listing of these, with descriptions, is given below:

❑ **index.php** – This is the home page for this module. It'll present the user with a list of topic titles to explore. That list will be dependent on whether the person is logged in or not, and what his/her view type (refers to the user's choice of seeing all topics or just his or her favorites) is.

❑ **showreply.php** – On this page, the visitors will see the topic they are interested in along with the replies associated with it. Furthermore, users will have the option of posting a reply to the topic.

❑ **starttopic.php** – This is the page that will allow users to start their own topics. If visitors try to access this page, they'll automatically be redirected to the accounts section where they can log in.

❑ **postreply.php** – Here, users can post replies to topics. They'll be able to see the topic they are replying to. Again, if visitors try to access this page without being logged in, they'll be sent to the accounts section.

On each page, there will be a bit of procedural PHP code. This will serve to check on things such as whether people are logged in or not, and then to instantiate and use the data objects that we've created according to what is discovered. Fortunately, since we've developed a lot of functionality in our objects, we won't need a lot of code on any of the display pages. This corresponds with our goal of keeping the presentation and business layers of our application separate.

The HTML layout that we'll create will make use of the framework defined in Chapter 3. Specifically, we'll be including /site/tpl_unsecure.php on our pages and using it to generate menus, banner advertisements, and the footer for the page. We'll only need to write three more PHP functions along the way. These will be responsible for generating HTML, for topics and for replies, based on the data returned from our classes. With this in mind, let's start with the /site/forums/index.php file.

index.php

Here is a 'To Do' list of objectives that we need to accomplish on this page:

- ❑ Check to see if the person viewing the page is logged in
- ❑ See if the user has a preference for page view
- ❑ Add or remove favorites if necessary
- ❑ Get the IDs for the topics to display
- ❑ Get the information needed for the paging functionality
- ❑ Display the corresponding content to the user

We'll start off this page by including the files we need. This includes the `tpl_unsecure.php` file that helps us with the UI, the `accounts` class (created in Chapter 5), and the `forumtopic` class shown previously:

```php
<?php

// File Location: /site/forums/index.php

require_once("tpl_unsecure.php");
require_once("class.accounts.php");
require_once("class.forumtopic.php");
```

Next we'll instantiate a topic object to use, since we'll always need one for this page:

```php
// we'll need a forumtopic object on this page
$oForumTopic = new forumtopic;
```

The next thing we need to do is to check if we have a user or a visitor. We can do this by creating an accounts object that can be used to check on the person's state, by first checking to see if the accounts cookie is defined, and then (assuming it is) checking to make sure the person has a valid session. This ensures that people can't fool the system by simply creating a false cookie:

```php
///////////////////////////////////////////////////////////////////////////////
// get session if the user is logged in
///////////////////////////////////////////////////////////////////////////////

$oAccounts = new accounts;

if( isset($_COOKIE["cACCOUNT"]) && $oAccounts->validateSession() ) {
    $aSess = $oAccounts->getSession();
```

Remember that if users are logged in, they have the option of two different types of page views – they can see all topics or just the ones they've designated as favorites. Therefore, we need to check to see what their preferred view is. The default will be all topics, but we can set a cookie if they want to customize their view:

```php
///////////////////////////////////////////////////////////////////////////////
// handle viewing of recent vs. favorites
///////////////////////////////////////////////////////////////////////////////
```

```
    if( $_GET["view"] ) {

        $sView = $_GET["view"];
        setcookie("cFORUMVIEW", $_GET["view"], time()+(TIMEOUT / 2), "/",
                  "", "");

    } elseif ( isset($_COOKIE["cFORUMVIEW"]) ) {
        $sView = $_COOKIE["cFORUMVIEW"];

    } else {
        $sView = "recent";
    }
```

If the user is not logged in, then the view defaults to all topics:

```
    } else {
        $sView = "recent";
    }
```

Now we're going to check and see if we need to add or remove any favorites for this user. We don't have to check to see if the user is logged in for this. Users see a form that allows them to submit a POST request for the desired action. All that we need to do is to check if the correct POST variables exist in $_POST. Visitors won't even have the form presented to them, so they won't have the option:

```
///////////////////////////////////////////////////////////////////////////
// add or remove from favorites if posted
///////////////////////////////////////////////////////////////////////////

$sAddFavorites = "btn_addfavs.gif";
$sDelFavorites = "btn_remfavs.gif";

if( !strcmp($_POST["submitFavorites"],$sAddFavorites) &&
    count($_POST["favorite"]) ) {
    $oForumTopic->addFavorites($_POST["favorite"] , $aSess["Account Id"]);
}

if( !strcmp($_POST["submitFavorites"],$sDelFavorites) &&
    count($_POST["favorite"]) ) {
    $oForumTopic->delFavorites($_POST["favorite"] , $aSess["Account Id"]);
}
```

This code will make a little more sense later down the page when we create the form. For now, the general idea is clear – we check for specific POST variables, and then use the 'add' and 'delete' methods that we built into the forumtopic class.

Next on our list of objectives for this page is getting the IDs of the topic titles that we want to display. Again, this is made easy due to our forumtopic class:

```
// now, let's grab the topic IDs and titles for the
// topics we'll be displaying
$aTopic = $oForumTopic->getTopicDisplay($iCursor,$sView,
                                        $aSess["Account Id"]);
```

Now we have all the necessary IDs stored in the $aTopic array. You'll remember that the $iCursor variable is given to us by the tpl_unsecure.php file. It helps keep track of the position in the result set.

The last thing to do before we get to the HTML is to set a variable that is needed for the paging. Yet again, the topic object makes this very easy to do:

```
// we'll need this for paging
$iTotalTopics = $oForumTopic->getTotalTopics($sView,$aSess["Account Id"]);
```

Since this is the first page we are looking at, we'll go through all the code and HTML; later on we'll only examine the interesting parts. We start the page with functions from tpl_unsecure.php, and then there is some (almost) static HTML:

```
setHeader();
openPage(true);

?>

<table border="0" cellpadding="0" cellspacing="0">
    <tr>
        <td><div class="header"><?php print ENTITY; ?> Forums</div></td>
    </tr>

    <tr>
        <td>
            <table cellpadding="6" cellspacing="0" border="0">
```

Now, it's time for some conditional logic. If a user is logged in, then the $aSess variable will be set and populated with session information. This type of user should have options for the view type and for starting a new topic. If there is no $aSess variable, then the user should just see a link to the login page:

```
<table cellpadding="6" cellspacing="0" border="0">

    <?php if( count($aSess) ) { ?>
        <tr>
          <td><a href="<?php print SELF; ?>?view=recent">
              Recent Topics</a></td>
          <td><a href="<?php print SELF; ?>
              ?view=favorites">Favorites</a></td>
          <td><a href="starttopic.php">Start a Topic</a></td>
        </tr>

    <?php } else { ?>
        <tr>
          <td colspan="3"><a href="/site/accounts/">Login</a>
           to create or reply to the forums!</td>
        </tr>
    <?php } ?>
```

We have some more HTML and PHP, it finishes out the current table (and writes out any errors generated), and then starts a form and the next table on the page:

```
          </table>
        </td>
      </tr>

      <tr>
        <td><div class="error"><?php writeErrors(); ?></div></td>
      </tr>

   </table>

   <form name="favourites" method="post" action="<?php print SELF; ?>">
   <table width="608" border="0" cellpadding="0" cellspacing="0">
```

Now, it's time to write out our links onto the page, using the writeTopicLink() method (shown shortly). For now, you just need to know that it takes the submitted arguments and prints out the requested HTML:

```
<?php

for( $i=0 ; $i < count($aTopic) ; ++$i ) {
    writeTopicLink($aTopic[$i]["Id"],$aTopic[$i]["Name"],
                   $aTopic[$i]["ReplyCount"]);
}
?>

    <tr>
        <td>
        <!--| paging |-->
        <table border="0" cellpadding="0" cellspacing="0" width="100%">
        <tr>
            <td align="left">
```

It was pointed out earlier that if users were not logged in, then they would not be able to submit the favorites form. The easiest way to keep them from submitting the form is to not expose any SUBMIT form elements to them. To accomplish this, we'll check for the existence of the $aSess array. If it's there, then the user is logged in and is shown a submit button. If not, then we have a visitor who will not be shown this button:

```
        <?php if( count($aSess) ) { ?>
            <input type="submit"
            value="<?php !strcmp($sView,"recent") ?
            print $sAddFavorites : print $sDelFavourites; ?>"
            name="submitFavorites">
        <?php } ?>
```

Here, there is a little bit of sneakiness on our part. If the user's view is recent, then we show the user an ADD FAVORITES button to add topics to the favorites list. If the view is not recent then he or she is already in the favorites mode. In this case, we show the user a REMOVE FAVORITES button to remove the selected items.

All that's left is to render the HTML needed for our pager. The `renderPaging()` function defined in `/_lib/_base/elements.php` takes care of the work for us. As usual, we need to supply it with the cursor position and the total number of items we're dealing with (stored in `$iTotalTopics`):

```
            </td>

            <td align="right">
                <?php renderPaging($iCursor,$iTotalTopics); ?>
             </td>

        </table>
        <!--| paging |-->
        </td>
    </tr>
</table>
</form>

<?php closePage(); ?>
```

In just a moment, you'll see what all of this looks like but, before that, let's return to the `writeTopicLink()` function that we used earlier that had the responsibility of printing out topic titles to the screen. Additionally, if the user was logged in, the function had to create checkboxes that the user could click on to add or remove favorites.

We've avoided using our data objects for generating any kind of output to be displayed to the end user. This brings up the question, "Is it better to create functions to generate display markup, or should we extend the data object classes and write markup writer methods in those new classes?" This is a matter of personal preference. In this case, we'll only need three functions, and we already have a file (`/_lib/_base/elements.php`) of functions dedicated to generating page elements, so we're going to add our functions to that file.

It's not very complicated, so let's look at it first and then talk about it:

```
// write an element of the topic list
function writeTopicLink($topicId,$topicTitle,$replyCount) {
    global $aSess;

    ?>
    <tr>
        <td>
            <table border="0" cellpadding="0" cellspacing="0" width="100%">
                <tr>
                    <td align="left">
                    <div class="section">
                        <?php if( count($aSess) ) { ?>
                            <input type="checkbox" name="favorite[]"
                             value="<?php print $topicId; ?>" />
                            <img src="../../_img/spc.gif"
                             width="10" height="1" alt="" border="0" />
                        <?php } ?>
```

```
                        <a href="showtopic.php?topicId=
                        <?php print $topicId; ?>">
                        <?php print format($topicTitle); ?></a>
                    </td>

                    <td align="right">
                    [ <?php print $replyCount; ?> replies ]
                    </div>
                    </td>
                </tr>
            </table>
        </td>
    </tr>

    <tr>
        <td class="dotrule"><img src="../../_img/spc.gif"
        width="1" height="15" alt="" border="0" /></td>
    </tr>

<?php
}
```

Most of this function prints HTML out to the screen, inserting the supplied argument data where necessary. We get the $aSess global variable and use it to conditionally include the checkboxes for the form. Again, if a user isn't logged in, he or she simply isn't presented with the option of viewing the favorites list.

This brings us to the end of the index.php page. A visitor would see a page like this:

As you can see, the visitor doesn't have any real options outside of looking at the topic replies and going to the login page. This is in line with the idea of giving visitors read-only access.

A user who is logged in will see a page like this:

As desired, the user has options to start new topics and set his or her view type.

starttopic.php

Since we've now provided a link to let logged-in users start topics, we should probably create the page that will actually let them perform this function, which is the /site/forums/starttopic.php script.

Our 'To Do' list for this page is a little shorter than it was for the previous example:

- ❑ Ensure that the user is logged in, and send him or her to the login page if he/she is not
- ❑ If the user submitted any form data, ensure that it's valid
- ❑ If it's valid, insert the data in the database and redirect the user to the home page
- ❑ If nothing was posted or if there was invalid data, generate a form where the user can start a new topic

Let's get right into the PHP code at the top of the page:

```php
<?php

require_once("tpl_unsecure.php");
require_once("class.accounts.php");
```

People must be logged in to be able to start a new topic. Therefore, the code will check this, and send them to the login page so they can log in or register, if not. If they're logged in, it'll put the session information in the familiar $aSess array:

```
// if the person isn't logged in, send him or her to login page
$oAccounts = new accounts;

// if user is logged in, add his/her session information to the $aSess array
$oAccounts->validateSession()
            ? $aSess = $oAccounts->getSession() :
            header("Location: /site/accounts/index.php");
```

To handle any form data that may have been submitted, we need two pieces of information – the topic title and the topic entry – so we need to make sure that these were entered:

```
// see if they posted anything
if( $_POST ) {
```

To ensure that the data entered is formatted well, we'll first use trim() to remove any leading or trailing whitespace, and then use stripslashes() to take care of any escaped quotation marks:

```
// first remove leading and trailing whitespace, then
// strip unwanted slashes
$sTopicTitle = stripslashes(trim($_POST["topictitle"]));
$sTopicText = stripslashes(trim($_POST["topictext"]));

// make sure they put something in for the title
if( !strcmp($sTopicTitle,'') ) {

    catchErr("Topic needs a title.");
}

// make sure they put something in for the entry
if( !strcmp($sTopicText,'') ) {

    catchErr("Topic needs an entry.");
}
```

Once again we're using the catchErr() function to handle errors. If there are any, then they'll be printed out automatically for the user to see when the writeErrors() function is called in the page.

Now, if there are no errors, we can instantiate a topic object and use the defined methods to put this data into the database:

```
// if there are no errors, create the topic
    if( !count($ERRORS) ) {

        // we can include this now since we know we'll need it
        require_once("class.forumtopic.php");
        $oForumTopic = new forumtopic();

        // set the account ID, topic name, and topic text
        $oForumTopic->setAccountId($aSess["Account Id"]);
```

```
        $oForumTopic->setTopicName($sTopicTitle);
        $oForumTopic->setTopicText($sTopicText);

        // now create the topic in the db
        if( $oForumTopic->createTopic() ) {
            header("Location: index.php");
        }
    }
}
```

The methods we have defined make this task very easy to accomplish. Here we redirect the user with the `header()` function. Note that we are careful to ensure that no other output has been sent to the browser at this point.

Having done this, the rest of the page is basically the trivial task of setting up an HTML form with the proper fields to use. We're not going to cover this since we have already done the real work for this page. Refer to the file in the code bundle, to see the specifics. When done, it'll display a page like this:

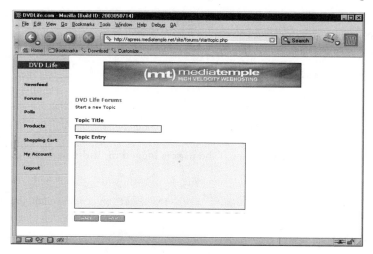

showtopic.php

Now we have the ability to view a topic listing and to create new topics. The next step is to add the ability to look at any replies that are available for the topics. We'll do this in the `/site/forums/showtopic.php` file.

Our list of objectives is very similar to the 'To Do' list for the `index.php` page:

❑   Ensure that there is a GET variable defining the topic ID

❑   See if the user is logged in, and if so get his/her session information

❑   Get information about the topic we want to display so that we can show it to the user

❑   Get the IDs of the replies that we're going to show on this page

❑   Show the full topic

❑   Show the appropriate replies for this page

This page starts out a little differently than the previous pages. Any user who comes here should have an identifier for the topic ID that is passed as a GET variable. If this isn't set, then we'll send the user back to the forums home page:

```php
<?php

// we should always have a $_GET["topicId"] set on this page.
// Redirect them if we don't
if( !isset($_GET["topicId"]) ) {
    header("Location: index.php");

} else {
    $iTopicId = $_GET["topicId"];
}
```

Having done that, we'll include the required files and instantiate two objects that we'll need a little later on:

```php
require_once("tpl_unsecure.php");
require_once("class.accounts.php");
require_once("class.forumreply.php");
require_once("class.forumtopic.php");

// we'll need these objects on this page
$oForumReply = new forumreply;
$oForumTopic = new forumtopic;
```

As with the home page, we'll check to see if the user is logged in. If the user is logged in, then we'll get the session information:

```php
// if user is logged in, get the session information in the $aSess array
$oAccounts = new accounts;

if( isset($_COOKIE["cACCOUNT"]) && $oAccounts->validateSession() ) {

    $aSess = $oAccounts->getSession();
}
```

Now, on every page where we see replies it would be useful to show the topic in full so that the user can quickly reference anything that the repliers are talking about. To do this, we'll need to get the topic information from the database by using the `$oForumTopic` object:

```php
// we'll want to show the topic on every page
// so that the users can see what they're replying to
$aHeaderArgs = $oForumTopic->getTopicFromDb($iTopicId);
```

And, of course, we'll need to retrieve the IDs of the replies that we are going to show on this page:

```php
// now, get the IDs for the replies we're going to show
$aReplyId = $oForumReply->getReplyIds($iCursor,$iTopicId);
```

Again, we aren't going to go through the entire HTML. The first interesting part is in the following lines:

```php
<?php if( count($aSess) ) { ?>

    <a href="postreply.php?topicId=<?php print $iTopicId; ?>">
     Post a reply</a>

<?php } else { ?>

    <a href="/site/accounts">Login</a> to post replies.
<?php } ?>
```

This is analogous to what we did on the index.php page before. If the user is logged in, then he or she is shown a link (with a $topicId GET variable defined) to a page where the user can post a reply. Otherwise, he or she sees a link to the login screen.

The next thing worth examining is where we print out the full topic. Here we'll use the writeTopic() method. For now we just need to know that it's used to print the form header:

```php
<?php
// print out the forum header
writeTopic($aHeaderArgs["ScreenName"],$aHeaderArgs["CreatedDate"],
           $aHeaderArgs["ReplyCount"],$aHeaderArgs["TopicName"],
           $aHeaderArgs["TopicText"]);
?>
```

Of course, the purpose of our writeTopic() method will be to generate appropriate HTML to display the topic based on these arguments. Immediately following this, we'll invoke another currently undefined function (writeReply()) to write out the replies. We'll do this by looping through the reply IDs and getting the necessary data from the database using class methods. Then, our undefined function will generate the necessary markup:

```php
<?php

// now print out our replies
for( $i=0 ; $i < count($aReplyId) ; ++$i ) {
    $aReplyArgs = $oForumReply->getReplyFromDb($aReplyId[$i]);
    writeReply($aReplyArgs["ScreenName"] , $aReplyArgs["PostDate"] ,
               $aReplyArgs["Reply"]);
}
?>
```

The rest of the page is not involved enough to review in detail. Instead, let's go ahead and write the two display functions – writeTopic() and writeReply(). Both of these functions go in the /_lib/_base/elements.php file just as our previous display function did.

The writeTopic() function is very simple. It just generates some HTML and inserts the arguments where necessary:

```php
// write a topic element
function writeTopic($sPoster,$sDate,$iReplies,$sTitle,$sText) {
    ?>
```

```
    <tr>
        <td><div class="forumhead">
            [ posted by <?php print $sPoster; ?> on <?php print $sDate; ?> ]
            [ <?php print $iReplies; ?> replies ]<br />
            <br />
            <b><?php print format($sTitle); ?></b><br />
            <br />
            <?php print format($sText); ?>
        </div></td>
    </tr>

    <tr>
        <td class="dotrule"><img src="../../_img/spc.gif"
         width="1" height="15" alt="" border="0" /></td>
    </tr>
<?php
}
```

The writeReply() function is a bit more complicated. It has two optional arguments – $bDelete and $iReplyId – that are relevant in the context of the admin and need explanation. The purpose of the admin for the forums is to allow web masters to delete topics or individual replies that are in some way unwanted. In the case of the topics display, we already have a mode with checkboxes for each topic, which is used for adding or removing favorites. It's easy to imagine adapting this same interface for the admin, along with the functionality to remove any topics that are checked. In fact this is exactly what is done.

To keep the interfaces uniform, we would, therefore, like to be able to have checkboxes for specific replies that would allow the web master to select the replies checked for deletion. That is what the $bDelete variable does. If it is not set to TRUE, then no checkbox will appear. If it is, then a checkbox is created with the value of the reply ID. We didn't supply values for these arguments above because the checkboxes shouldn't be visible to both users and visitors:

```
// write a reply element
function writeReply($sPoster,$sDate,$sReply,
                    $bDelete = FALSE, $iReplyId = -1) {
    ?>
    <tr>
        <td>
        <div class="forumreplyhead">
            [ posted by <?php print $sPoster; ?> on <?php print $sDate; ?> ]
        </div>
        <div class="copy">
            <?php print format($sReply); ?>
        </div>
```

If $bDelete is set, then we want to display a checkbox form element for use in the admin side of the forum:

```
        <?php if( $bDelete ) { ?>
            <br>
            <div class="error">Delete:: <input type="checkbox"
                name="deletereply[]" value="<?php print $iReplyId; ?>">
            </div>
        <?php } ?>

        </td>
```

```
        </tr>

        <tr>
            <td class="dotrule"><img src="../../_img/spc.gif"
            width="1" height="15" alt="" border="0" /></td>
        </tr>

<?php
}
```

This covers everything for the showtopic.php page. For a user, the display will look like this:

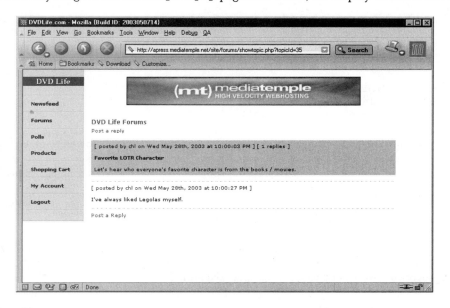

postreply.php

We need to create one more file in order to have a fully functioning forum system. The users need some way of posting replies to topics, and this will require the creation of the /site/forums/postreply.php file. This file operates almost identically to the starttopic.php file that we created earlier.

Here is the list of objectives for this page:

❑ Ensure that there is a GET variable defined, which specifies the topic to reply to

❑ Ensure that the user is logged in and redirect him/her if not

❑ Get the content for the topic the user is replying to, so we can show it to him/her while the entry is being made

❑ Validate any form data that might have been submitted, and put it in the database if it passes validation

❑ Display the form if there was no data submitted, or if there were errors

The beginning of the page should be very familiar at this point:

```php
<?php

// File Location: /site/forums/postreply.php

// we should always have a $_GET["topicId"] or $_POST["topicID"] set
// on this page. Redirect the user if we don't
if( isset($_POST["topicId"]) ) {
    $iTopicId = $_POST["topicId"];

} elseif ( isset($_GET["topicId"]) ) {
    $iTopicId = $_GET["topicId"];

} else {
    header("Location: index.php");
}

require_once("tpl_unsecure.php");
require_once("class.accounts.php");
require_once("class.forumtopic.php");
```

Next, we make sure the user is logged in, since only logged-in users are allowed to make replies:

```php
// if they're trying to come here not logged in, send them to login page
$oAccounts = new accounts;
$oAccounts->validateSession()
            ? $aSess = $oAccounts->getSession() :
            header("Location: /site/accounts/index.php");
```

Until this point the code was very similar to the page where users could start a new topic. We hit one twist here, however, as when the user is making a reply, it would be good if we could show the user the full topic. Therefore, we'll need to get the display data for this topic:

```php
// we'll want to print out the topic,
// so that the users can see what they are replying to
$oForumTopic = new forumtopic;
$aHeaderArgs = $oForumTopic->getTopicFromDb($iTopicId);
```

Now it's time to start examining any data that has come in as a POST submission from the form:

```php
// see if they posted anything
if($_POST) {
    $sReplyText = stripslashes(trim($_POST["replytext"]));

    // make sure they put something in for the entry
    if( !strcmp($sReplyText,'') ) {
        catchErr("Topic needs an entry.");
    }
```

If there are no errors, we'll create a reply object and use it to put the data into the database:

```php
    // if there are no errors, create the topic
    if( !count($ERRORS) ) {
```

```
          // we can include this now since we know we'll need it
          require_once("class.forumreply.php");

          // Note: Opening and reading the file is a fairly 'expensive'
          // operation for the server, so we do have some performance gain
          // by including the class only when and if we need to.

          $oForumReply = new forumreply($aSess["Account Id"] , $iTopicId);

          // set the creator ID, topic name, and topic text
          $oForumReply->setReply($sReplyText);

          // now create the reply in the db
          if( $oForumReply->createReply() ) {
              // put them back looking at the same topic they replied to
              header("Location: /site/forums/showtopic.php?topicId=$iTopicId");
          }
      }
  }
```

This is basically all of the work we need to do. The HTML for this page is again not worth examining in detail. We do display the topic to the user, but that is accomplished with the same writeTopic() function that we used earlier.

When finished, the page will look like in the following screenshot:

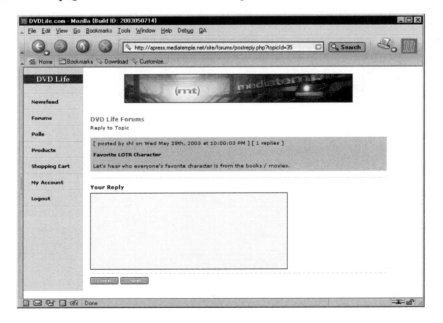

Summary

In this chapter we constructed a forum system. At this point, we have successfully built an application module that accomplishes the goals we set out to achieve. It makes use of the authentication that we developed earlier to differentiate between users who are logged in and those who aren't. Visitors have read-only abilities, whereas users can post new topics and replies. The users can also put topics they like into a grouping of favorites. The UI is generated largely with the system defined in Chapter 2, with our data objects being employed to get the rest of the data needed for the display.

These forums should provide a nice community building aspect of the site. Furthermore, it'll encourage new users to register with the site so that they'll have the option of interacting with the forum beyond the read-only access offered to visitors. Additionally, it gives us another place to display banner advertisements.

The administrative side that we have not covered is constructed in a fashion very similar to the forum itself. The data objects we created contain methods that can be used to selectively delete topics and/or replies. So the basic difference is that we use those methods instead of the `create*()` methods we saw here, which put data into the database. The code for the admin facility is included with the code bundle for the rest of the site.

11

Newsletters and Mailing Lists

Keeping the user informed and up to date is the most important job of a web site, and adding newsletter functionality to the web site is an effective way of getting this information across in a simple and controlled fashion. In this light, e-mail is an effective direct marketing tool, which can be used to help build an online community by ensuring that each user is receiving the same vital information. It can also help drive traffic back to our web site by informing the user about site changes and allowing the user to directly link back to a feature or update. Here, our primary focus in developing a mailing list is to provide a medium for keeping users informed about the latest DVD releases and related industry information.

In this chapter, we'll look at:

❑ The technical and business logic problems that come up when building a mailing system

❑ The marketing and functional problems that evolve out of the use and misuse of newsletters

❑ Using pre-built PEAR objects to make the job easier

❑ Tackling difficult system administration issues

We'll first identify and illustrate the key problems involved with building a newsletter system, and then look at some simple and concise ways of solving these issues. Once these issues are resolved, we'll begin to produce a design layout of how this system will work. Finally, we'll build and implement a mailing list program and place it into the unified framework of our Content Management System (CMS).

The Problem

One of the problems with adding a newsletter to the site is ensuring that this tool is not over-used. People do not enjoy receiving a massive amount of e-mail from any particular web site, and we do not want to force people to receive unsolicited e-mail from our organization. So the base purpose of our system would be to ensure that these intermittent newsletters are sent to only those users who choose to receive them.

Since the newsletter is used as a routine tool, we'll need to provide a convenient workflow system for the web master. We'll also need to provide an e-mail queuing system so that site members can grow accustomed to receiving our newsletter in a routine and timely manner. To provide a better reading experience, we'll want to develop a way of templating the newsletter so that the user can expect a certain amount of consistency when reading it.

A major issue that we've touched on in previous chapters is customization. Customization can be built into mailing lists in many ways depending upon the focused goal and the intended use. Since we're not trying to provide more than simple informative updates, we'll only be implementing a bare minimum of customization in our system. A simple example of e-mail customization is to start the e-mail with "Hello $Username". You could of course use these methods and design illustrations to build marketing-based customization into your mailing system.

The accounts and preferences tables (apress_accounts and apress_account_prefs, created in Chapter 5) that we have already set up will provide us with all the required data needed for this application. Since our web site already requires the visitor to sign up and create an account for increased interaction, we will have the user's e-mail address irrespective of the newsletter. Thus we won't need a separate provision for e-mail sign-up, since the account creation and administration process is based around this. It should be noted that out newsletter will only be received by those who have opted to receive it by setting their preferences accordingly from the /site/accounts/prefs.php page. Although this information has been created and stored, we'll need to develop a simple class method to pull out and return e-mail addresses from the pre-existing data tables.

One of the technical issues when building a mailing list in a shared environment is building around PHP's **safe mode**. While developing a site on a typical hosted platform, the server is most often running with the PHP safe mode enabled. This limits the use of certain core platform functionalities within the PHP environment, thus preventing users from opening and/or exploiting any security holes that may be present within the host system. PHP's safe mode alters the programming environment in many ways, including limiting the use and altering of environment variables and limiting the available readable files to a specific directory tree. The most prevalent issue from our standpoint, when building this application, will be to work around the inability to spawn off child processes with the use of a system shell – specifically, the inability to use the PHP shell_exec() method which is prevented by PHP's safe mode.

> Since PHP's entire execution process is completed prior to the output and display of a page, it's not possible to send a large number of e-mail messages prior to the timeout of a single page view.

When sending a message to a large userbase, we must take into consideration the time required for building and sending thousands of messages. This is something that does not usually take place in the time of a single page view and we'll need to work around this issue while avoiding the use of PHP's command line and system calls that are not available to us in our shared hosting environment. Furthermore, executing a process from the system's shell allows a time-lengthy process, such as a large mail send, to be activated by our CMS application. This allows the lengthy process to take as long as it needs to execute, rather than limiting it to the environment-defined maximum execution time.

The Design

The first thing to do while designing an application is to break it into smaller, more manageable modules. We'll divide our system into three main parts:

❑ **The data object layer** – This is the base to all of our data manipulation. In this case it will be a single PHP class.

❑ **The web master interface** – This will provide a means for the web masters to build and manage outgoing newsletters as well as queue them for sending.

❑ **The newsletter send daemon** – This will then pick up the newsletters and send them out to the site's mailing list while returning statistics to the CMS web master interface for later use.

A daemon is a program that runs in the background and is not invoked explicitly, but lies dormant waiting for some condition(s) to occur. The idea is that the program creating the condition need not be aware of a daemon, though often a program commits an action knowing that it will implicitly invoke the daemon.

We'll build the newsletter send daemon using a simple PHP script being executed by a server-side `crontab` running on an incremented time-table. When building this system in a Windows environment, we'll need to use the Scheduled Tasks Manager or AT to create the same effect. We'll talk about these two items in detail in the *Building the Send Daemon* section.

cron is a way of automating tasks under UNIX. The cron daemon looks at each other's crontab file every minute and checks to see if it needs to perform any actions.

Since both the CMS and the newsletter send daemon will be accessing and modifying data from the same tables, we'll build a singular data object that contains the functions for both the user interface and the `cron`-executed script. Some of the methods that we define will be used in only one of the two execution environments; however, the reuse of a few core methods will make this decision worthwhile.

> The send daemon is not a true daemon by definition, as it does not maintain an executed state at all times. We'll be calling it a daemon to imply that it is a background process that commits an action when specific changes are made to the data.

We'll use the PEAR::Mail objects for all of our outgoing e-mails. We'll explain the usage of this object in the *Implementing the Data Object* section; however, we'll not go into the details on the inner working of this object because of the depth of detail that it encompasses.

The following diagram illustrates the structure of our mailing system:

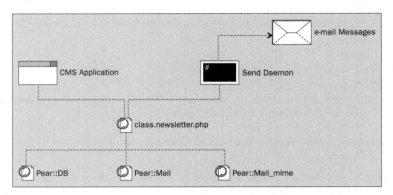

Designing the Data Layer

The database design for this application will be relatively simple. We'll use the predefined `apress_accounts` table, which will be joining `apress_account_prefs` to return our mailing list and user preferences. Both of these tables were created in Chapter 5.

The only table that we'll need to add is the `apress_newsletters` table, which will store our outgoing e-mail newsletters and returned usage statistics. The `apress_newsletters` table will also include the predefined table column constants that will be used to place the new data into our existing application security and presentation framework.

The data layer will consist of the following three tables:

❑ `apress_newsletters` to store the individual newsletters and their associated data

❑ `apress_accounts` to store the user's basic account information

❑ `apress_account_prefs` to hold the account user's application preferences

The Newsletters Table

The `apress_newsletters` table will store the newsletter content as well as log data returned by the e-mail send program, such as the number of recipients, the time it took to complete the send, as well as the web master that sent the message:

Field	Type	Description
newsletter_id	INT(10)	The unique identifier for the newsletter
admin_user_id	INT(10)	The identifier of the web master who sent the newsletter

Field	Type	Description
newsletter_subject	VARCHAR(255)	The subject of the newsletter
newsletter_body_text	TEXT	The newsletter text
newsletter_body_html	TEXT	The newsletter HTML bit
newsletter_send	DATETIME	Date that the newsletter should be sent
newsletter_sent	DATETIME	Date that the newsletter was sent
newsletter_send_complete	DATETIME	Date that the newsletter send process was completed
newsletter_recp_cnt	INT(10)	Number of recipients who will receive the newsletter
newsletter_send_status	INT(1)	Stores the send status of the newsletter
status	INT(1)	Flag to identify the newsletter status
deleted	INT(1)	Flag to set a 'deleted' status to the newsletter
deleted_dt	DATETIME	The date the newsletter was deleted
created_dt	DATETIME	The date the newsletter was created

Its primary key is newsletter_id, which will be used throughout the system to reference specific newsletters.

The Accounts Table

This apress_accounts table stores the user's basic account information. Its primary key is the account_id, which along with account_email will be the only data that we'll retrieve from this table:

Field	Type	Description
account_id	INT(1)	The unique identifier for each account record
account_pass	VARCHAR(32)	Password value with MD5 encryption
account_remind	VARCHAR(100)	Password value as plaintext
account_email	VARCHAR(100)	Unique e-mail address
account_screenname	VARCHAR(15)	Unique screen name
last_login_ip	VARCHAR(15)	IP address from last account login
last_login_host	VARCHAR(100)	Host name from last account login
last_login_dt	DATETIME	Date/time value from last account login

Table continued on following page

Field	Type	Description
status	INT(1)	Boolean value for account status
deleted	INT(1)	Boolean value for deleted account
deleted_dt	DATETIME	Date/time value when account was deleted
created_dt	DATETIME	Date/time value when account was created
modified_dt	DATETIME	Date/time value when account was last modified

The Account Preferences Table

The `apress_account_prefs` will be used to retrieve the user's mailing list preference, which is held in a field labeled `newsletter_recipient`:

Field	Type	Description
account_pref_id	INT(10)	The unique identifier for each account preferences record
account_id	INT(10)	Account reference ID
newsletter_recipient	INT(1)	Boolean flag for newsletter recipients
newsletter_format	VARCHAR(50)	Format type for newsletter
created_dt	DATETIME	Date/time value when the address record was created in the database table
modified_dt	DATETIME	Date/time value when address was last modified

Designing the Data Object

The newsletter program's data object will use three PEAR objects:

❏ The PEAR::DB object for database connectivity

❏ The PEAR::Mail object for all of its SMTP communications

❏ The PEAR Mail_mime object that'll allow us to create multi-part e-mails, thus allowing us to send HTML and plain-text bodies in the same e-mail

We'll build this PHP class using the same standards and methodology as described in previous chapters, but the implementation will be modified to suit our desired usage.

The Newsletter Class

This class handles all the assumed functionality that we could perform on/with a newsletter. As with the other classes that we've introduced, this class will include the creation, management, and removal of items (newsletters) within the context of our application framework. Unlike the other classes that we've introduced, this class will include all queuing and send management functions designed to be used from a shell-based environment.

Let's look at the outline and purpose of our desired class methods and properties.

> **A property or method description beginning with an asterisk mark (*) implies that this item is only to be used from the newsletter send daemon's `cron`-executed environment.**

Let's look at the private members first:

newsletter Class Variable	Description
$_iNewsletterId	Private variable containing the current newsletter's unique identifier
$_oMail	Private variable containing the PEAR::Mail object reference
$_oConn	Private variable containing the PEAR::DB object reference

Here's a listing of the public members of the class:

newsletter Class Method	Description
_statusToString (integer status)	Converts the send status integer to an English string representation
newsletter()	Constructor method which instantiates any parent objects and sets our global configuration variables
setNewsletterId($iNewsletterId)	Sets the $_iNewsletterId class variable
checkSend()	*Checks to see whether a newsletter is currently being sent by the newsletter send daemon
sendTest(email)	Sends a test message of the defined newsletter to the specified e-mail address
sendNewsletter()	*Sends the defined newsletter to the mailing list and writes log data back into the database
getNewsletterToSend()	*Checks to see if there are any messages waiting to be sent and returns the first one it finds or FALSE if none is found

Table continued on following page

`newsletter` Class Member	Description
`getMailingList()`	*Returns a multi-dimensional array of user accounts that have opted to receive our newsletter
`getNewsletter()`	Returns all data associated with the defined newsletter
`getNewsletters($sSort,` `            $iPage[optional])`	Accepts a string for the sort column and an optional numeric value for the row number to begin with and returns an array of active newsletters
`getNewslettersCount()`	Returns a numeric value representing the number of active newsletters in the database; it's used for pagination
`addNewsletter($aArgs)`	Accepts an array of newsletter information used to add a single newsletter to the system
`updateNewsletter($aArgs)`	Accepts an array of newsletter information used to update a single newsletter to the system
`markToBeSent()`	Marks a newsletter to be sent by the newsletter send daemon
`draftNewsletter()`	Marks a newsletter to not be sent by the newsletter send daemon if the send has not already begun
`deleteNewsletter()`	Updates the database setting the newsletter status as having been deleted (soft delete)

The Solution

Now that we've defined our problems and have a basic understanding of the application design, we'll begin the process of developing our solutions. We'll start the development at the core level by defining our mailing method (Simple Mail Transport Protocol; that is, SMTP) and by designing a simple but effective database schema.

This table describes the location and functional purpose of each file we use:

> As detailed in Chapter 2, the `_lib` directory contains files like the shared function libraries and custom classes. It includes a `_base` subdirectory that includes the common function libraries and the global configuration file, and a `classes` subdirectory that includes the custom classes that are written through the book. All our application modules fall into the `site` directory. The `core` directory includes the admin tools used to control the site, and its `newsletters` subdirectory includes the newsletter bit of the CMS.

File Name	File Path	Description
config.php	/_lib/_base/	Configuration values for the application.
funcs.php	/_lib/_base/	Utility functions for the application.
elements.php	/_lib/_base/	Reusable generic elements such as error display functions. This file also assigns the common GET variables of – $op and $id.
tpl_unsecure.php	/site/	Template framework file for pages outside the CMS application. It implements banner advertisements into the page framework.
tpl_secure.php	/core/	Template framework file for pages inside the CMS application.
handlers.php	/_lib/_base/	Data input validation functions.
index.php	/core/newsletters/	Displays a paginated list of all active newsletters in our database.
form.php	/core/newsletters/	Used for all viewing and editing of single records.
hourly.mailsend.php	/_lib/_bin/	Send daemon script invoked from cron.
class.newsletter.php	/_lib/_classes/	Data object used for all assumed newsletter functionality.

All the above listed scripts are available as part of the book's code download from http://www.apress.com.

This diagram shows the different relationships and dependencies of the files within our application framework that are necessary to implement the newsletter module:

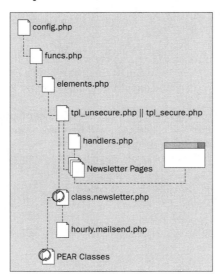

Let's turn our proposed solution into a working codebase. In *The Design* section, we described three primary parts of the development process. For implementation, let's divide these into six smaller key development tasks:

- ❏ Defining configuration constants
- ❏ Creating the database
- ❏ Creating the data object
- ❏ Building the newsletter send daemon
- ❏ Running the newsletter send daemon
- ❏ Building the CMS newsletter application

We start the development process by building up from our core data level, and then continue working through the presentation and execution within the two environments (User/CMS and cron/Shell). Let's start by defining the configuration variables using a text editor.

Defining Configuration Constants

While building the data object for this application, we'll use SMTP. To do this, let's define some global variables and add them to the `/_lib/_base/config.php` file.

We need a server that provides SMTP mail relaying from our server's IP address. In a standard hosting environment, the host server on which we run our application should be able to relay e-mail messages originating from its own IP address. This is similar to setting up a POP mail client. When setting up a mail client, we need to define an outgoing SMTP server to provide us with mail relaying. This is what we're doing by setting these global variables.

Open the `/_lib/_base/config.php` file and add the following configuration line items:

```
define("SMTP_HOST", "localhost");
define("SMTP_PORT","25");
```

By defining our `SMTP_HOST` variable as `localhost`, we're stating that we'll use our local server as the mail relay for our newsletters. We've also defined the `SMTP_PORT` constant to be 25, which is the standard port for SMTP traffic. This value should only be changed if the host provider specifies so.

While keeping this file open, we'll also need to add two other configuration constants. These two constants, labeled `FROM_NAME` and `FROM_EMAIL`, will be placed into the header of every outgoing newsletter to define the 'from address' of the sender:

```
define("FROM_NAME","DVD Life");
define("FROM_EMAIL","info@apress.mediatemple.net");
```

Implementing the Data Layer

Since the `apress_accounts` and `apress_account_prefs` tables have already been created (refer to the *Implementing the Data Layer* section in Chapter 5), we need to add just one table to our `apress` database to store the data needed for this application. The SQL script is created in the same manner as the previous chapters, by hand coding our table schema. Assuming that the readers are familiar and comfortable with their own approach in building up databases and their associated tables, we'll only look at the design from a standard SQL import approach.

apress_newsletters

Here is the script to create the `apress_newsletters` table:

```
CREATE TABLE apress_newsletters (
    newsletter_id            INT(10)       NOT NULL auto_increment,
    admin_user_id            INT(10)       NOT NULL default '0',
    newsletter_subject       VARCHAR(255)  default NULL,
    newsletter_body_text     TEXT,
    newsletter_body_html     TEXT,
    newsletter_send          DATETIME      default NULL,
    newsletter_sent          DATETIME      default NULL,
    newsletter_send_complete DATETIME      default NULL,
    newsletter_recp_cnt      INT(10)       default NULL,
    newsletter_send_status   INT(1)        NOT NULL default '0',
    status                   INT(1)        NOT NULL default '0',
    deleted                  INT(1)        default '0',
    deleted_dt               DATETIME      default NULL,
    created_dt               DATETIME      NOT NULL default '0000-00-00 00:00:00',
    modified_dt              DATETIME      NOT NULL default '0000-00-00 00:00:00',
                             PRIMARY KEY  (newsletter_id)
) TYPE=MyISAM;
```

Implementing the Data Object

The data object will be the base of the CMS application as well as the newsletter send daemon. As mentioned earlier, we'll use the PEAR::DB object as the interface for all of our database queries and the PEAR::Mail object for all of our SMTP interface functionality.

class.newsletter.php

Let's start our application by ensuring that these objects are included in the codebase:

```php
<?php

//File Location: /_lib/_classes/class.newsletter.php

// the Mail.php, Mail/mime.php, and DB.php scripts are in the PEAR library
// and they'll include and extend the PEAR.php class object automatically
require_once ("Mail.php");
require_once ("Mail/mime.php");
require_once ("DB.php");
```

We'll directly access the functions of the application framework and configuration files. Though these files may already be included by another object, we'll use the `require_once` statement to safeguard against multiple inclusions. This will also ensure that these functions are made available to the script when our class is instantiated from the `cron`-executed newsletter send daemon.

Let's continue with the script:

```php
// configuration values for the application
require_once("config.php");

// utility functions for the application
require_once("funcs.php");
```

Now that we have all the global constants, application functions, and parent objects in place, let's start our class by defining the object variables:

```php
class newsletter {

    // property containing the PEAR::Mail object reference
    var $_oMail;

    // property containing the PEAR::DB object reference
    var $_oConn;

    // property containing the newsletter unique identifier
    var $_iNewsletterId;
```

We've instantiated the PEAR::Mail and PEAR::DB objects into our private class variables, similar to the way we handled some of the previous data objects in this book (see Chapter 5, *Implementing the Data Object* section). The difference in this case is the use of the PEAR::Mail object as a direct gateway to the SMTP protocol rather than using a simple interface with the built-in PHP mail function. We do this by instantiating the mail object with the first argument ($backend) being set to `smtp` and the second set to an associative array containing our SMTP preferences:

```php
    // CONSTRUCTOR
    function newsletter() {

        // instantiate the PEAR::Mail object and set the mail method, SMTP
        // Server and SMTP Port. We use "smtp" for our mail method so that
        // we can use an external SMTP server for relaying messages if needed
        $this->_oMail = & Mail::factory("smtp", array("host" => SMTP_HOST,
                                                      "port" => SMTP_PORT));

        // check and capture returned exceptions if present
        if( Mail::isError($this->_oMail) ) {

            catchExc($this->_oMail->getMessage());
        }

        // instantiate the PEAR::DB module for database connectivity. This
        // will accept our 'DSN' global that we defined in our
```

```
           // /_lib/_base/_config.php configuration file.
           $this->_oConn = & DB::connect(DSN);

           // check and capture returned exceptions if present
           if( DB::isError($this->_oConn) ) {

                catchExc($this->_oConn->getMessage());
           }
      }
```

Private Method

We have only one private method, _statusToString, employed in this class:

```
function _statusToString($iStatus) {

      // make sure that the iStatus variable is an integer
      settype($iStatus, "int");

      // determine the value of the passed integer and select the correct
      // string representation to return
      switch($iStatus) {

           case 3:
                $return = "Sent";
                break;

           case 2:
                $return = "Sending";
                break;

           case 1:
                $return = "Pending";
                break;

           default:
                $return = "Not Sent";
      }

      return $return;
}
```

The apress_newsletters database table contains the newsletter_send_status field. This field is used as a primary integer for queuing newsletters to be sent. The data type of this field is an integer, which cannot be directly displayed as the status of a newsletter to the web master, since it wouldn't convey the meaning. So we include a private function to return a human readable string representation of the newsletter's integer send status.

We've defined a newsletter's Send Status by the following string representation:

- ❑ 0 – Not Sent
- ❑ 1 – Pending
- ❑ 2 – Sending
- ❑ 3 – Sent

> The 'Pending' state is used to define a newsletter that has been marked to be sent, but has not yet been picked up by our send daemon.

These integers will be used to define different methods within the data object, to queue the newsletter for sending, or to define the send state.

Public Methods

In this section we'll look at all the public methods in the class.newsletter.php file.

The first public method we see here is used to set the private $_iNewsletterId variable. This variable needs to be set if we want to use almost any of the class member functions. The function returns a Boolean indicating the success:

```
function setNewsletterId($iNewsletterId) {

    // set default return value
    $return = FALSE;

    // make sure that the newsletter ID is an integer
    settype($iNewsletterId, "int");

    // if the newsletter ID is a valid integer, then set the class
    // variable
    if( $iNewsletterId ) {

        $this->_iNewsletterId = $iNewsletterId;
        $return = TRUE;
    }

    // return success status
    return $return;
}
```

The checkSend() function will be used by the newsletter send daemon to check and see if the send program is already running. This function works by using the apress_newsletter's newsletter_send_status field to set a newsletter's status as 'currently sending'. When the send function is invoked, the first thing that the daemon does is to change the status of the newsletter that it's sending out. Once the send is complete, it changes the status again to define that the newsletter has been sent.

This function simply checks to see if there are any newsletters that have a status of 2 (Sending) and if so, returns the newsletter's unique identifier. If there are no newsletters currently being sent, the method will return FALSE:

```
function checkSend() {

        // set default return value
        $return = FALSE;

        // build SQL query
```

```
    $sql = "SELECT
                newsletter_id
            FROM
                ".PREFIX."_newsletters
            WHERE
                newsletter_send_status = 2 AND
                deleted = 0
            LIMIT 1";

    // run the query and capture returned exceptions if any
    if( DB::isError($rsTmp = $this->_oConn->query($sql)) ) {

        catchExc($rsTmp->getMessage());
    } else {

        // check the returned number of active send processes
        if( $rsTmp->numRows() > 0 ) {

            // fetch the first record
            $aTmpRow = $rsTmp->fetchRow();

            // set the return variable to the newsletter ID value
            $return = $aTmpRow[0];
        }
    }
    return $return;
}
```

The sendTest() method is used to send a test message to the web master who is registered in the CMS. As we've not extended the sessions class (created in Chapter 4), we don't have the user's e-mail address, so we pass it to the function upon execution.

This method will be the first to employ the use of PEAR's Mail_mime object, which we will be using to build our multi-part (text/HTML) messages. Its usage is simple and straightforward – we'll simply need to instantiate the object, set our two bodies, set our headers, and then have the class return the same body and headers in multi-part format with MIME-types included. Because of this we do not need to have two messages and a preference for each user. We simply create a single multi-part message.

Here is the sendTest() script:

```
function sendTest($sEmail) {

    // retrieve all data associated with the defined newsletter
    $aNewsletter = $this->getNewsletter();

    // build standard headers array
    $aHead = array(
                "From" => FROM_NAME."<".FROM_EMAIL.">",
                "Subject" => $aNewsletter["Subject"]
            );

    // build multi-part message
    // "\r\n" defines what characters to use as a line-break
    $oMime = new Mail_mime("\r\n");
```

```
        // set the plain-text body
        $oMime->setTxtBody($aNewsletter["Body Text"]);

        // set the HTML body
        $oMime->setHTMLBody($aNewsletter["Body HTML"]);

        // get multi-part body
        $sBody = $oMime->get();

        // get multi-part headers
        $aHeaders = $oMime->headers($aHead);

        // send multi-part message to the passed recipient address
        // then check and capture returned exceptions if present
        if( Mail::isError($mailTmp = $this->_oMail->send($sEmail,
                                            $aHeaders, $sBody)) ) {
            catchExc($mailTmp->getMessage());
            $return = FALSE;
        } else {

            $return = TRUE;
        }
        // return success status
        return $return;
    }
```

The `sendNewsletter()` class method is one of the most complicated functions in this data object. It should be executed only by the newsletter send daemon, because it will take a great deal of time to process if the mailing list contains more than a small number of names.

> *Note that before running this function, the `setNewsletterId()` function would have defined the newsletter to be sent. This is common for many other methods in this class.*

Let's go through this function one step at a time. The function starts by gathering all of the data required to send a newsletter and places it into two associative arrays. These arrays are labeled in association to the data that they represent:

```
function sendNewsletter() {

        // set the default return value
        $return = TRUE;

        // retrieve all data associated with the defined newsletter
        $aNewsletter = $this->getNewsletter();

        // retrieve all e-mail addresses subscribed to our mailing list
        // we'll see getMailingList() function's details later
        $aMailingList = $this->getMailingList();
```

Once the data is in place, we begin the sending process by setting the `newsletter_send_status` of a selected newsletter. Applying the send status to the selected newsletter will allow the CMS to flash a message to the web masters that the newsletter has begun its sending process. It will also avoid a second instance of the newsletter send daemon from spawning and taking up system resources:

```
                // update the newsletter_send_status for the defined newsletter and
                // update the sent time for the record. This will prevent any other
                // newsletters from being sent while the current one is being sent.
                $sql = "UPDATE
                            ".PREFIX."_newsletters
                        SET
                            newsletter_send_status = 2,
                            newsletter_sent = NOW()
                        WHERE
                            newsletter_id = '".$this->_iNewsletterId."'";

                // check and capture returned exceptions if present
                if( DB::isError($rsTmp = $this->_oConn->query($sql)) ) {

                    catchExc($rsTmp->getMessage());
                    $return = FALSE;
                }
```

Once we've set the send status of the newsletter, we can begin the e-mail message and headers build. This process begins by defining the header variables that will be used by all outgoing messages.

All of our messages will contain some common information, so we need to define our body and header variables only once. For this we will take the From and Subject attributes and store them into an associative array for later use:

```
                // build static headers
                $aHead = array(
                            "From" => FROM_NAME."<".FROM_EMAIL.">",
                            "Subject" => $aNewsletter["Subject"]
                        );
```

Once we have our static headers defined, we'll need to start our process of building a multi-part message. Building a multi-part message will enable us to send the same message to every recipient on our e-mail list. Depending on the recipient's e-mail program, the message will be displayed in text or HTML. This saves us from creating separate messages for each message type and the users from selecting the type of message they want to receive in their preferences. This building of a multi-part message will be taken care of by PEAR's Mail_mime object.

We start the build by instantiating the Mail_mime object and stating the characters to be used for line breaks within the mail message. We have decided to use the default value of "\r\n", but have defined it just to show you how to change it, should you choose to use something else:

```
                // build multi-part message
                // "\r\n" defines what characters to use as a line-break
                $oMime = new Mail_mime("\r\n");
```

Next we will set the two mail message bodies by passing the respective arrays to the two methods:

```
// set the plain-text body
$oMime->setTXTBody($aNewsletter["Body Text"]);

// set the HTML body
$oMime->setHTMLBody($aNewsletter["Body HTML"]);
```

Now we get these text and HTML parts as a single multi-part body string from the `get()` method included in the Mail_mime object:

```
// get the multi-part body string
$sBody = $oMime->get();
```

Once we have the message body taken care of, we need to set the headers. To do this we'll simply pass the static headers array, which we previously defined, to Mail_mime's `header()` method. This will return a headers array with all of the required MIME-types and header values needed for a multi-part e-mail message:

```
// get multi-part headers array
$aHeaders = $oMime->headers($aHead);
```

Once we build up the static information, we'll need to begin the loop through the mailing list to build up the rest of the header and body information. We then finish the process by sending it out to the SMTP server:

```
// loop through the mailing list and send to each recipient
$i=0;
$iRecpCnt = count($aMailingList);
while($i < $iRecpCnt) {

    $sEmail = $aMailingList[$i];

    // check and capture returned exceptions if present
    if( Mail::isError($mailTmp = $this->_oMail->send($sEmail,
                                                     $aHeaders,
                                                     $sBody)) ) {
        catchExc($mailTmp->getMessage());
        $return = FALSE;
        break;
    }
    $i++;
}
```

After this process has completed, we finish up the mail send routine by setting the newsletter's send status to 3 (Sent) and by returning some basic log information to the database.

Notice that when we set the `newsletter_send_status` at the beginning of the method, we also had the database log the time that the message was being sent (`newsletter_sent = NOW()`). The same thing is repeated in this query here, except that we're logging the time at send completion (`newsletter_send_complete = NOW()`). This information makes it possible, with some simple subtraction, to calculate the time that it took to mail the list out. This is useful when added with the final piece of information to be logged, which is the number of e-mail recipients (`newsletter_recp_cnt`):

```
                // set the number of e-mails sent
                $iNumSent = $i;

                // update the newsletter_send_status to unlock the send process and
                // allow other sends to begin. Also, update the completed time and
                // the number of recipients.
                $sql = "UPDATE
                            ".PREFIX."_newsletters
                        SET
                            newsletter_send_status = 3,
                            newsletter_send_complete = NOW(),
                            newsletter_recp_cnt = ".$iNumSent."
                        WHERE
                            newsletter_id = '".$this->_iNewsletterId."'";

                // check and capture returned exceptions if present
                if( DB::isError($rsTmp = $this->_oConn->query($sql)) ) {

                    catchExc($rsTmp->getMessage());
                    $return = FALSE;
                }
                return $return;
        }
```

Select Methods

The `getNewsletterToSend()` method is used by the newsletter send daemon to check if there are any newsletters currently marked for sending. This method will return the unique identifier of the first newsletter in queue if one exists; otherwise it will return FALSE:

```
function getNewsletterToSend() {

        // set the default return value
        $return = TRUE;

        // build the SQL query
        $sql = "SELECT
                    newsletter_id
                FROM
                    ".PREFIX."_newsletters
                WHERE
                    newsletter_send_status = 1 AND
                    deleted=0 AND
                    status=1 AND
                    newsletter_send < NOW() AND
                    ISNULL(newsletter_sent)
                ORDER BY
                    modified_dt DESC
                LIMIT 1";

        // check and capture returned exceptions if present
        if( DB::isError($rsTmp = $this->_oConn->query($sql)) ) {
```

```
                catchExc($rsTmp->getMessage());
                $return = FALSE;
        } else {

            // check to see if there are returned records
            if( $rsTmp->numRows() > 0 ) {

                // fetch the first returned row
                $aTmpRow = $rsTmp->fetchRow();

                // set the return value to the newsletter ID of the returned
                // record
                $return = $aTmpRow[0];
            }
        }
        // return a newsletter ID or FALSE
        return $return;
    }
```

The getMailingList() function is called from within the sendNewsletter() function. Many people might choose to make it a private method due to this; however, there are many uses in making it publicly available. This function returns an array containing all e-mail addresses of users who would like to receive our newsletters:

```
function getMailingList() {

    // build the SQL query
    $sql = "SELECT
                account.account_email
            FROM
                ".PREFIX."_accounts as account,
                ".PREFIX."_account_prefs as prefs
            WHERE
                account.account_id = prefs.account_id AND
                account.deleted = 0 AND
                account.status = 1 AND
                prefs.newsletter_recipient = 1";

    // check and capture returned exceptions if present
    if( DB::isError($rsTmp = $this->_oConn->query($sql)) ) {

        catchExc($rsTmp->getMessage());
        $return = FALSE;

    } else {

        // for each record, push the e-mail addr into the return array
        while( $aTmpRow = $rsTmp->fetchRow(DB_FETCHMODE_ASSOC) ) {

            array_push($return, $aTmpRow["account_email"]);
        }
```

```
        }
        // return the mailing list array
        return $return;
    }
```

The `getNewsletter()` function will be used by the CMS application framework as well as by both the newsletter send daemon and other member methods within the class. It's important that we maintain consistency within our main data element. We must verify the data and check for empty text and date fields before doing any string manipulation such as setting variable types and converting string formats:

```
function getNewsletter() {

        // build the SQL query
        $sql = "SELECT
                    admin_user_id,
                    newsletter_subject,
                    newsletter_body_text,
                    newsletter_body_html,
                    newsletter_send,
                    newsletter_sent,
                    newsletter_recp_cnt,
                    newsletter_send_status,
                    newsletter_send_complete,
                    status,
                    created_dt,
                    modified_dt
                FROM
                    ".PREFIX."_newsletters
                WHERE
                    deleted = 0 AND
                    newsletter_id = ".$this->_iNewsletterId;
```

Check and capture any returned exceptions:

```
        if( DB::isError($rsTmp = $this->_oConn->query($sql)) ) {

            catchExc($rsTmp->getMessage());
            $return = FALSE;

        // check and make sure that there were records returned
        } elseif ( $rsTmp->numRows() > 0 ) {

            // fetch the first returned record
            $aTmpRow = $rsTmp->fetchRow(DB_FETCHMODE_ASSOC);

            // set all array key values that need no manipulation
            $return["Newsletter Id"] = $iMsgId;
            $return["User Id"] = $aTmpRow["admin_user_id"];
            $return["Subject"] = $aTmpRow["newsletter_subject"];
            $return["Body Text"] = $aTmpRow["newsletter_body_text"];
            $return["Body HTML"] = $aTmpRow["newsletter_body_html"];
            $return["Recipients"] = $aTmpRow["newsletter_recp_cnt"];
            $return["Send Status Int"] = $aTmpRow["newsletter_send_status"];
            $return["Status"]          = $aTmpRow["status"];
```

Next, we set all array key values that need checking or manipulation:

```
                // check for a newsletter_send date string
                if( !strcmp($aTmpRow["newsletter_send"],"") ) {
                    $return["Send"] = FALSE;
                } else {

                    // convert datetime to a UNIX timestring
                    $return["Send"] = strtotime($aTmpRow["newsletter_send"]);

                }

                // check for a newsletter_sent date string
                if( !strcmp($aTmpRow["newsletter_sent"],"") ) {
                    $return["Sent"] = FALSE;
                } else {

                    // convert datetime to a UNIX timestring
                    $return["Sent"] = strtotime($aTmpRow["newsletter_sent"]);

                }

                // check for newsletter_send_complete date string
                if( !strcmp($aTmpRow["newsletter_send_complete"],"") ) {
                    $return["Completed"] = FALSE;
                } else {

                    // convert date to a UNIX timestring
                    $return["Completed"] =
                        strtotime($aTmpRow["newsletter_send_complete"]);

                }

                // convert the send status to a string using the private method
                $return["Send Status"] =
                    $this->_statusToString($aTmpRow["newsletter_send_status"]);

                // convert date to a UNIX timestring
                $return["Created Date"]  = strtotime($aTmpRow["created_dt"]);

                // convert date to a UNIX timestring
                $return["Modified Date"] = strtotime($aTmpRow["modified_dt"]);

            } else {

                $return = FALSE;

            }
            // return an associative array or FALSE
            return $return;

        }
```

The getNewsletters() method will return an array of newsletter data arrays. These arrays will contain the same data as defined in the previous function, and they will be grouped into a singular data array.

The required $sSort argument and the optional $iPage will be used by the CMS framework (described in Chapter 4) to paginate the list of active newsletters in the database. We will use the ROWCOUNT defined constant (Chapter 4) to determine the number of records to display on each page. This function will only be used from within the CMS application framework:

```
function getNewsletters($sSort, $iPage=0) {

        // build the SQL query
        $sql = "SELECT
                        newsletter_id,
                        admin_user_id,
                        newsletter_subject,
                        newsletter_body_text,
                        newsletter_body_html,
                        newsletter_send,
                        newsletter_sent,
                        newsletter_recp_cnt,
                        newsletter_send_status,
                        status,
                        created_dt,
                        modified_dt
                FROM
                    ".PREFIX."_newsletters
                WHERE
                    deleted = 0
                ORDER BY
                    ".$sSort."
                LIMIT
                    ".$iPage.", ".ROWCOUNT;
```

Next, check and capture any returned exceptions:

```
        if( DB::isError($rsTmp = $this->_oConn->query($sql)) ) {

            catchExc($rsTmp->getMessage());
            $return = FALSE;
        } else {

            $i = 0;
            while( $aTmpRow = $rsTmp->fetchRow(DB_FETCHMODE_ASSOC) ) {

                // set all array key values that need no manipulation
                $return[$i]["Newsletter Id"] = $aTmpRow["newsletter_id"];
                $return[$i]["User Id"] = $aTmpRow["admin_user_id"];
                $return[$i]["Subject"] = $aTmpRow["newsletter_subject"];
                $return[$i]["Body Text"] = $aTmpRow["newsletter_body_text"];
                $return[$i]["Body HTML"] = $aTmpRow["newsletter_body_html"];
                $return[$i]["Recipient Count"] =
                    $aTmpRow["newsletter_recp_cnt"];
                $return[$i]["Send Status Int"] =
                    $aTmpRow["newsletter_send_status"];
                $return[$i]["Status"] = $aTmpRow["status"];
```

Next, we set all array key values that need the data to be checked::

```
                    // check for a newsletter_send date string
                    if( !strcmp($aTmpRow["newsletter_send"],"") ) {
                        $return[$i]["Send"] = FALSE;
                    } else {

                        // convert to a UNIX timestring
                        $return[$i]["Send"] =
                            strtotime($aTmpRow["newsletter_send"]);
                    }

                    // check for a newsletter_sent date string
                    if( !strcmp($aTmpRow["newsletter_sent"],"") ) {
                        $return[$i]["Sent"] = FALSE;
                    } else {

                        // convert to a UNIX timestring
                        $return[$i]["Sent"] =
                            strtotime($aTmpRow["newsletter_sent"]);
                    }

                    // convert the send status integer to a string
                    // representation
                    $return[$i]["Send Status"] =
                     $this->_statusToString($aTmpRow["newsletter_send_status"]);

                    // convert to a UNIX timestring
                    $return[$i]["Created Date"] =
                        strtotime($aTmpRow["created_dt"]);

                    // convert to a UNIX timestring
                    $return[$i]["Modified Date"] =
                        strtotime($aTmpRow["modified_dt"]);

                    $i++;
                }

                // return the array of newsletters and associated data
                return $return;
            }

        }
```

After creating a method to build a paginated list of active newsletters, the CMS will also require a count of all of the active newsletters in the database. Let's construct a basic query to count the non-deleted records in the database and return the count as a single integer value:

```
function getNewsletterCount() {

        // build the SQL query
        $sql = "SELECT
                    count(newsletter_id)
                FROM
```

```
                          ".PREFIX."_newsletters
              WHERE
                  deleted = 0";

      // use the PEAR::DB's getOne() method to return the first value of
      // the first returned array and then free the result set
      $iCnt = $this->_oConn->getOne($sql);

      // return a count of the active newsletters in the database
      return $iCnt;
  }
```

Insert Method

The only insert method in this data class is the addNewsletter() function:

```
function addNewsletter($aArgs) {

      // build the SQL query
      $sql = "INSERT INTO ".PREFIX."_newsletters (
                  admin_user_id,
                  newsletter_subject,
                  newsletter_body_text,
                  newsletter_body_html,
                  newsletter_send,
                  created_dt,
                  modified_dt
              ) VALUES (
                  '".$aArgs["User Id"]."',
                  '".$aArgs["Subject"]."',
                  '".$aArgs["Body Text"]."',
                  '".$aArgs["Body HTML"]."',
                  '".date("Y-m-d H:i:s", $aArgs["Send"])."',
                  NOW(),
                  NOW()
              )";
```

Since many of the fields in the database will be updated at a later time and are not set at the time of insert, we've set default values for all of them and only included the newsletter-specific data for the INSERT statement. The arguments that are passed to this function will be contained in a single associative array and will have been checked for errors prior to the point of entry. The array keys are defined as follows:

Argument Array Key	Description
User ID	Property containing the admin_user_id of the web master adding the newsletter
Subject	Property containing the e-mail subject
Body Text	Property containing the plaintext e-mail body
Body HTML	Property containing the HTML e-mail body
Send	Property containing the desired UNIX timestring value that the administrative user would like to use to send the newsletter

Let's continue with the script:

```
            // check and capture returned exceptions if present
            if( DB::isError($rsTmp = $this->_oConn->query($sql)) ) {

                catchExc($rsTmp->getMessage());
                $return = FALSE;
            } else {

                // get the ID of the record that we just inserted
                $sql = "SELECT LAST_INSERT_ID()";
                $iMsgId = $this->_oConn->getOne($sql);
                $return = $iMsgId;
            }
```

If the item was inserted successfully, the function returns the unique identifier of the added newsletter; otherwise the function will return FALSE:

```
            // return an ID for the inserted record or FALSE
            return $return;
        }
```

Update Methods

The first update method is updateNewsletter(). This method accepts the same array input as the previous addNewsletter() function and updates the same database fields. The only change to the query is the removal of the created_dt field. It will return a Boolean value of TRUE on success and FALSE on failure:

```
    function updateNewsletter($aArgs) {

        // set the default return value
        $return = TRUE;

        $sql = "UPDATE
                ".PREFIX."_newsletters
                SET
                admin_user_id = '".$aArgs["User Id"]."',
                newsletter_subject = '".$aArgs["Subject"]."',
                newsletter_body_text = '".$aArgs["Body Text"]."',
                newsletter_body_html = '".$aArgs["Body HTML"]."',
                newsletter_send = '".date("Y-m-d H:i:s",$aArgs["Send"])."',
                modified_dt = NOW()
                WHERE
                newsletter_id = '".$this->_iNewsletterId."'
                ";

        // check and capture returned exceptions if present
        if( DB::isError($rsTmp = $this->_oConn->query($sql)) ) {

            catchExc($rsTmp->getMessage());
            $return = FALSE;
        }

        // return the update success state
        return $return;
    }
```

The next update function will mark a newsletter to be sent. This class method will serve as the activation function within the CMS. This will update both the `newsletter_send_status` field to set the newsletter as being ready for sending, and the status field to inform the CMS application that the newsletter has been `published`:

```
function markToBeSent() {

        // set the default return value
        $return = FALSE;
        // retrieve all data associated with the defined newsletter
        $aNewsletter = $this->getNewsletter();

        // check to make sure that the message has not already been sent
        if( ($aNewsletter["Send Status Int"]) > 0 ) {

            catchExc("This newsletter has already been sent");
        } else {

            // build the SQL query
            $sql = "UPDATE
                    ".PREFIX."_newsletters
                SET
                    status = 1,
                    newsletter_send_status = 1,
                    modified_dt = NOW()
                WHERE
                    newsletter_id = '".$this->_iNewsletterId."'";

            // check and capture returned exceptions if present
            if( DB::isError($rsTmp = $this->_oConn->query($sql)) ) {

                catchExc($rsTmp->getMessage());
            } else {

                $return = TRUE;
            }
        }

        // return update success/failure status
        return $return;
}
```

The `draftNewsletter()` method is used to cancel the change of the send state or to return the newsletter back to its original state. One of the issues that we need to keep in mind while building this function is to ensure that we don't interfere with the newsletter send daemon, which may have accessed the data since the time the newsletter was staged. Thus we need to write in a small database check to see if the send status has changed. We'll do this by checking if the send status is greater than one. If so, we'll exit the function and return FALSE. Otherwise, update the status and set it back to 0 (Not Sent) and return TRUE.

Note that the amount of time that a message can stay staged will depend on the time increment that is set in the `crontab` file. This will be covered in detail in the *Running the Send Daemon* section.

Here is the code for the method:

```
function draftNewsletter() {

        // set the default return value
        $return = FALSE;

        // retrieve all data associated with the defined newsletter
        $aNewsletter = $this->getNewsletter();

        // check to make sure that the message has not already been sent
        if( ($aNewsletter["Send Status Int"]) > 1 ) {

            catchExc("This newsletter has already been sent");
        } else {

            // build the SQL query
            $sql = "UPDATE
                        ".PREFIX."_newsletters
                    SET
                        status = 0,
                        newsletter_send_status = 0,
                        modified_dt = NOW()
                    WHERE
                        newsletter_id = '".$this->_iNewsletterId."'";

            // check and capture returned exceptions if present
            if( DB::isError($rsTmp = $this->_oConn->query($sql)) ) {

                catchExc($rsTmp->getMessage());
            } else {

                $return = TRUE;
            }
        }
        // return the update success status
        return $return;
    }
```

Delete Methods

We have only one delete method to write into the class. The delete function will remove a single newsletter from the database. Since we're not using hard deletes anywhere else in the site, we'll follow the same methodology and only update the delete field to show that this is a record that we no longer wish to use:

```
function deleteNewsletter() {

        // set the default return value
        $return = TRUE;

        // build the SQL query
        $sql = "UPDATE
```

```
                    ".PREFIX."_newsletters
                SET
                    deleted = 1,
                    deleted_dt = NOW()
                WHERE
                    newsletter_id = '".$this->_iNewsletterId."'";

        // check and capture returned exceptions if present
        if( DB::isError($rsTmp = $this->_oConn->query($sql)) ) {

            catchExc($rsTmp->getMessage());
            $return = FALSE;
        }
        // return the update success status
        return $return;
    }
```

Now that we've successfully created all of our class methods and properties, let's start building the newsletter daemon and the CMS application.

Building the Send Daemon

Now that all of our data object methods have been created, we can proceed with the building of our newsletter send daemon. The newsletter send daemon is no more than a small script invoked by cron (or Scheduled Tasks Manager or AT) on an incremented time-table. Since PHP has no execution time limits set when running from the command line, we can run large send processes using this script rather than the limited execution time of the web server module.

When running our script as a cron job, we will not be able to change PHP configuration values via the .htaccess file, as we detailed in Chapter 2 – this is because we will not be executing our script through Apache. So we'll need to rebuild our previously defined include path so that we are able to correctly include our data object, application functions, configuration variables, and parent objects. This is done by using PHP's ini_set() function and appending the current include_path to our custom required include paths:

```
ini_set("include_path",ini_get("include_path").":/var/www/html/_lib/_base/:/var/www
/html/_lib/_classes/:/var/www/html/site/:/var/www/html/core/");
```

Earlier, our .htaccess file included this:

".:/usr/lib/php/:/var/www/html/_lib/_base:/var/www/html/_lib/_classes:/var/www/html/site:/var/www/html/core:/var/www/html/pear"

Once this is done, we can successfully instantiate our primary data object created in the previous section. Since for our site we'll only need to send e-mail newsletters on an hourly basis, we're going to call this the hourly.mailsend.php script:

The hourly timeframe would be used to execute our cron program to check for outgoing messages marked to be sent.

```php
<?php

// File Location: /_lib/_bin/hourly.mailsend.php

require_once("class.newsletter.php");

$oNewsletter = new newsletter;
```

Now that all of our tools are in place, the first step in implementing our class is to check for newsletters that need to be sent. We've already built the stageNewsletter() function to do this for us, so we need to run that method and assign the returned data to the $iNewsletterId integer variable:

```php
// get the Newsletter ID of a Message that needs to be sent
$iNewsletterId = $oNewsletter->getNewsletterToSend();
```

Now that we've defined the $iNewsletterId variable, let's run a second method to check and see if there is another send process already running. Let's run a conditional statement on these two pieces of data to determine if we can continue the send process. If we determine that there is no other process running, and we have a valid newsletter's unique identifier, we can continue by setting the _iNewsletterId class variable and running the sendNewsletter()method:

```php
if( $iNewsletterId && !$oNewsletter->checkSend() ) {

    // set the Newsletter Id and begin to send
    $oNewsletter->setNewsletterId($iNewsletterId);
    $oNewsletter->sendNewsletter();
}
exit;
?>
```

Running the Send Daemon

The newsletter send daemon can run on UNIX-and Windows based-platforms. Next we'll look at the implementation of the newsletter send daemon on both of these systems.

UNIX

For applications running on a UNIX-compatible platform, we need to add the path and time variables to the user account's crontab file. To set this up, either we need shell access to the box, or we need to send the cron script to the system administrator to place the file for us. If shell access to the server is possible, log in and type the following command:

```
$ crontab -e
```

This will open the default editor and display the current `crontab file`. This file will most likely contain nothing. Type the following into the file:

```
1 * * * * /usr/bin/php /var/www/html/_lib/_bin/hourly.mailsend.php
```

This will execute the `crontab` file changes and begin to run the script every hour. However, make sure you only add this to the `crontab`. If something already exists, simply add your changes to a new line.

Windows

When using the Windows environment we need to use the built-in Scheduled Tasks Manager or AT. This can only be accessed if we have remote desktop access or physical access to the server. If we don't, then we need the system administrator to set up the routine for us.

The AT command is the Windows NT equivalent of the Linux `cron`. It allows you to automate commands under Windows 2000, XP, and NT. There is no `crontab/AT` mechanism for Windows 95/98/ME. Instead we have the Scheduled Tasks Manager. For more information on how to set this up, refer to Chapter 20 in *Professional PHP4* from *Apress* (*ISBN 1-861006-91-8*) that deals with non-web PHP programming.

Building the CMS Newsletter Application

The CMS application is built just as we've done for all of the past applications that we've covered in the book. All the files will be placed in the `/core/newsletters` directory, and we need to register this path and application with the database to start implementing the framework security:

```
mysql> INSERT INTO apress_admin_apps (admin_app_name, admin_app_path)
       VALUES ('Newsletters','/core/newsletters/');
```

We also need to update the user permissions using the CMS web master application. The `class.users.php` section in Chapter 4 details how this can be done.

CMS Application Files

In this section we'll detail the two CMS application files that we require:

- ❏ **index.php** – CMS newsletter listing
- ❏ **form.php** – CMS Newsletter Management (Add/Edit) Form

CMS Newsletter Listing

This file will display a paginated list of all active newsletters in our database. We will display the subject of the newsletter as the 'Item Name' and follow the same methodologies as in previous chapters by including the created date of the record as well as edit and delete buttons.

```php
<?php

// File Location: /core/newsletters/index.php

// template framework file for pages inside of the CMS application
require_once ("tpl_secure.php");

// data object for all newsletter functionality
require_once ("class.newsletter.php");

// instantiate the newsletter object
$oNewsletter = new newsletter;

// get a limited array of newsletters (Limited for pagination)
$aNewsletters = $oNewsletter->getNewsletters("newsletter_send_status, created_dt
DESC", $iCursor);

// get a total count of all active newsletters used for pagination
$iCnt = $oNewsletter->getNewsletterCount();
```

The if loop checks for returned records:

```php
if( count($aNewsletters)>0 ) {

    // push newsletter data into the CMS display array
    $i = 0;
    while( $i < count($aNewsletters) ) {
        $aData[$i]["Id"] = $aNewsletters[$i]["Newsletter Id"];
        $aData[$i]["Name"] = $aNewsletters[$i]["Subject"];
        $aData[$i]["Status"] = $aNewsletters[$i]["Status"];
        $aData[$i]["Created"] =$aNewsletters[$i]["Created Date"];
        ++$i;
    }
}

// check for an incoming "id" variable
if( $id ) {

    // set the $_iNewsletterId member variable to the current $id
    settype($id, "integer");
    $oNewsletter->setNewsletterId($id);

    // if the incoming "op" variable is set to "del"
    // then delete the selected newsletter.
    if( !strcmp($op, "del") ) {

        $oNewsletter->deleteNewsletter();
        header("Location: ".SELF);

    // if the incoming "op" variable is set to "act" then
    // mark the current newsletter to be sent by the send daemon
    } elseif ( !strcmp($op, "act") ) {
```

```
        $oNewsletter->markToBeSent();
        header("Location: ".SELF);

    // if the incoming "op" variable is set to "deact" then
    // mark the current newsletter to not be sent by the send daemon
    } elseif ( !strcmp($op, "deact") ) {

        $oNewsletter->draftNewsletter();
        header("Location: ".SELF);
    }
}

setHeader();
openPage();
?>
```

Here is the HTML part of the script:

```
<table width="608" border="0" cellpadding="0" cellspacing="0">
    <tr>
        <td colspan="2"><div class="header">
         <?php print ENTITY ?> Newsletter Administration</div></td>
    </tr>

    <tr>
        <td colspan="2"><div class="copy">To manage newsletters,
         select a user action from the list below.</div></td>
    </tr>

    <tr>
        <td><div class="error"><?php writeErrors() ?></div></td>
        <td align="right" valign="top"><?php if( $iPerm > 1 ) { ?>
         <a href="form.php?op=add">
          <img src="../../_img/buttons/btn_additem.gif"
            width="58" height="15" alt="" border="0" /></a><?php } ?></td>
    </tr>

</table>

<?php renderList($iCnt, $aData) ?>
<?php closePage(); ?>
```

As of now, the newsletter listing page looks like this:

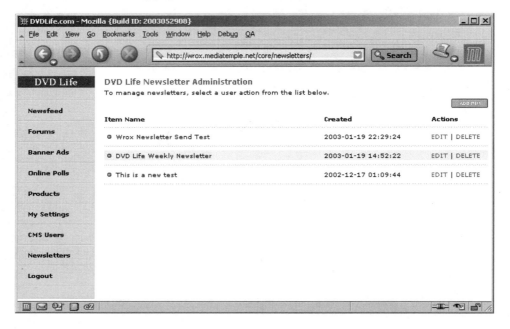

CMS Newsletter Management Form

The form.php script will be used for all viewing and editing of single records and will follow the format requirements defined in Chapter 4:

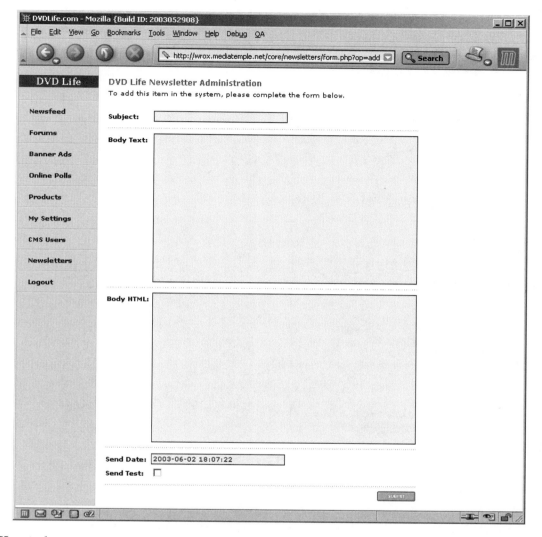

Here is the script:

```php
<?php

// File Location: /core/newsletters/form.php

/* include required libraries */

// template framework file for pages inside of the CMS application
require_once ("tpl_secure.php");

// form handlers used for error reporting and data manipulation
require_once ("handlers.php");
```

```
// data object for all newswletter functionality
require_once "class.newsletter.php";

// instantiate the newsletter object
$oNewsletter = new newsletter;

// check for in incoming newsletter ID
if( $id ) {

    // set the current newsletter ID member variable
    settype($id, "integer");
    $oNewsletter->setNewsletterId($id);
}
```

Next, check for posted data:

```
if( $_POST ) {

    // if an item is being updated, get the origional item to check the
    // current send status of the item.  If the newsletter has been sent,
    // then we need to make sure that it is locked for editing.
    $aCheckNewsletter = $oNewsletter->getNewsletter();

    // set page variables from posted values
    $sSubject = $_POST["subject"];
    $sBodyText = $_POST["body_text"];
    $sBodyHTML = $_POST["body_html"];
    $sSend = strtotime($_POST["send"]);

    // error reporting - check for valid subject
    if( !strcmp("",$sSubject) ) {
        catchErr("Enter a Subject");
        $FORMOK = FALSE;
    }

    // error reporting - check for valid body
    if( !strcmp("",$sBodyText) ) {
        catchErr("Enter Body Text");
        $FORMOK = FALSE;
    }

    // if there are no errors, then continue with the process
    if( $FORMOK ) {

        // fill the argument array that will be passed to the object method
        $aArgs["User Id"] = $iUserId;
        $aArgs["Subject"] = $sSubject;
        $aArgs["Body Text"] = $sBodyText;
        $aArgs["Body HTML"] = $sBodyHTML;
        $aArgs["Send"] = $sSend;

        // if we are updating a record then use the updateNewsletter method
        if( !strcmp("edit", $op) ) {
```

```
            if( $aCheckNewsletter["Send Status Int"]==0 ) {

                $FORMOK = $oNewsletter->updateNewsletter($aArgs);
            } else {

                $FORMOK = TRUE;
            }

        // if we are adding a record then use the addNewsletter method
        } elseif (!strcmp("add", $op)) {

            $FORMOK = $oNewsletter->addNewsletter($aArgs);
        }
```

If the page has still not come across any errors then finish up the page logic:

```
            if( $FORMOK ) {

                // if the "Send Test" checkbox has been checked,
                // then e-mail a copy of the message to the web master
                if( !strcmp("1",$_POST["send_test"])) {
                    $aUser = $oSess->getUser($iUserId);
                    $oNewsletter->sendTest($aUser["Email"] );
                }

                // forward the user to the newsletter list page
                header("Location: index.php");
            }
        }

// do the following if no posted data is detected
} else {

    // set the send date to now
    $sSend = time();

    // if no posted data is found and we are trying to edit a newsletter,
    // then fetch the newsletter that we are trying to edit and fill the
    // page variables
    if( !strcmp("edit", $op) ) {

        $aNewsletter = $oNewsletter->getNewsletter();
        $sSubject = $aNewsletter["Subject"];
        $sBodyText = $aNewsletter["Body Text"];
        $sBodyHTML = $aNewsletter["Body HTML"];
        $sSend = $aNewsletter["Send"];
    }
}

// get all applications that the user has access to (CMS menu system)
$aApps = $oSess->getApps();

setHeader();
openPage();
```

The HTML of our page will display a form that will be populated by the page variables that we have defined throughout the application:

```
?>

<table border="0" cellpadding="0" cellspacing="0">
    <tr>
        <td><div class="header"><?php print ENTITY ?>
        Newsletter Administration</div></td>
    </tr>

    <tr>
        <td><div class="copy">To <?php print $op ?> this item in the system,
        please complete the form below.</div></td>
    </tr>

    <tr>
        <td><div class="error"><?php writeErrors() ?></div></td>
    </tr>
</table>

<form action="<?php print SELF ?>?op=<?php print $op ?>
            &id=<?php print $id ?>" method="post" name="apressform">

<table border="0" cellpadding="0" cellspacing="0">

    <tr>
        <td><div class="formlabel">Subject:</div></td>
        <td><input type="text" name="subject"
        value="<?php print clean($sSubject) ?>" class="textfield" /></td>
    </tr>

    <tr>
        <td class="dotrule" colspan="2"><img src="../../_img/spc.gif"
        width="1" height="15" alt="" border="0" /></td>
    </tr>

.....
    <?php if( strcmp($aNewsletter["Send Status"], "") ) { ?>
    <tr>
        <td><div class="formlabel">Send Status:</div></td>
        <td><?php print clean($aNewsletter["Send Status"]) ?></td>
    </tr>

    <?php } ?>

    <?php if( strcmp($aNewsletter["Sent"], "") ) { ?>
    <tr>
        <td><div class="formlabel">Sent Date:</div></td>
        <td><?php print clean(date("Y-m-d H:i:s",$aNewsletter["Sent"]))
        ?></td>
    </tr>

    <?php } ?>

    <?php if( strcmp($aNewsletter["Completed"], "") ) { ?>

    <tr>
```

```
        <td><div class="formlabel">Completed Date:</div></td>
        <td><?php print clean(date("Y-m-d H:i:s",$aNewsletter["Completed"]))
          ?></td>
    </tr>

    <?php } ?>

    <?php if( strcmp($aNewsletter["Recipients"], "") ) { ?>

    <tr>
        <td><div class="formlabel">Recipients:</div></td>
        <td><?php print clean($aNewsletter["Recipients"]) ?></td>
    </tr>

    <?php } ?>

.....

</table>
</form>
<?php closePage(); ?>
```

Summary

In this chapter we detailed the process of identifying, designing, and solving the problems associated with building an effective newsletter mailing system. We've developed a newsletter send daemon with a web-based interface via the command line and have executed it outside PHP's safe mode environment, and used technologies like SMTP and cron that helped us in creating the application. We thus created a complete mailing system that extends the classes and functions that were developed earlier in the book.

There are many things that we can do with a mailing system, especially when it comes to targeting content. Here we provided a basic knowledge of how to accomplish some of the key tasks involved with building a professional mailing system, and hope that you will explore the usage of this effective tool.

In the next chapter we'll design, build, and implement a product management system and cookie-based shopping cart. This will further help us in the final chapter, where we'll see how to implement an e-commerce check out system into our web site.

12

Shopping Carts

Selling your product over the Internet can be a difficult and complicated task. There are many problems involved with this process and there are many options to consider. In this chapter and the next we will look at some of the problems involved with building an online shopping system.

This chapter details the most notable part of our project – the shopping cart. We'll see how to build an informative and easy-to-use product database that will allow a user to purchase items directly from our web site.

In this chapter, we will:

- ❏ Build a products section for our user to browse through. We will make the front-end by:
  - ❏ Building a products list page
  - ❏ Building a product details page
- ❏ Build a CMS application for managing products in our database
- ❏ Build a client-based shopping cart

This shopping cart system will use the same standards that we have used throughout the book. We will employ the use of client-side cookies for storing products to be purchased (much in the same way that we used them in Chapter 5). We will also employ the use of our application framework defined in Chapter 4.

Chapters 12 and 13 together will cover the entire online shopping process. This chapter will deal with the creation of the products database and item selection process, whereas the next chapter will deal with the check out and fulfillment process.

The Problem

Since our site caters to the DVD enthusiast, we would like to enable our users to purchase DVDs and other DVD-related products from our web site. To do this we'll need a product database of the desired sales items, and will need to develop an easy-to-administer shopping cart system, which will allow users to browse and add items to it. This will allow our customers to order numerous products by going through the check out process (detailed in Chapter 13) just once. Of course, the shopping cart also should allow the user to denote the quantity of an item in a single session.

The most important aspect of a shopping cart system is a user-friendly interface. The average Internet user has grown accustomed to certain features and usability aspects of a shopping cart system like: adding items, deleting items, modifying the quantity, returning later to add more items, and an easy-to-use interface. We'll need to make sure that our customers can easily navigate our shopping cart and feel at ease while purchasing from our retail service.

Interface Requirements

There are some basic interface requirements that should be outlined prior to designing the data functionality of the site. These requirements will reflect our desired user experience while using the shopping system.

Products List

We'll want to create a paginated list of products that we offer for purchase. The list should also display some basic information about the product and a link to the product's detail page for more information. This should also be the first point of entry into the shopping system. This page should also contain an Add To Cart button so that the user can easily and quickly purchase the item.

Product Details

The product details page should contain all data associated with a specific product, including the movie credits, video formats, ratings, as well as the purchase price and number of units in stock. The Product Details page should also contain a picture of the selected DVD cover. The more information that we can provide to the customer, the better the site will be. This will cause the customer to begin to use the site as a reference when gathering information on a specific title and in turn may lead to the sale of a larger number of units in the long run.

This page should also include an Add To Cart button, which will add the item to the user's shopping cart. If a product is out of stock or not published in the CMS, the user should not be able to add this item to the shopping cart.

View Shopping Cart

We should design a shopping cart page that will display the DVDs that users add to the cart, remove from the cart, as well as change the number of copies of a certain DVD that they would like to purchase. This page should be accessible from anywhere on the site and should therefore be added as a root menu item.

Other Features

There are many other features that you can add to a shopping cart system. You can easily add 'user wish lists' or 'similar users have bought...' sections. You could also add user reviews of the products, utilizing the same methodology as we did when building comments for Chapter 6.

Application Requirements

We'll need an application for administering the products in our database. This application will manage every product and its relationship to our web site. The editable information in our application should represent the information that is used for the public (user front-end) side of the site. Furthermore, it should hold information that will be used by us for business purposes, more specifically the number of copies that we have in stock and the date the product was added.

Add/Edit Product

Each product should be editable in the same manner in which it was added. We should be able to update all information pertaining to the sales of the item. Furthermore, besides the textual information, we should be able to add (optionally) an associated image of the DVD cover to the database, for display on the site.

View Products

The CMS application should be able to present an easy-to-use paginated list of all the active products in our database. From this list the administrator should be able to edit, delete, publish, or stage the selected item. This view should be the entry point to the product administration CMS application.

Publish/Stage Product

The CMS application should publish or un-publish (stage) a product for display in the front-end of the web site. If a product is marked as staged, then the product should not be displayed in the products section of the web site and should not be allowed to be purchased. In other words, the user should not be aware of the product unless the product has been 'published'.

The Design

Now that we have defined our problem and the development requirements, we can start with our design. We will split up the design process into smaller sections to make the process easier to follow and to allow for greater understanding of the usage of data.

Designing the Data Layer

Let's start the design process by defining our database and looking at the specific information that we'll require to build this application.

Our database design for this application will be rather simple. Since we are keeping it simple, we will only use a `apress_products` table in the database.

The Products Table

This table will hold all the data associated with a certain product, and it will be referenced throughout the shopping system. The following is an outline of the information that we need in the database:

Field	Data Type	Description
product_id	INT(10)	This will be the primary ID for the product table and will serve as a referencing index for all the page views and transactions related to a product.
product_sku	VARCHAR(10)	The product SKU (Stock Keeping Unit) number is unique to each item. This number is assigned to the product by the distributor or manufacturer of the product, and proves useful when attempting to order more units of a given item.
product_name	VARCHAR(200)	The display name of the product. This will typically be the name of the DVD title.
product_desc	TEXT	The main text field used to hold a description of the item for sales purposes. In the case of a DVD we will be using this to hold the plot description as well as a list of credits and cast members. *If you plan on standardizing the data in this field, you may find it useful to split it into separate more specific text fields. MySQL will perform better with smaller data columns.*
product_rating	VARCHAR(5)	The voluntary movie rating given to the film by the Motion Picture Association of America (MPAA). It can hold one of these values: G, PG, PG-13, R, NC-17, NR.
product_format	VARCHAR(20)	The video format of the DVD. This field should be one of the following (NTSC, PAL, SECAM). (This will be different for each region/country.)
product_release_dt	DATE	The release date of the DVD.
product_img_path	VARCHAR(200)	The name of the image file associated with the DVD. This is usually an image of the DVD cover and should be NULL if there is no image available. Since checking for the field in the database is less work for the system than checking it on the file system for each query, we will be storing our images in the file system rather than in the database to help maintain data integrity and to facilitate faster queries.

Field	Data Type	Description
product_price	FLOAT	The price of the DVD. This is the price that will be used as the retail price of the item.
product_quantity	INT(5)	The quantity of this title currently in stock. This is very important for both the customer side and the administrative side of the system.
status	INT(1)	The state of the row item. This field is defined by the CMS and is used to see if the DVD is published on the front-end.
deleted	INT(1)	To see if a record has been deleted (soft delete) or not. This field is defined by the CMS. *A soft delete just marks the record as deleted and makes it invisible on the user front-end. To retrieve information on the soft-deleted product, the administrator can manually query for the associated data that will be present in the database.*
deleted_dt	DATETIME	The date that a record was deleted. This field should be NULL if the record is still active. The column is defined by the CMS.
created_dt	DATETIME	The date when the record was created. This field is defined by the CMS.
modified_dt	DATETIME	The last date that a record was modified. This field is defined by the CMS.

Designing the Data Objects

For our products module we'll break up our data functionality into two data objects, which will be instantiated as and when they are used. The first one will be used to manage the products in our database and the second will be used to administer the items to be held in the client-side cookie.

We'll employ the use of the PEAR::DB class for all database connectivity. We'll also be employing the use of our presentation libraries that we developed in earlier chapters.

The Products Class

The products class will manage all the assumed functionality that we could perform on or with a product. This will include the creation, management, and removal of items within the context of our application framework, and will also manage the publishing and staging of items for public viewing and shopping cart functionality.

Let's take a look at the members that we will need in order to build a products management system:

products Class Member	Description
_iProductId	Property containing the product unique identifier.
_oConn	Property containing the PEAR database object reference.
products()	Constructor method that instantiates any parent objects and sets global configuration variables.
_checkQuantity(quantity)	Checks to see if the requested quantity is available.
setProductId(product id)	Public method to set the $_iProductId class variable.
getProduct()	Returns all data associated with the defined product.
getProducts(sort, rows[optional], status[optional])	Accepts a string for the sort column, an optional numeric value for the row number to begin and an optional Boolean value for whether or not to display non-published items. This method returns an array of active products.
getProductsCount(status[optional])	Accepts a numeric value for whether or not to display non-published items, and returns a numeric value representing the number of active products in the database; it's used for pagination.
addProduct(product data)	Accepts an array of product information used to add a single product to the system.
updateProduct(product data)	Accepts an array of product information used to update a single product in the system.
publishProduct()	Marks a product to be displayed on the web site.
stageProduct ()	Marks a product so that it is not displayed on the web site.
deleteProduct()	Updates the database by setting the deleted (soft delete) status for a particular product.

The Shopping Cart Class

The second data object is the shopping_cart class, which will extend the products class and implement all the assumed functionality that can be associated with the shopping cart. This will include the addition, modification, and deletion of all records in the user's shopping cart. The shopping cart will be based on a cookie variable, which is nothing more than a serialized string containing the data of a simple associative array. The array's key would be the product's unique identifier and the value the quantity of the selected item that the user would like to purchase.

Let's take a look at all of the class members that will be included in this data object:

`shopping_cart` Class Member	Description
`$_iTotalPrice`	Property containing the total price of all items in the shopping cart.
`shopping_cart()`	Constructor method that instantiates any parent objects and sets our global configuration variables.
`_getCart()`	Retrieves the set cookie string and returns an associative array; that is, it parses the cookie into a useable associative array containing the product and its associated quantity.
`setCart(cart data)`	Replaces the entire shopping cart with a new array. This is used to commit any changes that have been made to the shopping cart.
`_getQuantity(product id)`	Checks to see if a product is in the user's shopping cart. If so, it returns the quantity of the product desired by the user.
`getTotalPrice()`	Returns the sum total of all product prices in the user's shopping cart.
`getCartItems()`	Returns an array containing all necessary data associated with the user's shopping cart items and also builds the `$_iTotalPrice` member variable.
`addCartItem(product id, quantity)`	Adds a product to the user's shopping cart.
`updateCartItem()`	Updates the quantity of a specific item in the user's shopping cart.
`deleteCartItem(product id)`	Removes the specified product from the user's shopping cart.
`clearCart()`	Deletes everything in the user's shopping cart.

Designing the Customer Interface

The customer interface is one of the most important parts of developing a successful online store. The user's experiences in the store is going to determine if the user will shop with us in the future, which will be the determining factor of how well our sales fare in the long run. If we can provide the user with a simple yet informative product catalogue, and make the purchasing process as painless as possible, then we'll get good returns for our hard work and investment.

The Products List Page

Our web site will feature only a small number of products and won't need an intricate browsing system. For our purpose, a paginated list of available DVDs will be more than sufficient, and it will serve as the entry point of our store. It should include the following items in this list:

397

- ❑ Title
- ❑ Release date
- ❑ Purchase item/stock status
- ❑ Add To Cart button

We would like our customers to be able to sort the list page by title or release date, as well as be able to add the product to their shopping cart directly from the list page for quick and easy purchasing. For now, since we'll not be featuring a large number of products, we will not include a search function from within the viewable products list. However, we could look into adding in this functionality as our product list gets larger. For information on building search engines, refer to *Professional PHP4 Web Development Solutions* from *Apress (ISBN 1-861007-43-4)*.

The Product Details Page

Each product displayed in the product list page should have an associated product details page, where all the associated DVD information is displayed. Users can add items to their shopping cart from this page. Furthermore, this page will also be linked to from the shopping cart view page, so that the users can go back and make sure that they have selected the correct DVD. Along with all of the text on this page, we will also include an image of the DVD's cover so that users can easily associate the product with the item that they are looking for.

The Add To Shopping Cart button of this page leads to the shopping cart section, which includes a quantity field (it defaults to 1) that allows the users to easily add multiple quantities of an item to their cart during a single purchase. Note that the shopping cart section should only be displayed if there is one or more of the selected items in stock.

The View Shopping Cart Page

This page will assume all of the functionality involved with adding, modifying, and deleting products from the user's shopping cart. This page will be accessible from the main menu bar and will allow users to view all of the items in their shopping cart. The page will also include links for each item so that users can go back and view more information on a product that they are purchasing. It will also include the CHECKOUT button that will serve as an end to the user's shopping and begin the check out process (detailed in the next chapter).

The view shopping cart page should include the following display items for each product:

- ❑ Product title (If clicked, this should link to the selected product details page.)
- ❑ An input field for the desired quantity
- ❑ Product unit price
- ❑ Combined price (quantity * unit price)
- ❑ The DVD title
- ❑ A DELETE button that will remove a product from the user's shopping cart

This page should also include the total sum price of all items in the user's shopping cart, as well as an UPDATE button for updating any changed quantity values and a CHECKOUT button for when the user is finally ready to check out.

Designing the Administration Interface

This administration interface will be placed inside the designed CMS framework and will be used to administer the product database. Similar to the CMS applications that we have built till now, this application will contain two main parts – the products list page, and the add/edit product page. The first of these will be used to display a list of items that we have access to viewing or editing, and the latter will be used to view or edit a specific product.

Products List

The products list page will be used as the primary entrance point to the products CMS application and will contain a list of all the active products in the database. This page will allow the web master to view all products as well as link to the edit page for any specific product.

Since the application framework has already been defined, we'll stick to the same standards and permission structure. If the web master has permissions to add a product to the database, then an ADD ITEM button will be displayed on this page, which will allow him or her to add DVDs to the database. If you are unclear on the use of our CMS permissions, please refer to Chapter 4.

The Add/Edit Page

The add/edit product form will be the same. If a unique ID is passed to the form page, the page will be filled with the ID's associated data. If an ID is not present, then the form will be blank and will simply add a product.

The form page should include fields for both the customer presentation data as well as administration specific data such as the quantity of the given product that is currently in stock. All of the fields on this page should be defined by user input, except for the rating and format fields that have the following options:

- ❏ Rating – G, PG, PG-13, R, NC-17, NR
- ❏ Video Format – NTSC, PAL, SECAM

The Solution

Now that we have defined our problems and have a basic understanding of the application design, let's begin the process of developing our solutions. We will use many of the tools and global methods that have been used throughout the development process. We'll start the development process by building up from our core data level. We'll then work through the presentation and execution of the web site and CMS.

Implementing the Data Layer

We've already designed the database table and defined the fields that we need to add, so at this point all we need to do is create the actual table.

apress_products

Run the following script on the MySQL command prompt to create the `apress_products` table:

```
DROP TABLE IF EXISTS apress_products;

CREATE TABLE apress_products (
    product_id          INT(10)       NOT NULL auto_increment,
    product_sku         VARCHAR(10)   NOT NULL default '',
    product_name        VARCHAR(200)  NOT NULL default '',
    product_desc        TEXT          NOT NULL,
    product_rating      VARCHAR(5)    NOT NULL default '',
    product_format      VARCHAR(20)   NOT NULL default '',
    product_release_dt  DATE          default NULL,
    product_img_path    VARCHAR(200)  default NULL,
    product_price       FLOAT         NOT NULL default 0,
    product_quantity    INT(5)        NOT NULL default 0,
    status              INT(1)        NOT NULL default 0,
    deleted             INT(1)        NOT NULL default 0,
    deleted_dt          DATETIME      default NULL,
    created_dt          DATETIME      NOT NULL default '0000-00-00 00:00:00',
    modified_dt         DATETIME      NOT NULL default '0000-00-00 00:00:00',
                        PRIMARY KEY   (product_id)
) TYPE=MyISAM;
```

Implementing the Data Objects

The data objects will be used as the base to both our CMS application as well as to the user front-end of the web site. Because of this we have designed our classes to be flexible and easy-to-use for multiple purposes. The shopping cart class will be used only on the user front-end since it manages the user's session, and does not contain modifying methods needed for use within the CMS application. However, the products class will be used on both the front-end and from within the CMS framework.

class.products.php

This data object has been built in much the same way that other objects have been made in the earlier chapters. Once again we are using the PEAR::DB object for all database connectivity.

Include Base Libraries

We'll start the class by requiring the PEAR and user includes that are required for this object to work:

```php
<?php
// require PEAR objects
require_once "DB.php";

// require USER objects
require_once "config.php";
require_once "funcs.php";
```

Define Member Variables

Now that all the libraries have been imported, let's start the class and define our member variables:

```php
class products {
```

The $_oConn member variable is defined in the constructor method and is the database connectivity handle used for all queries executed from within this data object:

```
var $_oConn;
```

The $_iProductId is used in almost every method in this class. It needs to be set to a valid product identifier reference in order to modify, delete, stage, publish, or get a product's related information:

```
var $_iProductId;
```

Constructor Method

Let's begin the data object by instantiating the database connection via the use of the DB::connect() method executed from within the constructor method. This will define the $_oConn member variable as the database connectivity handle:

```
function products() {

        // Instantiate the database connection
        $this->_oConn =& DB::connect(DSN);

        // Check for DB class exceptions
        if (DB::isError($this->_oConn)) {

            // Report class exceptions if present
            catchExc($this->_oConn->getMessage());
        }
    }
```

Private Methods

At this point all of our libraries have been included and our database connectivity has been established, so let's begin the process of creating the private and public data methods that will be used in the development of these applications.

This data object will only require the use of a single private method. The _checkQuantity() method will be used to determine if the desired number of products is currently in stock. This method will simply return Boolean and will be used in the check out process described in the next chapter:

```
function _checkQuantity($iQuantity) {

        // Set default return value
        $return = FALSE;

        // Build SQL query
        $sql = "SELECT
                    product_quantity
                FROM
                    ".PREFIX."_products
                WHERE
                    product_id = '".$this->_iProductId."'
```

401

```
                        ";

            // Get the returned quantity and check for DB errors
            if (DB::isError($iNum = $this->_oConn->getOne($sql))) {

                // Report class exceptions if present
                catchExc($iNum->getMessage());
            } else {

                // Return true if quantity exists
                if($iNum >= $iQuantity) {
                    $return = TRUE;
                }
            }

            // Return Boolean value
            return $return;
    }
```

Public Methods

The first public data method that we'll create is the `setProductId()` method. This method sets the `$_iProductId` member variable, which is used in almost every method in this class:

```
    function setProductId($iProductId) {

            // Make sure that the product identifier is an integer
            settype($iProductId, "int");

            // If there is a valid product ID, then set the member variable and
            // return TRUE, else return FALSE
            if($iProductId != 0) {
                $this->_iProductId = $iProductId;
                $return = TRUE;
            } else {
                $return = FALSE;
            }

            // return Boolean value
            return $return;
    }
```

Select Methods

The select methods will be used to return data from the database to our CMS application and the user front-end. These are the functions that will be used for the majority of our database workload and should return data that is easy to integrate into many situations. Note that all of the return data is converted to the PHP standard data types and is in the most portable data format possible. For dates we'll always transport the data in a standard Unix timestamp format, so that it can be easily formatted in many locations and data situations.

The first method in this section is the `getProduct()` method. This will be used in both the CMS application and in the web site front-end to display products and their associated data:

```php
function getProduct() {

        // Set default return value
        $return = FALSE;

        // Build SQL query
        $sql = "SELECT
                    product_sku,
                    product_name,
                    product_desc,
                    product_rating,
                    product_format,
                    product_release_dt,
                    product_img_path,
                    product_price,
                    product_quantity,
                    status,
                    created_dt,
                    modified_dt
                FROM
                    ".PREFIX."_products
                WHERE
                    deleted = 0 AND
                    product_id = '".$this->_iProductId."'
            ";

    // Check for DB class exceptions
    if (DB::isError($rsTmp = $this->_oConn->query($sql))) {

        // Report exceptions if present
        catchExc($rsTmp->getMessage());

    // If the query returns a record set then begin to build the array
    } elseif ($rsTmp->numRows()>0) {

        // Get the first record
        $aTmpRow = $rsTmp->fetchRow(DB_FETCHMODE_ASSOC);

        // Set the product ID from the member variable
        $return["Product Id"] = $this->_iProductId;

        // Set the array key/value pairs that need no manipulation
        $return["SKU"] = $aTmpRow["product_sku"];
        $return["Name"] = $aTmpRow["product_name"];
        $return["Description"] = $aTmpRow["product_desc"];
        $return["Rating"] = $aTmpRow["product_rating"];
        $return["Format"] = $aTmpRow["product_format"];
        $return["Image"] = $aTmpRow["product_img_path"];
        $return["Price"] = $aTmpRow["product_price"];

        // Cast the quantity variable as an integer
        $return["Quantity"] = (int) $aTmpRow["product_quantity"];

        // Convert the release date to a Unix timestring
        $return["Release Date"] =
                        strtotime($aTmpRow["product_release_dt"]);
```

```
                    // Cast the status variable as an integer
                    $return["Status"] = (int) $aTmpRow["status"];

                    // Convert the created date to a Unix timestring
                    $return["Created Date"]  = strtotime($aTmpRow["created_dt"]);

                    // Convert the modified date to a Unix timestring
                    $return["Modified Date"] = strtotime($aTmpRow["modified_dt"]);

            }

            // free the result set
            $rsTmp->free();

            // Return the array or FALSE
            return $return;
    }
```

The next method that we look at will also be used by both the CMS and the user front-end section. It's used to return and display a list of products in the database. The data returned will have the same associated key names but this time they will be grouped into a numbered array. The number of items returned will depend on the ROWCOUNT configuration variable defined in the /_lib/_base/config.php file.

Notice that we are passing three arguments to the method. The first argument is a standard SQL ORDER BY statement and will be similar to many of the other data methods that we have used throughout the book. The second argument is used to offset the returned data array and will be used for pagination. The third and final argument will be used to specify whether or not we would like to return only published products or all products. The argument will be used as follows:

❑   TRUE – returns only published products

❑   FALSE – returns all products

Here is the getProducts() method:

```
function getProducts($sSort, $iPage=0, $iStatus=FALSE) {

        // Set the default return value
        $return = FALSE;

        // Build SQL filter
        // If $iStatus is TRUE, then only return published products
        $iStatus ? $sFilter = " AND status = 1" : $sFilter = "";

        // Build the SQL query
        $sql = "SELECT
                        product_id,
                        product_sku,
                        product_name,
                        product_desc,
                        product_rating,
                        product_format,
                        product_release_dt,
                        product_img_path,
                        product_price,
```

```
                product_quantity,
                status,
                created_dt,
                modified_dt
        FROM
            ".PREFIX."_products
        WHERE
            deleted = 0
            ".$sFilter."
        ORDER BY
            ".$sSort."
        LIMIT
            ".$iPage.", ".ROWCOUNT;
```

Next, check for DB class exceptions:

```
if (DB::isError($rsTmp = $this->_oConn->query($sql))) {

    // Report exceptions if present
    catchExc($rsTmp->getMessage());

// If there are no class exceptions, then begin to build the array
} else {

    $i = 0;
```

Now loop through the returned records:

```
while ($aTmpRow = $rsTmp->fetchRow(DB_FETCHMODE_ASSOC)) {

    // Cast the product id variable as an integer
    $return[$i]["Product Id"] = (int) $aTmpRow["product_id"];

    // Set the array key/value pairs that need no manipulation
    $return[$i]["SKU"] = $aTmpRow["product_sku"];
    $return[$i]["Name"] = $aTmpRow["product_name"];
    $return[$i]["Description"] = $aTmpRow["product_desc"];
    $return[$i]["Rating"] = $aTmpRow["product_rating"];
    $return[$i]["Format"] = $aTmpRow["product_format"];
    $return[$i]["Image"] = $aTmpRow["product_img_path"];
    $return[$i]["Price"] = $aTmpRow["product_price"];

    // Convert the release date to a Unix timestring
    $return[$i]["Release Date"] =
                strtotime($aTmpRow["product_release_dt"]);

    // Cast the quantity variable as an integer
    $return[$i]["Quantity"] = (int)
                        $aTmpRow["product_quantity"];

    // Cast the status variable as an integer
    $return[$i]["Status"] = (int) $aTmpRow["status"];

    // Convert the created date to a Unix timestring
    $return[$i]["Created Date"] =
                strtotime($aTmpRow["created_dt"]);
```

```
                // Convert the modified date to a Unix timestring
                $return[$i]["Modified Date"] =
                    strtotime($aTmpRow["modified_dt"]);

                $i++;
            }

            // free the result set
            $rsTmp->free();

            // Return the built array or FALSE
            return $return;
        }
    }
```

The final select method returns a total number of active records in the database, which is used for paginating the product list in the CMS product application and the user front-end.

Much like the previous method, we will include an argument that will determine whether or not we want to return only published products or all active products in the database:

```
function getProductsCount($iStatus=FALSE) {

        // Set the default return value
        $return = 0;

        // Build SQL filter. If $iStatus is TRUE, then only return a count
        // of the published products
        $iStatus ? $sFilter .= " AND status = 1" : $sFilter .= "";

        // Build SQL query
        $sql = "SELECT
                    COUNT(product_id)
                FROM
                    ".PREFIX."_products
                WHERE
                    deleted = 0
                ".$sFilter;

        // Check for DB class exceptions
        if (DB::isError($return = (int) $this->_oConn->getOne($sql))) {

            // Report exceptions if present
            catchExc($return->getMessage());
        }

        // Return the number of (active?) products in the database
        return $return;
    }
```

Insert Method

The products data object includes one insert method, which is used for adding product information to the designed database. Here we'll need to handle the raw data and upload the associated file image as well.

Since we are passing this method as an associative array of arguments we should define in greater detail the data that will need to be passed. The following is a table of the associated array keys and their desired data types:

Argument Array Key	Description
SKU	Property containing the unique SKU number for the product.
Name	Property containing the name of the product; the title of the DVD, for instance.
Description	Property containing the product description. This will be a text field containing the cast list as well as a brief description of the movie plot.
Rating	Property containing a string representation of the MPAA rating (G, PG, PG-13, R, NC-17, NR) for the movie.
Format	Property containing the video format (NTSC, PAL, SECAM) of the DVD.
Release Date	Property containing a Unix timestamp of the original release date of the DVD. An strtotime() function should be executed on this property prior to it being passed to the method.
Price	Property containing the price of the DVD. This should be a floating integer with only two decimal points.
Quantity	Property containing the number of units that are currently available for sale.
Image	Property containing the passed $_FILE[Key] data for the passed file. If no file has been uploaded then this field should be null.

Since we are dealing with file uploads in this data object, ensure that the directory to which the fields are being moved is writable by the web server. You will also need to be aware of the image size constraint defined by your server's php.ini file.

Here is the code for the method:

```php
function addProduct($aArgs) {

    // Set default return value
    $return = FALSE;

    // Build SQL query
    // Convert the release date to a SQL date format
    $sql = "INSERT INTO ".PREFIX."_products (
                product_sku,
                product_name,
                product_desc,
                product_rating,
```

```
                         product_format,
                         product_release_dt,
                         product_price,
                         product_quantity,
                         created_dt,
                         modified_dt
                    ) VALUES (
                         '".$aArgs["SKU"]."',
                         '".$aArgs["Name"]."',
                         '".$aArgs["Description"]."',
                         '".$aArgs["Rating"]."',
                         '".$aArgs["Format"]."',
                         '".date("Y-m-d",$aArgs["Release Date"])."',
                         '".$aArgs["Price"]."',
                         '".$aArgs["Quantity"]."',
                         NOW(),
                         NOW()
                    )";
```

Next, check for DB class exceptions:

```
if (DB::isError($rsTmp = $this->_oConn->query($sql))) {

    // Report exceptions if present
    catchExc($rsTmp->getMessage());

// If there are no DB class exceptions, then get the insert ID
} else {

    // Use MySQL's LAST_INSERT_ID() method to query for the insert ID
    $sql = "SELECT LAST_INSERT_ID()";

    // Check for DB class exceptions
    if (DB::isError($iProductId = $this->_oConn->getOne($sql))) {

        // Report exceptions if present
        catchExc($iProductId->getMessage());

        // Unset the product id
        unset($iProductId);
    }
```

Check that the file is uplaoded and that the product has been inserted into the database successfully:

```
if (strcmp("",$aArgs["Image"]["name"]) &&
    is_uploaded_file($aArgs["Image"]["tmp_name"]) &&
    $iProductId) {

    // Move the uploaded file to the correct location
    move_uploaded_file($aArgs["Image"]["tmp_name"],
        BASE_DIR."/_img/_products/".$iProductId.".jpg");

    // Build update query to include the image path in the
    // database
```

```
                    $sql = "UPDATE
                            ".PREFIX."_products
                        SET
                            product_img_path = '".$iProductId.".jpg'
                        WHERE
                            product_id = '".$iProductId."'";

                    // Check for DB class exceptions
                    if (DB::isError($rsTmp = $this->_oConn->query($sql))) {

                        // Report exceptions if present
                        catchExc($rsTmp->getMessage());
                    }
                }

                // Set the return value as the inserted product ID
                $return = $iProductId;
            }

        // Return either the inserted ID or FALSE
        return $return;
    }
```

Update Methods

The update methods are used to modify a record, from updating the published status to uploading a new image for a product. All of these functions will require that the setProductId() method be executed prior to running.

The updateProduct() method is used to update a product record in the database. This will accept the same data array that we used when adding a product. We'll again need to take into consideration the image file upload and data formatting that we did in the addProduct() method:

```
function updateProduct($aArgs) {

    // Set default return value
    $return = FALSE;

    // Build the SQL query
    // Convert the release date to an SQL date format
    $sql = "UPDATE
            ".PREFIX."_products
        SET
            product_sku = '".$aArgs["SKU"]."',
            product_name = '".$aArgs["Name"]."',
            product_desc = '".$aArgs["Description"]."',
            product_rating = '".$aArgs["Rating"]."',
            product_format = '".$aArgs["Format"]."',
            product_release_dt = '".date("Y-m-d",$aArgs["Release Date"])."',
            product_price = '".$aArgs["Price"]."',
            product_quantity = '".$aArgs["Quantity"]."',
            modified_dt = NOW()
```

```
                    WHERE
                      product_id = '".$this->_iProductId."'
                    ";
```

The `if` loop checks for DB class exceptions, and if there are none it checks for an uploaded file:

```
    if (DB::isError($rsTmp = $this->_oConn->query($sql))) {

        // Report exceptions if present
        catchExc($rsTmp->getMessage());

    } else {

        // Check for the uploaded file
        if (strcmp("",$aArgs["Image"]["name"]) &&
            is_uploaded_file($aArgs["Image"]["tmp_name"])) {

            // Move the uploaded file to the correct path location
            move_uploaded_file($aArgs["Image"]["tmp_name"],
                    BASE_DIR."/_img/_products/".$this->_iProductId.".jpg");

            // Build update query to include the image path in the database
            $sql = "UPDATE
                        ".PREFIX."_products
                    SET
                        product_img_path = '".$this->_iProductId.".jpg'
                    WHERE
                        product_id = '".$this->_iProductId."'";

            // Check for DB class exceptions
            if (DB::isError($rsTmp = $this->_oConn->query($sql))) {

                // Report exceptions if present
                catchExc($rsTmp->getMessage());
            }
        }

        // If no exceptions are present then set return = TRUE
        $return = TRUE;
    }

    // Return TRUE on success
    return $return;
}
```

The `publishProduct()` method updates the status field in the `apress_products` table. Setting this variable to 1 tells the system that we would like this record to show up on the web site and be accessible to public viewing and functionality. This method is run from the CMS administration application and is used by clicking on the publish/un-publish (soft delete) button defined by our CMS framework in Chapter 4:

```
function publishProduct() {

        // Build the SQL query
        $sql = "UPDATE
                    ".PREFIX."_products
```

```
                SET
                    status = 1,
                    modified_dt = NOW()
                WHERE
                    product_id = '".$this->_iProductId."'
                ";

        // Check for DB class exceptions
        if (DB::isError($rsTmp = $this->_oConn->query($sql))) {

            // Report exceptions if present
            catchExc($rsTmp->getMessage());

            // Set return = FALSE
            $return = FALSE;

        } else {

            // If there are no exceptions then set return = TRUE
            $return = TRUE;
        }

        // return TRUE on success
        return $return;
    }
```

The `stageProduct()` method is used to deactivate and prevent it from being displayed on the front-end. This method is also executed from the CMS application framework by clicking on the publish/un-publish (soft delete) button in the products list view (Chapter 4), which will cause the user front-end to ignore this record and not allow a user to view or purchase it:

```
function stageProduct() {

        // Build the SQL query
        $sql = "UPDATE
                ".PREFIX."_products
            SET
                status = 0,
                modified_dt = NOW()
            WHERE
                product_id = '".$this->_iProductId."'
            ";

        // Check for DB class exceptions
        if (DB::isError($rsTmp = $this->_oConn->query($sql))) {

            // Report exceptions if present
            catchExc($rsTmp->getMessage());

            // Set return = FALSE
            $return = FALSE;
        } else {
```

```
                // If there are no exceptions then set return = TRUE
                $return = TRUE;
        }

        // Return TRUE on success
        return $return;
    }
```

Delete Method

The `deleteProduct()` method is used to delete (soft delete) products from the database. It uses a `UPDATE` query to set the `deleted` flag field to 1:

```
function deleteProduct() {

        // Build SQL query
        $sql = "UPDATE
                    ".PREFIX."_products
                SET
                    deleted = 1,
                    deleted_dt = NOW(),
                    modified_dt = NOW()
                WHERE
                    product_id = '".$this->_iProductId."'
                ";

        // Check for DB class exceptions
        if (DB::isError($rsTmp = $this->_oConn->query($sql))) {

            // Report exceptions if present
            catchExc($rsTmp->getMessage());

            // Set return = FALSE
            $return = FALSE;
        } else {

            // If there are no exceptions, then set return = TRUE
            $return = TRUE;
        }

        // Return TRUE on success
        return $return;
    }
```

Now that all the necessary data objects have been created, let's close the class:

```
} // end products class
?>
```

class.shopping_cart.php

The `shopping_cart` class is an extension of the `products` class, which allows us to access all the products methods from within this new class. We'll use the `shopping_cart` class to manage all the products in a user's shopping cart.

Include Base Libraries

First let's include the necessary parent object – the `class.products.php` script:

```php
<?php
// require USER objects
require_once("class.products.php");
```

Define Member Variables

Let's extend the class and define our member variables:

```php
class shopping_cart extends products {
```

The `$_iTotalPrice` variable will be the only member variable added in this class extension and will be calculated when the `getCartItems()` function is executed. This will be the total price of all the items in the user's shopping cart:

```php
var $_iTotalPrice = 0;
```

Constructor Method

The constructor method executes the `products()` constructor method of the parent object, which in turn instantiates the database connectivity:

```php
function shopping_cart() {

    // Execute constructor for parent object
    $this->products();
}
```

Since we are going to use a cookie for storing the user's shopping cart, we'll need to convert our associative array to a string. This is since a cookie can only be a string or an integer value. For our purposes a cookie fits great as a simple client-side storage container. PHP sessions would work just as well, if not more effectively than the cookie; however, sessions carry pros and cons of their own and are not necessary for us here.

To do this we will create two methods – the `_getCart()` method and the `setCart()` method. These methods will use the PHP `serialize()` and `unserialize()` functions to convert our associative array into and out of a storable string representation.

The `_getCart()` method is used to parse the cookie into a useable associative array containing the product and its associated quantity:

```php
function _getCart() {

    // Convert the shopping cart cookie to a useable associative array
    return unserialize($_COOKIE["cart"]);
}
```

The setCart() is used to convert and store the associative array as a client-side cookie. Unlike the _getCart() method, this method is public and can be used directly by the CMS application to replace the entire cart with new variables. This will be important when we get to the *Update Cart* section later in the chapter.

Here is the code for the setCart() method:

```
function setCart($aCart) {

    // Covert the passed array to a storable string and set it in a cookie
    setcookie("cart", serialize($aCart), FALSE, "/" , "", "");

    // Always return TRUE.
    return TRUE;
}
```

Private Methods

The next method checks if a specific product exists in the user's shopping cart. If the item does exist, then the method will return the quantity of product that the user has requested. It can be used to display the quantity on the user interface:

```
function _getQuantity($iProductId) {

    // Get the current cookie array
    $aCart = $this->_getCart();

    // Check for the product ID and return the quantity
    if($aCart[$iProductId] > 0) {

        $return = $aCart[$iProductId];
    } else {

        // return FALSE if the item does not exist in the user's cart
        $return = FALSE;
    }
    return $return;
}
```

Public Methods

The getCartItems() method fetches and returns the items in a shopping cart, which is used to build the View Shopping Cart page. It builds a query using the shopping cart array and the SQL IN() statement to return data from the database and associates it with the data stored in the user's cookie:

```
function getCartItems() {

    // Set default return value
    $return = array();

    // get the current shopping cart array
```

```
                    $aCartItems = $this->_getCart();

                    // Check for cart items
                    if($aCartItems) {
```

Build the SQL filter:

```
            if(count($aCartItems)){

                // get a list of all product IDs in the shopping cart
                $aKeys = array_keys($aCartItems);

                $i=0;
                while($i<count($aKeys)){

                    if($i != 0){
                        $sFilter .= ",";
                    }

                    $sFilter .= $aKeys[$i];
                    $i++;

                }
            }
```

Build the SQL query:

```
        $sql = "SELECT
                    product_id,
                    product_name,
                    product_price
                FROM
                    ".PREFIX."_products
                WHERE
                    status = 1 AND
                    deleted = 0 AND
                    product_id IN (".$sFilter.")
                ";
```

Check for DB class exceptions:

```
            if(DB::isError($rsTmp = $this->_oConn->query($sql))){

                catchExc($rsTmp->getMessage());
                $return = FALSE;
            } else {

                $i=0;
                while ($aTmpRow = $rsTmp->fetchRow(DB_FETCHMODE_ASSOC)) {

                    $return[$i]["Product Id"] = $aTmpRow["product_id"];
                    $return[$i]["Name"] = $aTmpRow["product_name"];
                    $return[$i]["Price"] =
                            round($aTmpRow["product_price"],2);
                    $return[$i]["Quantity"] = (int)
                            $aCartItems[$aTmpRow["product_id"]];
```

```
                    // Multiply the quantity and price to get a combined price
                    $return[$i]["Combined Price"] = $return[$i]["Quantity"]
                                                    * $return[$i]["Price"];

                    // Add the combined price to the total
                    $iTotal = $iTotal + $return[$i]["Combined Price"];

                    $i++;
                }
            }

            // Set class member variable to the added total price
            $this->_iTotalPrice = $iTotal;

            if(count($return) == 0) { $return = array(); }
        }
        // Return the array of cart items
        return $return;
    }
```

Note that we are continually adding the combined prices to build a final total price, which is set to the private member variable ($_iTotalPrice) so that we can display it to the user and also use it during the check out process.

The getTotalPrice() method returns the private member variable, which is created in the getCartItems() method, by adding up the items in the user's shopping cart. This means that we do expect the getCartItems() method to have executed prior to this method. We'll check for this here, and if the member variable contains no value, we will run the getCartItems() method, thus allowing the method to set the variable for our use:

```
function getTotalPrice() {

    // Check for a set member variable
    // getCartItems() has to be run prior to executing this method, so if a
    // value does not exist, then run the method
    if ($this->_iTotalPrice == 0) {
        $aCartItems = $this->getCartItems();
    }

    // return the member variable
    return $this->_iTotalPrice;

}
```

The next method adds items to the shopping cart. This method receives two variables – the product unique identifier and the desired quantity. If a quantity already exists in the user's cookie, the new quantity is added to the previous quantity to ascertain the final order:

```
function addCartItem($iProductId, $iQuantity) {

    // get the current shopping cart array
    $aCart = $this->_getCart();

    // add the desired item and quantity to the array
    $aCart[$iProductId] = ( $aCart[$iProductId] + $iQuantity );
```

```
        // set the cart
        $this->setCart($aCart);

        // always returns TRUE
        return TRUE;
    }
```

The `updateCartItem()` method updates the item quantity field in the user's shopping cart:

```
function updateCartItem($iProductId, $iQuantity) {

        // get the current shopping cart array
        $aCart = $this->_getCart();

        // replace the item's quantity with the new quantity
        $aCart[$iProductId] = $iQuantity;

        // set the cart
        $this->setCart($aCart);

        // always return TRUE
        return TRUE;
    }
```

The next method in this class will be used to delete an item from a user's shopping cart. Note that this will delete the total quantity of the product in the cart:

```
function deleteCartItem($iProductId) {

        // get the current shopping cart array
        $aCart = $this->_getCart();

        // remove the associated array key/value pair
        unset($aCart[$iProductId]);

        // set the cart
        $this->setCart($aCart);

        // always return TRUE
        return TRUE;
    }
```

For our final method in this data object, we will create a function to clear the shopping cart entirely. This will simply replace the shopping cart array with a blank array and commit it using the `setCart()` method:

```
function clearCart() {

        // set an empty cart
        $this->setCart(array());

        // always return TRUE
        return TRUE;
    }
```

Now let's close the class and get started on building the CMS application and user front-end for this application.

```
} // end shopping_cart class
```

Building the CMS Application

The CMS application for administering products is built using the same methodology that we have used to build all of the other administration applications in this book.

CMS Product Listing

This is the product list on the CMS section of the site:

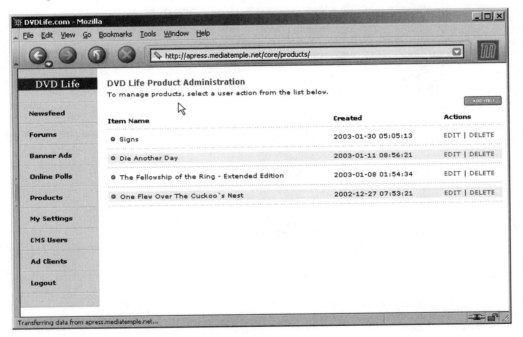

And here is the script:

```php
<?php

//File Location: /core/products/index.php

require_once("tpl_secure.php");
```

```php
require_once("class.products.php");

$oProducts = new products;

$aProducts = $oProducts->getProducts("created_dt DESC", $iCursor);
$iCnt = $oProducts->getProductsCount();

if (count($aProducts)>0) {

    $i = 0;
    while ($i < count($aProducts)) {
        $aData[$i]["Id"] = $aProducts[$i]["Product Id"];
        $aData[$i]["Name"] = $aProducts[$i]["Name"];
        $aData[$i]["Status"] = $aProducts[$i]["Status"];
        $aData[$i]["Created"] =$aProducts[$i]["Created Date"];
        ++$i;
    }
}

if ($id) {

    settype($id, "integer");
    $oProducts->setProductId($id);

    if (!strcmp($op, "del")) {

        $oProducts->deleteProduct();
        header("Location: ".SELF);

    } elseif (!strcmp($op, "act")) {

        $oProducts->publishProduct();
        header("Location: ".SELF);

    } elseif (!strcmp($op, "deact")) {

        $oProducts->stageProduct();
        header("Location: ".SELF);
    }
}

setHeader();
openPage();
?>
```

Next, is the HTML part of the script:

```html
<table width="608" border="0" cellpadding="0" cellspacing="0">
    <tr>
        <td colspan="2"><div class="header"><?php print ENTITY ?>
        Product Administration</div></td>
    </tr>
    <tr>
        <td colspan="2"><div class="copy">To manage products,
        select a user action from the list below.</div></td>
```

```
            </tr>
            <tr>
                <td><div class="error"><?php writeErrors() ?></div></td>
                <td align="right" valign="top"><?php if ($iPerm > 1) { ?>
                <a href="form.php?op=add">
                 <img src="../../_img/buttons/btn_additem.gif"
                    width="58" height="15" alt="" border="0" /></a><?php } ?></td>
            </tr>
    </table>

    <?php renderList($iCnt, $aData) ?>

    <?php closePage(); ?>
```

CMS Add/Edit Product Page

This the form page where the web master can add and/or edit products:

```php
<?php

// File Location: /core/products/form.php

require_once("tpl_secure.php");
require_once("class.products.php");

$oProducts = new products;

$aProducts = $oProducts->getProducts("created_dt DESC", $iCursor);
$iCnt = $oProducts->getProductsCount();

if (count($aProducts)>0) {

    $i = 0;
    while ($i < count($aProducts)) {
        $aData[$i]["Id"] = $aProducts[$i]["Product Id"];
        $aData[$i]["Name"] = $aProducts[$i]["Name"];
        $aData[$i]["Status"] = $aProducts[$i]["Status"];
        $aData[$i]["Created"] =$aProducts[$i]["Created Date"];
        ++$i;
    }
}
```

Next, depending on the 'status' returned, the product is activated or deactivated:

```php
if ($id) {

    settype($id, "integer");
    $oProducts->setProductId($id);

    if (!strcmp($op, "del")) {

        $oProducts->deleteProduct();
        header("Location: ".SELF);

    } elseif (!strcmp($op, "act")) {
```

```php
        $oProducts->publishProduct();
        header("Location: ".SELF);

    } elseif (!strcmp($op, "deact")) {

        $oProducts->stageProduct();
        header("Location: ".SELF);
    }
}

setHeader();
openPage();

?>
```

Here is the HTML part of the script:

```html
<table width="608" border="0" cellpadding="0" cellspacing="0">
    <tr>
        <td colspan="2"><div class="header"><?php print ENTITY ?>
         Product Administration</div></td>
    </tr>
    <tr>
        <td colspan="2"><div class="copy">To manage products,
         select a user action from the list below.</div></td>
    </tr>
    <tr>
        <td><div class="error"><?php writeErrors() ?></div></td>
        <td align="right" valign="top"><?php if ($iPerm > 1) { ?>
         <a href="form.php?op=add">
          <img src="../../_img/buttons/btn_additem.gif"
           width="58" height="15" alt="" border="0" /></a><?php } ?></td>
    </tr>
</table>

<?php renderList($iCnt, $aData) ?>

<?php closePage(); ?>
```

This screenshot displays the edit functionality of the form:

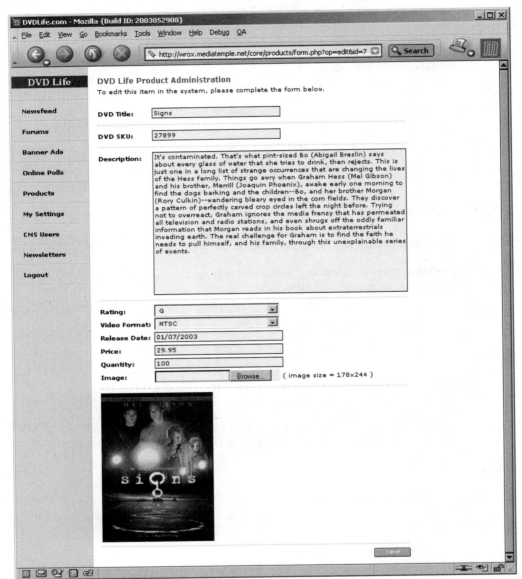

Building the User Front-End

All the shopping cart functionality is implemented in the user front-end. We'll build links to the shopping cart page from a number of different places on the site; however, all shopping cart functionality will be executed from the single /site/shopping_cart/index.php page. This page lists all the items in the user's shopping cart, and allows the user to update, add, and delete items from the cart.

Site Product List Page

This is how a user's shopping cart page would look:

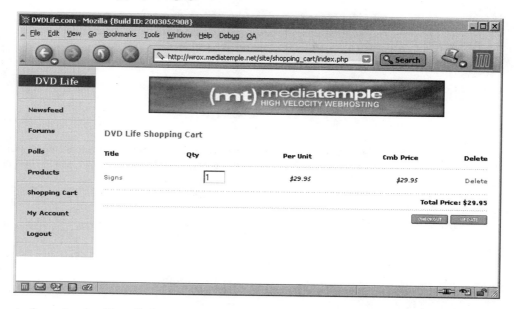

Here is the script that lists all the items in the user's shopping cart, and allows the user to update, add, and delete items from the cart:

```php
<?php

File Location: /site/shopping_cart/index.php

// get the tpl_unsecure.php file that has the necessary
// functions for the rest of this page
require_once("tpl_unsecure.php");
require_once("class.shopping_cart.php");

$oCart = new shopping_cart;
```

All of our assumed functionality will take place by assessing the incoming $_GET variables. Thus we'll set up three different script operations, which will be executed if the $_GET["opt"] variable is equal to one of the following:

❑ add – increments the given product ID by 1

❑ del – deletes all quantities associated with the given ID

❑ edit – checks the posted form variables and updates accordingly

Note that after each operation call, the page is refreshed using the header() function. We do this because a cookie can only be used on the next page view.

Let's continue with the script:

```
//add item
if(!strcmp("add",$_GET["opt"]) && $id > 0){

    $oCart->addCartItem($id, 1);
    header("Location: ".SELF);

// delete item
} elseif(!strcmp("del",$_GET["opt"]) && $id > 0) {

    $oCart->deleteCartItem($id);
    header("Location: ".SELF);
```

The next bit of code will update the entire cookie so we will want to check each incoming $_POST variable before placing it into an associative array and passing it to the setCartItems() class method:

```
} elseif(!strcmp("edit",$_GET["opt"]) && $POSTED ) {

    $aCartItems = array();

    while(list($sKey,$sVal) = @each($_POST)){

        if(ereg("^update_[0-9]+$",$sKey)){

            $id = str_replace("update_","",$sKey);
            $iQnt = $sVal;
            settype($id,"integer");
            settype($iQnt,"integer");

            if($iQnt == 0) {

                unset($aCartItems[$id]);
            } else {

                $aCartItems[$id] = $iQnt;
            }
        }
    }

    $oCart->setCart($aCartItems);

    header("Location: ".SELF);
}

// get cart items
$aProducts = $oCart->getCartItems();

// generate the header information
setHeader();

// start a new page with a banner advertisement
openPage(TRUE);
?>
```

This is the HTML part of the script:

```
<!-- main content -->
<table border="0" cellpadding="0" cellspacing="0">
    <tr>
        <td><div class="header"><?php echo ENTITY; ?> Shopping
        Cart</div></td>
    </tr>

    <tr>
        <td><div class="error"><?php writeErrors(); ?></div></td>
    </tr>
</table>

<form name="apressform" action="<?php print SELF ?>?opt=edit" method="post">
<table width="608" border="0" cellpadding="0" cellspacing="0">
    <?php

    if (count($aProducts)) {
    ?>

    <tr>
        <td align="left" class="copy"><b>Title<b/></td>
        <td align="center" class="copy"><b>Qty</b></td>
        <td align="right" class="copy"><b>Per Unit<b/></td>
        <td align="right" class="copy"><b>Cmb Price<b/></td>
        <td align="right" class="copy"><b>Delete<b/></td>
    </tr>
    <tr>
        <td colspan="5" class="dotrule"><img src="../../_img/spc.gif"
        width="1" height="15" alt="" border="0" /></td>
    </tr>

    <?php
        $i = 0;
        while ($i < count($aProducts)) {
    ?>
    <tr>
        <td><div class="section"><a href="../products/detail.php?id=
        <?php print $aProducts[$i]["Product Id"] ?>">
        <?php print format($aProducts[$i]["Name"]) ?></a></div></td>

.....

    <?php
            ++$i;
        }
    ?>

    <tr>
        <td colspan="5" align="right"><b>Total Price: $
        <?php print $oCart->getTotalPrice() ?></b></td>
    </tr>
```

```
    <tr>
        <td colspan="5" class="dotrule"><img src="../../_img/spc.gif"
        width="1" height="15" alt="" border="0" /></td>
    </tr>

    <tr>
        <td colspan="5" align="center"><a href="checkout.php">Check Out</a>
        | <a href="javascript:document.apressform.submit();">Update</a></td>
    </tr>
```

If there aren't any products in the user's database, an appropriate message is displayed:

```
    <?php
    } else {
    ?>

    <tr>
        <td><div class="copy">I am sorry, there are no products in your
        shopping cart.</div></td>
    </tr>

    <?php } ?>
</form>
</table>
</form>

<?php

// print out footer information
closePage();
?>
```

Building the Products Display

We'll split the functionality of the product display pages into a products list page and a products details page. Since we have integrated all of the data methods required for pagination into our data class, we should have no problem simply parsing out the data and building a basic list page.

The two important items to note are the add-to-cart functionality and the stock checks:

❑   The add-to-cart functionality is integrated by creating a link to the already created shopping cart view page and passing two get variables to it – an opt variable of the add operation, and an id variable of the product the user wants to add.

❑   The stock check looks at the returned records and checks to see if the item's Quantity field is greater than 0. If so, the program will place the Add To Cart link to the page; otherwise, it'll inform the user that the product is out of stock.

Product Display List Page

This is the script to display the product list:

```php
<?php

//file Location: /products/index.php

// get the tpl_unsecure.php file that has the needed
// functions for the rest of this page
require_once("tpl_unsecure.php");
require_once("class.products.php");

$oProducts = new products;

// get products and count
$aProducts = $oProducts->getProducts("product_release_dt DESC", $iPage=0, TRUE);
$iCnt = $oProducts->getProductsCount(TRUE);

// generate the header information
setHeader();

// start a new page with a banner advertisement
openPage(TRUE);

?>
```

Following is the HTML part of the script:

```html
<!-- main content -->
<table border="0" cellpadding="0" cellspacing="0">
    <tr>
        <td><div class="header"><?php echo ENTITY; ?> Products</div></td>
    </tr>
    <tr>
        <td><div class="error"><?php writeErrors(); ?></div></td>
    </tr>
</table>

<table width="608" border="0" cellpadding="0" cellspacing="0">
    <?php

    if (count($aProducts)) {

        $i = 0;
        while ($i < count($aProducts)) {
    ?>
    <tr>
        <td><div class="section"><a href="detail.php?id=
        <?php print $aProducts[$i]["Product Id"] ?>">
        <?php print format($aProducts[$i]["Name"]."
        (".date("Y",$aProducts[$i]["Release Date"]).")") ?></a></div></td>
```

```
            <td align="right"><div class="copy">$
             <?php print $aProducts[$i]["Price"] ?></div></td>
            <td align="right" width="80">
                <div class="copy">
                    <?php if ($aProducts[$i]["Quantity"] > 0) { ?>
                        <i><a href="../shopping_cart/index.php?opt=add&id=
                            <?php print $aProducts[$i]["Product Id"] ?>">
                            Add To Cart</a></i>
                    <?php } else { ?>
                        <i>Out Of Stock</i>
                    <?php } ?>
                </div>
            </td>
        </tr>
        <tr>
            <td colspan="3" class="dotrule"><img src="../../_img/spc.gif"
            width="1" height="15" alt="" border="0" /></td>
        </tr>
        <?php
            ++$i;
        }
        ?>
        <tr>
            <td colspan="3"><?php renderPaging($iCursor, $iCnt, "&type=".$iType)
            ?></td>
        </tr>
```

If there aren't any products, an appropriate message will be displayed:

```
    <?php
    } else {
    ?>
    <tr>
        <td><div class="copy">I am sorry, there are no products
        available.</div></td>
    </tr>
    <?php } ?>
</table>
</form>

<?php

// print out footer information
closePage();

?>
```

Product Display Details Page

This is the script that handles the product details page:

```php
<?php

// File Location: /products/details.php

require_once("tpl_unsecure.php");
require_once("class.products.php");

$oProducts = new products;

// set product ID
$oProducts->setProductId($id);

// get product array
$aProduct = $oProducts->getProduct();

// generate the header information
setHeader();

// start a new page with a banner advertisement
openPage(TRUE);

?>
```

This is the HTML part of the script:

```html
<!-- main content -->
<table border="0" cellpadding="0" cellspacing="0">
    <tr>
        <td><div class="header"><?php echo ENTITY; ?> Products</div></td>
    </tr>
</table>

<form action="<?php print SELF ?>?id=<?php print $id ?>" method="post"
 name="apressform">
<table width="608" border="0" cellpadding="0" cellspacing="0">
    <?php if (is_array($aProduct)) { ?>
    <tr>
        <td colspan="2"><div class="section">
         <?php print format($aProduct["Name"]."
         (".date("Y", $aProduct["Release Date"]).")") ?></div></td>
    </tr>
    <tr>
        <td colspan="2">
            <div class="copy">
                <?php if(strcmp("",$aProduct["Image"])) { ?>
                <img src="../../_img/_products/
                <?php print $aProduct["Image"] ?>"
                align="right" style="padding:10px"/><?php } ?>
```

```
                    <?php print format($aProduct["Description"]) ?>
              </div>
          </td>
      </tr>

.....

      <tr>
          <td><div class="copy">Price: $<?php print $aProduct["Price"]
          ?></div></td>
          <td>
              <div class="copy">
                  <?php if($aProduct["Quantity"]>0) { ?>
                      <a href="../shopping_cart/index.php?opt=add&id=
                      <?php print $aProduct["Product Id"] ?>">
                      Add To Shopping Cart</a>
                  <?php } else { ?>
                      Out of Stock
                  <?php } ?>
              </div>
          </td>
      </tr>
      <tr>
          <td colspan="2" class="dotrule"><img src="../../_img/spc.gif"
          width="1" height="15" alt="" border="0" /></td>
      </tr>
      <?php
      } else {
      ?>
      <tr>
          <td><div class="copy">I am sorry, the product you have requested
          cannot be found.</div></td>
      </tr>
      <?php } ?>
  </table>
  </form>

  <?php

  // print out footer information
  closePage();
  ?>
```

Summary

At this point we have walked through the entire process of creating a products display, a management system, and a full shopping cart process. The customers should be able to browse your product catalog and add products that they would like to purchase. They should be able to update their quantities as well as delete specific items from their cart. With the addition of the product management CMS application, the web master should be able to manage products in the database and keep important stock-keeping information that is associated with those products.

Building the product database and the shopping cart is just the first part of building an online store. In the next chapter we will cover how to check out and implement e-commerce into our site. We will continue where we left off by describing the check out process and many of the problems involved with online purchases, data security, and credit card transactions.

13

Checking Out

Implementing e-commerce on a web site is one of the most complicated tasks online. Whenever we are dealing with money and transactions, we need to make sure that each process has been checked thoroughly. In Chapter 12, we described how to build a shopping cart interface for our web site. In this chapter, we'll start from where we left off in the last chapter. We'll look at how to finish the shopping process by defining the problems involved with online commerce and build a simple but efficient solution.

Since the purpose of this book is not specifically to build an e-commerce application, we are going to show you a very basic example of building a product ordering, checking out, and fulfillment system. We are going to utilize one of the most well-known credit card validation APIs, **Payflow Pro**. Note that when working with secure applications, we should always work within the mod_ssl environment (http://www.modssl.org/) and be mindful of our development environment as well as our data transfers and manipulations.

In this chapter, we will be using VeriSign's Payflow Pro API to implement the financial transactions. There are many different methods and services for processing credit card transactions, but the Payflow Pro methods will work best for our code base and business model. To follow this chapter, you will need the following:

❑ Payflow Pro module compiled into Apache (http://www.php.net/manual/en/ref.pfpro.php)
❑ Merchant bank account
❑ VeriSign Payflow Pro account

We aren't going to describe compiling Payflow Pro with our Apache module, and if this is not provided, we suggest contacting your Internet hosting provider.

Once all of this is in place we can begin the process of implementing VeriSign's Payflow Pro.

The Problem

In this chapter, we deal with different pieces of information that we need from different places. First, we need to develop a check out process, which will help us in getting the user input data. Next, we'll need a way of gathering information about users' preferences from their account. Then we will develop a way to combine all the gathered information. Since we are dealing with money and sensitive information like credit card numbers, security is an important aspect that needs serious attention.

Interface Requirements

There are some basic interface requirements that should be outlined prior to designing the data functionality of the site. These requirements will reflect our desired user experience when checking out of our online store. Since we have already developed the shopping cart, we already have an array of desired products and now we only have to think about the process of purchasing and storing the desired products.

Account Preferences

Since all of the information being used will be tied to the user, it's important that all data for the user is stored in the user's preferences. We'll need to add a number of fields, such as their billing address and shipping address, to the user's preferences.

We'll not be storing the user's credit card information, as we do not want to worry about having it compromised. Credit card information is definitely the most worrisome information that could possibly be compromised, but it should also be noted that details like billing/shipping addresses and phone numbers should be made as secure as possible. Upon check out, our application first checks the login status of the current user. If the user is not already logged in, he/she will be taken to the account registration (login) page.

Check Out Page

The check out page will confirm the user's shipping preferences and shopping cart items. If any information needs to be changed, then the user will be linked to the correct page to modify the data they need to change. If all the information is correct, then the user will be able to input their credit card information and click SUBMIT. All error reporting and processing should be done on this page.

My Orders List

The 'My Orders' list page will be used for the account holder to check on their order status and view all of their past orders. This will simply be a list of all orders that the user has submitted. Each item on the list can be selected to show a detailed page consisting of all information associated with the order.

My Orders Details Page

This page will be used to display the associated order information to a user. This enables users to use this page as a receipt for their purchase. If a purchase is successful, users will be shown this page as a confirmation.

Application Requirements

We'll only have one application requirement for this section of the web site. The application for fulfillment can be complicated; however, for our site, we'll simply build a single application for viewing orders.

Fulfillment deals with the packaging and shipping of ordered items.

If you are building a large e-commerce site, you may want to build applications for refunds, shipping interaction, inventory, and workflow processes. You may also want to include features such as a PDF generator for building and printing shipping slips and receipts.

View Orders

Since we are just shipping a small number of items, the only application that we'll be developing will create a paginated list of orders and their associated shipping data. The page will simply list the purchase date and the account e-mail of the user that will be receiving the package. The order name is linked with the associated 'View Orders' page.

Order Details

The 'Order Details' page will give a detailed list of products that need to be shipped, along with the shipping address and other user information required to ship the packages.

Order Delivery Status

The CMS application marks a specific order as being fulfilled when the package has been shipped. Then this shows up on the user's 'My Orders' page stating that their package is on the way. This will be activated by using the application framework's publish/stage (soft delete, that is) button.

The Design

Now that we have defined our problem and development requirements, we'll design our application and plan the development process in great detail.

To better understand the process that we'll need to create, here is a simple diagram illustrating the layout of the check out process:

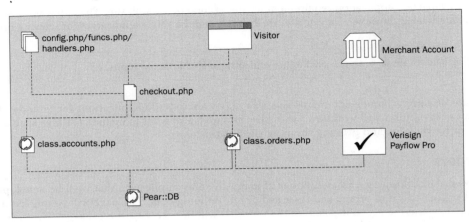

We'll start the process by designing the database tables that will hold all the order information and serve as a backbone to the check out process.

Designing the Data Layer

We'll start the design process by defining our database and look at certain information that we require to build our application.

Our database design for this application will be based on two tables:

- ❑ apress_orders to store the orders
- ❑ apress_order_items to store the order items

Let's look at our tables in detail to get a better understanding of the relative data.

The Orders Table

This table contains the associated user, order date, and order number, as well as the total price billed to the user:

Column Name	Data Type	Description
order_id	INT(10)	This is the primary key for the apress_orders table, and serves as a reference column for all page views and transactions related to a specific order.
account_id	INT(10)	Contains the associated account ID of the user that submitted the order.
order_total_price	FLOAT	Contains the total price billed to the user's credit card.

Column Name	Data Type	Description
order_cc_number	VARCHAR(4)	Contains an abbreviated representation of the user's credit card number. Typically we would set this to the last four digits of a user's credit card number. We do not want to store the entire number for security reasons. This can be used to manually confirm the transferred funds.
order_cc_exp_dt	DATE	Holds the expiration date of the user's credit card.
order_ship_dt	DATETIME	Is set at the time when the web master fulfills the order.
order_pfp_confirm	VARCHAR(120)	Contains the Payflow Pro confirmation number.
status	INT(1)	Is used to state whether the order has been completed.
created_dt	DATE	Contains the date in which the order was submitted.

The Order Items Table

The second table that we are creating contains all of the products that the user is purchasing and associates them with a specific order. We'll be storing the prices and descriptions along with the product identifier so the correct purchased price is shown if the sales price of an item changes in the database.

The following table shows all the fields in the apress_order_items table:

Column Name	Data Type	Description
item_id	INT(10)	This is the primary key for the apress_order_items table, and serves as the referencing column for all page views and transactions related to a specific order item.
order_id	INT(10)	Contains the associated order, which is a unique identifier that this item will be associated with.
product_id	INT(10)	Contains the unique identifier of the purchased product.
item_name	VARCHAR(200)	Contains the product name at the time of purchase. We'll store this column and the following ones, as product information alters with time.
item_price	FLOAT	Contains the product's price at the time of purchase.
item_quantity	INT(4)	Contains the quantity of the item selected by the customer.

Designing the Data Object

For the check out stage of our application, we'll be utilizing a number of data objects that have already been created. We'll be utilizing the accounts, products, and shopping cart classes throughout the entire process. The only data object that is still required is one to process the credit card transactions and add the orders to our database for processing. As we have already designed the database tables for these processes, we now need to design our data object that will access these tables.

The Orders Class

Here are the member properties that we will need to build to make a successful check out system:

orders Class Member	Description
_iOrderId	Property containing the order's unique identifier.
_oConn	Property containing the PEAR database object reference.
orders()	Constructor method that instantiates any parent objects and sets our global configuration variables.
setOrderId(order ID)	Public method to set the _iOrderId class variable.
processCreditCard($CCNumber, $iCCDate, $iAmount, $iTest=0)	Processes a credit card transaction using the Payflow API. The credit card number, expiration date, and the amount to bill information is passed to it. Returns TRUE on success and FALSE on failure.
getOrder()	Returns all data associated with the defined order.
getOrders($sSort, $iPage=0, $iStatus)	Accepts a string for the 'sort' column and an optional numeric value for the row number to begin with. It returns an array of active orders.
getOrdersCount()	Returns a numeric value representing the number of active orders in the database.
getOrderItems()	Returns an array of items and data related to a pre-determined order ID.
getAccountOrders($iAccountId)	Accepts a string representing the current user and returns all associated orders made by that user.
addOrder($aArgs)	Accepts an array of order information used to add a single order to the system.
addOrderItem($aArgs)	Accepts an array of order item data used to add and associate a desired item with an order.
confirmPayment($sConfirm)	Updates the record to include the payment confirmation number.

`orders` Class Member	Description
`completeOrder()`	This method sets the shipping date to the present date and changes the status to show completion.
`deleteOrder()`	Permanently deletes an order. This is primarily used in the check out page to delete a record if the payment does not go through.

Since we are dealing with purchases, many of the theories used throughout the rest of the book have changed to be more finite. An order is deleted only when it is not going to be used at all and is removed completely from the database. Also, you will notice that there is no 'unpublish (stage)' method, since there is no way to take back an order or not ship one.

Designing the Check Out Process

When dealing with money and fulfillment, we must always double check everything. Our check out process will be rather simple from a design perspective. The difficult part is the massive error checking that we'll have to do while actually building it.

In this module, all the processing for purchasing an item will be done from the check out page. This means that we will need to import all profile (used for shipping) and shopping cart data, and double check it before allowing the user to fill in their credit card information. Once we know that all of our data is valid, we will simply display their shipping information, the products they would like to purchase, the legal disclaimer, and a form for the user to fill in their credit card information.

All processing, business logic, and form handling should be done from this page, and all incoming data should be checked for validity prior to being sent to any data objects instantiated from within the page. If all data and credit card information is valid, then the user will be billed and the products will be added to the orders database for processing.

The credit cards information will not be compromised during transit, since all data will be transferred using HTTPS.

A sample of what the check out page should look like is shown over-leaf. It contains everything needed for the check out process and allows you to edit each item individually. The edit features should simply link to the page where the data was originally created. This is to say that the Shipping Info [Edit] link should simply link to the My Shipping Info page, and the Selected Products [Edit] link should take the user back to the Shopping Cart page.

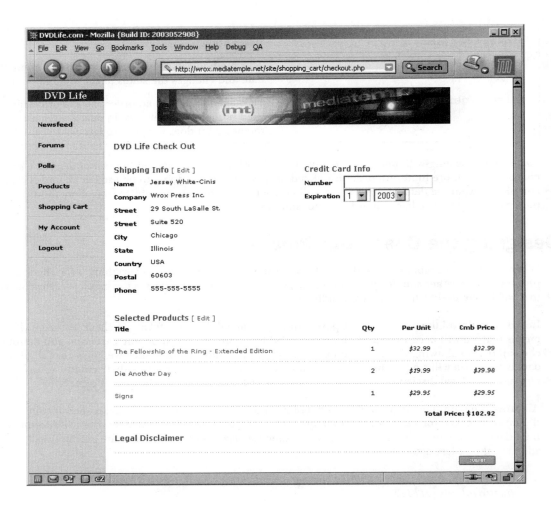

The Solution

Now that we have defined and designed all aspects of our check out process, we can begin our implementation. Once again we will start the process of building this application by working from the ground up.

The following diagram shows the different relationships and dependencies of files within our application framework that are necessary to implement the check out and fulfillment module:

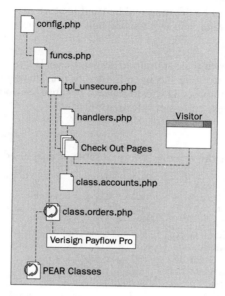

The following table describes the location and functional purpose of each file:

File Name	File Path	Description
config.php	/_lib/_base/	Configuration values for the application
funcs.php	/_lib/_base/	Utility functions for the application
tpl_unsecure.php	/site/	Template framework file for pages outside the CMS application
handlers.php	/_lib/_base/	Data input validation functions
checkout.php	/site/shopping_cart/	Check out page that confirms the user's shipping preferences and shopping cart items
orders.php	/site/accounts/	Orders list page for the account holder to check on their order status and view all of their past orders
order.php	/site/accounts/	Order details page to give a detailed list of products that need to be shipped, along with the shipping address and other user information required to ship the packages
class.orders.php	/_lib/_classes/	Data object for check out and fulfillment logic

Implementing the Data Layer

The database tables that we will be creating will be used to store orders and their associated items. As we will not be modifying this data, you will not see fields such as `modified_dt` that you have seen in past table creation statements.

All orders will be associated with their submitted account user ID, as seen in the `account_id` column. Also note that the `order_cc_number` has been limited to four characters so that the whole credit card number is not stored in the database. This is important because we do not want anyone in our organization to be able to access customer information.

apress_orders

The following SQL will create the `apress_orders` table as described in the *The Design* section:

```
CREATE TABLE apress_orders (
    order_id          INT(10)        NOT NULL auto_increment,
    account_id        INT(10)        NOT NULL default '0',
    order_total_price FLOAT          NOT NULL default '0',
    order_cc_number   VARCHAR(4)     default NULL,
    order_cc_exp_dt   DATE           NOT NULL default '0000-00-00',
    order_ship_dt     DATETIME       default NULL,
    order_pfp_confirm VARCHAR(120)   default NULL,
    status            INT(1)         NOT NULL default '0',
    created_dt        DATE           NOT NULL default '0000-00-00',
                      PRIMARY KEY (order_id)
) TYPE=MyISAM;
```

apress_order_items

The next table will be used to store associated products being purchased by the user. We are storing the price, name, and description, along with the product ID. This is important because we do not want the purchase data to change if the product changes in our products table:

```
CREATE TABLE apress_order_items (
    item_id        INT(10)        NOT NULL auto_increment,
    order_id       INT(10)        NOT NULL default '0',
    product_id     INT(10)        NOT NULL
    item_name      VARCHAR(200)   default NULL,
    item_price     FLOAT          default '0',
    item_quantity  INT(4)         default '1',
                   PRIMARY KEY (item_id)
) TYPE=MyISAM;
```

Now that we have our tables created, we can go on to describe the building of our data object.

Implementing the Data Object

The one data object that we will be creating in this chapter will be used for both credit card transactions as well as for processing the order within our own system. For the credit card transaction method in our class, we will be using the Payflow Pro API. This is just our method of choice; however, you can achieve this by means of many different credit card processing solutions. We will get into more detail on how this process works when we discuss the method.

class.orders.php

To begin this class, we need to include all of the libraries that we are using. Similar to previous chapters, we are using the PEAR::DB object for all database connectivity. We also require the use of all of our global configuration variables that we have defined in config.php:

```php
<?php

// File Location: /_lib/_classes/class.orders.php

// include PEAR objects
require_once("DB.php");

// include USER libraries
require_once("config.php");
```

Class Definition

Now that we are certain that all of our tools are in place, we can start our object and set all of our method variables:

```php
class orders {
```

Member Variables

The $_oConn variable is used in the same way that it was previously. It is used to house the object referenced by the PEAR::DB database object. This is set by our constructor method:

```php
var $_oConn;
```

The $_iOrderId() method property is set publicly by the setOrderId() method to define the current order's unique identifier:

```php
var $_iOrderId;
```

Constructor Method

The constructor method has one functionality – to instantiate our database connectivity. This method instantiates the object and defines it as our $_oConn member variable:

```php
function orders() {

    $this->_oConn =& DB::connect(DSN);

    if( DB::isError($this->_oConn) ) {
        catchExc($this->_oConn->getMessage());
    }
}
```

Public Methods

The first public method that we are building for this class is the `setOrderId()` method. This is used to define the current order that we are working with:

```
function setOrderId($iOrderId) {

    settype($iOrderId, "integer");

    if( $iOrderId != 0 ) {

        $this->_iOrderId = $iOrderId;
        $return = TRUE;
    } else {

        $return = FALSE;
    }

    return $return;
}
```

Building the Credit Card Processor

The second public method that we are creating is possibly the most vital of all. Let's call it `processCreditCard()`. This function is used to process all credit card transactions. The layout of the method is rather simple, but the execution must be bug free every time. All error reporting for this function will be done in the 'check out' script. This function simply returns the payment confirmation if the transaction goes through, otherwise it returns `FALSE`.

Up until version 4.x, MySQL did not accept the use of SQL transactions. A transaction is to be used where you have multiple queries that need to take place, all of which are contingent on the other's success or failure. Since we are not able to use transactions in our system, we need to write some extra logic into the check out script that allows us to roll back our queries if the credit card processor returns with a failure.

Since we need to test this system thoroughly, we'll create a number of test returns so that we can check to make sure that the rest of the process is working. For this we will use a single integer value between 0 and 3.

The meaning for each of the test options is given below:

- ❑   0 – Live transaction
- ❑   1 – Test transaction
- ❑   2 – No transaction and returns TRUE
- ❑   3 – No transaction and returns FALSE

Now let's write the function definition, by defining its arguments, which we have shown on the following page. The simplicity of this method makes it easy to implement the credit card processing from the live script.

The arguments are as follows:

- ❏ `$sCCNumber` – The credit card number
- ❏ `$iCCDate` – The credit card expiration date
- ❏ `$iAmount` – The amount to bill the credit card
- ❏ `$iTest` – The method to be used for testing

Note that there is no credit card type because the format of the card number will define the card type.

The arguments and the function are defined as follows:

```
function processCreditCard($sCCNumber, $iCCDate, $iAmount, $iTest = 0) {
```

Now we set the Payflow Pro server. Payflow Pro provides two servers for processing credit card transactions. The first server is used to test if a transaction is valid and the second is used to make the actual transaction. We are going to define these servers by using the `$iTest` parameter:

```
// define server
        if( $iTest == 1 ) {
            $sServer = "test-payflow.verisign.com";
        } else {
            $sServer = "connect.signio.com";
        }
```

Since we are using this code only for one site, we'll statically define our Payflow Pro user information. You may choose to put this in your configuration file for security reasons, but for our purposes we will avoid doing this.

This information is provided to you when you set up your Payflow Pro account with VeriSign. We will not be walking through how to create this account, but this should be done prior to setting up this method.

> **VeriSign account setup:**
> **http://www.verisign.com/products/payflow/pro/index.html**

Let's continue with the script:

```
if( $iTest == 0 || $iTest == 1 ) {

        pfpro_init();

        // this will define your transaction as well as
        // your VeriSign user information
        $aTransArgs = array(
            'USER' => 'mylogin',
            'PWD'  => 'mypassword',
            'PARTNER' => 'VeriSign',
            'TRXTYPE' => 'S',
```

```
                'TENDER'   => 'C',
                'AMT'      => $iAmount,
                'ACCT'     => $sCCNumber,
                'EXPDATE'  => date("my",$iCCDate)
        );

        $aResp = pfpro_process($aTransArgs, $sServer);

        if( !$aResp ) {

            $return = FALSE;
        } else {

            $return = $aResp['RESULT'];
        }

            pfpro_cleanup();
```

The last two else clauses are used strictly for testing purposes. The first is used to have the method return TRUE, and the second to return FALSE:

```
        } elseif ( $iTest == 2 ) {

            $return = "TEST CONFERMATION STRING";
        } else {

            $return = FALSE;
        }

        return $return;
}
```

Select Methods

The first select method that we define will be used to return a single order and its associated data. This requires that the setOrderId() method be run prior to execution:

```
        function getOrder() {

            $sql = "SELECT
                        account_id,
                        order_total_price,
                        order_cc_number,
                        order_cc_exp_dt,
                        order_ship_dt,
                        order_pfp_confirm,
                        status,
                        created_dt
                    FROM
                        ".PREFIX."_orders
                    WHERE
                        order_id = '".$this->_iOrderId."'
```

```
                   ";

    if( DB::isError($rsTmp = $this->_oConn->query($sql)) ) {

        catchExc($rsTmp->getMessage());
        $return = FALSE;

    } elseif ( $rsTmp->numRows() > 0 ) {

        $return = $rsTmp->fetchRow(DB_FETCHMODE_ASSOC);

        $return["order_id"] = $this->_iOrderId;

        // check for ship date
        if(!strcmp("",$return["order_ship_dt"])){
            $return["order_ship_dt"] = FALSE;
        } else {
            $return["order_ship_dt"] =
                                      strtotime($return["order_ship_dt"]);
        }

        $return["created_dt"] = strtotime($return["created_dt"]);

    } else {

        $return = FALSE;
    }

    return $return;
}
```

One might ask, "Where is the benefit in storing the data in DATETIME format if you always convert it to UNIX timestamps?" But in fact, there are many reasons for storing the date format as a datetime string in the database:

- ❏ It allows us to use all of MySQL's date/time functionality.
- ❏ It allows us to query based on the year/month/day/hour.
- ❏ It allows us to store dates before and after the ~60 year timeframe that a timestamp will cover.
- ❏ It allows us to maintain a standard date/time format spanning multiple languages. We needn't worry about having an API to support timestamps from within our desired programming language (one may not choose to use PHP for external reporting).
- ❏ Since this is an ordering system, it may need to interface with other systems (other databases, shipping/tracking systems, stock keeping systems).

The getOrders() method is used for the CMS application to build a list of all orders based on their process status. This is created the same way that we have created the past return arrays:

```
function getOrders($sSort, $iPage=0, $iStatus=FALSE) {

    $sql = "SELECT
```

```
                   order_id,
                   account_id,
                   order_total_price,
                   order_cc_number,
                   order_cc_exp_dt,
                   order_ship_dt,
                   order_pfp_confirm,
                   status,
                   created_dt
             FROM
                   ".PREFIX."_orders
             WHERE
                   status = 1
             ORDER BY
                   ".$sSort."
             LIMIT
                   ".$iPage.", ".ROWCOUNT;

      if( DB::isError($rsTmp = $this->_oConn->query($sql)) ) {

          catchExc($rsTmp->getMessage());
          $return = FALSE;

      } elseif ( $rsTmp->numRows() > 0 ) {

          $i=0;
          while( $aTmpRow = $rsTmp->fetchRow(DB_FETCHMODE_ASSOC) ) {

              // copy row to return array
              $return[$i] = $aTmpRow;

              $return[$i]["order_cc_exp_dt"] =
                  strtotime($return[$i]["order_cc_exp_dt"]);

              // check for ship date
              if( !strcmp("",$return[$i]["order_ship_dt"]) ) {
                  $return[$i]["order_ship_dt"] = FALSE;
              } else {
                  $return[$i]["order_ship_dt"] =
                              strtotime($return[$i]["order_ship_dt"]);
              }

              $return[$i]["created_dt"] =
                          strtotime($return[$i]["created_dt"]);

          $i++;
          }
      } else {
          $return = FALSE;
      }
      return $return;
  }
```

The next method we build is used to retrieve an integer representation of all records in the `apress_orders` table. This is required for pagination from within our CMS application:

```
function getOrdersCount() {

    $sql = "SELECT
                COUNT(order_id)
            FROM
                ".PREFIX."_orders
            ";

    $iCnt = $this->_oConn->getOne($sql);

    return $iCnt;
}
```

The `getOrderItems()` method is used on both the front and back-ends to display items that are associated with a specific order. The order unique identifier will be pre-set by the `setOrderId()` function:

```
function getOrderItems() {

    $sql = "SELECT
                item_id,
                order_id,
                item_name,
                item_price,
                item_quantity
            FROM
                ".PREFIX."_order_items
            WHERE
                order_id = '".$this->_iOrderId."'
            ";

    if( DB::isError($rsTmp = $this->_oConn->query($sql)) ) {

        catchExc($rsTmp->getMessage());
        $return = FALSE;

    } elseif ( $rsTmp->numRows() > 0 ) {

        $i=0;
        while($aTmpRow = $rsTmp->fetchRow(DB_FETCHMODE_ASSOC)) {

            // copy row to return array
            $return[$i] = $aTmpRow;

            $i++;
        }

    } else {

        $return = FALSE;
    }
    return $return;
}
```

Since we are creating a page for users to view their orders, we want to create a function that returns all orders that the specific user has created. Also, since we are not extending the accounts class, we need to pass the user's account ID to return their associated orders:

We do not extend the class because we are using this class from both the CMS and the front-end, and it is not necessary to extend it for a single needed variable.

```
function getAccountOrders($iAccountId) {

    $sql = "SELECT
                order_id,
                account_id,
                order_total_price,
                order_cc_number,
                order_cc_exp_dt,
                order_ship_dt,
                order_pfp_confirm,
                status,
                created_dt
            FROM
                ".PREFIX."_orders
            WHERE
                account_id = '".$iAccountId."'
            ORDER BY
                order_id DESC
            ";

    if( DB::isError($rsTmp = $this->_oConn->query($sql)) ) {

        catchExc($rsTmp->getMessage());
        $return = FALSE;

    } elseif ( $rsTmp->numRows() > 0 ) {

        $i=0;
        while($aTmpRow = $rsTmp->fetchRow(DB_FETCHMODE_ASSOC)) {

            // copy row to return array
            $return[$i] = $aTmpRow;

            $return[$i]["order_cc_exp_dt"] =
                strtotime($return[$i]["order_cc_exp_dt"]);

            // check for ship date
            if( !strcmp("",$return[$i]["order_ship_dt"]) ) {
                $return[$i]["order_ship_dt"] = FALSE;
            } else {
                $return[$i]["order_ship_dt"] =
                        strtotime($return[$i]["order_ship_dt"]);
            }
```

```
                    $return[$i]["created_dt"] =
                               strtotime($return[$i]["created_dt"]);

         $i++;
         }

     } else {

         $return = FALSE;
     }

     return $return;
}
```

Insert Methods

At this point, we have created methods for gathering information from the designed database and setting basic required class objects and variables. We have also created a method for processing and testing our credit card transactions. Now we need to create the methods that will be used to insert orders and their associated items into our database.

For this application, we will need to create two insert methods – one method to create base orders and another one to add items to that order.

For us to associate added items to a specific order, we need to have the addOrder() function return its insert ID so that we can pass it to the addOrderItems() method. This method accepts an array key of data used to insert the order record:

❏ account_id – The user's unique account identifier

❏ order_total_price – The total cost that will be charged to the user

❏ order_cc_number – The last four characters of the credit card

❏ order_cc_exp_dt – The credit card's expiration date

Let's continue with the script:

```
function addOrder($aArgs) {

    $sql = "INSERT INTO ".PREFIX."_orders (
               account_id,
               order_total_price,
               order_cc_number,
               order_cc_exp_dt,
               status,
               created_dt
           ) VALUES (
               '".$aArgs["account_id"]."',
               '".$aArgs["order_total_price"]."',
               '".$aArgs["order_cc_number"]."',
               '".date("Y-m-d",$aArgs["order_cc_exp_dt"])."',
```

```
                        '1',
                    NOW()
                )";

        if( DB::isError($rsTmp = $this->_oConn->query($sql)) ) {

            catchExc($rsTmp->getMessage());
            $return = FALSE;
        } else {

            $sql = "SELECT LAST_INSERT_ID()";
            $iOrderId = $this->_oConn->getOne($sql);
            $return = $iOrderId;
        }
        return $return;
    }
```

The addOrderItem() function is used to associate a desired item with an order. This method also handles the subtraction of the item quantity from the stocked inventory. It accepts an array with the following keys:

❑   item_name – The product name of the purchased item

❑   item_price – The price of the item at the time of purchase

❑   item_quantity – The quantity ordered of the selected item

❑   product_id – The product_id of the ordered product

Now that we have defined what data needs to be passed, let's take a look at the code used to build this method:

```
function addOrderItem($aArgs) {

        $sql = "INSERT INTO ".PREFIX."_order_items (
                    order_id,
                    item_name,
                    item_price,
                    item_quantity
                ) VALUES (
                    '".$this->_iOrderId."',
                    '".$aArgs["item_name"]."',
                    '".$aArgs["item_price"]."',
                    '".$aArgs["item_quantity"]."'
                )";

        if( DB::isError($rsTmp = $this->_oConn->query($sql)) ) {

            catchExc($rsTmp->getMessage());
            $return = FALSE;

        } else {
```

```
            $sql = "SELECT LAST_INSERT_ID()";
            $iItemId = $this->_oConn->getOne($sql);
            $return = $iItemId;

            $sql = "UPDATE
                        ".PREFIX."_products
                    SET
                        product_quanity = product_quantity -
                            ".$aArgs["item_quantity"]."
                    WHERE
                        product_id = '".$aArgs["product_id"]."'
                ";

            if( DB::isError($rsTmp = $this->_oConn->query($sql)) ) {

                catchExc($rsTmp->getMessage());
                $return = FALSE;
            }
        }

        return $return;
    }
```

Update Methods

The first of the two update methods is the payment confirmation method. This function simply takes a string argument of the Payflow Pro order confirmation and add it to the database. This is stored for use from within the Payflow Pro management console:

```
    function confirmPayment($sConfirm) {

        $sql = "UPDATE
                    ".PREFIX."_orders
                SET
                    order_pfp_confirm = '".$sConfirm."',
                    status = 1
                WHERE
                    order_id = '".$this->_iOrderId."'
            ";

        if( DB::isError($rsTmp = $this->_oConn->query($sql)) ) {

            catchExc($rsTmp->getMessage());
            $return = FALSE;
        } else {

            $return = TRUE;
        }
        return $return;
    }
```

The second update method that we see below is used in the CMS administration application to mark an order as fulfilled. This sets the records as completed and sets the 'shipped date' so that the user can know that the package is on the way:

```
function completeOrder() {

    $sql = "UPDATE
            ".PREFIX."_orders
        SET
            order_ship_dt = NOW(),
            status = 0
        WHERE
            order_id = '".$this->_iOrderId."'
        ";

    if( DB::isError($rsTmp = $this->_oConn->query($sql)) ) {

        catchExc($rsTmp->getMessage());
        $return = FALSE;
    } else {

        $return = TRUE;
    }
    return $return;
}
```

Delete Methods

The one delete method that we are now creating is used to permanently delete an order record from the database. We are creating this method so that we could add the order prior to billing the user, and if the payment fails, we remove the attempted transaction from the database:

```
function deleteOrder() {

    $sql = "DELETE
        FROM ".PREFIX."_orders
        WHERE order_id = '".$this->_iOrderId."'";

    if( DB::isError($rsTmp = $this->_oConn->query($sql)) ) {

        catchExc($rsTmp->getMessage());
        $return = FALSE;
    } else {

        $return = TRUE;
    }
    return $return;
}
}
```

Building the Check Out Process

Now that we have all of our tools in place, we can start writing our check out process. We will start by building a single page with all the required data and a lot of error handling code. We will walk through this process one step at a time, as it becomes quite complicated.

Check Out Page

We start this page just as we have started any of the other front-end pages, by including the `tpl_unsecure.php` file. This provides us with all of our front-end design templates and methods:

```php
<?php

//File Location: /site/shopping_cart/checkout.php

// get the tpl_unsecure.php file that has the needed
// functions for the rest of this page
require_once("tpl_unsecure.php");
```

Now we need to include all of our necessary data objects and instantiate them into usable object pointers. We need to require accounts for accessing all of our shipping information, a shopping cart for accessing all products desired by the user, and orders for all of our order processing methods:

```php
require_once("class.accounts.php");
require_once("class.shopping_cart.php");
require_once("class.orders.php");

$oAccounts = new accounts;
$oCart = new shopping_cart;
$oOrders = new orders;
```

The next step we have to take is to check our passed cookie for a valid account ID. If an account user is not logged in, then the user should be prompted to log in before going through the check out process.

If an account is present, then we follow through with checking that they have valid shipping address information and set our `$iShippingOK` variable accordingly:

```php
// validate session get account information
if( isset($_COOKIE["cACCOUNT"]) && $oAccounts->validateSession() ) {

    $aSess = $oAccounts->getSession();
    $aAddress = $oAccounts->getAccountAddress();

    // error handling
    if  (
        !strcmp("",$aAddress["Address Name"]) ||
        !strcmp("",$aAddress["Address Street"]) ||
        !strcmp("",$aAddress["Address City"]) ||
        !strcmp("",$aAddress["Address State"]) ||
        !strcmp("",$aAddress["Address Country"]) ||
        !strcmp("",$aAddress["Address Postal"]) ||
        !strcmp("",$aAddress["Address Phone"])
        ) {

        catchErr("Your shipping info is not valid. Please correct it.");
        $iShippingOK = FALSE;
```

```
        } else {

            $iShippingOK = TRUE;
        }
    } else {
        catchErr("You must be logged in to purchase products");
    }
```

Once we have determined that a user has logged in and has valid associated address information, we can continue to gather the next set of data, which happens to be the desired items in the user's shopping cart. We need to populate both our products array as well as our total price variable so that we can use them later in the script:

```
// get cart items
$aProducts = $oCart->getCartItems();
$iTotalPrice = $oCart->getTotalPrice();
```

Now we need to check the products array for valid data. If no products are present in the user's shopping cart, then we need to set our $iProductsOK variable to FALSE and report an error prompting the user that his or her cart contains no products:

```
// error reporting
if( !strcmp("",$aProducts[0]["Product Id"]) ) {

    catchErr("Your shopping cart is empty.");
    $iProductsOK = FALSE;
} else {
    $iProductsOK = TRUE;
}
```

Handle Posted Data

This section of the script handles all of the posted data and processes the order. Before starting any data manipulation, we need to check to make sure that all of our data is correct and intact, as well as making sure that we have all posted data that we require:

```
// check for all needed session variables and check for posted data
if( $_POST && $aSess && $iShippingOK && $iProductsOK ) {

    // error checking
    $sCCExpDate = $_POST["cc_exp_y"]."-".$_POST["cc_exp_m"]."-01";
    is_numeric($_POST["cc_number"]) ? $sCCNumber = $_POST["cc_number"] :
            catchErr("Please enter a valid credit card number.");
```

Now that we know we have all the required information, we will begin to populate our parameter array that will be passed to the addOrder() function. First we insert the order into the database so that we can make sure that no customers are unreportedly being billed if the process dies somewhere along the way. You will notice later in the script that we delete the added order if the purchase fails. If the add order returns without any errors, then we set the order ID and continue with the payment process:

```
        // fill argument array
        $aArgs["account_id"]        = $aSess["Account Id"];
        $aArgs["order_total_price"] = $iTotalPrice;
        $aArgs["order_cc_number"]   = substr($sCCNumber,-4,4);
        $aArgs["order_cc_exp_dt"]   = strtotime($sCCExpDate);

        // add order to database if credit card is processed
        $iOrderId = $oOrders->addOrder($aArgs);
        $oOrders->setOrderId($iOrderId);

        // reset argument array
        $aArgs = array();
```

If our order insert method returns successfully, we can go ahead and process the credit card and add all of the purchased items to the order. You will notice that we have set the processCreditCard() to test mode by setting the final argument to 1. This should only be removed when you have tested the process thoroughly, and you know that your application is ready to be used in production.

If the credit card process returns successfully and the order was entered correctly, then we can confirm the payment and start to loop through the products while adding them to the order. If the credit card returns in failure, then we need to document the error and delete the order from the database:

```
    if( $sConfirm = $oOrders->processCreditCard ($sCCNumber, $sCCExpDate,
            $iTotalPrice, 1) && $iOrderId ) {

        $oOrder->confirmPayment($sConfirm);

        if( !$ERRORS && $iOrderId > 0 ) {

            // loop through products adding them to the order.
            $i=0;
            while($i < count($aProducts)) {

                $aArgs["product_id"]    = $aProducts[$i]["Product Id"];
                $aArgs["item_name"]     = $aProducts[$i]["Name"];
                $aArgs["item_price"]    = $aProducts[$i]["Price"];
                $aArgs["item_quantity"] = $aProducts[$i]["Quantity"];
                $oOrders->addOrderItem($aArgs);
                $i++;
            }

            $oCart->clearCart();
        }
    } else {
        catchErr("Your credit card was not accepted, please check your
                                        submission and try again");
        $oOrders->deleteOrder($iOrderId);
    }
```

At this point, the order has been added to the database and the user's credit card has been billed for the product. If there were no errors in the entire process, then we can forward the user to the confirmation page of the specific order. Otherwise, we need to print the errors and allow the user to change some of their data:

```
        // if no errors, then forward to confirmation page
        if( !$ERRORS ) {
            header("Location: ../accounts/order.php?id=".$iOrderId);
        }
    }

    // generate the header information
    setHeader();

    // start a new page with a banner advertisement
    openPage(TRUE);

?>

<!-- main content -->
<table border="0" cellpadding="0" cellspacing="0">
  <tr>
    <td><div class="header"><?php echo ENTITY; ?> Check Out</div></td>
  </tr>
  <tr>
    <td><div class="error"><?php writeErrors(); ?></div></td>
  </tr>
</table>

<?php

// check to see if the account user is logged in
if( $aSess ) {

?>

<form name="apressform" action="<?php print SELF ?>" method="post">

<table width="608" border="0" cellpadding="0" cellspacing="0">
  <tr>
    <td align="left" valign="top" width="304">
      <table border="0" cellpadding="0" cellspacing="0">
```

The [Edit] link that we placed next to the Shipping Info allows users to go to their account setup page and change their billing information:

```
        <tr><td align="left" colspan="2">
          <div class="header"> <b>Shipping Info</b>
            <a href="../accounts/shipping.php">[ Edit ]</a></div>
        </td></tr>
        <tr><td align="left"><div class="formlabel"><b>Name</b></div></td>
            <td align="left"><div class="copy">
               <?php print $aAddress["Address Name"] ?></div>
        </td></tr>
        <tr><td align="left">
         <div class="formlabel"><b>Company</b></div></td>
            <td align="left"><div class="copy">
```

```
                        <?php print $aAddress["Address Company"] ?></div>
            </td></tr>

        .....

        </table>
      </td>

      <td align="left" valign="top" width="304">
        <table border="0" cellpadding="0" cellspacing="0">
          <tr><td align="left" colspan="2">
            <div class="header"><b>Credit Card Info</b></div>
          </td></tr>
          <tr><td align="left"><div class="formlabel">Number</div></td>
              <td align="left"><input type="text" name="cc_number" value=""/>
          </td></tr>
          <tr>
            <td align="left"><div class="formlabel">Expiration</div></td>
              <td align="left">
                <select name="cc_exp_m" style="padding-right:5px;">
                  <option value="1">1</option>
                  <option value="2">2</option>
                  <option value="3">3</option>

                  .....

                </select>
                <select name="cc_exp_y" style="padding-right:5px;">
                  <?php

                      $i = date("Y");
                      $j = $i+6;
                      while($i <= $j) { ?>
                       <option value="<?php print $i ?>">
                        <?php print $i ?></option>
                      <?php
                        $i++;
                      } ?>
                </select>
              </td>
          </tr>
        </table>
      </td>
    </tr>
  </table>

<br/>
<br/>

<table width="608" border="0" cellpadding="0" cellspacing="0">
  <?php if( $aProducts[0]["Product Id"] ) {    ?>
```

The [Edit] link that we placed next to the **Selected Products** allows users to go to their shopping cart and edit the values:

```
<tr><td align="left" colspan="4"><div class="header"><b>
Selected Products</b>
      <a href="../shopping_cart/">[ Edit ]</a></div></td></tr>

<tr>
  <td align="left" class="copy"><b>Title<b/></td>
  <td align="right" class="copy"><b>Qty</b></td>
  <td align="right" class="copy"><b>Per Unit<b/></td>
  <td align="right" class="copy"><b>Cmb Price<b/></td>
</tr>
<tr>
 <td colspan="4" class="dotrule">
   <img src="../../_img/spc.gif"
    width="1" height="15" alt="" border="0" />
 </td>
</tr>
```

Here we loop through the products in the user's shopping cart and display the total price to the user:

```
<?php
  $i = 0;
  while( $i < count($aProducts) ) {
?>
<tr>
  <td><div class="section"><a href="../products/detail.php?id=
   <?php print $aProducts[$i]["Product Id"] ?>">
   <?php print format($aProducts[$i]["Name"]) ?></a>
  </div></td>
  <td align="right"><div class="copy">
   <input type="hidden"
     name="purchase_<?php print $aProducts[$i]["Product Id"] ?>"
     value="<?php print $aProducts[$i]["Quantity"] ?>" size="2"/>
     <?php print $aProducts[$i]["Quantity"] ?>
  </div></td>
  <td align="right"><div class="copy"><i>$
   <?php print $aProducts[$i]["Price"] ?></i></div></td>
  <td align="right"><div class="copy"><i>$
   <?php print $aProducts[$i]["Combined Price"] ?></i></div></td>
  </tr>
  <tr>
      <td colspan="4" class="dotrule"><img src="../../_img/spc.gif"
       width="1" height="15" alt="" border="0" /></td>
  </tr>
  <?php
        ++$i;
      }
  ?>
  <tr>
```

```
        <td colspan="4" align="right"><b>Total Price: $
          <?php print $iTotalPrice ?></b></td>
    </tr>
    <tr>
        <td colspan="4" class="dotrule"><img src="../../_img/spc.gif"
          width="1" height="15" alt="" border="0" /></td>
    </tr>
```

When building an e-commerce site, it is important that you correctly lay out your legal obligations to the customer who is purchasing products from your store. This should be written by a licensed attorney and reflect the current laws associated with online stores:

```
<tr><td colspan="4"><div class="header" style="padding-top:
  10px"><b>Legal Disclaimer</b></div></td></tr>
    <tr>
        <td colspan="4">
            // Legal Disclaimer goes here.<br/><br/>
        </td>
    </tr>

    <tr>
        <td colspan="4" class="dotrule"><img src="../../_img/spc.gif"
          width="1" height="15" alt="" border="0" /></td>
    </tr>
```

Since we do not want people to continue with the purchasing process in case of any errors in the required data, we make the form so that it can only be submitted when all the data is correct and there are no errors on the page:

```
<?php if( !$ERRORS || ($iShippingOK && $iProductsOK) ) { ?>
    <tr>
        <td colspan="4" align="right"><input type="image"
          src="../../_img/buttons/btn_submit.gif"
          width="58" height="15" alt="" border="0" onfocus="this.blur();" />
        </a></td>
    </tr>
<?php } ?>

<?php

} else {

?>
    <tr>
        <td><div class="copy">I am sorry, there are no products in your
                        shopping cart.</div></td>
    </tr>
<?php } ?>
</form>
</table>
```

```php
<?php

// if account user is not logged in
} else {

?>

<div class="copy">Please <a href="../accounts/">log in</a> if you would like to
purchase products</div>

<?php } ?>

<?php

// print out footer information
closePage();
?>
```

Building the 'My Orders' Page

The My Orders page is used by the user to look at all orders that they have submitted. This is important so that the user can easily gain access to any information that the web site might have and check on the status of their order. This page is simply a list of all the orders that they have made, and each record is selectable so that the user can gain more information on the purchase.

Orders List Page

For this we need to build two pages. The first page is used to list all of the purchases that the user has made. Here is the code for that page:

```php
<?php

// File Location: /site/accounts/orders.php

require_once("tpl_unsecure.php");
require_once("class.accounts.php");
require_once("handlers.php");
require_once("class.orders.php");

$oAccounts = new accounts;
$oAccounts->validateSession() ? $aSess = $oAccounts->getSession() :
header("Location: index.php");
$oOrders = new orders;

// initialize page variables
$aOrders = $oOrders->getAccountOrders($aSess["Account Id"]);

setHeader();
openPage(TRUE);
?>
```

Let's start with the HTML part of the script:

```html
<table border="0" cellpadding="0" cellspacing="0">
    <tr>
        <td class="dotrule"><img src="../../_img/spc.gif"
         width="1" height="15" alt="" border="0" /></td>
    </tr>
    <tr>
        <td>
            <a href="manage.php">My Settings</a> |
            <a href="prefs.php">My Preferences</a> |
            <a href="shipping.php">My Shipping Info</a> |
            <a href="orders.php">My Orders</a>
        </td>
    </tr>

.....

    <?php
    if( $aOrders[0] ) {

        $i = 0;
        while( $i < count($aOrders) ) {
    ?>

    <tr>
        <td align="center"><div class="copy"><a href="order.php?id=
         <?php print $aOrders[$i]["order_id"] ?>">
         <?php print date("l, F jS, Y",$aOrders[$i]["created_dt"]) ?>
        </a></div></td>
        <td align="center"><div class="copy">
         <?php print $aOrders[$i]["item_count"] ?></div></td>
        <td align="center"><div class="copy">$
         <?php print $aOrders[$i]["order_total_price"] ?></div></td>
        <td align="center">
            <div class="copy">
                <?php if( $aOrders[$i]["order_ship_dt"] ) { ?>
                    <i><?php print "Shipped
                     ".date("m/d/Y",$aOrders[$i]["order_ship_dt"]) ?></i>
                <?php } else { ?>
                    <i>Has Not Shipped</i>
                <?php } ?>
            </div>
        </td>
    </tr>

.....

<?php closePage(); ?>
```

Order Details Page

Now that we have created the orders list page, we need to build a page for detailing each order. This page needs to include all information associated with the order as well as all of the items that have been ordered. We also want to display the shipping status so that the user can come here to check on the status of their order.

The following screenshot details the information that we would like to display:

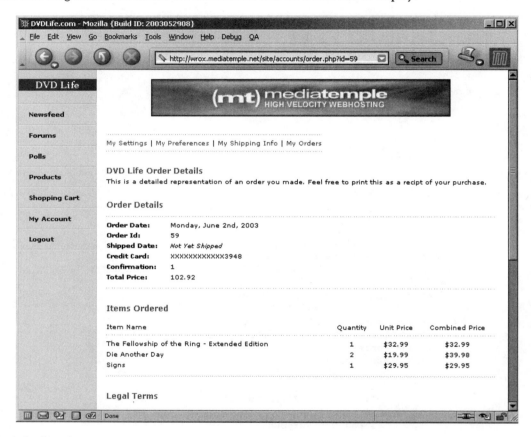

Let's look at the script:

```php
<?php

// File Location: /site/accounts/order.php

// required libraries
require_once("tpl_unsecure.php");
require_once("class.accounts.php");
require_once("handlers.php");
require_once("class.orders.php");

$oAccounts = new accounts;
```

```
$oAccounts->validateSession() ? $aSess = $oAccounts->getSession() :
header("Location: index.php");

// Instantiate Orders
$oOrders = new orders;
```

Since this page accepts an ID value to identify the order, we need to make sure that the user cannot view the orders of other account users by simply changing the ID in the URL path. For this, we check the returned order array, $aOrder, for the account_id and make sure that it matches the Account Id of the current session. If they do not match, we redirect the user back to their account orders page:

```
// check for an ID
if( strcmp($_GET["id"],"") ){

    $id = $_GET["id"];

    // initialise page variables
    $oOrders->setOrderId($id);
    $aOrder = $oOrders->getOrder($id);
    $aItems = $oOrders->getOrderItems();

    if($aOrder["account_id"] != $aSess["Account Id"]){

        $aOrder = FALSE;
        $aItems = FALSE;

        header("Location: orders.php");
    }
} else {

    $id = FALSE;
}

setHeader();
openPage(TRUE);
?>
```

Here's the HTML part of the script:

```
<table border="0" cellpadding="0" cellspacing="0">
    <tr>
        <td class="dotrule"><img src="../../_img/spc.gif"
        width="1" height="15" alt="" border="0" /></td>
    </tr>
    <tr>
        <td>
            <a href="manage.php">My Settings</a> |
            <a href="prefs.php">My Preferences</a> |
            <a href="shipping.php">My Shipping Info</a> |
            <a href="orders.php">My Orders</a>
```

```
                </td>
        </tr>
        <tr>
            <td class="dotrule"><img src="../../_img/spc.gif"
             width="1" height="15" alt="" border="0" /></td>
        </tr>
</table>

<br />

<table border="0" cellpadding="0" cellspacing="0">
    <tr>
        <td><div class="header"><?php print ENTITY ?>
         Order Details</div></td>
    </tr>
    <tr>
        <td><div class="copy">This is a detailed representation of an
         order you made.  Feel free to print this as a recipt of your
         purchase.</div></td>
    </tr>
    <tr>
        <td><div class="error"><?php writeErrors() ?></div></td>
    </tr>
</table>

<div class="header">Order Details</div>
<table border="0" cellpadding="0" cellspacing="0" width="608">
    <tr>
        <td class="dotrule" colspan="2"><img src="../../_img/spc.gif"
         width="1" height="15" alt="" border="0" /></td>
    </tr>

.....

    <?php

    $i=0;
    while( $i<count($aItems) ) {

        ?>
        <tr>
            <td align="left"><div class="copy">
             <?php print format($aItems[$i]["item_name"]) ?></div></td>
            <td align="center"><div class="copy">
             <?php print format($aItems[$i]["item_quantity"]) ?></div></td>
            <td align="center"><div class="copy">$
             <?php print format($aItems[$i]["item_price"]) ?></div></td>
            <td align="center"><div class="copy">$
             <?php print number_format($aItems[$i]["item_price"] *
             $aItems[$i]["item_quantity"],2) ?></div></td>
        </tr>
        <?
        $i++;
    }
    ?>

.....

<?php closePage(); ?>
```

Building the CMS Application

The CMS application for fulfillment is created using the same methodology as all the other CMS applications that we have created up to this point. We will be using a single function for displaying a paginated list of records and allowing you to select a single record to view the associated data.

The only difference between this application and the others that we have built, is that once an order is published (fulfilled) in the CMS framework, it can no longer be staged (un-fulfilled). This is to say that once the product has been sent, it cannot be 'un-sent'.

When displaying an order in the CMS, we need to combine the use of three primary methods:

- ❑ `$oOrders->GetOrder()` – To display all of the order information
- ❑ `$oOrders->getOrderItems()` – To get all of the items associated with the order
- ❑ `$oAccount->getAccountAddress()` – To get the shipping information for the site user

The workflow process for your fulfillment will differ depending on your use.

Summary

In this chapter, we defined the problems associated with implementing the checking out process into our web site. We then produced a logical design concept to adhere to the intended functionality that we decided upon, and then preceded to code our design solution into a functional application that seamlessly plugged into the CMS architecture for easy management.

At this point, you should be aware of the following aspects and be comfortable with implementing them in your application:

- ❑ The problems and considerations needed when building a shopping cart with a check out process
- ❑ The importance of efficiency and performance considerations while designing the application data objects and database
- ❑ Writing the background application functionality, keeping the interface and display of contents in mind

Building e-commerce applications is a large and complicated task. It is important to be very detail – oriented and thorough while building any application that processes financial information. Since this book is not oriented towards building an online store, we have provided a basic means for purchasing items. For more information about building an online store in greater detail, we suggest reading *Professional PHP4 Web Development Solutions* from *Apress* (*ISBN 1-861007-43-4*).

14

The Road Ahead

Having deployed the site on our ISP or local machine, and having tinkered with it and browsed the code, we are done with the task that had been set for us at the beginning of this book – building an application-driven PHP MySQL web site.

Now let's review what we have done.

Our Finished Site

After laying out the basic plan for the site, in Chapters 1 and 2, we looked at the creation of a solid foundation for the UI that could be employed throughout the design of our application. In Chapter 3 we created a file that uniformly creates the header, navigation, and footer HTML for any given page.

Then in Chapters 4 and 5 we looked at laying the foundation for our application by implementing a user management system for the Content Management System (CMS) as well as the web site's visitor accounts.

Finally, it was time to build on to the core framework by implementing vertical applications.

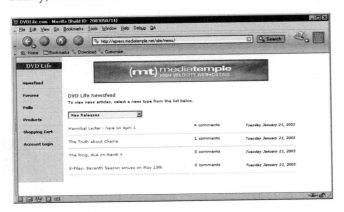

Browse Through the Latest News Items

Chapter 6 built a simple news management and delivery system, and also laid the groundwork for ou RSS news syndication, which we then detailed in Chapter 7.

To encourage community presence we made a provision for users to post opinions about news articles as well.

We also discussed different options to implement reliable, practical, and effective advertising systems into the web site to supplement our revenue model, in Chapter 8.

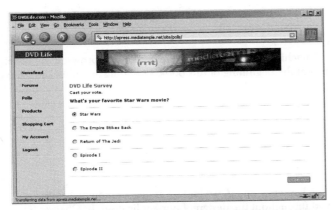

Cast Your Vote in the Polls

Chapter 9 built the polling system, attempting to make sure it was close to one-person, one-vote, while not discouraging visitors from participating i the poll.

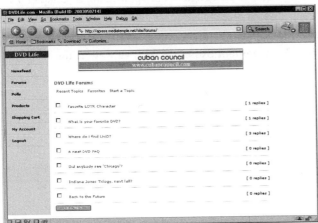

Browse Through the Forums

Chapter 10 built the discussion forums, where visitors could browse the message in the forums, ask questions and reply to those of others, and share ideas and tips.

e-mail is an effective direct marketing tool, and Chapter 11 added newsletter functionality to the web site to get information across to our users in a simple and controlled fashion.

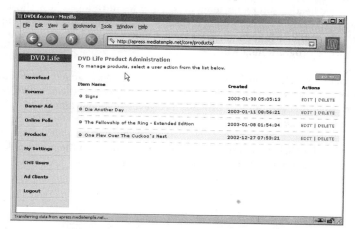

Look Through the Shop and Pick Some Products

Chapter 12 built a products list and the item selection process.

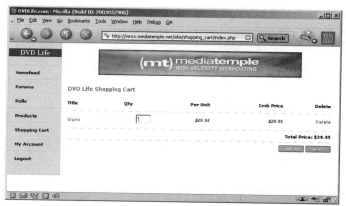

Buy Some Products

Chapter 13 finished the shopping process by building a product ordering and fulfillment system, and utilized VeriSign's PayFlow Pro API to implement the financial transactions.

Now Create an Account and Start Making Posts to the Site

Built early on in Chapter 5, we showed how to authenticate and store user accounts.

Over the course of our investigation into building dynamic, interactive web sites using PHP and MySQL, we've discussed a number of technologies that can help us to accomplish this. We started with building libraries of useful components, like our basic header and footer templates. Then we introduced how classes can be used to modularize code relating to database access, making it easier to reuse, rather than rebuilding it from scratch each time we wish to implement similar functionality. These are core programming concepts that are useful no matter what language we're programming with.

Now that we've created a working site that meets all of our functional requirements, this is an excellent time to reflect on how well we've done and whether we could have done better. In most projects this is called **refactoring**, and is done continuously during the development process. However since our aim is not to throw you into the deep end, we have left this stage to the very end of the book.

A lot of the concepts that we will explore in the chapter on refactoring will be used more in the next book in this series, in which we'll examine building e-commerce sites with PHP and MySQL.

Refactoring

Like many other aspects of programming, refactoring is not an exact science; suggestions and ideas that are introduced during refactoring have both advantages and disadvantages. It's up to you as the programmer to decide if any of the refactoring ideas would be beneficial in your application.

So let's dive in and take a look at what we have done.

Our Base Structure

In Chapter 2, we laid out our files and grouped them according to function or purpose, either as modules or shared resources. This is a common method in many open source projects; you may have seen similar layouts before if you've browsed around existing PHP applications.

As you've read this book, you may have noticed that we introduced early on the idea of using functions like:

```
openPage();
```

to accomplish tasks that are often repeated.

As the application codebase grew, remembering where this was defined (in Chapter 3) became more difficult. In most projects it is also important that when somebody looks at the code you have written, that person will be able to find function definitions and change them quickly. One of the more common methods of facilitating this is by writing classes that act as wrappers for often-reused functions.

```
Site_Elements::openPage();
```

By defining the function as a method of the Site_Elements class, we can help the casual reader of the code to have a reasonable chance of working out where openPage() is actually defined.

It's a good idea to place class definitions in include files with appropriate names such as `Site_Element.class.php`. *However, even wrapper classes/methods shouldn't be arbitrary – they should model a logical component of the application.*

You may also notice here that we have named our class very similarly to the directory in which it resides. As you explore PEAR, you will realize this is their standard, and makes locating classes and code very easy.

Real Life Annoyances

Like all perfect designs, real life has a horrible habit of coming back and biting us. You may have noticed early on that we stored some user information in cookies.

```
if( isset($_COOKIE["cUSER"]) ) {
    ....
```

This offers a very easy way to deal with storing variables and passing them from page to page. But what happens if the end user has read some horror story about Internet Explorer and viruses and thought that turning off cookies was a good idea? How do we deal with such a case?

Like most advanced server application languages, PHP has a built-in feature known as sessions, which can be configured to use automated URL rewriting if the user has turned off cookies in his/her browser.

In order to enable a user session, all we have to do is add this code to the start of any page.

```
session_start();
```

Once you've done this, you can access any session variable using the PHP superglobal `$_SESSION` array. For example:

```
if( isset($_SESSION["cUSER"]) ) {
    // .....
}
```

You can also store object instances, like the data objects we created in Chapter 4, in the session, making it easy to manage large amounts of data about a user.

For more information about sessions in PHP, see *Professional PHP4 Programming* from *Apress* (*ISBN 1-861006-91-8*). It would also be good to refer to the session handling section in the PHP Manual at http://www.php.net/manual/en/ref.session.php.

Looking for More Flexibility in Look and Feel

In Chapter 3 we used Cascading Style Sheets (CSS) in our header and footer code. This served us very well throughout the book, and is likely to work well in most simple situations. But what if you wanted to provide a different look and feel for affiliate DVD shops, so they could use your online shop, but with their own logos, layout, and color scheme?

Well, you could go down the road of writing an individual template file for each affiliate, but over time this broken up HTML and PHP file is very difficult to maintain, since you cannot instantly get an idea of what the site will look like when editing the HTML.

This is where **templating** in PHP comes in – although PHP really started off as a way to add 'variables' to HTML, it's now far more than that, as you can see from the site we have developed. Templating solutions were developed to try and solve the issue of mixing PHP and HTML. The great advantage of this is that you can design your web pages in WYSISYG tools like Macromedia Dreamweaver, which also allows you preview PHP pages live on a development server. This static HTML can then be easily integrated with the web site's PHP code.

While there is not enough space in this book to cover all of the available packages, or even tell you about the detailed benefits of each, we will provide a general overview of the two main types and their advantages and disadvantages.

For a more detailed discussion of PHP templating, look out for the *PHP Templating Handbook (ISBN 1-861008-96-1)* currently under development by this publisher.

HTML Tag Replacers

In the HTML file, we can put in comments and tags indicating the start and end of blocks or where to show variables:

```
<!-- BLOCK: START someloop -->
<td>{somevariable}</td>
```

These engines are usually very easy to write templates for in WYSISYG editors, and the person designing the HTML page does not require any real knowledge of writing PHP applications.

A lot of the work is done by the PHP program when displaying the page by replacing the tags with PHP variables or values, often using the PHP's `str_replace` function. For simple tasks this type of template is very easy to use; however, it can become difficult to work with if you have many complex loops and other programming blocks. You should also be aware that if performance is a concern, some packages that use this method can be very slow.

PHP Code Replacers

The second approach for templates is to take a template (similar to the one we saw earlier) and replace it with PHP code:

```php
<?php foreach($someblock as $somevariable) { ?>

    <td><?php echo $somevariable ?></td>

<?php } ?>
```

This method is significant in terms of performance, since the file is converted only when it's modified, and can allow template engines to have considerably more features.

Hopefully this gives you a start on understanding templates and how they could be implemented with our DVD site; you will be seeing more of this in the next book on e-commerce.

Other than these resources, you may want to explore XSLT in the *PHP4 XML* book from *Apress (ISBN 1-861007-21-3)*. As is often the case, there is no single 'right' way to do this, just a lot of excellent alternatives for you to make your own choice based on your circumstances and requirements:

- ❑ PEAR (http://pear.php.net/) includes a number of template packages
- ❑ Smarty is a well developed engine (http://smarty.php.net/)
- ❑ The PHP Classes site has a mix of various template engines (http://www.phpclasses.org/)

More PEAR

Throughout this book we have used the PEAR::DB abstraction layer rather than PHP's own MySQL functions. From a programming perspective this "reduce each database's API feature set to the lowest common denominator" feature is extremely advantageous. Since PEAR is closely tied to PHP, there are a considerable number of users supporting, improving, and fixing the packages. With the release of PHP 4.3, PEAR is being more closely integrated with PHP itself, and the forthcoming *Professional PHP5* book from *Apress (ISBN 1-861007-85-X)* will contain a lot more information on the other packages available.

The purpose of this book was to learn how to design a dynamic web site, rather than a PEAR tutorial. But now that we are considering refactoring, we should take a look at some of the packages in PEAR that might help to improve our application.

The first of these is the PEAR error handler, part of the base PEAR system. PEAR_ERROR or an extended version is really the best method to store and retrieve error messages. In our application, we do use PEAR_ERROR everywhere we can, and, once we get the error messages, trap them in our own way so that we can display them in reasonably friendly ways.

In the application we created for this book, we implemented our own error handler; when something went wrong, we called our 'print out an error page'. Using PEAR, we normally check to see if there was a PEAR error. Furthermore, PEAR has the ability to set a callback function for errors, and PEAR's `raiseError()` method can also emit our own application's error messages.

At the time of writing there were over 100 PEAR packages, offering a multitude of tools for databases like data objects and query builders, for XML parsing, for sending e-mail, and many more. It's well worth a look to see if any of those packages could be used to replace or extend our existing code:

- ❑ PEAR home page (http://pear.php.net/)
- ❑ The CVS repository of PEAR code (http://cvs.php.net/cvs.php/pear)
- ❑ PEAR tutorials listing (http://php.weblogs.com/php_pear_tutorials/)

Classes Everywhere

We've used classes heavily for implementing our data objects, and our page output remained as straight-through output. You may have noticed a lot of similarity in the code on different pages; a lot of it took input, and called a related object to create, update, list, or delete it. This commonality is what the classes thrive on.

Examining our page output code, you can see that a base set of methods, say for redirecting to the add or update functionality, would save considerable code. While you could create a function library to do this, using classes will make the code considerably easier to read later, and just by extending this base page library class, you can very quickly provide the functionality in each module.

Going on a lot further here, we might be able to offer a different solution to browser redirection on submitting data. If we became less dependent on global and context variables, we could just pass control of our application from one object to another.

As mentioned early on, we have assumed that `register_globals` is turned off (as it is by default beginning with PHP version 4.2.0). Sometimes, however, people may end up turning it back on so they can run that 'cool' webmail application they really like – so it can be a very dangerous assumption to make. We could program defensively by using classes, which don't inherit the global variable scope or take precautions against this.

The following is a list of some excellent online resources exploring the many facets of PHP' s object-oriented (OO) coding:

- ❏ PHP Patterns (http://www.phppatterns.com/)
  A site devoted to helping PHP developers learn and employ object-oriented programming (OOP) patterns in their applications

- ❏ Object-Oriented PHP (http://www.phpbuilder.com/columns/luis20000420.php3 and http://www.phpbuilder.com/columns/mark20000727.php3)
  A pair of articles from PHPBuilder – the first is intended for developers with OOP experience but who might be new to PHP, and the second is for PHP users who are new to OOP

- ❏ PHP Classes (http://www.phpclasses.org/)
  A more general collection of PHP programming classes, of varying quality, often a useful to base for your own classes

Also Apress's forthcoming *Professional PHP 5* book (*ISBN 1-861007-85-X)* is expected to cover the enhanced OOP functionality of PHP 5.

The Little Details

If you have ever written a document and given it to somebody to check, looking for deep and meaningful analysis, but ended up with them dissecting on your spelling and grammar, you are going to love this.

No refactoring is complete without going through your code line by line. So let's take a look at some of ours and see if we could have done better.

We used the following code bit throughout to send queries to the database. Since MySQL and most other databases use persistent connections, there is no real overhead in connecting; in fact, if you have connected already and try to do it again, nothing actually happens. So we don't really need to store that connection object; we could just create a `query()` method in the base data object and keep calling it:

```
$this->_oConn = &DB::connect(DSN)
....
$this->_oConn->query(...);
```

Note that this is true in our own context only if PHP and MySQL are configured to do so. However, it is true that connections last for the lifetime of the script in which they're created.

You may have noticed in Chapter 4 that we used the $POSTED flag to indicate if anything had been posted:

```
if (_$POST) $POSTED = TRUE;

if ($POSTED) { ...
```

This is set in the handlers.php file. However, as with some of the other functions we've created, it's easy to forget after a while where we defined this variable. This becomes evident when you return to the project after six months. Could we perhaps have done without it?

As we progressed through the steps required to build our application, we noticed that we were creating a potential for bugs to creep in by employing user-defined arrays, rather than just using the column names from the database. In the later stages, you will have seen that we changed this, and the code became a lot clearer and required less documentation. Also, it was less susceptible to nothing appearing on the page when someone accidentally typed 'Name' in the wrong case:

```
while(list($a,$b,$c) = $rsTmp->fetchRow(DB_FETCHMODE_ORDERED)) {
    $return[$i]['App Name'] = $a;
    $return[$i]['App Path'] = $b;
}
```

In the following example, you can see that we have created a temporary $ret variable, yet we do not do anything with it except return it:

```
if ($something) {
    $ret = TRUE;
} else {
    $ret = FALSE;
}
return $ret;
```

When you consider the performance of the application, one of the aims is to reduce both code and temporary variables. If this code is called a lot, then simply returning directly could double the speed of the operation.

A considerable amount of our code is concerned with SQL statements, and returning the results. It is likely that some form of query-building tool may reduce our code size considerably and hence reduce the time to develop:

```
$sql = "SELECT
            account_id,
            order_total_price,
            order_cc_number,
            order_cc_exp_dt,
            order_ship_dt,
            order_pfp_confirm,
            status,
            created_dt
        FROM
            ".PREFIX."_orders
        WHERE
            order_id = '".$this->_iOrderId."'
        ";
```

In the following example:

```
header("Location: ".SELF);
```

our page redirects to itself; however, you cannot be certain where the constant SELF is actually defined. Our application uses constants as configuration items. To change the settings of the program, we must edit the file where all these are defined. Are there other alternatives like XML configuration or .ini files that could be used?

The above example is also good for demonstrating that at times using a constant is unnecessary and it's better just to use something that's already supplied by the environment ($PHP_SELF, for example).

As mentioned at the beginning of the section, refactoring is not an exact science; the choices you make as a programmer to use specific methods like strcmp():

```
if (!strcmp($op, "deact")) {
```

where an '==' or a 'switch/case' might work are really a mix of personal preference, experience, and style.

Hopefully we have given you an idea of what could be done to the PHP code here to improve it. But at the end of the day, when you write your application, you will end up with the same situation. It's always possible to improve what you've written, but at some point you just have to stop and say 'this works', and realize that making more changes has diminishing returns.

> **Strike a balance between elegance, efficiency, reusability, and simply getting the job done.**

Pushing MySQL to the Edge

As you can see from the web site we have developed, we are making great use of MySQL, in almost every aspect of the site. However we have only scratched the surface of what MySQL can do.

In the early chapters we started using table locking to ensure that when we added a record, other processes were temporarily prevented from writing. However, the latest versions of MySQL now support full rollback and transactions. Could we have made use of this in the shopping cart system?

Using this in conjunction with replication, we can start to think about preventing an avalanche of e-mails in the morning from DVD enthusiasts wondering why they can't get to the site, or worse still, wondering if you are still in business and will be delivering their orders.

We have also skipped over the more precise details of database optimization; in some instances we have deliberately done a few more queries than are necessary just to make the code more readable.

A lot of this is explored in the *MySQL Transactions and Replication Handbook* from *Apress* (*ISBN 1-861008-38-4*). Although we focus on MySQL, most of the code in this book will work just as well on other databases, like PostgreSQL, Oracle, or Microsoft SQL server.

Getting Too Busy

Once the web site is set up, and if it's fairly user-friendly, people start visiting and joining in. Membership and traffic grow, and we spend more time adding lots of cool new features to the site. At some point, you'll consider listing on NASDAQ, but that's for another book. Meanwhile, you have to work out how to deal with this increasing load. Your server is overheating and you are losing potential sales.

Apart from using MySQL, you'll need to look at page caching, usually by working out which pages are really dynamic, and which ones can be stored and updated only upon the occurrence of a relevant event occurring, like somebody adding a comment to a forum. Again have a look around PEAR and you will see a few examples.

Apache also offers features to help us out. Reverse proxies enable us to use multiple servers to do the CPU-intensive work, and to use one machine relay the output to the user. The *Professional Apache 2* book from *Apress (ISBN 1-861007-22-1)* covers a lot of the tricks on how to make the most out of Apache.

There are also a number of PHP accelerators available, and we can take our pick from Zend, Ioncube, or APC. All these tools turn the PHP code into bytecode (like Java), and some do optimizations to make your code faster still:

❑ Zend Performance Suite (http://www.zend.com/)

❑ IonCube PHP Accelerator (http://www.ioncube.com/)

❑ APC Alternative PHP Cache (http://apc.communityconnect.com/)

More XML

We've illustrated the use of XML for syndicating news content and employing it in conjunction with XSLT for creating templates, but this only touches the surface, and there are many more ways in which we could have used XML. Here are just a few ideas:

❑ Configuration
It's becoming quite common to see XML configuration files offering a very flexible method to store and retrieve settings for your site. There are PEAR libraries to support these as well.

❑ Importing
It's time-consuming to type in all the new DVD titles available into your database. Your DVD wholesale supplier will be only too happy to provide you with an inventory for you to offer on your site, and these days the best way to get the data is in XML format.

❑ Exporting
In most places, you will need to pay taxes on all the income generated from your DVD site. Usually this involves working with an accountant or some kind of accounting package. These days importing of XML-based accounting data is becoming a common feature of modern accounting packages.

❑ Point of Sale (POS) systems
Perhaps you run a small 'real shop' alongside your DVD web site. If you don't want to have two inventory systems, one for the Web and one for the shop, you could use XML RPC or SOAP so the POS system can talk to your DVD site. You may even want to use PHP-GTK on the POS.

As you can see, there are a multitude of uses for XML in our site that we have yet to explore, and the following references may prove worthwhile:

❑   XML @ W3C (http://www.w3.org/XML/)

❑   XMLHack (http://www.xmlhack.com/)

❑   XML-RPC home page (http://www.xmlrpc.com/)

❑   *PHP 4 XML* from *Apress Press* (*ISBN 1-861007-21-3*)

❑   ActiveState's Simple Web Services API (SWAPI) for PHP
    (http://aspn.activestate.com/ASPN/WebServices/SWSAPI/phptut)

❑   UDDI.org (http://www.uddi.org)
    Universal Description Discovery and Integration – for Web Services publication and discovery

❑   phpUDDI (http://phpuddi.sourceforge.net/)
    PHP classes for Web Services Discovery

❑   W3C's Web Services Activity Page (http://www.w3.org/2002/ws/)

❑   *PHP Web Services* from *Apress Press* (*ISBN 1-861008-07-4*)

❑   Resource Definition Format @ W3C (http://www.w3.org/RDF/)

❑   RSS Specs (http://web.resource.org/rss/1.0/ and http://backend.userland.com/rss/)

Get Building

We have come out of this book with a basic methodology for creating a dynamic web site using PHP and MySQL, along with a knowledge of why we built the site the way we did. We can easily borrow these techniques to create a PHP web site from design to deployment. However, it is by no means the end of the road. On the other hand, it is a milestone for the road ahead.

The next step is to build your own site. This book will have given you a framework and some modules to use or modify. Now you just need to tailor the modules and templates that we've provided to fit your own needs.

We also hope that you will build your own modules in the framework we created here. A lot of our design work went into providing new modules that are easy to add and modify – and you will be able to link your modules to our central accounts system, modify our header and footer controls, or add some of the ideas discussed in refactoring. This book will thus serve as a reference of how similar projects are built, so you can have a better understanding of how to contribute to this and many other projects, with the aim of rapidly delivering your own web site.

Join the Community

No developer works in isolation, nor would we expect you to. There are many online communities where you can get assistance with obtaining, learning, and improving your skills with the Web technologies discussed in this book. We provide one in conjunction with this book.

Our DVD Life application includes a discussion forum. Although this forum was built for the purpose of discussing DVD-related news, we could have book-specific discussions emerging here in the form of posts and replies from readers and the authors themselves (http://apress.mediatemple.net/site/forums/).

You'll be able to find solutions there to your problems and to share ideas. Also, if you're looking for modules, adapted from those in the book or using our framework, you can find out if someone else hasn't already written the one you need, or can help you do so yourself. You could also tell everybody about the sites that you've developed.

Through the forum at DVD Life we hope to build up a list of the best web sites built with the help of this book. If you do something really impressive, we might even ask you to write for us about it!

Mailing Lists

PHP already has a huge following, as you can see by browsing the various PHP mailing lists. Sign up for the php-general and the pear-general lists at php.net, and the PEAR developer's list to get involved in the development of PEAR itself.

These groups are full of helpful people with similar interests and extensive experience:

❑   Sign up to a PHP Mailing list (http://www.php.net/mailing-lists.php)

❑   Search the archives (http://marc.theaimsgroup.com/)

Is There More to Come?

Yes! We are already planning a sequel to this book, which we're tentatively calling 'PHP E-Commerce Problem – Design – Solution', that will be written with the intent of showcasing the key design and development issues for applying PHP to e-commerce solutions. By using an ongoing case study we will cover all the common issues relating to e-commerce and impart developer know-how specific to solving problems in this area of application development. We encourage your valuable feedback and inputs into this sequel, by making relevant posts at DVD Life.

Index

A Guide to the Index

The index is arranged hierarchically, in alphabetical order, with symbols preceding the letter A. Most second-level entries and many third-level entries also occur as first-level entries. This is to ensure that users will find the information they require however they choose to search for it.